LABOR RELATIONS AND PUBLIC POLICY SERIES

REPORT NO. 12

NLRB REMEDIES FOR UNFAIR LABOR PRACTICES

by

DOUGLAS S. MCDOWELL

and

KENNETH C. HUHN

with the assistance of
KEVIN S. MCGUINESS
and
PETER A. JANUS

LEGES SINE MORIBUS VANAE

INDUSTRIAL RESEARCH UNIT
The Wharton School, Vance Hall/CS
University of Pennsylvania
Philadelphia, Pennsylvania 19174
U.S.A.

Foreword

In 1968, the Industrial Research Unit inaugurated its Labor Relations and Public Policy monographs as a means of examining issues and stimulating discussions in the complex and controversial areas of collective bargaining and the regulation of labor-management disputes. The first four studies, and the eighth and ninth, in the series dealt with aspects of the National Labor Relations Board and its administration. The fifth report contained papers read at the fiftieth anniversary conference of the Industrial Research Unit, at which many aspects of labor relations and public policy were discussed. The sixth monograph—*Welfare and Strikes*—was the first empirical analysis of the impact of government payments to strikers on the American collective bargaining system and on the settlement of disputes under that system. The seventh in the series, *Opening the Skilled Construction Trades to Blacks*, was the initial attempt to determine, by detailed field analysis, what actually occurs when the federal government insists that the skilled construction trades make a serious effort to increase the number and percentage of Negroes in their work force. The tenth, *The Davis-Bacon Act*, dealt with another aspect of construction in that it involved a critical analysis of the impact and administration of the little known law under which "prevailing wages" are established in the construction industry. The eleventh monograph in the series marked the Industrial Research Unit's first published work in the public employee field since the publication of Michael H. Moskow's pioneering work, *Teachers and Unions*, in 1966. It presented the results of a study of the labor relations climate in the Philadelphia School System as it impacted upon the management of human resources.

This, the twelfth in our series, marks a return to the general subject matter of six of the previous monographs, National Labor Relations Board (NLRB) policy. The NLRB has been empowered by Congress to prevent persons from engaging in unfair labor practices. To this end, the NLRB exercises broad authority to remedy such violations by ordering respondents to cease and desist from proscribed activities and to take such other affirmative action as will effectuate the policies of the National Labor Relations Act. This study describes and analyzes various NLRB-ordered remedies developed under this Congressional mandate. This report also discusses and evaluates many of the criticisms directed both at the Board's remedial policies and the analytical methods under which those policies have been developed. This study, therefore, not only describes NLRB remedies, but also provides a basis for evaluating their effectiveness in carrying out the national labor policy.

Douglas S. McDowell, the senior author of this study, received his J.D. from the University of Michigan Law School in 1970. He has been admitted to practice before the United States Supreme Court, and is a member of the Michigan and District of Columbia Bars. From 1971 to 1975, Mr. McDowell served as an attorney in the appellate court branch of the NLRB General Counsel's office. He now practices law in Washington, D. C. Kenneth C. Huhn, the other major author, drafted chapters of this study while serving as Legal Research Associate with the Industrial Research Unit. He received his J.D. from Rutgers-Camden Law School and is a member of the Pennsylvania Bar. He presently serves as labor counsel on the legal staff of a private corporation. Messrs. McDowell and Huhn were assisted by Peter A. Janus who wrote major portions of the chapters dealing with *Gissel* bargaining orders. Mr. Janus is a member of the Connecticut Bar, received his J.D. from the Boston University School of Law, served as an officer in the Adjutant General Corps, U.S. Army, and was awarded the MBA degree from the Wharton Graduate Division in May 1974. He formerly was a Legal Research Associate with the Industrial Research Unit, is now manager of labor relations for a major industrial corporation. Kevin S. McGuiness was of major assistance in research and drafted several chapters. Mr. McGuiness received his BA in history from the University of California at Irvine, after which he was an instructor in Renaissance history and English literature at Shapley *Scuola di Firenze* in Florence, Italy. He is now working as a research associate in Washington, D. C.

This study was funded by a number of specific and general grants. Initial research money was provided by grants from the General Electric and Gulf Oil Foundations in support of the general research program of the Industrial Research Unit, and by the unrestricted funds provided by the fifty-five companies represented on the Unit's Research Advisory Group. A specific grant in support of this study was then provided by the ALCOA Foundation.

The final costs, including publishing, were met by a generous grant from the Pew Memorial Trust in support of the Labor Relations and Public Policy Series.

The authors would like to express their appreciation to Robert E. Williams who advised them in outlining the scope and purpose of the study, and in evaluating the arguments advanced by the authors. Mr. Williams also reviewed each chapter in final draft form and repeatedly offered helpful suggestions. The authors and the Industrial Research Unit also wish to thank Maria Dwyer who did the bulk of the typing, Michael J. McGrath and Rochelle R. Bookspan who edited the manuscript and prepared the case index, and Mrs. Margaret E. Doyle, who handled the administrative matters concerning the project. The research and the views expressed are, of course, the sole responsibility of the authors.

HERBERT R. NORTHRUP, *Director*
Industrial Research Unit
The Wharton School
University of Pennsylvania

Philadelphia
January 1976

TABLE OF CONTENTS

PART FIVE

REMEDYING ILLEGAL DOMINATION OF,
OR ASSISTANCE TO, LABOR ORGANIZATIONS
BY EMPLOYERS

PART SEVEN

NLRA SANCTIONS AGAINST THE PERSISTENT,
FLAGRANT, OR FRIVOLOUS VIOLATOR

PART EIGHT

CONCLUSION

PART ONE

Introduction

CHAPTER 1

Scope and Purpose of the Study

A legal remedy is the means by which a right is enforced, or the violation of a right is prevented, redressed, or compensated. The remedies provided by the National Labor Relations Act are of paramount importance to employees because through such remedies their congressionally-created rights are protected and preserved. Indeed, it has long been recognized that "[t]he Act is essentially remedial." [1] The National Labor Relations Board (NLRB) has been delegated the task of devising appropriate remedies to protect the rights of employees to engage freely in collective bargaining, choose a bargaining representative, and engage in or refrain from other concerted activities protected by the Act. [2] The Board's task is not an easy one; well established guidelines provide that the Board must adequately protect these statutory rights while it fashions orders that are purely remedial in nature, not so harsh as to be punitive or confiscatory. [3]

This study of NLRB remedies has several objectives. The first purpose is to discuss the broad range of NLRB remedies in a single volume because, while hundreds of decided cases, law review articles, and critical commentaries exist, individual decisions and articles often deal with only a few aspects of the Board's remedial authority. Specific remedies, therefore, may tend to be viewed in isolation rather than in the context of the overall purposes and policies of the National Labor Relations Act. This single volume will provide a convenient source of reference material to acquaint the reader with the many ways in which unfair labor practices are remedied.

---

[1] Republic Steel Corp. v. NLRB, 311 U.S. 7, 9-11, 7 L.R.R.M. 287, 289 (1940).

[2] NLRB v. Pennsylvania Greyhound Lines, Inc., 303 U.S. 261, 271, 2 L.R.R.M. 600, 603 (1938); NLRB v. The Falk Corp., 308 U.S. 453, 461, 5 L.R.R.M. 677, 681 (1940).

[3] See, e.g., Virginia Electric & Power Co. v. NLRB, 319 U.S. 533, 540, 12 L.R.R.M. 739, 742 (1943).

Second, the text is intended to provide an introduction for persons unfamiliar with this area of labor law, and a guide for those needing their knowledge refreshed. More particularly, one aim is to provide the labor relations specialist, personnel officer, union official, and labor law practitioner with a comprehensive reference to Board remedies so that those persons can predict the remedial consequences of actions which concern them. To achieve this end, we have attempted to make the text understandable and readable to the nonlawyer, while at the same time preserving technical, legal accuracy.

Third, this study is designed to provide sufficient detail for use as a research tool for the labor lawyer who requires precedential authority in cases before the NLRB and courts. We have cited a great many legal authorities in the hope of providing the practitioner with substantial research in readily usable form. Even though it is not possible to anticipate every legal issue, we have tried to provide a thorough explanation of basic principles, exceptions thereto, and recurring issues which arise in NLRA litigation. Recurring issues have been augmented by numerous, and at times exhaustive, case citations. We have also noted areas of significant disagreement between the Board and the courts of appeals over the Board's exercise of its remedial authority. We hope that an explanation of these differences will not aid simply in preparing cases, but will also assist the reader in evaluating the effectiveness of the Board's remedial decisions. Further, we have tried to indicate areas where the law is uncertain, and anticipate where changes in Board membership may result in changes in Board remedial policy. In these areas especially, the practitioner is urged to supplement our work with independent research to satisfy himself that the law has not changed significantly.

In implementing our first three objectives, we have found it useful to discuss individual remedies in the context of the substantive illegal unfair labor practices they are designed to correct. Although this facilitates the possibility of digressing into areas not strictly germane to the remedies themselves, we hope that, overall, we clarify the reasons the remedies are employed. This method, also, will assist readers who are unfamiliar with specific actions proscribed by the National Labor Relations Act.

To fulfill the above objectives, we have attempted to describe the existing state of the law without advancing our own personal views. A somewhat different approach was necessary to achieve our final goal of evaluating the efficacy of existing NLRB remedies. Proposals for change have been advanced by critics of both the NLRB and the Act which this agency administers; we have analyzed these proposals in the light of our evaluation. In doing so, we found it necessary to depart from a pure recitation of legal principles and to make personal judgments and form conclusions. Although criticisms or suggestions are made periodically throughout this study, we have attempted to maintain a clear textual delineation between our own views and the existing law as found in the Act and in the decided cases.

A discussion of proposals to modify NLRB remedial authority seems particularly timely because these issues have been the subject of continuous oversight hearings conducted over the past several months by the Labor Subcommittee on Labor-Management Relations of the U.S. House of Representatives. These hearings have been especially concerned with remedies dealing with employers and unions shown to have flagrantly and repeatedly violated the Act. The subcommittee is also considering methods to alleviate the harmful effects on NLRA remedies allegedly caused by the Board's increasing caseload and the time delay between the date of filing of an unfair labor practice charge and final disposition of the case either by the NLRB or the courts.

We think, however, that before these criticisms and proposals for change can be analyzed properly, it is necessary to examine the Board's existing remedial authority and the present implementation of the Board's congressionally-granted power to remedy specific violations of the Act. Our initial undertaking in Chapter II is a discussion of the broad discretion given the Board to fashion appropriate remedies to effectuate the purposes of the Act.

The Remedial Authority of the NLRB

Congress has granted to the National Labor Relations Board the sole authority to prevent the commission of unfair labor practices described in Section 8 of the National Labor Relations Act.[1] Section 10(c) states that if the Board should find that an employer or union has engaged in, or is engaging in an unfair labor practice, then:

> . . . the Board shall state its findings of fact and shall issue and cause to be served on such person an order requiring such person to cease and desist from such unfair labor practice, and to take such affirmative action including reinstatement of employees with or without back pay, as will effectuate the policies of this Act. . . .[2]

THE STATUTORY PROVISIONS AND NLRB DISCRETION

Within the limits set forth in the National Labor Relations Act, Congress has given the Board a relatively free hand and broad discretion in determining which remedy will best effectuate the purposes of the Act.[3] The Supreme Court has cautioned the lower courts against substituting their judgment for that of the Board's in determining how the effects of unfair labor prac-

---

[1] Section 10(a) of the Act (29 U.S.C. § 160(a) (1970), provides that the "Board is empowered, as hereinafter provided, to prevent any person from engaging in any unfair labor practice affecting commerce. This power shall not be affected by any other means of adjustment or prevention that has been or may be established by agreement, law, or otherwise . . . ."

[2] *Id.* at § 160(c).

[3] *See* NLRB v. Mine Workers (P.M.W.), Local 403, 375 U.S. 396, 55 L.R.R.M. 2084 (1964); Republic Aviation Corp. v. NLRB, 324 U.S. 793, 16 L.R.R.M. 620 (1945); NLRB v. P. Lorillard Co., 314 U.S. 512, 9 L.R.R.M. 410 (1942). Fibreboard Paper Products Corp., 379 U.S. 203, 216, 57 L.R.R.M. 2609 (1964).

6

tices may best be expunged.[4] The Court has indicated that under the regulatory scheme of the Act, the function of the appellate courts is limited to reviewing questions of law.

> Because the relation of remedy to policy is peculiarly a matter for administrative competence, courts must not enter the allowable area of the Board's discretion and must guard against the danger of sliding unconsciously from the narrow confines of law into the more spacious domain of policy.[5]

The Court has explained that the requirement that the courts defer to the judgment of the Board in matters of remedial policy concurs with the congressional intent to vest the Board alone with remedial authority,[6] in order to take advantage of the "expert judgment"[7] by "experienced officials with an adequate appreciation of the complexities of the subject,"[8] who would be able to "draw on enlightenment gained from experience,"[9] in reaching their decision.

The United States circuit courts of appeals have repeatedly observed that their function in reviewing the Board's exercise of its remedial authority is limited. For example, the Second Circuit stated:

> There is no need to ring the changes on the agency's broad discretion in the selection of remedies, and the deference paid by reviewing courts when such choices have been deliberately and rationally made. That much is now engrained in Board law.[10]

On the other hand, the Supreme Court has been unwilling to require either the parties or the courts to place blind trust in the Board's decisions. The Court expects the Board to ex-

---

[4] *E.g.*, NLRB v. Link-Belt Co., 311 U.S. 584, 7 L.R.R.M. 297 (1941); Machinists, Lodge 35 v. NLRB, 311 U.S. 72, 7 L.R.R.M. 282 (1940); *cf.* NLRB v. Seven-Up Bottling Co., 344 U.S. 344, 31 L.R.R.M. 2237 (1953).

[5] Phelps Dodge Corp. v. NLRB, 313 U.S. 177, 194, 8 L.R.R.M. 439, 446 (1941).

[6] NLRB v. Seven-Up Bottling Co., 344 U.S. 344, 346, 31 L.R.R.M. 2237, 2238 (1953).

[7] Machinists, Lodge 35 v. NLRB, 311 U.S. 72, 82, 7 L.R.R.M. 282, 287 (1940).

[8] Republic Aviation Corp. v. NLRB, 324 U.S. 793, 800, 16 L.R.R.M. 620, 624 (1945).

[9] NLRB v. Seven-Up Bottling Co., 344 U.S. 344, 346, 31 L.R.R.M. 2237, 2238 (1953).

[10] Russell Motors, Inc., Amalgamated Local Union 355 v. NLRB, 481 F.2d 996, 1006, 83 L.R.R.M. 2849, 2857 (2d Cir. 1973), and cases cited therein.

hibit the expertise it is presumed to possess. Thus, the Court has pointed out that where the statute is silent as to the appropriateness of a remedy, the NLRB has the duty to explain how the implementation of the proposed remedy furthers the policies of the Act.[11]

BOARD REMEDIES MUST BE DESIGNED TO EFFECTUATE THE POLICIES OF THE ACT

The Board's authority is limited by the statutory requirement that its orders must consist only of that "which can fairly be said to effectuate the policies of the Act."[12] Stated another way, the relief granted by the Board must bear some rational relationship to the unfair labor practice(s) committed,[13] or must be a function of the purposes it is expected to accomplish.[14]

The statutory command that the Board's remedy must effectuate the policies of the Act is usually the focal point of debates concerning the pros and cons of a particular remedy. Standing alone, this requirement obviously is vague and gives scant assistance in determining the propriety of Board remedies. Consequently, it is necessary that further guidance be obtained from the language of the National Labor Relations Act. The "policies" which the Board is directed to "effectuate" were outlined by Congress in Section 1 of the Act.

> It is hereby declared to be the policy of the United States to . . . mitigate and eliminate . . . [obstructions to the freeflow of commerce] . . . when they have occurred *by encouraging the practice and procedure of collective bargaining and by protecting the exer-*

---

[11] Phelps Dodge Corp. v. NLRB, 313 U.S. 177, 196-197, 8 L.R.R.M. 439, 447 (1941). *Cf.* NLRB v. Seven-Up Bottling Co., 344 U.S. 344, 348, 31 L.R.R.M. 2237, 2239 (1953), wherein the Court stated that the Board was "created for the purpose of using its judgment and its knowledge." It should also be noted, however, that the assumption that the Board possesses a unique expertise has not gone unchallenged. *See, e.g.,* Getman & Goldberg, *The Myth of NLRB Expertise*, 39 U. Chi. L. Rev. 681 (1972).

[12] Virginia Electric & Power Co. v. NLRB, 319 U.S. 533, 540, 12 L.R.R.M. 739 (1943).

[13] *See* NLRB v. MacKay Radio & Telegraph Co., 304 U.S. 333, 348, 2 L.R.R.M. 610, 615 (1938), where the Court stated that "the relief which the statute empowers the Board to grant is to be adapted to the situation which calls for redress." *Cf.* Republic Steel Corp. v. NLRB, 311 U.S. 7, 7 L.R.R.M. 287 (1940).

[14] NLRB v. Seven-Up Bottling Co., 344 U.S. 344, 346, 31 L.R.R.M. 2237, 2238 (1953).

> *cise by workers of full freedom of association, self-organization and designation of representatives of their own choosing, for the purpose of negotiating the terms and conditions of their employment or other mutual aid or protection.*[15]

Pursuant to this declaration of purpose, it is apparent that Congress contemplated that the Act accomplish three basic objectives: (1) free collective bargaining; (2) free choice in the selection of bargaining representatives; and (3) freedom to engage in, or refrain from, concerted activities for the mutual aid and protection of the employees. Board remedies, therefore, must accord with and further these statutory objectives. Conversely, there are two situations in which the failure of the Board's relief to fall within the statutory framework invalidates the remedy. First, the relief granted must not be in conflict with any one of the primary statutory objectives. Second, the remedy must not be an attempt to achieve ends other than those set forth in the statute. Several case examples will be helpful in demonstrating how these principles have been applied by the Board and courts.

Shortly after the passage of the Act, a number of Supreme Court decisions dealt with the issue of whether a proposed Board remedy was in harmony with one of the three primary objectives of the Act listed above. In one case, in order to implement the statutory policy which guarantees employees the right to choose freely their bargaining representatives, the Supreme Court approved a Board order directing the disestablishment of an employer-dominated union and its exclusion from the ballot in a subsequent representation election.[16] In another case, the Court approved an order designed to effect the same policy by directing an employer to bargain with a minority union whose loss of majority status to a rival union was presumptively the result of unfair labor practices.[17] Conversely, the Court has rejected Board remedies which infringe upon the employees' freedom of choice. In *Consolidated Edison Co. of N.Y. v. NLRB*,[18] the Court refused to sanction an order that required an employer to abrogate col-

---

[15] 29 U.S.C. § 151 (1970) (emphasis added). *Cf.* NLRB v. Jones & Laughlin Steel Corp., 301 U.S. 1, 1 L.R.R.M. 703 (1937).

[16] NLRB v. The Falk Corp., 308 U.S. 453, 5 L.R.R.M. 677 (1940).

[17] *See* NLRB v. P. Lorillard Co., 314 U.S. 512, 9 L.R.R.M. 410 (1942); Machinists, Lodge 35 v. NLRB, 311 U.S. 72, 7 L.R.R.M. 282 (1940).

[18] 305 U.S. 197, 3 L.R.R.M. 645 (1938).

lective bargaining contracts absent a finding of domination or interference. The agreements had been executed on the behalf of employees who were members of an unaffiliated union that had not been certified as the employees' exclusive representative by the Board. The Court concluded that absent an order directing a representation election, the Board did not possess the authority to direct the recision of the contracts since such a remedy would imperil the interests of the employees in exercising their freedom of choice in selecting a bargaining representative.[19]

Two landmark Supreme Court decisions illustrate the complexity involved in implementing the congressional policy of promoting free collective bargaining. In *Fibreboard Paper Products Co. v. NLRB*,[20] the issue concerned whether the Board was empowered to direct an employer to resume a maintenance operation that had been subcontracted without prior bargaining with the union representing the maintenance employees. Finding that the Board's order was designed to promote collective bargaining by restoring the status quo prior to the unfair labor practice, the Court held that the remedy was within the Board's statutory grant of authority to promote the policies of the Act.[21] The fact that the remedy was clearly an imposition on management's right to conduct its business was held not to invalidate the order since the NLRB was engaged in effectuating a primary policy of the Act.[22] The Supreme Court's decision does suggest, however, that the economic burden on the employer is a factor

---

[19] *Id.* at 238, 3 L.R.R.M. at 657. *Cf.* Local 57, ILGWU v. NLRB (Garwin Corp.), 374 F.2d 295, 64 L.R.R.M. 2159 (D.C Cir. 1967), which provides an excellent illustration of the problems which may arise when an apparent conflict in basic statutory policies exists. In attempting to implement the bargaining obligation of a runaway New York employer who had moved his operations to Florida, the Board had ordered the employer to bargain with the same union in the new Florida plant. Recognizing that the Board was faced with a difficult remedial problem, the court refused to enforce the order since the remedy wrongfully deprived the Florida workers of their freedom to select their own bargaining representative.

[20] 379 U.S. 203, 57 L.R.R.M. 2609 (1964).

[21] *Id.* at 216, 57 L.R.R.M. at 2614.

[22] The employer had argued that the proviso to § 10(c) which specifically enjoins the Board from ordering reinstatement of employees who were suspended or discharged for cause prevented the Board from requiring the reinstatement of the employees and consequently the resumption of the operation. The Court pointed out that the legislative history of the proviso indicated that it was designed to preserve an employer's right to discharge employees for their misconduct, not as an incident to management rights. *Id.* at 217 n.11, 57 L.R.R.M. at 2614.

which may limit the Board's remedial authority in other circumstances. But the Court found the facts of *Fibreboard* showed that no undue economic burden had been imposed on the employer.[23] It concluded that the restoration order was not inimical to the policies of the Act.

In the second case, *H.K. Porter Co. v. NLRB*,[24] the Supreme Court declined to enforce a Board order, premised upon a refusal to bargain violation, which would have imposed a substantive contractual term on one of the parties to the negotiations. Similar to the *Fibreboard* case, the Court based its decision in *H.K. Porter* upon the primacy of the policy of free collective bargaining, stating:

> The Board's remedial powers under § 10 of the Act are broad, but they are limited to carrying out the policies of the Act itself. One of these fundamental policies is freedom of contract. While the parties' freedom of contract is not absolute under the Act [*e.g.*, contracts entered into by the majority representative bind the minority employees as well], allowing the Board to compel agreement when the parties themselves are unable to agree would violate the fundamental premise upon which the Act is based—private bargaining under governmental supervision of the procedure alone, without any official compulsion over the actual terms of the contract.[25]

Significantly, the majority opinion in *H.K. Porter*, unlike the dissent,[26] had regarded the alleged merits of the remedy as irrelevant. Instead, the sole grounds for holding that the Board had exceeded its remedial authority was based on the conflict with the policy of free collective bargaining which the remedy created.

Finally, in fashioning unfair labor practice remedies, the Board must be careful not to advance one statutory policy so strongly

---

[23] The maintenance operation was being performed in much the same manner as it was prior to the subcontracting agreement. Since the maintenance operation would be continued, regardless of the identity of the employees who did the work, and because the subcontract was terminable upon 60 days notice, the Board found that the reinstatement of the operation would not impose an undue burden on the employer. *See* Fibreboard Paper Products Corp., 138 N.L.R.B. 550, 555 n. 19, 51 L.R.R.M. 1101, 1102 (1962).

[24] 397 U.S. 99, 73 L.R.R.M. 2561 (1970).

[25] *Id.* at 108, 73 L.R.R.M. at 2564.

[26] *Id.* at 110, 73 L.R.R.M. at 2565 (J. Douglas, dissenting). In his dissent, Justice Douglas with whom Justice Stewart concurred, would have enforced the Board's order as "affirmative action" necessary to remedy the allegedly flagrant refusal of the employer to bargain.

that it thereby would defeat other statutory policies. As the Supreme Court has pointed out, "[I]t is the business of the Board to give coordinated effect to the policies of the Act." [27]

BOARD REMEDIES MUST BE REMEDIAL, NOT PUNITIVE

The Supreme Court has explained that the affirmative remedial power of the Board "is merely incidental to the primary purpose of Congress to stop and prevent unfair labor practices." [28] For this reason, the Board must closely restrict its remedies to undoing the effects of the unfair labor practices committed. In other words, its orders may not be punitive or confiscatory. [29]

Conceptually, this remedial-punitive distinction is perhaps more troublesome than the requirement that the Board relief must not conflict with the policies of the Act, because, in a sense, each order directing a violator to take affirmative action contains an element of punishment, at least in the subjective judgment of the party required to comply with the Board's order.

At the outset, it should be noted that the terminology employed by the Court in describing nonremedial orders as "punitive" is unfortunate in that it implicitly introduces considerations which are not relevant to the issue. The Supreme Court itself, in *NLRB v. Seven-Up Bottling Co.* [30] referred to the remedial-punitive debate as a "bog of logomachy" into which it preferred not to enter. The punitive label is actually shorthand for the concept that a Board order is invalid where it is shown to be a

---

[27] NLRB v. Seven-Up Bottling Co., 344 U.S. 344, 348, 31 L.R.R.M. 2237, 2239 (1953). *Cf.* NLRB v. Flotill Products, Inc., 180 F.2d 441, 25 L.R.R.M. 2463 (9th Cir. 1950).

[28] International Union, UAW v. Russell, 356 U.S. 634, 643, 42 L.R.R.M. 2142, 2145 (1958).

[29] *See e.g.,* Local 60, Carpenters v. NLRB, 365 U.S. 651, 655, 47 L.R.R.M. 2900 (1961) where the Court ruled that "reimbursing of a lot of old-time union men by refunding their dues is not a remedial measure in the competence of the Board to impose, unless there is support in the evidence that their membership was induced, obtained, or retained in violation of the Act. It would be difficult, even with hostile eyes, to read the history of trade unionism except in terms of voluntary associations formed to meet pressing needs in a complex society." *See also* Virginia Electric & Power Co. v. NLRB, 319 U.S. 533, 540, 12 L.R.R.M. 739, 742 (1943); Cantainair Systems Corp. v. NLRB, —— F.2d ——, 89 L.R.R.M. 2685, 2690 (2d Cir. 1975).

[30] 344 U.S. 344, 348, 31 L.R.R.M. 2237, 2239 (1953).

"patent attempt to achieve ends other than those which can fairly be said to effectuate the policies of the Act." [31]

The Court first defined the limits of the Board's remedial jurisdiction in *Consolidated Edison Co. of N.Y., Inc. v. NLRB*,[32] stating:

> The power to command affirmative action is remedial, not punitive, and is to be exercised in aid of the Board's authority to restrain violations and as a means of removing or avoiding the consequences of violation where those consequences are of a kind to thwart the purposes the Act.[33]

Although the application of this formula has undergone minor modifications through the ensuing years, as the circumstances of particular cases have dictated, the general principles stated therein have retained their validity.

For example, the Supreme Court has often upheld Board decisions which have the legitimate purpose of removing or avoiding the effects of an unfair labor practice. Thus, the Court has approved remedies which purport to restore the status quo as a means of depriving the violator of the advantage gained by the unfair labor practice,[34] or returning the parties to the position which would have existed, but for the illegal conduct.[35] The so-called make-whole remedies also are justified under this principle.[36] Alternatively, the Board's relief may be justified on the grounds that it prevents the consequences of a violation from thwarting the purposes of the Act. Thus, the Court has held that a lesser order would be ineffective,[37] or that the relief is necessary

---

[31] Virginia Electric & Power Co. v. NLRB, 319 U.S. 533, 540, 12 L.R.R.M. 739, 742 (1943).

[32] 305 U.S. 197, 3 L.R.R.M. 645 (1938).

[33] *Id.* at 236, 3 L.R.R.M. at 655.

[34] *See* Virginia Electric & Power Co. v. NLRB, 319 U.S. 533, 541, 12 L.R.R.M. 739, 743 (1943).

[35] Phelps Dodge Corp. v. NLRB, 313 U.S. 177, 194, 8 L.R.R.M. 439, 446 (1941).

[36] *See, e.g.,* Nathanson v. NLRB, 344 U.S. 25, 27, 31 L.R.R.M. 2036, 2037 (1952), wherein the Court stated, "A back pay order is a reparation order designed to vindicate the public policy of the statute by making the employers whole for losses suffered on account of an unfair labor practice."

[37] NLRB v. Pennsylvania Greyhound Lines, Inc., 303 U.S. 261, 265, 2 L.R.R.M. 600, 601 (1938).

to prevent future enjoyment of the fruits of an unfair labor practice.[38]

Conversely, the Court in *Local 60, Carpenters v. NLRB*,[39] declared that where "no 'consequences of violation' are removed . . .; and no 'dissipation' of the effects of the prohibited action is achieved, . . . [t]he order . . . becomes punitive and beyond the power of the Board." [40]

In *Republic Steel Corp. v. NLRB*,[41] the Supreme Court held that a Board order, which directed the employer to pay to appropriate governmental agencies an amount of money equal to that which had been earned by discriminatorily discharged employees on "work relief projects" and to credit that amount of money to a backpay award, was beyond the Board's remedial authority. Such payments, the Court claimed, had neither the effect of making employees whole nor of assuring them of their right to bargain collectively. Hence, the remedy served no statutory purpose.[42] Indeed, the Court felt that such payments were in the nature of an exaction, since the "work relief" payments constituted consideration for valuable services which the government received.[43]

Significantly, in *Republic Steel* the Court also rejected the Board's argument that the remedy was permissible since it would have the effect of deterring others from violating the Act. Although a remedy may incidentally act as a deterrent, the Court felt that if the NLRB was permitted to impose remedies *solely* on the basis of acting as a deterrent, the Board would be free to set up any system of penalties which it could deem adequate to that end.[44] The Court's holding reflects the principle that the rational relationship between unlawful conduct and the relief which is granted is not satisfied when the remedy purports to achieve ends other than those contemplated by the statute.[45]

---

[38] National Licorice Co. v. NLRB, 309 U.S. 350, 6 L.R.R.M. 674 (1940).

[39] 365 U.S. 651, 47 L.R.R.M. 2900 (1961).

[40] *Id.* at 655, 47 L.R.R.M. at 2901.

[41] 311 U.S. 7, 9-11, 7 L.R.R.M. 287, 289 (1940).

[42] *Id.* at 12-13, 7 L.R.R.M. at 290.

[43] *Id.,* 7 L.R.R.M. at 290.

[44] *Id.* at 12, 7 L.R.R.M. at 290. *See also* NLRB v. Coats & Clark, Inc., 241 F.2d 556, 561, 39 L.R.R.M. 2405 (5th Cir. 1957).

[45] As the Court pointed out, an unfair labor practice is not a crime; the Board may not impose remedies to compensate injuries it has deemed the body politic to have suffered. Republic Steel v. NLRB, 311 U.S. 7, 10, 7 L.R.R.M. at 289.

As shown above, even the Supreme Court, which enunciated this punitive-remedial test, has been critical of its use to attempt to analyze the propriety of NLRB orders, because its use often results in a semantic battle.[46] However, this test is consistently employed by the Board [47] and courts and must be dealt with when discussing the propriety of Board orders.[48]

---

[46] NLRB v. Seven-Up Bottling Co., *supra*, 344 U.S. 344, 348, 31 L.R.R.M. 2237, 2239 (1953).

[47] *See* Russell Motors, Inc., Amalgamated Local Union 355, 198 N.L.R.B. No. 58, 80 L.R.R.M. 1757, 1758, 1760 (1972), *enforced as modified*, 481 F.2d 996, 83 L.R.R.M. 2849 (2d Cir., 1973).

[48] *See NLRB Damage Awards*, 84 HARV. L. REV. 1670, 1679-1683 (1971) for a highly critical commentary of the courts' application of this remedial-punitive distinction. This article argues that "since the [Supreme] Court has never articulated a meaningful rationale for the doctrine, its application in any given case is usually problematic." *Id.*, at 1680. The article also suggests that the courts have applied the rule against punitive orders in an objectionable conclusory fashion. *Id.* The article further states that if the "Supreme Court would reject the uncritical application of the punitive doctrine and allow the policy considerations to come into the open, the Board could explore new remedies that are now apparently barred." *Id.* at p. 1682.

PART TWO

The Proper Scope of Board Orders

CHAPTER III

Cease and Desist Orders—The Appropriate Use of "Narrow" and "Broad" Orders

The most common of all NLRB remedial orders is the "cease and desist" order, i.e., an order directing a party found to have engaged in an unfair labor practice to cease and desist from the particular conduct found to be unlawful. Sometimes, the Board goes further and orders the offender also to cease and desist from "any other conduct" violative of rights guaranteed in the Act. The principles governing the award of such "broad" cease and desist orders are discussed below.

THE EXPRESS PUBLISHING DOCTRINE

Very early in the history of the Act, the Supreme Court recognized that the scope of cease and desist orders entered pursuant to the Act is important to the employer, as well as the employee, since the potentiality of contempt proceedings and penalties for future violations "adds sufficient additional sanctions to make material the difference between enjoined and nonenjoined employer activities." [1] Similar considerations arise in regard to the legality of broad injunctions against unions found to have engaged in unlawful secondary activity. The courts have consistently reminded the Board that it must clarify its orders and must tailor them so that they do not go beyond the circumstances, places, or persons involved in the proceedings.

In 1941, the Supreme Court, in *NLRB v. Express Publishing Co.*,[2] set out the doctrine that the Board must consider the nature and seriousness of the unfair labor practices found, the offender's past history of violations, and the probability of

---

[1] May Department Stores Co. v. NLRB, 326 U.S. 376, 388, 17 L.R.R.M. 643, 648 (1945).

[2] 312 U.S. 426, 8 L.R.R.M. 415 (1941).

recurrence. These guiding principles, still valid today, are the bases upon which the Board can rely in order to justify its issuance of a broad cease and desist order. In that case, the Board issued an order which restrained from committing "any act in violation of the statute" an employer who had unlawfully refused to bargain. The Board argued that because a violation of Section 8(5) is also a technical violation of Section 8(1), it was free to restrain not only violations of the type committed by the employer, but also any other unfair labor practices which infringe upon the rights of employees enumerated in Section 7. The Board proposed that this could be done however unrelated those practices were to the actual misconduct proven before the Board.[3]

The Court, however, rejected the Board's argument, reasoning that the apparent intent of Congress in enacting a statute which defined and classified unfair labor practices was that unlawful acts are not always so similar or related that the commission of one will necessitate an order restraining them all.[4] The Court noted that since the Act had granted exclusive power to the Board to prevent unfair labor practices, it was apparent that ". . . Congress did not contemplate that the courts should, by contempt proceedings, try alleged violations . . . not in controversy and not found by the Board. . . ."[5] Moreover, the Court believed that since the federal judiciary is not permitted to enjoin future violations of a statute which are unlike and unrelated to those originally charged,[6] the Board, which must act through the courts, could not have this broad authority either. Instead, the Court stated that:

> [t]he breadth of the order, like the injunction of a court, must depend upon the circumstances of each case, the purpose being to prevent violations, the threat of which in the future is indicated because of their similarity or relation to those unlawful acts which the Board has found to have been committed by the employer in the past.[7]

---

[3] *Id.* at 432-433, 8 L.R.R.M. at 418.

[4] *Id.* at 434, 8 L.R.R.M. at 418.

[5] *Id.* at 435, 8 L.R.R.M. at 419.

[6] *Id.* at 436, 8 L.R.R.M. at 419. *See* New York, N.H. & H.R. Co. v. Interstate Commerce Comm'n, 200 U.S. 361, 404 (1906); Swift & Co. v. United States, 196 U.S. 375 (1905).

[7] 312 U.S. at 436-437, 8 L.R.R.M. at 420.

As indicated above, the *Express Publishing* doctrine rests on two independent tests: (1) whether there is a likelihood that the violator will engage in future unlawful practices; or (2) whether the violations restrained bear some resemblance to the violation(s) found. In applying the first of these tests— the likelihood of the recurrence of future violations [8]—evidence showing either a pattern of numerous violations [9] or past instances in which an employer has committed unfair practices [10] has also been held sufficient to justify broad NLRB orders.

In an interesting extension of this doctrine, the Board issued a broad order not only against the employer but also against an individual representing the employer. The representative was found to have engaged in a pattern of bad-faith bargaining which resulted in numerous findings of Section 8(a)(5) and (1) violations against other employers who had been represented by that individual as a labor relations consultant. The Board ordered the individual to cease and desist from "[r]efusing to bargain in good faith with any labor organization when she is agent for any employer subject to the jurisdiction of the Board, that has an obligation under the Act to bargain with said labor organization." The order also required the individual to refrain from interfering "in any manner" with the Section 7 rights of employees. The Ninth Circuit enforced the Board's order except for the "in any other manner" provision which it ordered deleted.[11]

Alternatively, pursuant to the *Express Publishing* doctrine, the Board may justify a broad order where the additional

---

[8] Fremont Newspapers, Inc. v. NLRB, 436 F.2d 665, 76 L.R.R.M. 2049, 2056-2057 (8th Cir. 1970). The Board's order enjoining the employer from engaging in unlawful inducements and promises of benefits in violation of § 8(a)(1) was properly extended to "any other labor organization" since it was forseeable that new efforts would be made at union organization attempts.

[9] NLRB v. Great Atlantic and Pacific Tea Co., 406 F.2d 1173, 1175, 70 L.R.R.M. 2438 (5th Cir. 1969); Singer Company v. NLRB, 429 F.2d 172, 182, 74 L.R.R.M. 2669 (8th Cir. 1970); NLRB v. Kirk & Son, 154 F.2d 110, 18 L.R.R.M. 2177 (9th Cir. 1946) (per curiam) (general intent to violate all provisions of the Act warranted by specific findings of § 8(a)(1), (2), (3), and (5), and § 9(a) and (b) violations).

[10] *E.g.*, Kentucky Utilities Co., 76 N.L.R.B. 845, 849, 21 L.R.R.M. 1258, 1261 (1948).

[11] West Coast Liquidators and Mrs. Gladys Selvin, 205 N.L.R.B. 512, 517, 84 L.R.R.M. 1249 (1973), *enforced as modified*, NLRB v. Selvin, —— F.2d ——, 90 L.R.R.M. 2829, 2832 (9th Cir. 1975); Chalk Metal Co. and Mrs. Gladys Selvin, 197 N.L.R.B. 1133, 80 L.R.R.M. 1516 (1972).

violations restrained bear some resemblance to the violation(s) found. For example, in *Windsor Mfg. Co. v. NLRB*,[12] the court held that a broad order couched in the language of Section 7 was justified where, in addition to a Section 8(5) violation, there was evidence of other misconduct violative of Section 8(1). In another case, *Marshfield Steel Co. v. NLRB*,[13] the employer had challenged an order directing him to cease and desist from discouraging membership in the United Steelworkers of America "or in any other labor organization," on the grounds that the company had not engaged in violations against members of any union other than the Steelworkers. The court reasoned that the employer's reliance on *Express Publishing* was misplaced, stating that the doctrine stood for the proposition that the Board could not restrain an employer from committing *"other unfair labor practices in which it has not been found to be engaged . . . ,"* while the order in the case at bar "merely restrains (the employer) from conducting against other labor organizations the same unfair labor practices in which it has been found to be engaged."[14] The court concluded that the order was fully within the guidelines of *Express Publishing,* as the restrained violations bore complete resemblance to those which the employer had already committed.[15]

Generally, when faced with a challenge to a broad Board order on the grounds that it is overdrawn, the courts have indicated that "the order should not go beyond the evidence supporting unfair labor practices alleged."[16] Therefore, if the order restrains conduct violative of the Act and unrelated to the

---

[12] 118 F.2d 486, 8 L.R.R.M. 566 (3d Cir. 1941). *See also* NLRB v. Entwistle Mfg. Co., 120 F.2d 532, 536, 8 L.R.R.M. 645, 650 (4th Cir. 1941) (§ 8(3) violation coupled with violations of § 8(1)).

[13] 324 F.2d 333, 54 L.R.R.M. 2648 (8th Cir. 1963).

[14] *Id.* at 339, 54 L.R.R.M. 2653 (emphasis in the original); *cf.* NLRB v. Morrison Cafeteria Co., 311 F.2d 534, 52 L.R.R.M. 2150 (8th Cir. 1963).

[15] 324 F.2d at 339, 54 L.R.R.M. at 2653. *See* Allegheny Pepsi-Cola Bottling Co. v. NLRB, 312 F.2d 529, 52 L.R.R.M. 2019 (3d Cir. 1962); General Motors Corp. v. NLRB, —— F.2d ——, 89 L.R.R.M. 2431, 2432 (6th Cir. 1975).

[16] NLRB v. Cleveland Cliffs Iron Co., 133 F.2d 295, 302, 12 L.R.R.M. 550, 555 (6th Cir. 1943). *See* NLRB v. American Rolling Mill Co., 126 F.2d 38, 42, 10 L.R.R.M. 389, 393 (6th Cir. 1942); *cf.* Morrison-Knudsen, Inc. v. NLRB, 270 F.2d 864, 865, 44 L.R.R.M. 2680, 2681 (9th Cir. 1959) (employer practice of conditioning employment upon union "clearance" through its hiring hall, even though unlawful, did not justify a broad § 8(a)(1) and (3) cease and desist order when other forms of encouragement of union membership and loyalty could not be fairly anticipated).

unfair labor practices actually committed,[17] if the injunction goes beyond the threatened danger,[18] if there is no evidence that future unfair labor practices are likely,[19] or if the prior labor relations history of the offender shows no proclivity to violate the Act,[20] a broad order would be improper.

When unfair labor practices engaged in by an employer are of a pro forma nature, the courts are reluctant to enforce broad cease and desist orders to remedy such violations. For example, under the Act an employer may not obtain direct appellate court review of NLRB election case rulings, since these rulings are not considered to be *final* orders as required by Section 10(c) of the Act. An employer in such circumstances must commit a "technical" Section 8(a)(5) refusal to bargain violation in order to gain access to court review.[21]

In *May Department Stores Co. v. NLRB*,[22] the Supreme Court stated that:

> [A]lthough there is a violation of 8(1) as well as 8(5), the violation of 8(1) is so intertwined with the refusal to bargain with a unit asserted to be certified improperly that, without a clear determination by the Board of an attitude of opposition to the pur-

---

[17] *E.g.*, NLRB v. Walt Disney Productions, 146 F.2d 44, 50, 15 L.R.R.M. 691, 697 (9th Cir. 1944); NLRB v. Great Atlantic & Pacific Tea Co., 406 F.2d 1173, 70 L.R.R.M. 2438, 2439-2440 (5th Cir. 1969). *Cf.* NLRB v. Whitfield Pickle Co., 374 F.2d 576, 583, 64 L.R.R.M. 2656, 2661-2662 (5th Cir. 1967), wherein the court refused to enforce that part of the Board's order directing the employer to bargain collectively since the only reference to collective bargaining was a statement by a company official to the effect that he would not sign any agreement with the union. Although the statement violated § 8(a)(1), it did not violate § 8(a)(5), and therefore no bargaining order could be based upon it.

[18] NLRB v. Consolidated Machine Tool Corp., 163 F.2d 376, 379, 20 L.R.R.M. 2439, 2441 (2d Cir. 1947), *cert. denied*, 332 U.S. 824, 21 L.R.R.M. 2043 (1947).

[19] NLRB v. Standard Metal Fabricating Co., 297 F.2d 365, 367, 49 L.R.R.M. 2309, 2310 (8th Cir. 1961).

[20] *E.g.*, Fremont Newspapers, Inc. v. NLRB, 436 F.2d 665, 675, 76 L.R.R.M. 2049, 2056 (8th Cir. 1970); Southwire Co. v. NLRB, 383 F.2d 235, 237, 65 L.R.R.M. 3042, 3045 (5th Cir. 1967). The Board itself has narrowed the scope of an order recommended by a trial examiner on identical grounds. Central Rigging and Contracting Corp., 129 N.L.R.B. 342, 343 n.3, 46 L.R.R.M. 1548, 1549 (1960).

[21] As the Fifth Circuit noted, the courts attach no opprobrium to the employer's refusal to bargain where it is the only means of inveighing the Board's findings in an underlying representation case. NLRB v. Genesco, Inc., 406 F.2d 393, 70 L.R.R.M. 2252, 2253 (5th Cir. 1969).

[22] 326 U.S. 376, 17 L.R.R.M. 643 (1945).

poses of the Act to protect the rights of employees generally, the decree need not enjoin Company actions which are not determined by the Board to be so motivated.[23]

Accordingly, the Board also has refused to issue broad orders in such cases.[24]

The importance of the Board's applying the proper scope to its cease and desist orders cannot be overestimated. The threat to an employer who must live under an unjustifiably broad order is formidable, considering that he may thereafter become the target of contempt of court proceedings for future violations of that order.[25]

UNION VIOLATIONS OF SECTION 8(b)

With the enactment of the Taft-Hartley Amendments,[26] and the revisions found in the Landrum-Griffin Act,[27] labor organizations became subject to, *inter alia,* the Section 8(b) restrictions which prohibit certain kinds of secondary activities. As was the case in issuing remedies for employer violations, the permissible scope of remedial orders enjoining union violations is tested under the guidelines enunciated in *Express Publishing.*

In *IBEW, Local 501 v. NLRB,*[28] the Supreme Court reviewed a broad Board order issued upon a finding of a violation of Section 8(b)(4)(A), whereby the union had induced, through picketing, the employees of one construction project subcontractor to engage in a strike. The object of the strike was to force the general contractor to terminate his business relationship with a nonunion subcontractor. The union had objected to the breadth of the Board's order, which in pertinent part provided that the union:

---

[23] *Id.* at 392, 17 L.R.R.M. at 650.

[24] Southeastern Envelope Co., 206 N.L.R.B. 933, 84 L.R.R.M. 1577, 1580 (1973); Crucible Steel Co., 66 N.L.R.B. 1157, 1162, 17 L.R.R.M. 397, 398 (1946) (refusal to bargain undertaken on grounds that the determination of the appropriate bargaining unit was erroneous); *see also* United Fryer & Stillman, Inc., 139 N.L.R.B. 704 n.1, 51 L.R.R.M. 1385, 1386 (1962) (dispute as to appropriateness of multi-employer unit).

[25] May Department Stores Co. v. NLRB, 326 U.S. 376, 388, 17 L.R.R.M. 643, 648 (1945).

[26] 61 Stat. 136 (1947).

[27] 73 Stat. 541 (1959).

[28] 341 U.S. 694, 696-698, 28 L.R.R.M. 2115, 2116-2117 (1951).

[c]ease and desist from inducing or encouraging the employees of Nicholas Deltorto [the struck subcontractor] *or any employer*, by picketing . . . strike or a concerted refusal . . . to perform any services, where an object thereof is to force or require Giorgi Construction Co. [the general contractor] *or any other employer or person* to cease doing business with Samuel Langer [the non-union subcontractor].[29] (emphasis added)

The union contended that the language, herein italicized, rendered the order overly broad because it prohibited secondary activity not only by the employees of Deltorto but also of "any other employer," and that the condemned objective was to break business relations not only between Giorgi and Langer, but also with "any other employer" doing business with Langer.[30] The Court overruled the union's objections, pointing out that if the order were limited to Deltorto or Giorgi, it would still expose Langer or any other employers doing business with him to the same type of unlawful pressure through other "comparable channels."[31] The Court justified the decision on the principle that "when the purpose to restrain trade appears from a clear violation of law, it is not necessary that all of the untraveled roads to that end be left open and that only the worn one be closed."[32] This holding clearly falls within the test enunciated in *Express Publishing* that permits broad restraint on future violations which bear some resemblance to the violation(s) found.

The permissible scope of Section 8(b) Board orders was further defined by the Court in *Communication Workers v. NLRB*,[33] decided nearly a decade later. In that case, the union, during the course of a strike, had coerced employees of the Ohio Consolidated Telephone Company in the exercise of their right to refrain from participation in union activity, thereby violating Section 8(b)(1)(A). In its order, the Board had directed the union to cease and desist from such violations affecting not only the employees of Ohio Consolidated, but also employees of "any other employer." In a per curiam opinion, the Supreme Court modified the order by striking the words

---

[29] *Id.* at 698-699, 28 L.R.R.M. at 2117.

[30] *Id.* at 705, 28 L.R.R.M. at 2120.

[31] *Id.* at 705-706, 28 L.R.R.M. at 2120.

[32] *Id.* at 706, 28 L.R.R.M. at 2120, *quoting from* International Salt Co. v. United States, 332 U.S. 392, 400 (1947).

[33] 362 U.S. 479, 46 L.R.R.M. 2033 (1960) (per curiam).

"or any other employer," reasoning that without evidence the union had violated the rights of the employees of any other employer, the order went beyond the violation found and could not be justified on the principles of *Express Publishing*.[34]

In general, the *IBEW, Local 501* and *Communication Workers* cases teach that the scope of the Board's order should be directed only toward protecting the union's intended victim and those with whom he does business.[35] Thus, when the order purports to enjoin misconduct by a union with the object of affecting its relationship not only with a neutral or primary employer, but also with any other neutrals or primary employers who are unrelated to the participants in the dispute, the Board has been found to have exceeded its authority.[36]

When the union's illegal conduct, however, involves a contract into which the union has entered not only with the subject employer but with other employers as well, the Board and courts are more likely to perceive the desirability and necessity of expanding the impact of the Board's order beyond the immediate employer in the case.[37]

The aforementioned guideline must be further qualified to take into account other aspects of the *Express Publishing* doctrine. Illustrative of this point is the case of *Local 469, Plumbers*

---

[34] *Id.* at 480-481, 46 L.R.R.M. at 2034.

[35] *Cf.* NLRB v. Carpenters District Council (Kaaz Woodwork, Co.), 383 F.2d 89, 66 L.R.R.M. 2177 (8th Cir. 1967).

[36] *See, e.g.*, Plumbers, Local 519 v. NLRB, 416 F.2d 1120, 70 L.R.R.M. 3300 (D.C. Cir. 1969); NLRB v. Hatters Union (Korber Hats, Inc.), 286 F.2d 950, 47 L.R.R.M. 2752 (4th Cir. 1961); NLRB v. Carpenters Union (Midwest Homes, Inc.), 276 F.2d 694, 45 L.R.R.M. 3014 (7th Cir. 1960); NLRB v. Local 926, Operating Engineers, 267 F.2d 418, 44 L.R.R.M. 2200 (5th Cir. 1959); NLRB v. Int'l Hod Carriers, Local 1140, 285 F.2d 394, 396, 47 L.R.R.M. 2311 (8th Cir. 1960), and 285 F.2d 397, 404-405, 47 L.R.R.M. 2345 (8th Cir. 1960), *cert. denied* 366 U.S. 903; NLRB v. Enterprise Ass'n, Local Union No. 638, 285 F.2d 642, 47 L.R.R.M. 2189 (2d Cir. 1960); NLRB v. Local Union No. 25, IBEW, 491 F.2d 838, 85 L.R.R.M. 2499, 2501 (2d Cir. 1974).

[37] *See* NLRB v. Local 294, Teamsters (Van Transport Lines, Inc.), 298 F.2d 105, 49 L.R.R.M. 2315, 2317 (2d Cir. 1961); NLRB v. Shuck Construction Co., 243 F.2d 519, 39 L.R.R.M. 2322, 2326 (9th Cir. 1957), and cases cited therein; NLRB v. Sun Tent-Leubbert Co., 151 F.2d 483, 17 L.R.R.M. 515, 521-522 (9th Cir. 1945) *cert. denied sub nom.* Merchants & Mfgrs. Ass'n v. NLRB, 329 U.S. 714, 18 L.R.R.M. 2468; Milk Drivers and Dairy Employees Union Local No. 471, Int'l Bro. of Teamsters, (Ronco Delivery) 209 N.L.R.B. No. 10, 86 L.R.R.M. 1239 (1974); Teamsters, Local Union No. 631, 154 N.L.R.B. 67, 70, 59 L.R.R.M. 1716 (1965); Milk Drivers and Dairy Employees, Local Union No. 537 (Sealtest Foods), 147 N.L.R.B. 230, 237, 56 L.R.R.M. 1193 (1964).

& *Pipefitters* (*Howard C. Johnson*),[38] wherein the union, in violation of Section 8(b)(4)(A), induced the employees of a general contractor (Thomas) at a construction project to engage in a work stoppage with the object of forcing Thomas to cease doing business with a nonunion subcontractor (Johnson). In its ititial hearing, the panel majority had held that, in light of the *Communication Workers* decision, a Board order which restrained the union from inducing the employees of Thomas "or any other employer" to engage in strikes directed at terminating a business relationship with Johnson was overdrawn. The evidence showed that the inducement was limited to the Thomas-Johnson subcontract.[39] Member Rodgers dissented on the grounds that the *Communication Workers* case was distinct because it had concerned only employee coercion, a violation of Section 8(b)(1)(A), while the instant case involved a Section 8(b)(4)(A) violation.[40] On the motion of the General Counsel for reconsideration, the Board amended its prior order, issuing a supplemental decision and order which, in effect, adopted the dissent of Member Rodgers.[41]

The union then sought and obtained judicial review of the proper scope of the Board's amended order.[42] On appeal, the Ninth Circuit refused to enforce the extension of the order on the grounds that the evidence required for a broad order under the *Express Publishing* doctrine was insufficient.[43] Since the general contractor, Thomas, was in a situation similar to that of the general contractor in the *IBEW, Local 501* case, a strict application of law, without regard to facts, would have rendered *IBEW, Local 501* the controlling precedent. The court, however, distinguished the *IBEW, Local 501* case on the grounds that the evidence therein showed a likelihood of further union secondary activity against the primary and secondary employers, whereas, in the case at bar, such evidence was lacking; hence

---

[38] 129 N.L.R.B. 36, 46 L.R.R.M. 1483 (1960).

[39] *Id.* at 37 n.1, 46 L.R.R.M. at 1483-1484.

[40] *Id.*, 46 L.R.R.M. at 1484 (Member Rodgers, dissenting).

[41] Local 469, Plumbers & Pipefitters, 130 N.L.R.B. 1289, 47 L.R.R.M. 1484 (1961).

[42] NLRB v. Local 469, Plumbers & Pipefitters, 300 F.2d 649, 49 L.R.R.M. 2862 (9th Cir. 1962).

[43] *Id.* at 653, 49 L.R.R.M. at 2865.

the Board failed to satisfy the requirements of the *Express Publishing* doctrine.[44]

When the evidence has been sufficient to meet the *Express Publishing* guidelines of similarity or likelihood of recurrence, the courts have sanctioned broad orders against unions. For example, in *NLRB v. Brewery Drivers, Local 830*,[45] the court enforced an order which prohibited the union from violating not only the rights of the employees of five beer distributors at whose places of business the unlawful practices had occurred, but also the rights of employees of any other employer. The court reasoned that the union's attack on the breadth of the order was unfounded [46] since the testimony had shown a pattern of unlawful conduct by the union which indicated that the danger of recurrence of such misconduct was great.[47] In the same vein, the Court of Appeals for the Second Circuit sustained a broad order where evidence was that the specific violations found had come from a generalized campaign of secondary pressure by the union. The court reasoned that an order limited solely to the employers involved would be an inadequate safeguard.[48]

In proving that a broad order is necessary because of a particular union's proclivity to violate the Act, it is evident that a record of past violations by the union is properly and consistently considered probative as a means of forecasting the union's likelihood of violating the Act in the future.[49] The

---

[44] *Id.*, 49 L.R.R.M. at 2865. *See e.g.*, Local 69, Sheet Metal Workers (Wind Heating Co.), 209 N.L.R.B. No. 154, 85 L.R.R.M. 1481 (1974); Carpenters, Local 690 (Moore Construction Co.), 190 N.L.R.B. 609, 77 L.R.R.M. 1271 (1971).

[45] 281 F.2d 319, 323, 46 L.R.R.M. 2732, 2735 (3d Cir. 1960).

[46] The Third Circuit did modify the scope of the order, limiting its effects so as to make it "applicable to the situation (both places and persons) which gave rise to this litigation." *Id.* at 323, 46 L.R.R.M. at 2735. *See* p. 36, *infra.*

[47] 281 F.2d at 323, 46 L.R.R.M. at 2735.

[48] NLRB v. Local 25, IBEW, 383 F.2d 449, 454-455, 66 L.R.R.M. 2355, 2359 (2d Cir. 1967). *See also* NLRB v. Local 3, IBEW, 477 F.2d 260, 268-269, 82 L.R.R.M. 3190 (2d Cir. 1973).

[49] *See e.g.*, NLRB v. Teamsters, Local 327 (Whale, Inc.), 432 F.2d 933, 934, 75 L.R.R.M. 2435 (6th Cir. 1970); NLRB v. Teamsters, Local 327 (Hartmann Luggage Co.), 419 F.2d 1282, 1284, 73 L.R.R.M. 2199, 2200 (6th Cir. 1970); Teamsters, Local 70 (Morris Draying Co.), 195 N.L.R.B. 957, 79 L.R.R.M. 1601, 1602 (1972); NLRB v. Carpenters District Council of Kansas City & Vic. (Kaaz Woodwork Co.), 383 F.2d 89, 96, 66 L.R.R.M. 2177 (8th

Board will also consider a union's proclivity to engage in violence and threats of violence.[50] As a matter of proof, it has been held that judicial notice could be taken of past violations of Section 8(b)(4) to justify a finding that a particular union has demonstrated a proclivity to violate the Act.[51] Although in at least one case the Second Circuit refused to enforce a broad Board order because the Court found no evidence "on the instant record" that the union had engaged in a violation against the employees of any employer,[52] it is well established by the overwhelming number of decided cases that the Board need not restrict itself to the record of the case before it in deciding that a broad order is warranted.

On the other hand, in *Teamsters, Local 70 (C&T Trucking Co.)*,[53] the Board, despite the urgings of the General Counsel, refused to issue a broad order against a union that had engaged in common-situs picketing which did not conform to the *Moore Dry Dock Co.* standards.[54] Unlike the trial examiner, who would only receive evidence in connection with the case at bar, the Board recognized that prior decisions could be considered. The Board refused, however, to issue a broad order

---

Cir. 1967); NLRB v. Int'l Union of Operating Engineers, Local 571, 317 F.2d 638, 644, 53 L.R.R.M. 2294 (8th Cir. 1963); NLRB v. Milk Drivers & Dairy Emp. Local Union 584 (Old Dutch Farms, Inc.), 341 F.2d 29, 33, 58 L.R.R.M. 2290 (2d Cir. 1965); NLRB v. Local 282, Int'l Bro. of Teamsters, Local 282, 344 F.2d 649, 652-653, 58 L.R.R.M. 2065 (2d Cir. 1965); NLRB v. Local 810, Fabricators & Warehousemen, Int'l Bro. of Teamsters (Advance Trucking Corp.), 299 F.2d 636, 637, 49 L.R.R.M. 2433 (2d Cir. 1962); NLRB v. Local 542, Int'l Union of Operating Engineers, 329 F.2d 512, 515-516, 56 L.R.R.M. 2028 (3d Cir. 1964); Amalgamated Local Union 355 v. NLRB (Russell Motors, Inc.), 481 F.2d 996, 1008, 83 L.R.R.M. 2849 (2d Cir. 1973) and cases cited therein; NLRB v. Sequoia District Council of Carpenters, etc., 499 F.2d 129, 86 L.R.R.M. 3001 (9th Cir. 1974).

[50] Teamsters Local 901 (Associated Federal Homes), 193 N.L.R.B. 591, 598, 78 L.R.R.M. 1377, 1379 (1971).

[51] *See* NLRB v. Local 85, Teamsters (Victory Transportation Service, Inc.), 454 F.2d 875, 879, 79 L.R.R.M. 2437, 2439 (9th Cir. 1972) (court had recently enforced broad order against Local 85, noting its propensity for illegal secondary activities accompanied by violence); NLRB v. Teamsters, Local 327 (Hartmann Luggage Co.), 419 F.2d 1282, 1284, 73 L.R.R.M. 2199, 2200 (6th Cir. 1970) (Board can take judicial notice of its own case involving same local).

[52] *See* NLRB v. Local Union No. 25, IBEW, 491 F.2d 838, 85 L.R.R.M. 2499, 2501 (2d Cir. 1974).

[53] 191 N.L.R.B. 11, 12, 77 L.R.R.M. 1336 (1971).

[54] 92 N.L.R.B. 547, 549, 27 L.R.R.M. 1108, 1110 (1950).

even though the particular Teamster's local had a history of some eighteen prior unfair labor practice dispositions against it.[55] The Board discounted seventeen of these as having no probative value, and held that one prior adverse Board decision was irrelevant, since it had involved only secondary activities for a recognitional purpose, whereas the illegal objective of the union in the case at bar was designed to force the secondary employer to cease doing business with the primary employer.[56] The decision is somewhat anomalous, since the Board in *C&T Trucking* approached the problem of determining the proper scope of its order in the same manner discredited by the Ninth Circuit in *NLRB v. Local 469, Plumbers & Pipefitters*,[57] by "simply . . . classifying the . . . case in one or another of the available statutory categories." [58]

Thus, even though the legal principles relating to the breadth of Board orders are quite well established, it is not necessarily easy to predict when the courts will agree with Board determinations that similar past violations justify the issuance of a broad order. Another interesting illustration is found in a series of Board decisions which were consolidated for court review in *San Francisco Local Joint Executive Board of Culinary Workers, et al. v. NLRB*.[59] There the Board found in three separate cases that the union had picketed three employers with a recognitional object in violation of Section 8(b)(7)(C), and ordered the union to refrain from so picketing "any other employer." Further, there was a similar fourth violation found in another unappealed Board decision. Despite this strong evidence of the union's tendency to violate this section of the Act, the Court found that the union was not engaged in "a generalized scheme to violate the Act." [60] The Court majority reasoned that the union was a sizable labor organization in a

---

[55] In support of his request for a broad order based upon the union's penchant to violate the Act, the General Counsel had cited thirteen settlement agreements, one Board decision, one trial examiner's decision to which no exceptions were filed, and another which was then pending to before the Board, a civil and criminal contempt adjudication in one case, and a preliminary injunction in another. 191 N.L.R.B. at 11, 77 L.R.R.M. at 1337.

[56] *Id.*, 77 L.R.R.M. at 1337-1338.

[57] 300 F.2d 649, 49 L.R.R.M. 2862 (9th Cir. 1962).

[58] *Id.* at 654, 49 L.R.R.M. at 2866.

[59] 501 F.2d 794, 86 L.R.R.M. 2828, 2833-2834 (D.C. Cir. 1974).

[60] *Id.*, 86 L.R.R.M. at 2834.

major metropolitan area, and that, within this context, its violations took on the "coloration of isolated instances," with the union simply being "somewhat overzealous in pursuing its legitimate organizational goals." [61] Judge MacKinnon strongly dissented from this holding and argued that "the repeated illegal picketing against four different employers" satisfied the requirement of a generalized scheme to violate the Act.[62] The uncertainty of the direction the Board sometimes receives from the courts is now highlighted by the very next broad 8(b)(7) (C) Board order [63] against the same union which came before the District of Columbia Circuit. In all relevant aspects, this case was identical to the previous one considered by the court, except that the union had committed one more violation. The union strenuously fought the broad order but the court enforced the Board's order in a summary per curiam opinion and did not even discuss the broad order issue that had so troubled the previous panel.[64]

BOARD ORDERS MUST CLEARLY INDICATE WHAT ACTIVITIES ARE PROHIBITED

In *Express Publishing,* the Supreme Court observed that Board orders, when judicially confirmed, may result in contempt proceedings; therefore, an order must "state with reasonable specificity the acts which the [violator] is to do or refrain from doing." [65] Shortly thereafter, in *J.I. Case Co. v. NLRB,*[66] the Court reaffirmed this principle, stating:

> Questions of construction had better be ironed out before enforcement orders issue than upon contempt proceedings. A party is entitled to a definition as exact as the circumstances permit of the acts which he can perform only on pain of contempt of court.[67]

---

[61] *Id.*

[62] *Id.,* 86 L.R.R.M. at 2835-2837.

[63] San Francisco Local Joint Executive Board of Culinary Workers, *et al.,* 207 N.L.R.B. No. 38, 84 L.R.R.M. 1604 (1973).

[64] *See* San Francisco Local Joint Executive Board of Culinary Workers, *et al.* v. NLRB, per curiam (D.C. Cir., Docket No. 73-2259, 1975).

[65] 312 U.S. at 433, 8 L.R.R.M. 415, 418.

[66] 321 U.S. 332, 14 L.R.R.M. 501 (1944).

[67] *Id.* at 341, 14 L.R.R.M. at 505-506.

Furthermore, although the Board has sole authority to institute contempt proceedings, the Court has held that ". . . Congress did not contemplate that the courts should, by contempt proceedings, try alleged violations of the [Act] not in controversy. . . ." [68] Accordingly, rather than being subjected immediately to contempt proceedings which encompass parties or events absent in the instant case, an offender charged with a violation at some future time generally will receive a Board hearing.[69] This relieves a court of appeals, by virtue of its contempt powers, from becoming a labor court of first instance.[70]

The Board's order must be limited to the facts appearing on the record. For example, in *NLRB v. Carpenters Union (Midwest Homes, Inc.)*,[71] the Board issued a broad order prohibiting not only secondary activities directed at the primary employer in the instant case, but also against all other primary employers. Claiming that the Board lacked sufficient facts upon which to act, the court stated that the Board in effect "merely announced a legal pattern, commanded 'Go and sin no more' and then washed its hands of the matter." [72] The objection of the courts was that such an order "would impose upon a court of appeals on a possible future hearing of contempt charges, the duty of resolving factual issues . . . [concerning] a particular primary employer not named in the present proceeding." [73] The court refused to undertake this duty

---

[68] 312 U.S. at 435, 8 L.R.R.M. at 419.

[69] *See* Reliance Mfg. Co. v. NLRB, 125 F.2d 311, 322, 9 L.R.R.M. 536, 547 (7th Cir. 1941) ; *accord*, NLRB v. Ford Motor Co., 119 F.2d 326, 8 L.R.R.M. 656 (5th Cir. 1941); NLRB v. Schill Steel Products, Inc., 480 F.2d 586, 83 L.R.R.M. 2386, 2393 (5th Cir. 1973).

[70] Teamsters, Local 554 v. NLRB, 262 F.2d 456, 463, 43 L.R.R.M. 2197, 2202 (D.C. Cir. 1958) ; *accord*, Morrison-Knudsen, Inc., 270 F.2d 864, 865, 44 L.R.R.M. 2680, 2681 (9th Cir. 1959).

[71] 276 F.2d 694, 45 L.R.R.M. 3014 (7th Cir. 1960).

[72] *Id.* at 699, 45 L.R.R.M. at 3017.

[73] *Id.*, 45 L.R.R.M. at 3017. *See also* NLRB v. Local 926, Operating Engineers, 267 F.2d 418, 421, 44 L.R.R.M. 2200, 2203 (5th Cir. 1959), wherein the court, recognizing the discretionary authority of the Board to fashion remedies, stated:

> We consider more important, and basic to a fair administration of the Act, the hard-won principle of Anglo-American law that a judgment or order must find adequate support in the record. An order of a court or federal agency that goes beyond the record to penalize an offender smacks too much of attainder to be acceptable to this Court.

on two grounds: first, that the determination should be made by the Board prior to entering its order; and second, that it was not the intent of Congress that the courts should be used in contempt proceedings to remedy the deficiencies of Board orders.[74]

Similarly, the order should not be susceptible to any possible misconstructions. For example, in *NLRB v. Stowe Spinning Co.*,[75] the Supreme Court rejected contentions that, implicit in the Board's decree was the word "reasonable" regarding the potential applicability of the decree to future violations. The Court astutely noted that if "reasonable" were implied, then a court would have to review that decision in order to determine its appropriate scope before making a decision on the case at hand. Since the Board should have determined the appropriate scope of the order originally, the Court concluded that a court review of the scope "makes the order itself a useless formality."[76] In another case, *J.I. Case Co. v. NLRB*,[77] the Supreme Court cautioned the Board against ordering a violator "to desist from more on the theory that he may violate the literal language and then defend by resort to the Board's construction of it [since] Court's orders are not to be trifled with, nor should they invite litigation as to their meaning."[78] On the other hand, it has been held that an order requiring an offender to cease and desist from interfering with employee rights in any *like* or *related* manner "is not subject to the construction of a scatter-gun charge subjecting [the offender] to the possibility of contempt proceedings for violations not substantially like or related to the subject matter specified in the Board's order. . . ."[79]

---

[74] 276 F.2d at 699, 45 L.R.R.M. at 3017, *see* text accompanying note 66, *supra*.

[75] 336 U.S. 226, 232-233, 23 L.R.R.M. 2371, 2374 (1949).

[76] *Id.* at 233, 23 L.R.R.M. at 2374.

[77] 321 U.S. 332, 14 L.R.R.M. 501 (1944).

[78] *Id.* at 341, 14 L.R.R.M. at 506. *Cf.* NLRB v. United Wire & Supply Corp., 312 F.2d 11, 13, 52 L.R.R.M. 2110, 2112 (1st Cir. 1962) (order directing employer to cease and desist from creating an "impression of surveillance" overly broad without qualifying language setting forth the conduct which is specifically objected to and forbidden).

[79] NLRB v. Great Atlantic & Pacific Tea Co., 277 F.2d 759, 765, 46 L.R.R.M. 2055, 2059 (5th Cir. 1960) (unlawful solicitation and distribution rules).

THE SCOPE OF THE REMEDY MAY VARY WITH THE SCOPE OF THE VIOLATOR'S OPERATIONS

Because many employers have several plants and multistate operations, and unions often operate on a regional or national basis, the Board has often ordered remedial action that extends beyond the immediate units involved in the case. Thus, where it had been shown that the employer had instituted a system-wide, centrally directed, and coordinated policy to commit unfair practices, the courts have found that the Board had properly included all the employer's plants within its order.[80]

Moreover, the Board may properly consider that, if not deterred, the employer would pursue the same discriminatory policies at every unit within a certain geographic area, and may apply its cease and desist order to that entire area.[81] Furthermore, when employers who have such a coordinated system-wide policy commit flagrant unfair labor practices, the application of Board orders to plants other than those at which the violations occurred has been found to be particularly appropriate.[82] When the employer controls several corporations, or one corporation with separate divisions, Board orders applying to more than one division or corporation have also been upheld by the courts.[83]

[80] NLRB v. Salant & Salant, Inc., 183 F.2d 462, 465, 26 L.R.R.M. 2234, 2236 (6th Cir. 1950); *cf.* United Aircraft Co. v. NLRB, 440 F.2d 85, 100, 76 L.R.R.M. 2761, 2773 (2d Cir. 1971) (general pattern of union hostility and discriminatory conduct at five of company's six plants located in a compact geographical area justified order directing that notices be posted at all six plants); Decaturville Sportswear Co. v. NLRB, 406 F.2d 886, 889, 70 L.R.R.M. 2472, 2474 (6th Cir. 1969); *accord* United Aircraft Co. v. NLRB, 440 F.2d 85, 76 L.R.R.M. 2761, 2773 (2d Cir. 1971).

[81] NLRB v. Lummus Co., 210 F.2d 377, 33 L.R.R.M. 2513, 2516 (5th Cir. 1954); Texas Gulf Sulphur Co. v. NLRB, 463 F.2d 779, 80 L.R.R.M. 3171 (5th Cir. 1972).

[82] *See e.g.,* NLRB v. Great Atlantic & Pacific Tea Co., 408 F.2d 374, 376, 70 L.R.R.M. 2829, 2830 (5th Cir. 1969) (per curiam); NLRB v. Great Atlantic & Pacific Tea Co., 409 F.2d 296, 70 L.R.R.M. 3246, 3248 (5th Cir. 1969); J. P. Stevens & Co. v. NLRB, 388 F.2d 896, 65 L.R.R.M. 2829, 2838 (2d Cir. 1967); J. P. Stevens & Co., 205 N.L.R.B. 1032, 84 L.R.R.M. 1092 (1973) (known antiunion attitude of employer justified posting notices in all of its plants in a three-state area even though violation had occurred only at one plant). *But cf.* J. P. Stevens & Co. v. NLRB, 461 F.2d 490, 80 L.R.R.M. 2609, 2612 (4th Cir. 1972). *See also* Heck's Inc., 191 N.L.R.B. 886, 887, 77 L.R.R.M. 1513, 1514-1515 (1971).

[83] NLRB v. Lipman Brothers, 355 F.2d 1966, 61 L.R.R.M. 2193, 2197 (1st Cir. 1966) (three brothers were officers and directors of all corporations in-

On the other hand, orders which would have applied to an employer's units other than those immediately involved in the case at hand have been found to be inappropriate in cases in which the misconduct was not pervasive, occurred only at an individual plant, and did not evidently affect the employees in the other units.[84] For example, in *NLRB v. Ford Motor Co.*,[85] the Board directed the company to post notices in all of its plants even though the violations committed by the employer occurred only in its Dallas plant. The court found that the system-wide scope of the Board's order was too broad and held that the "Board was without jurisdiction to make the order operate as generally as it did." [86]

---

volved, were considered joint employers, and formulated and administered a common labor policy); NLRB v. Sunbeam Electric Mfg. Co., 133 F.2d 856, 861, 11 L.R.R.M. 820, 826 (7th Cir. 1943) (broad order enforced, even though the distribution of illegal circulars was limited to one division, since a contemporaneous oral campaign directed at all employees had made them aware of the issues, placing them within the scope of the employer's propaganda campaign); Schramm & Schmieg Co., 67 N.L.R.B. 980, 993-994, 18 L.R.R.M. 1032, 1033 (1946) (employees of two factories, owned by a common employer and located in the same building, given notice since the individual found to have violated the Act was the superintendent of both factories).

[84] Dover Corp., 211 N.L.R.B. No. 98, 86 L.R.R.M. 1607, 1612 (1974); Albert's Inc., 213 N.L.R.B. No. 94, 87 L.R.R.M. 1682 (1974); United Mercantile Inc., 204 N.L.R.B. 663, 83 L.R.R.M. 1562 (1973); *But cf.* Kellwood Co., 199 N.L.R.B. 756, 82 L.R.R.M. 1015, 1016 (1972), wherein the Board denied the General Counsel's request that Kellwood be enjoined from further § 8(a)(1) violations at all of its plants and that notices be posted for the fifty-one plants in the Kellwood complex, although the Board recognized the propensity of the employer to engage in unfair labor practices.

[85] 119 F.2d 326, 8 L.R.R.M. 656 (5th Cir. 1941).

[86] *Id.* at 330-331, 8 L.R.R.M. at 659. *See also* Reliance Mfg. Co. v. NLRB, 125 F.2d 311, 321-322, 9 L.R.R.M. 536, 547 (7th Cir. 1941), wherein the court, relying on *Ford Motor Co.*, refused to enforce an order requiring posting of notices in all of the plants operated by the employer (the original charges claimed violations at ten of thirteen plants—subsequently, the Board dismissed charges as to one plant for lack of evidence and severed as to another), holding that when a charge is filed complaining of violations at plants not included in the instant proceeding, the employer is entitled to a Board hearing. *Cf.* NLRB v. F. H. McGraw & Co., 206 F.2d 635, 641, 32 L.R.R.M. 2220, 2225 (6th Cir. 1953). *And see* NLRB v. Jack Smith Beverages, Inc., 202 F.2d 100, 102, 31 L.R.R.M. 2366, 2368 (6th Cir. 1953), *cert. denied*, 345 U.S. 995, 32 L.R.R.M. 2247 (1953). The employer had violated § 8(a)(2) by rendering unlawful assistance to an incumbent union, the order was strictly limited by the court to apply to the one plant where the violations were found to have occurred on the rationale that to render a broad order on the basis of the *Express Publishing* doctrine would impose an unlawful restraint on the employees' freedom of choice in choosing their representatives in other plants within the system.

Many of the relevant factors to be considered in determining whether or not to expand the scope of the remedy beyond the immediate parties involved were outlined in *Teamsters Local No. 386 (Valley Employers Ass'n, et al.)*[87] where the Board reversed the trial examiner and struck his recommendation that all of the members (about 400) of the employers' association be required to post the notice to remedy the union's violation. The Board stressed that the member employers were engaged in various industries, many without union organization, and many were engaged only in intrastate commerce. Moreover, none of the other association members belonged to the industry group involved, none were covered by the same collective bargaining agreement, and most of them did not have a contract with the respondent union.

In cases involving union violations, the courts have limited the scope of the Board's orders to the "local" union in order to make it consonant with both the places and persons which have given rise to the litigation.[88] Thus, in *NLRB v. Teamsters, Local 327 (Hartmann Luggage Co.)*,[89] the Sixth Circuit held that a Board order restraining the union from "coercing the employees of Hartmann Luggage Company *or the employees of any other employer within its jurisdictional territory*" in their Section 7 rights, posed both conceptual and practical problems for a court which seriously contemplated enforcing the order. The court reasoned that the order violated the provisions of Rule 65(d) of the Federal Rules of Civil Procedure,[90] in that it contained no limitation in time, was both too broad and too vague in relation to persons expected to obey it, and did not define the jurisdiction of Local 327, thus providing no means for ascertaining the individuals for whom protection was sought.[91]

---

[87] 145 N.L.R.B. 1475, n. 1, and 55 L.R.R.M. 1186 (1964).

[88] NLRB v. Brewery Drivers, Local 830, 281 F.2d 319, 323, 46 L.R.R.M. 2732, 2735 (3d Cir. 1960).

[89] 419 F.2d 1282, 1283, 73 L.R.R.M. 2199, 2200 (6th Cir. 1970) (per curiam).

[90] *See* Fed. R. Civ. P. 65(d), which provides in pertinent part that: "Every order granting an injunction . . . shall be specific in terms; shall describe in reasonable detail, and not by reference to the complaint or other document, the act or acts sought to be restrained . . . ."

[91] 419 F.2d at 1283, 73 L.R.R.M. at 2200. *See* NLRB v. Teamsters, Local 327 (Whale, Inc.), 432 F.2d 933, 934-935, 75 L.R.R.M. 2435, 2436 (6th Cir.

As has been pointed out previously, p. 30, *supra,* care should be taken not to assume that one can easily predict how broad Board orders will fare at the hands of the courts. For example, in *Teamsters Local 554 (Clark Bros. Transfer Co.) v. NLRB,*[92] the court found overly broad a Board order which was designed to protect not only the employers involved, but also "all other employers in the area over which the Union has jurisdiction." The court pointed out that no threat had been made to use illegal methods against all other employers. Moreover, since the basic function of the union was to unionize the area within its jurisdiction, the court felt that the broad order might conflict with the purpose of the Act to protect the right of the employees to organize and engage in collective bargaining. The very next year, however, a similar Board order, based on similar violations came before the District of Columbia Circuit in *Central States Drivers Council v. NLRB (Clark Bros. Transfer Co.).*[93] The Board's cease and desist order ran against the union's unlawful activity as it might affect the Clark Company "or any other similar carrier." [94] The union cited the Court's earlier opinion and argued that the Board's order was too broad. The court disagreed, however, and enforced the Board's order, construing " 'any other similar common carrier' " to mean any "other 'nonunionized motor truck common carriers' " within the "jurisdiction" of the union.[95] The disposition of these two cases is confusing; the court in the second case approved the Board's order by construing its language to mean the same as the first Board order which the court had found improper.

1970) (per curiam). *Accord* NLRB v. Miscellaneous Drivers, Local 610 (Funeral Directors of Greater St. Louis, Inc.), 293 F.2d 437, 441; 48 L.R.R.M. 2816, 2820 (8th Cir. 1961) (court found an insufficient evidentiary basis to approve an order covering all other employers within the "territorial jurisdiction" of the union, but indicated such an order might be approved in a proper case).

[92] 262 F.2d 456, 43 L.R.R.M. 2197, 2201-2202 (D.C. Cir. 1958).

[93] 267 F.2d 166, 168, 44 L.R.R.M. 2058, 2059 (D.C. Cir. 1959).

[94] *Id.* at 167, 44 L.R.R.M. at 2059.

[95] *Id.*

CHAPTER IV

The Significance of the Violation and the Necessity of the Order

Problems arise because of the delay between the filing of an unfair labor practice charge with the Board and the ultimate disposal of the case either by the Board or by the courts of appeals which review the Board's decisions and orders. (Chapter XVI elaborates upon various proposals to decrease this time lag.) One aspect of this delay which may be conveniently addressed at this time is whether the Board may or should refuse to issue remedial orders in cases involving only isolated or minimal violations. Many cases have been handled through the Board's processes in a manner which has magnified obscure aspects and resulted in the pursuit of administrative and judicial remedies against parties whose misconduct, if any, is de minimis. The pursuit of remedies in such circumstances contributes to the backlog of Board and court cases and thereby further delays the processing of cases genuinely needing remedies. Whatever the impact upon delaying the dispositions of the whole of Board and court cases, there is little reason for expending limited judicial and administrative resources to try, brief, argue, consider, and decide cases in which no meaningful order is at stake. The purpose of this chapter is to exemplify opportunities for the Board and General Counsel to exercise self-restraint by not issuing or seeking a remedy and thereby curtailing unnecessary and unproductive litigation. This chapter also recognizes, on the other hand, that there are instances in which the circumstances surrounding a seemingly insignificant violation require the Board to invoke its remedial powers.

ISOLATED AND DE MINIMIS VIOLATIONS

In a report[1] of the labor law committee of the New York City Bar Association concerned with improved NLRB enforce-

---

[1] The Committee on Labor and Social Security Legislation, *Report, Improved Enforcement of the National Labor Relations Act*, 27 RECORD OF N.Y.C.B.A. 523, 530 (1972).

ment, one of the recommendations made to expedite cases at the Board level was the suggestion that the General Counsel should be actively encouraged to screen out de minimis or isolated violations. The Board itself has refused to issue remedial orders in many cases, even though violations have been found, where the unlawful practices are of such an isolated[2] or de minimis[3] nature that they do not warrant any remedial action. Thus, questions arise concerning how insignificant a violation must be to be deemed too isolated or de minimis in character that no remedial order is necessary. Moreover, some courts have questioned the authority of the Board to refuse to issue a remedial order when it has found a violation. Ever present in these cases is the implicit issue of why such admittedly minor misconduct has been brought before the Board for remedial action.

The NLRB has frequently held that it will not issue a remedial order when the circumstances are such that the isolated nature of a violation renders an order inappropriate because it will not effectuate the purposes of the Act.[4] In refusing to order a remedy, the Board has claimed that, although the conduct of an alleged offender may be violative of the Act in itself, the conduct must be viewed in its total context before a remedial order is issued.[5] For example, in *Country Cubbard Corp.,*[6] a restaurant

---

[2] *See, e.g.,* Decker Disposal, Inc., 171 N.L.R.B. 879, 880 n.1, 68 L.R.R.M. 1306, 1308 (1968) (unilateral change in starting time); Howell Refining Co., 163 N.L.R.B. 18, 19, 64 L.R.R.M. 1271, 1272 (1967) (coercion); Allied Chemical Corp., National Aniline Division, 143 N.L.R.B. 260, 263, 53 L.R.R.M. 1380, 1381 (1963) (interrogation); Frohman Mfg. Co., 107 N.L.R.B. 1308, 1315, 33 L.R.R.M. 1388, 1392 (1954) (veiled threat).

[3] *E.g.,* American Federation of Musicians, Local 76, 202 N.L.R.B. No. 80, 82 L.R.R.M. 1591, 1594 (1973). *See* cases cited at note 19, *infra,* p. 42.

[4] *See* Pepsi-Cola Allied Bottlers, Inc., 170 N.L.R.B. 1250, 67 L.R.R.M. 1603 (1968); Eaborn Trucking Service, 156 N.L.R.B. 1370, 1372, 61 L.R.R.M. 1268, 1269 (1966); Bridwell Oil Co., 172 N.L.R.B. 1635, 69 L.R.R.M. 1382, 1383 (1968); Nehi-Royal Crown Corp., 178 N.L.R.B. 93, 94, 71 L.R.R.M. 1666, 1668-1669 (1969); Mallory Battery Co., 176 N.L.R.B. No. 108, 71 L.R.R.M. 1320 (1969).

[5] Howell Refining Co., 163 N.L.R.B. 18, 19, 64 L.R.R.M. 1271, 1272 (1967); *cf.* Kohl Motors, Inc., 185 N.L.R.B. 324, 334, 76 L.R.R.M. 1747, 1748 (1970) (three unrelated instances of interrogation by a supervisor who was not otherwise improperly discussing a union campaign with a single employee); Poinsett Lumber & Mfg. Co., 147 N.L.R.B. 1197, 1201 n.5, 56 L.R.R.M. 1381, 1384 (1964) (alleged interrogation of employee while both he and a supervisor were socializing at a local tavern).

[6] 179 N.L.R.B. 53, 72 L.R.R.M. 1255 (1969).

manager, in violation of Section 8(a)(1), threatened to "write up" the employees in the future because of their resort to the union. The Board adopted the recommendation of the trial examiner that no remedy was necessary for several reasons: (1) the successful contractual relationship between the employer and union; (2) the employer's cooperative attitude in administering the collective agreement; (3) the fact that no subsequent attempt was made to visit reprisals on, or "write up," any of the employees; and (4) the lack of any other evidence that the employer had a propensity to interfere with the employees' rights under the Act [7]—in short, the lack of any employer labor union animus.

Under Section 19(c), the Board is directed to fashion remedies that "will effectuate the policies of this Act. . . ." [8] Consequently, the NLRB has in some cases seized upon the notion, implicit in this broad statutory command, that where no useful purpose is served by issuing a remedy, the Board has the discretion to withhold granting a remedial order. [9]

A typical situation in which the usefulness of a Board order is doubtful arises when either the supervisor who uttered an unlawful statement or the employee who heard the remark is no longer in the employ of the company now charged with an unfair labor practice. In *Leonard Refineries, Inc.*, [10] a supervisor, since deceased, was charged with violating Section 8(a)(1) when he remarked to several employees that if the union won an upcoming election, the employees would lose their Christmas bonuses. The trial examiner had recommended that no remedial order should be issued on the grounds that the supervisor's death obviated any possible recurrence of the violation, that his

---

[7] *Id.* at 54-55, 72 L.R.R.M. at 1255-1256.

[8] 28 U.S.C. § 160(c) (1970). *Cf.* General Asbestos & Rubber Division, 168 N.L.R.B. 396, 406, 67 L.R.R.M. 1012 (1967). The Board, relying on its established policy to encourage settlements, refused to issue an order remedying a minor unilateral change which was subsequently altered during negotiations.

[9] *See, e.g.*, Eaborn Trucking Service, 156 N.L.R.B. 1370, 61 L.R.R.M. 1268 (1966). In *Eaborn*, the employer granted a unilateral wage increase to one employee during the pre-election period in violation of § 8(a)(1). The Board, however, held that no remedy was necessary when the union, upon winning the election, demanded union scale, and the employer, who was in dire economic circumstances, refused, whereupon all the employees quit their jobs. *Cf.* Braswell Motor Freight Lines, 107 N.L.R.B. 761, 33 L.R.R.M. 1243 (1954).

[10] 147 N.L.R.B. 488, 56 L.R.R.M. 1285 (1964).

remark was the sole incident of unlawful conduct attributable to the employer during the campaign, and that it was an isolated statement to only three employees out of a unit comprised of 169 employees. The Board disagreed, pointing out that the Christmas bonus issue was significant because it was of primary concern to the employees' supervisor and the supervisor's statement was likely to receive wide and prompt circulation. The Board held that the supervisor's death six months after the election did not alter the effect of the violation.[11] In a later case, however, the Court of Appeals for the Fifth Circuit, in *Hill-Behan Lumber Co. v. NLRB,*[12] refused to enforce an order of the Board based on a Section 8(a)(1) violation where the author of the coercive statement had died before trial, because the violation "[could not] by its very nature reoccur." Moreover, in other recent cases wherein the employee who was the object of the unlawful statements had either retired or quit, the Board has refused to issue a remedial order.[13] These apparent inconsistencies can perhaps be explained as results of applying different standards of requisite conduct when the Board is considering the necessity of directing a second election, as in *Leonard Refineries.*[14]

When an employer has technically violated Section 8(a)(1) by threatening an employee for filing a grievance, the Board has taken the broad view that such threats must be viewed in the total context of the labor-management relationship.[15] In so doing, the Board has focused upon the realities of this un-

---

[11] *Id.* at 489, 56 L.R.R.M. at 1285-1286. *But cf.* Shulman's Inc., of Norfolk v. NLRB, —— F.2d ——, 89 L.R.R.M. 2729, 2731 (4th Cir. 1975) wherein the court refused to enforce an NLRB bargaining order because the only supervisor who was found to have violated the Act had departed the employer.

[12] 396 F.2d 807, 68 L.R.R.M. 2384 (5th Cir. 1968) (per curiam), *amended on other grounds,* 68 L.R.R.M. 2974 (5th Cir. 1968).

[13] *See* Rosella's Fruit & Produce Co., 199 N.L.R.B. No. 109, 82 L.R.R.M. 1080 (1972); Craftsman Electronic Products, Inc., 179 N.L.R.B. 419, 72 L.R.R.M. 1345 (1969).

[14] *Cf.* WILLIAMS, JANUS & HUHN, NLRB REGULATION OF ELECTION CONDUCT 244 (LAB. REL. & PUB. POL. SER., REP. NO. 8, 1974). *See also* Advance Envelope Mfg. Co., 170 N.L.R.B. 1459, 1470 n.8, 68 L.R.R.M. 1023 (1968), wherein the Board, refusing to issue a bargaining order based on coercive statements prior to an election which the union subsequently lost, pointed out that another election is always available.

[15] Consolidated Freightways Corp., 181 N.L.R.B. 856, 862, 74 L.R.R.M. 1038, 1039 (1970).

certain and sometimes antagonistic relationship, and has rejected the notion that a violation, however isolated, should
automatically be the basis for a remedial order.[16] For example,
in *International Paper Co.*,[17] a supervisor unlawfully threatened
to fire a union steward for filing a grievance for another employee. The Board held, however, that a remedial order was
not warranted, stating that: (1) the threat was based on a
good faith belief that the contract did not permit stewards to
file grievances for other employees; (2) the employer, during
a subsequent grievance proceeding, receded from the position
that stewards could not file grievances for unit employees; (3)
the evidence reflected an atmosphere of employee freedom in
voicing complaints and filing grievances; and (4) the supervisor's threat was isolated.[18]

As with isolated violations, the Board has also refused to issue
remedial orders because of the de minimis quality of certain
violations.[19]

In such cases involving de minimis and isolated violations
where the Board has found an order unnecessary, the Board has
encountered some opposition from courts which have claimed that
any time the Board determines that a violation has occurred,

---

[16] *See* International Harvester Co., 180 N.L.R.B. 1038, 1039, 73 L.R.R.M.
1331 (1970), wherein the Board adopted the following analysis of the trial
examiner:

> [T]he free exchange of views by company and union representatives in
> processing of grievances would be severely limited if the refinements of
> diplomatic language were required of factory personnel concerned with
> the day-to-day operations of a collective-bargaining agreement.

[17] 184 N.L.R.B. No. 38, 74 L.R.R.M. 1438 (1970).

[18] *Id.*, 74 L.R.R.M. at 1438. In a similar situation, where there had been
a finding of isolated instances of unfair labor practices engaged in by supervisors, but contrary to management instructions, the Board felt that a remedial
order was unnecessary. *See* Craftsman Electronic Products, Inc., 179 N.L.R.B.
419, 72 L.R.R.M. 1345 (1969); Allied Chemical Corp., National Aniline
Division, 143 N.L.R.B. 260, 263, 53 L.R.R.M. 1380, 1381 (1963).

[19] *See, e.g.*, O'Neil Moving and Storage, Inc., 209 N.L.R.B. No. 82, 85
L.R.R.M. 1488 (1974); Fearn International, Inc., Eggo Foods Division, 209
N.L.R.B. No. 37, 85 L.R.R.M. 1534 (1974); Walgreen Co. d/b/a Globe
Shopping City, 203 N.L.R.B. No. 36, 83 LR.R.M. 1059 (1973). American
Federation of Musicians, Local 76, 202 N.L.R.B. No. 80, 82 L.R.R.M. 1591
(1973).

it must issue a remedy.[20] Hence, in recent years, a conflict between the Board and the courts and among Board members themselves [21] has arisen over whether the NLRB has been granted sufficient discretionary powers under the Act to refuse to remedy certain types of de minimis violations.

The statutory language governing the issuance of remedial orders by the Board is found in Section 10(c), and provides, in pertinent part, that:

> . . . the Board *shall* state its findings of fact and *shall* issue and cause to be served on such person an order requiring such person to cease and desist from such unfair labor practice, and to take such affirmative action including reinstatement of employees with or without back pay, *as will effectuate the policies of this Act . . . .*[22]

As is apparent on the surface of the statute, the Board is "authorized to frame an order in two parts: (1) [a] negative part, ordering the party found guilty of unfair labor practices to cease and desist . . . [; and] (2) [a]n affirmative part, directing

---

[20] *See* UAW v. NLRB (Omni Spectra, Inc.), 427 F.2d 1330, 74 L.R.R.M. 2481 (6th Cir. 1970); Woodworkers, Local 3-10 v. NLRB, 380 F.2d 628, 65 L.R.R.M. 2633, 2635 n.2 (D.C. Cir. 1967); Steelworkers v. NLRB (Wagner Industrial Products Co.), 386 F.2d 981, 66 L.R.R.M. 2417 (D.C. Cir. 1967); Eichleay Corp. v. NLRB, 206 F.2d 799, 32 L.R.R.M. 2628, 2634 (3d Cir. 1953). While the Second Circuit has stated that it would not pass judgment on the propriety of these decisions, on one occasion it did "assume, without deciding" that "the Board in an appropriate case can balance the detrimental effects of an order [,] if issued [,] on labor-management relations and refuse to issue one." *See* Luxuray of N.Y., Div. of Beaunit Corp. v. NLRB, 447 F.2d 112, 114, 77 L.R.R.M. 2820, 2822 (2d Cir. 1971).

[21] Carolina American Textiles, Inc., 219 N.L.R.B. No. 51, 90 L.R.R.M. 1074 (1975) (Chairman Murphy dissenting); Interlake, Inc., 218 N.L.R.B. No. 154, 89 L.R.R.M. 1794 (1975) (Member Kennedy dissenting); Thermalloy Corp., 213 N.L.R.B. No. 26, 87 L.R.R.M. 1081, 1082 (1974) (Member Jenkins dissenting); Triangle Publications, Inc., 204 N.L.R.B. No. 108, 83 L.R.R.M. 1382, 1384 (1973); Deringer Mfg. Co., 201 N.L.R.B. No. 94, 82 L.R.R.M. 1607, 1608 (1973). *And see* O'Neil Moving and Storage, Inc., 209 N.L.R.B. No. 82, 85 L.R.R.M. 1488, 1490-1491 (1974) (Members Fanning and Jenkins, dissenting); Las Vegas Sun, 209 N.L.R.B. No. 38, 85 L.R.R.M. 1536, 1538 (1974) (Member Fanning, dissenting); Fearn International Inc., Eggo Foods Division, 209 N.L.R.B. No. 37, 85 L.R.R.M. 1534, 1535-1536 (1974) (Member Fanning, dissenting); Walgreen Co., d/b/a Globe Shopping City, 203 N.L.R.B. No. 36, 83 L.R.R.M. 1059, 1060-1061 (1973) (Member Fanning, dissenting). In each of these cases, Members Fanning and Jenkins would have issued a remedy, once a violation was found, regardless of its de minimis nature.

[22] 29 U.S.C. § 160(c) (1970) (emphasis added).

the action required to remedy the violation."[23] The issue concerns whether the language "as will effectuate the policies of this Act," was meant to operate solely as a limitation on permissible affirmative action, or whether it is a contingent condition which must be satisfied before either negative or affirmative relief can be directed.

In *Eichleay Corp. v. NLRB*[24] the Court of Appeals for the Third Circuit held that the language of Section 10(c) meant "that the Board *must* issue a cease and desist order once it has held a hearing and determined that a prohibited practice exists, but is allowed some discretion in ordering other affirmative action, to wit, discretion to determine what will or will not effectuate the policies of the Act."[25] In the *Eichleay* case, it was the offender and not the Board that asserted the discretionary authority of the Board to withhold a remedy. In a similar situation, however, the court in *J.J. Newberry Co. v. NLRB*[26] refused to enforce a Board order; it held that, in light of the isloated nature of the unlawful practice and the company's otherwise lawful conduct, the violation was de minimis and hence no order was necessary. Thus there is fundamental disagreement not only concerning the Board's discretion to decline to issue an order, but also concerning a court's authority to deny enforcement of a Board order on the grounds that the violation is de minimis.

The issue which has attracted most attention is the dichotomy of opinion as to whether a Board remedy in the case of a de minimis violation is mandatory.[27] One faction, represented by the courts of appeals for the Sixth and District of Columbia Circuits, has held that once the Board has found a violation,

---

[23] McGuiness, How To Take a Case Before the NLRB 261 (3d ed. 1967.

[24] 206 F.2d 799, 32 L.R.R.M. 2628 (3d Cir. 1953).

[25] *Id.* at 805, 32 L.R.R.M. at 2633 (emphasis in the original).

[26] 442 F.2d 897, 901, 77 L.R.R.M. 2097, 2100 (2d Cir. 1971).

[27] *See, e.g.,* UAW v. NLRB (Omni Spectra, Inc.), 427 F.2d 1330, 1333, 74 L.R.R.M. 2481, 2483-2484 (6th Cir. 1970), wherein the court stated:

There can be no doubt about the clarity of the statutory language. . . . The statute authorizes (and requires) the dismissal of a complaint *only* when the Board finds that no unfair labor practice has occurred. . . . Congress could surely have written the words "may issue" if it had wished the Board to have the discretion to issue or not to issue a cease and desist order once it has found that an unfair labor practice has occurred.

the de minimis character of the violation is irrelevant since the statute commands the Board to issue a remedy.[28] Nonetheless, these same courts have properly indicated that, should the Board determine that the alleged misconduct is of such a de minimis nature that no violation need be found, then the Board is, of course, not obligated to issue a remedy.[29]

Taking a completely opposite approach, the Fifth Circuit, in *NLRB v. Big Three Industrial Gas Co.*,[30] refused to enforce an order of the Board that would have remedied what the court saw as minimal violations of Section 8(a)(3). The court stated:

> The maxim *de minimis non curat lex* is well known in the law and stands for the proposition that courts do not care for trifles. This rede is particularly applicable to the instant situation. The loss by two employees of a few dollars pay is simply too picayune to warrant setting aside a long and costly election process involving hundreds of voters or, indeed, even to warrant a cease and desist and back pay order for the men involved. Conceding arguendo, that the Company's practice was discriminatory, it would be such a rank unfairness to the remaining electors and so clearly

---

[28] *See* cases cited at note 20, *supra*. These courts construe the word "shall" in Section 10(c) as meaning that the Board "must" issue an order once a violation is found. It should be noted that the courts have taken an entirely different approach in construing the word "shall" contained in Section 9(c)(1). Section 9(c)(1) provides that once the Board finds that there is a question of representation, it "shall" direct an election and "shall" certify the results thereof. But a series of consistent court decisions have held that Section 9(c)(1) has never been interpreted to impose upon the Board a series of mandatory steps which it must follow in processing representation petitions. *See* National Maritime Union v. NLRB, 267 F. Supp. 117, 121-122, 65 L.R.R.M. 2065 (S.D.N.Y. 1967) and cases cited therein; National Maritime Union v. NLRB, 375 F. Supp. 421, 86 L.R.R.M. 2510, 2518-2520 (E.D.Pa. 1974) and cases cited therein, *affirmed* 506 F.2d 1052, 87 L.R.R.M. 3275, (1974) *cert. denied* —— U.S. ——, 89 L.R.R.M. 2248 (1975).

[29] Woodworkers Local 3-10 v. NLRB, *supra*, note 20, 380 F.2d at 631 n.2, 65 L.R.R.M. at 2635. In the *Woodworkers* case, the D.C. Circuit distinguished each of the following cases because they involved misconduct of such a de minimis character that no unfair labor practice finding could be validly predicated upon it. Caribe General Electric, Inc. v. NLRB, 357 F.2d 664, 666, 61 L.R.R.M. 2513, 2514 (1st Cir. 1966); NLRB v. Clegg Machine Works, 304 F.2d 168, 176, 50 L.R.R.M. 2524, 2530 (8th Cir. 1962); NLRB v. Grunwald-Marx, Inc., 290 F.2d 210, 47 L.R.R.M. 2940 (9th Cir. 1961); NLRB v. Mississippi Products, Inc., 213 F.2d 670, 674, 34 L.R.R.M. 2431, 2343-2344 (5th Cir. 1954). *See also* UAW v. NLRB (Omni Spectra Inc.), *supra*, note 27. 427 F.2d at 1333 n.2, 74 L.R.R.M. at 2483.

[30] 441 F.2d 774, 778, 77 L.R.R.M. 2120, 2123 (5th Cir. 1971), *reh. denied* 77 L.R.R.M. 3155.

beneath the dignity of the Board's function, that we hold this triviality could not support any order.

ENFORCEMENT DENIED.

By the same token, in *Hill-Behan Lumber Co. v. NLRB*,[31] the same court denied enforcement of a Section 8(a)(1) remedy because of the inconsequential nature of the violation found and the death of one who participated in the coercive conversation.

As a matter of statutory interpretation, there are strong reasons why the Board should be permitted to refrain from issuing orders that would remedy only minor and unimportant violations. Thus, the Board is entitled to consider not only the literal language of Section 10(c) but also the object of the statute—i.e., to provide remedies which will effectuate the purposes of the Act.[32] As the Supreme Court has stated, "In fashioning remedies to undo the effects of violations of the Act, the Board must draw on enlightenment gained from experience . . . [and] mould remedies suited to practical needs."[33]

The Board has argued that implicit in its sole authority to seek enforcement of its orders is the corollary that it also has the authority to decline to issue a remedy when it believes that enforcement would be meaningless.[34] Some courts have answered this objection by claiming that different considerations bear upon the decision to seek enforcement.[35] Such reasoning begs the question, however, because the "different considerations" spoken of by the courts would not be present if no Board remedy were fashioned. The pointlessness of these rationalizations was illustrated in the *UAW v. NLRB* (*Omni Spectra,*

---

[31] 396 F.2d 807, 68 L.R.R.M. 2384 (5th Cir. 1968).

[32] It is interesting that this issue is even raised, since Board remedies are usually challenged on the grounds that they are in excess of the Board's authority. *See, e.g.,* H. K. Porter Co. v. NLRB, 397 U.S. 99, 73 L.R.R.M. 2561 (1970) (Board cannot compel concession or agreement); May Department Stores Co. v. NLRB, 326 U.S. 376, 17 L.R.R.M. 643 (1945) (cannot go beyond evidence); Republic Steel Corp. v. NLRB, 311 U.S. 7, 7 L.R.R.M. 287 (1940) (order must be remedial and not punitive); *cf.* NLRB v. Mine Workers, Local 403, 375 U.S. 396, 55 L.R.R.M. 2084 (1964) (question of remedy within Board's discretion).

[33] NLRB v. Seven-Up Bottling Co., 344 U.S. 344, 346, 352, 31 L.R.R.M. 2237, 2238, 2240 (1953).

[34] *E.g.,* Woodworkers, Local 3-10 v. NLRB, 380 F.2d 628, 631, 65 L.R.R.M. 2633, 2636 (D.C. Cir. 1967).

[35] *Id.,* 65 L.R.R.M. at 2636.

Inc.)[36] case. The court, deciding that a cease and desist order was mandatory, remanded the case to the Board which held, upon reconsideration, that the violation found by the trial examiner and considered too insignificant to warrant the issuance of a remedial order in its initial decision, was not a violation at all.[37] Consequently, the Board can moot the issue merely by deciding on remand that no violation occurred.

As indicated above, however, the crux of the problem is more fundamental than a battle of competing legalistic definitions over the meaning of the statutory language of the Act. At stake is the issue of how the Board can best effectuate the Act through its remedial powers. In turn, two related questions arise: (1) why should the Board be forced to order a remedy when it seems unnecessary? (2) Is this the best allocation of the Board's time and resources?

One response to these questions was given by the Board in *American Federation of Musicians, Local 76.*[38] There, a union, through a temporary refusal to work, in violation of Section 8(b)(1)(B), interfered with management's right to select its representatives in dealing with the union. In refusing to issue a remedial order, the Board pointed out that "[T]he alleged misconduct . . . is of such obviously limited impact and significance that we ought not to find that it rises to the level of constituting a violation of our Act."[39] The Board then quoted extensively from two contemporary District of Columbia cases (which in themselves might indicate a sub silentio shift of opinion in that circuit) stating that the case involved was one of those "infinitestimally small abstract grievances that must give way to actual and existing legal problems if the courts (and the NLRB) are to dispose of their heavy calenders."[40]

---

[36] 427 F.2d 1330, 74 L.R.R.M. 2481 (6th Cir. 1970), *remanding,* Omni Spectra, Inc., 176 N.L.R.B. 165, 71 L.R.R.M. 1222 (1969)

[37] Omni Spectra, Inc., 186 N.L.R.B. 673, 75 L.R.R.M. 1402 (1970).

[38] 202 N.L.R.B. No. 80, 82 L.R.R.M. 1591 (1973).

[39] *Id.,* 82 L.R.R.M. at 1593. *But see* Georgia Hosiery Mills, 207 N.L.R.B. No. 117, 85 L.R.R.M. 1067 (1973), wherein the Board distinguished the *Musicians* case as pertaining to a single, isolated threat which was rescinded before any action was taken and hence was substantially remedied before the complaint was issued.

[40] 202 N.L.R.B. No. 80, 82 L.R.R.M. at 1593. *Accord,* NLRB v. Columbia Typographical Union, Local 101, 470 F.2d 1274, 81 L.R.R.M. 2668 (D.C. Cir. 1972); Dallas Mailer's Union, Local 143 v. NLRB, 445 F.2d 730, 76 L.R.R.M.

In conclusion, pointing to the court's concern about frivolous litigation,[41] the Board stated:

> [I]n view of the increasing need for expedition in the processing of cases, we have concluded that we ought not expend the Board's limited resources on matters which have little or no meaning in effectuating the policies of this Act. Thus, in this insubstantial case, we would find that the conduct involved, although it may have been in technical contravention of the statute as interpreted by this Board, was nevertheless so insignificant and so largely rendered meaningless by Respondent's subsequent conduct that we will not utilize it as a basis for either a finding of violation or a remedial order.[42]

Perhaps the answer to the questions we have raised—as the Board strongly implied in the *Musicians* case—is that cases involving isolated or de minimis violations should not reach the Board at all. For example, in the case of an isolated speech, which is alleged to be an independent violation of Section 8(a)(1), the Board and the courts have warned against too quickly regarding the remark of a supervisor as an expression of man-

---

2247, 2249 (D.C. Cir. 1971), where Judge Tamm stated in reluctantly enforcing the Board's order:

> Now [this case] has finally come to rest in the bosoms of three judges, who must pick their way through a quagmire of grammar totaling almost 300 pages of briefs, documents, and transcripts that will presumably aid us in determining whether Colston's manner was too overbearing or Cantrell's skin too thin.
> At a time when this court is confronted with an all-time high in caseload and backlog, it is most unfortunate that three of its judges must conscientiously spend the necessary time to do justice to a dispute that should have been settled long ago within the Company and Union family. We see no hope for the expeditious determination of appeals unless an effective method of weeding out cases of this sort is established to prevent others like it from receiving so much unearned attention. It seems elementary to the very existence of our judicial machinery that infinitesimally small abstract grievances must give way to actual and existing legal problems if courts are to dispose of their heavy calendars. We mention this only to encourage other members of the legal community to constructively think of ways to alleviate the problem. Any step in the right direction would be a giant service to us and the public at large.

[41] Citing the *Dallas Mailer's* case, the D.C. Circuit in *Columbia Typographical, Local 101*, stated:

> [I]t would seem that the Board also "could very well be spared the time consuming energy necessarily exhausted in the determination of [this] type of dispute . . . ."
> Under the circumstances, why the General Counsel filed his charge and the Board persists in this litigation is difficult to understand. 470 F.2d at 1275, 81 L.R.R.M. at 2668.

[42] 202 N.L.R.B. No. 80, 82 L.R.R.M. at 1594.

agement when the words are clearly gratuitous and are not made in concert with other statements, or against a background of unfair labor practices.[43] One possible explanation for the Board's tendency at times to seize upon isolated remarks as unfair labor practices is that the Board may fail to distinguish those isolated violations from situations in which minor improper occurrences constitute only a portion of a number of unlawful practices, which, when viewed in their totality, present a picture of an employer's determined antiunion conduct. Sometimes, authority for treating the remarks as independent violations is created while the supporting rationale is either forgotten or ignored.

Several Board members have argued that all violations of the Act should be remedied, using the theory that if small individual violations were ignored, an increase in the number and severity of violations might be encouraged.[44] On the other hand, there is the countervailing possibility that a policy of remedying each violation, regardless of consequence, merely encourages the filing of unfair labor practice charges rather than discourages their commission. Obviously, such results would misallocate the Board's resources by channeling them away from more serious and important offenses and thereby diminish the effectiveness of the Board. Moreover, it is arguable that when the General Counsel and the Board pursue minimal violations rather than utilize their discretionary authority to screen out those that are

---

[43] *See* Great Atlantic & Pacific Tea Co. 129 N.L.R.B. 757, 760, 47 L.R.R.M. 1059, 1061 (1960), wherein the Board cites NLRB v. Whittier Mills Co., 111 F.2d 474, 479, 6 L.R.R.M. 799, 803 (5th Cir. 1940), which stated:

> Isolated speeches . . ., though having some authority, in casual conversation with fellow employees, which are not authorized or encouraged or even known to the management, ought not to be too quickly imputed to the employer as his breaches of the law. When not made in the exercise of authority, but in personal conversation, they do not appear to be the sentiments of the employer nor his acts, and to make them such the circumstances ought to show some encouragement or ratification or such repetition as to justify the inference of a policy which they express.

See also Las Vegas Sun, 209 N.L.R.B. No. 38, 85 L.R.R.M. 1536 (1974); NLRB v. General Industries Electronics Co., 401 F.2d 297, 300, 69 L.R.R.M. 2455 (8th Cir. 1968); Metropolitan Life Ins. Co. v. NLRB, 371 F.2d 573, 580, 64 L.R.R.M. 2130 (6th Cir. 1967), *reh. denied* 374 F.2d 693, 64 L.R.R.M. 2768 (6th Cir. 1967).

[44] St. Regis Paper Co., 192 N.L.R.B. 661, 662, 77 L.R.R.M. 1878, 1879 (1971). Members Fanning, Jenkins, and Brown overruled the trial examiner and held that minor violations of the Act should be remedied. Chairman Miller and Member Kennedy dissented.

de minimis or isolated, they contribute unnecessarily to the Board's rising caseload. It is precisely this predicament of generating unfair labor practice charges with which the Board majority in the *Musicians* case [45] and the New York City Bar Association committee on reform [46] concerned themselves, and which prompted the District of Columbia Circuit in the *Columbia Typographical, Local 101* case to ask, "Under the circumstances [de minimis violation], why the General Counsel filed his charge and the Board persists in this litigation is difficult to understand." [47]

MOOTNESS

In one of its earliest labor decisions relating to the National Labor Relations Act, the Supreme Court in *NLRB v. Pennsylvania Greyhound Lines, Inc.,*[48] held that an order of the Board "lawful when made, does not become moot because it is obeyed or because changing circumstances indicate the need for it to be less than when made." [49] Observing that "[t]he Act does not require the Board to play hide and seek with those guilty of unfair labor practices," the Court added in a later case that compliance with a Board order does not render it moot either.[50]

---

[45] 202 N.L.R.B. No. 80, 82 L.R.R.M. at 1593-1594.

[46] *See Report,* 27 Record of N.Y.C.B.A. 523, 530 (1972) at note 1, *supra.*

　　The Board's load could be reduced without countervailing disadvantages by screening out de minimis or isolated violations. The fact that the investigation of a charge reveals some minor breaches of the Act should not necessarily call for the issuance of a complaint . . . the General Counsel should use the power granted to him in Section 3(d) to refuse to prosecute violations of minor or isolated character that do not warrant exercise of the Board's remedial powers.
　　. . . [W]ith the ever-expanding caseload, it is more important than ever that the Board be permitted to husband its limited resources and apply them where they have maximum impact in effectuating the Act. Otherwise time, energy, and manpower are dissipated in seeking to rectify situations of no moment while, backed up behind them, significant violations remain unremedied.

[47] 470 F.2d at 1275, 81 L.R.R.M. at 2668.

[48] 303 U.S. 261, 2 L.R.R.M. at 600 (1938).

[49] *Id.* 271, 2 L.R.R.M. at 603. *Cf.* Consolidated Edison Co. of N.Y., v. NLRB, 305 U.S. 197, 230, 3 L.R.R.M. 646, 653 (1938).

[50] NLRB v. Mexia Textile Mills, 339 U.S. 563, 567-568, 26 L.R.R.M. 2123, 2125 (1950). *See* NLRB v. Carpenters, District Council of Kansas City, 184 F.2d 60, 63, 26 L.R.R.M. 2480, 2483 (10th Cir. 1950), wherein the court pointed out that an order does not become moot because of compliance, chang-

The rationale for enforcing Board orders, even though enforcement may be contrary to accepted common law doctrines,[51] is that under the Act, the violation is of a continuing nature[52] and hence ". . . enforcement of the order provides an incentive for continued compliance through the possible sanction of contempt proceedings for violations."[53] Thus, for example, a refusal to sign an agreement is violative of the duty to bargain in good faith and requires a negative order[54] but will not be affirmatively remedied—i.e., by an order to sign—when the agreement has expired under its terms.[55] Since the Board has the discretion to decide whether a matter has been successfully concluded and thereby obviates the necessity of seeking enforcement,[56] private agreements between parties which purport to

---

ing circumstances, or discontinuance of the unfair practice, thereby depriving the Board of its right to secure enforcement. *Accord* G&W Electric Specialty Co. v. NLRB, 360 F.2d 873, 874, 62 L.R.R.M. 2085 (7th Cir. 1966).

[51] *See, e.g.,* NLRB v. Pacific Gas & Electric Co., 118 F.2d 780, 789, 8 L.R.R.M. 848, 857 (9th Cir. 1941). In this case, the court rejected the equitable (equity will not enjoin completed transactions) and constitutional (no case or controversy within the meaning of § 2 of Article III of the Constitution) contentions of the offender, citing the statement of the Supreme Court in IAM, Lodge 35 v. NLRB, 311 U.S. 72, 82, 7 L.R.R.M. 282, 287 (1940) that it "is for the Board not the courts to determine how the effect of prior unfair labor practices may be expunged." *See also* NLRB v. Ford Motor Co., 119 F.2d 326, 329, 8 L.R.R.M. 656, 658 (5th Cir. 1941) (rejection of equitable argument that injunctions will not issue to prevent practices that have not only been discontinued but of the recurrence of which there is no reasonable likelihood).

[52] *See, e.g.,* NLRB v. Jones & Laughlin Steel Corp., 331 U.S. 416, 20 L.R.R.M. 2115 (1947). *See also* NLRB Statements of Procedure, Series 8, *as amended,* § 101.13.

[53] NLRB v. Southern Household Products Co., 449 F.2d 749, 750, 78 L.R.R.M. 2597, 2598 (5th Cir. 1971); *accord,* NLRB v. Raytheon, 398 U.S. 25, 27, 74 L.R.R.M. 2177, 2178 (1970); NLRB v. Marsh Supermarkets, Inc., 327 F.2d 109, 111, 55 L.R.R.M. 2017, 2018 (7th Cir. 1963), *cert. denied,* 377 U.S. 944, 56 L.R.R.M. 2288 (1964); Modine Mfg. Co., 500 F.2d 914, 86 L.R.R.M. 3197, 3199 n.4 (8th Cir. 1974); NLRB v. Unoco Apparel, Inc., 508 F.2d 1368, 88 L.R.R.M. 2956, 2958 (5th Cir. 1975).

[54] *E.g.,* Henry I. Siegel Co. v. NLRB, 340 F.2d 309, 310-311, 58 L.R.R.M. 2182, 2183 (2d Cir. 1965).

[55] *See* NLRB v. Painters Union, Local 1385, 334 F.2d 729, 732, 56 L.R.R.M. 2648, 2650 (7th Cir. 1964); NLRB v. Cosmopolitan Studios, Inc., 291 F.2d 110, 112, 48 L.R.R.M. 2398, 2399 (2d Cir. 1961); NLRB v. Local 19, Longshoremen (AFL-CIO), 286 F.2d 661, 664, 47 L.R.R.M. 2420, 2422 (7th Cir. 1961), *cert. denied,* 368 U.S. 820, 48 L.R.R.M. 3110 (1961).

[56] NLRB v. T. W. Phillips Gas & Oil Co., 141 F.2d 304, 14 L.R.R.M. 509 (3d Cir. 1944).

constitute a final settlement of the dispute are not binding according to the Board.[57] However, it must also be pointed out that the Supreme Court has stated that there are situations where an enforcement proceeding will become moot because a party can establish that "there is no reasonable expectation that the wrong will be repeated." [58] But such circumstances have rarely been found by the Board and courts.

In *Raytheon,* however, the Court rejected the employer's mootness argument, and held that an intervening election did not bar enforcement of a Section 8(a)(1) order because there was nothing in the record to show that the specific acts complained of have not been repeated or to give any assurance that they would not be repeated in the future.

Compliance

In most cases, compliance with a Board order by either an employer [59] or a labor organization [60] does not moot an order

---

[57] *See* NLRB v. Prettyman, d/b/a Ann Arbor Press, 117 F.2d 921, 7 L.R.R.M. 469 (6th Cir. 1941); NLRB v. General Motors Corp., 116 F.2d 306, 7 L.R.R.M. 506 (7th Cir. 1940); Jerstedt Lumber Co., 209 N.L.R.B. No. 107, 85 L.R.R.M. 1460 (1974); Finishline Industries, Inc, 181 N.L.R.B. 756, 74 L.R.R.M. 1654 (1970); Superior Coach Corp., 175 N.L.R.B. 200, 70 L.R.R.M. 1514 (1969). Additionally, Section 10(a) of the Act confers upon the Board the statutory authority "to prevent any person from engaging in any unfair labor practice (listed in Section 8) affecting commerce" and further provides that this "power shall not be affected by any other means of adjustment . . . that has been . . . established by agreement. . . ."

[58] NLRB v. Raytheon Co., 398 U.S. 25, 27, 74 L.R.R.M. 2177, 2178 (1970), *citing* NLRB v. Jones & Laughlin Steel Corp., 331 U.S. 416, 428, 20 L.R.R.M. 2115 (1947), and United States v. W. T. Grant Co., 345 U.S. 629, 633.

[59] *E.g.,* NLRB v. Mexia Textile Mills, Inc., 339 U.S. 563, 26 L.R.R.M. 2123 (1950). *Cf.* NLRB v. Crompton-Highland Mills, 337 U.S. 217, 225, 24 L.R.R.M. 2088, 2091 (1949); G&W Electric Specialty Co. v. NLRB, 360 F.2d 873, 874, 62 L.R.R.M. 2085, 2086 (7th Cir. 1966).

[60] *See* NLRB v. Elevator Constructors, Local 8, 465 F.2d 794, 975-976, 81 L.R.R.M. 2091, 2093 (9th Cir. 1972); NLRB v. Teamsters, Local 364 (Light Co.), 274 F.2d 19, 25, 45 L.R.R.M. 2393, 2397 (7th Cir. 1960); NLRB v. Local 926, Operating Engineers, 267 F.2d 418, 420, 44 L.R.R.M. 2200, 2202 (5th Cir. 1959). *But cf.* NLRB v. Columbia Typographical Union, 470 F.2d 1274, 1275, 81 L.R.R.M. 2668 (D.C. Cir. 1972) where the court found the issue in the suit moot where the respondent union had vacated its alleged unlawful action and ended the dispute before the complaint of the General Counsel was even filed. The court complained that it was once again presented with one of those "infinitesimally small abstract grievances [that] must give way to actual and existing legal problems if the courts are to dispose of their heavy calendars," *citing* Dallas Mailers Union, Local No. 143 v. NLRB, 445 F.2d 730, 733, 76 L.R.R.M. 2247, 2249 (D.C. Cir. 1971).

for enforcement purposes. In *NLRB v. Mexia Textile Mills, Inc.*[61] the Supreme Court stated:

> [T]he employer's compliance with an order of the Board does not render the cause moot, depriving the Board of its opportunity to secure enforcement from an appropriate court. . . . A Board order imposes a continuing obligation; and the Board is entitled to have the resumption of the unfair practice barred by an enforcement decree.[62]

Moreover, compliance is generally considered to be a matter reserved for Board determination and is not a matter to be considered in an appellate enforcement proceeding.[63] Thus, in seeking enforcement of a bargaining order, the Board is under no obligation to show that subsequent to the issuance of its remedial order, an employer declined to bargain at the union's request.[64] Since a Board order has a preventive, as well as a remedial purpose, it is clear that enforcement of the negative part (cease and desist portion) of the order is best left to the discretion of the Board. To do otherwise would, in effect, give the violator "a second bite at the apple" before the Board could bring contempt proceedings against him for further violations. Some controversy has arisen over the question of whether a court should enforce the affirmative sections of a Board order when the violator has already complied.

Although the Supreme Court in *Mexia Textile Mills* stated broadly that an "employer's compliance with an order of the Board does not render the cause moot," the order specifically involved in that case merely enjoined the employer from further refusals to bargain in good faith—no affirmative duty was required.[65] Thereafter, the Court of Appeals for the Fifth Cir-

---

[61] 339 U.S. 563, 26 L.R.R.M. 2123 (1950).

[62] *Id.* at 567, 26 L.R.R.M. at 2125.

[63] Solo Cup Co. v. NLRB, 332 F.2d 447, 449, 56 L.R.R.M. 2383 (4th Cir. 1964) and cases cited therein.

[64] *See, e.g.*, NLRB v. Rippee, d/b/a Pacific Multiforms Co., 339 F.2d 315, 316, 58 L.R.R.M. 2054, 2055 (9th Cir. 1964) (rejecting employer's contention that it stands ready, willing, and able to bargain with union at any time upon the latter's request); NLRB v. Dworkin Electroplaters, 323 F.2d 934, 54 L.R.R.M. 2427 (3d Cir. 1963) (per curiam); NLRB v. Lettie Lee, Inc., 140 F.2d 243, 13 L.R.R.M. 782 (9th Cir. 1944); NLRB v. C. E. Hobbs Co., 132 F.2d 249, 11 L.R.R.M. 742 (1st Cir 1942).

[65] 339 US. at 566-567, 26 L.R.R.M. at 2125. In a similar vein, although the courts will not enforce a Board order requiring a labor organization to execute an agreement which would have expired by its terms, they will

cuit denied enforcement to the portion of a Board order in
NLRB v. Caroline Mills, Inc.[66] which required reinstatement of
one employee because the employee had not only already been
reinstated but had been given a better job. The Fifth Circuit
subsquently adopted a pro forma order which required an
employer to do only such things as have been left undone.[67]
Similarly, the Court of Appeals for the Third Circuit in *NLRB
v. National Biscuit Co.*[68] drew a clear distinction between the
"negative" and "affirmative" parts of a Board order, stating
that although the decision in *Mexia Textile Mills* required it to
grant the injunction against the employer's unfair labor practices, it would not enter a decree "requiring the [employer] to
do things which it has already done." On the other hand, the
Court of Appeals for the Ninth Circuit has taken a per se
approach, holding that compliance with a Board order, whether
negative or affirmative, is no defense against court enforcement
nor does it render the order moot.[69]

The courts have also held that an enforcement proceeding
initiated by the Board is not moot when the violator has
claimed that he has complied fully with the recommendation
of the trial examiner.[70] In so deciding, the court in *NLRB v.
Oregon Worsted Co.*[71] reasoned as follows:

---

enjoin the union from further bad-faith bargaining. *See* NLRB v. Painters,
Local 1385, 334 F.2d 729, 56 L.R.R.M. 2648 (7th Cir. 1964); NLRB v. Local 19,
Longshoremen (AFL-CIO), 286 F.2d 661, 47 L.R.R.M. 2420 (7th Cir. 1961),
cert. denied, 368 U.S. 820, 48 L.R.R.M. 3110 (1961).

[66] 167 F.2d 212, 214, 21 L.R.R.M. 2542, 2543 (5th Cir. 1948). Because the
employee in *Caroline Mills* had voluntarily left the employment of the company subsequent to his reinstatement, the court may have felt that it was
inequitable to force the company to extend a second offer to return.

[67] *See* NLRB v. Davis Lumber Co., 172 F.2d 225, 23 L.R.R.M. 2380 (5th
Cir. 1949) (per curiam); *accord*, NLRB v. American Thread Co., 188 F.2d
161, 162, 28 L.R.R.M. 2004, 2005 (5th Cir. 1951) (per curiam). *But see* NLRB
v. Patterson Menhaden Corp., d/b/a Gallant Man, 389 F.2d 701, 67 L.R.R.M.
2545 (5th Cir. 1968).

[68] 185 F.2d 123, 124, 27 L.R.R.M. 2086, 2087 (3d Cir. 1950).

[69] *See* NLRB v. Trimfit of California, Inc., 211 F.2d 206, 208, 33 L.R.R.M.
2705, 2706 (9th Cir. 1954); NLRB v. Ronney & Sons Furniture Mfg. Co., 206
F.2d 730, 32 L.R.R.M. 2635 (9th Cir. 1953), *cert. denied*, 346 U.S. 937, 33
L.R.R.M. 2394 (1954).

[70] *See* NLRB v. Hamel Leather Co., 135 F.2d 71, 72-73, 12 L.R.R.M. 655,
657 (1st Cir. 1943).

[71] 94 F.2d 671, 1A L.R.R.M. 638 (9th Cir. 1938).

> The remedy of the statute . . . is in the orders of the *Board* . . . [while t]he recommendations of the trial examiner are no more than *recommendations* to the Board as to its action . . . [which t]he Board may accept or reject . . . .
>
> While performance of all the recommendations by the examiner covering every phase of the complaint may lead the Board, in its administrative discretion, to dismiss the petition, such performance gives no right to the respondent to insist on such dismissal.[72]

Similarly, an order of the Board entered upon stipulation may not be denied enforcement on the grounds that an offender has not violated, nor does he intend to violate, the order.[73] Although it is true that the Board may seek enforcement of any of its orders in the courts of appeals, it is also true that Congress, in enacting Sections 10(c) and 10(e), granted the Board discretionary authority to seek enforcement.[74] Consequently, when a violator has fully complied with the Board's order and has no history of serious unfair labor practices, or a showing, as in the instant case, of a concerted or implacable position in defiance of the Act, the Board should carefully consider whether to seek enforcement. Recognizing that voluntary compliance with the Board's order, pursuant to *Mexia Textile Mills*, is no defense to enforcement, a discriminating use of appellate litigation resources by the Board should seem desirable to husband the resources of the Board and appellate courts. Even though enforcement has some preventive value in that it subjects the violator to contempt proceedings should further unlawful acts occur, it may also be, in many cases, that compliance by the violator indicates that he intends to abide by the Act, albeit under the duress of a potential enforcement proceeding. The Court of Appeals for the Sixth Circuit in *NLRB v. United States Gypsum*[75] alluded to this

---

[72] *Id.* at 672, 1A L.R.R.M. at 639 (emphasis added).

[73] NLRB v. Fickett-Brown Mfg. Co., 140 F.2d 883, 884-885, 13 L.R.R.M. 811, 812 (5th Cir. 1944).

[74] *See also* NLRB v. Local 926, Operating Engineers, 267 F.2d 418, 420, 44 L.R.R.M. 2200, 2202 (5th Cir. 1959); NLRB v. Newspaper & Mail Deliverer's Union, 246 F.2d 62, 65, 40 L.R.R.M. 2295, 2297 (3d Cir. 1957). *See* NLRB v. Marland One-Way Clutch Co., 520 F.2d 856, 89 L.R.R.M. 2721, 2725 (7th Cir. 1975), where the court observed that circumstances may arise where an enforcement proceeding will become moot because a party can establish that there is no reasonable expectation that a wrong will be repeated, but then declined to speculate on the issue in order to await Board compliance proceedings.

[75] 393 F.2d 883, 68 L.R.R.M. 2253 (6th Cir. 1968).

problem when it refused to enforce a Board order concerning a minor and subsequently remedied violation, and concluded that ". . . under the facts . . . this is a case in which a minimum amount of investigation by the Board would have avoided pursuing the enforcement petition on the heavily congested docket of this Court." [76] In short, when the likelihood of future violations is small and when voluntary compliance has occurred, the Board might do well to exercise its discretion and not continue further with enforcement proceedings.

Discontinuance of the Unfair Labor Practice

Respondents in Board proceedings will often argue that because they have stopped engaging in the sort of conduct that was found to violate the Act no further remedial action need be taken.

To illustrate from the facts of one case, prior to November 1936, the Consolidated Edison Company of New York had employed outside investigating agencies for the purpose of conducting industrial espionage on union attempts to organize. Even though the practice was voluntarily discontinued thereafter, the Supreme Court held that the Board possessed the requisite authority to have its order, which barred the resumption of the spying activities, enforced. [77] From this brief mention of the Board's authority to seek enforcement of cease and desist orders prohibiting unlawful conduct discontinued by the violator, has grown a labor law doctrine which denies mootness (the abandonment of unlawful practices) as a defense. [78]

For example, voluntary discontinuance of an unlawful no-distribution rule, [79] and the use of questionnaires soliciting a prospective employee's union membership, [80] do not moot a Board

---

[76] *Id.* at 884, 68 L.R.R.M. at 2254.

[77] Consolidated Edison Co. of N.Y., Inc., 305 U.S. 197, 230, 3 L.R.R.M. 646, 653 (1938).

[78] *See, e.g.,* NLRB v. Oertel Brewing Co., 197 F.2d 59, 30 L.R.R.M. 2236 (6th Cir. 1952).

[79] United Aircraft Corp., 67 N.L.R.B. 594, 18 L.R.R.M. 1009 (1946).

[80] NLRB v. F. H. McGraw & Co., 206 F.2d 635, 32 L.R.R.M. 2220 (6th Cir. 1953); Clark Printing Co., 146 N.L.R.B. 121, 55 L.R.R.M. 1269 (1964). *But see* National Freight, Inc., 154 N.L.R.B. 621, 633, 59 L.R.R.M. 1789, 1792 (1965), wherein the Board held that no remedial order was necessary, since the use of such application forms was discontinued when the employer learned that it might be in violation of the Act and where there was no evidence that the employer intended to use the form again.

order prohibiting such practices because an NLRB cease and desist order is viewed as having preventive as well as remedial purposes. Nor does a substantial lapse of time after the unlawful practices are abandoned and enforcement is sought operate as laches against the Board since it is entrusted with the sole power to prohibit violations in the future as well as to stop present violations.[81]

After the enactment of the Taft-Hartley Amendments, the Board held that discontinuance of unlawful activities, a defense unavailable to employers, was also invalid as a union defense.[82] Thus, a union claim that a primary dispute has been settled,[83] or that it has abolished its illegal hiring hall practices,[84] does not render the controversy moot, and a Board order may be properly issued and enforced. Unions have had some limited success in urging discontinuance as a defense during Section 10(1) proceedings.[85] In such cases, district courts have refrained from issuing temporary injunctions when they believe the danger of recurrence has abated because of the union's abandonment of its illegal acts.[86]

---

[81] NLRB v. Sewell Mfg. Co., 172 F.2d 459, 461, 23 L.R.R.M. 2323, 2325 (5th Cir. 1949) ; *cf.* NLRB v. Pool Mfg. Co., 339 U.S. 577, 580-582, 26 L.R.R.M. 2127, 2128 (1950).

[82] Teamsters, Local 145 (Howland Dry Goods Co.), 85 N.L.R.B. 1037, 1038 n.1, 24 L.R.R.M. 1513, 1515 (1949), *enforced,* 191 F.2d 65, 28 L.R.R.M. 2450 (2d Cir. 1951).

[83] *E.g.,* NLRB v. Local 751, Carpenters (Mengel Co.), 285 F.2d 633, 638, 47 L.R.R.M. 2425, 2429 (9th Cir. 1960) ; Teamsters, Local 688 (Acme Paper Co.), 121 N.L.R.B. 702, 703, 42 L.R.R.M. 1416, 1418 (1958). *See also* Local 1976, Carpenters v. NLRB (Sand Door & Plywood Co.), 357 U.S. 93, 97 n.2, 42 L.R.R.M. 2243, 2245 (1958).

[84] Funeral Directors of Greater St. Louis, Inc., 125 N.L.R.B. 241, 243, 45 L.R.R.M. 1103, 1104 (1959).

[85] *See* Greene v. Bangor Building Trades Council, 165 F. Supp. 902, 906, 42 L.R.R.M. 2713, 2716 (N.D. Me. 1958), wherein the court, noting the willingness of the labor organization to give written assurances that its unlawful conduct will not recur, concluded that Congress, in framing the Act, had intended that when illegal secondary activities had been proved, a district court was obligated to issue a temporary injunction.

[86] *See, e.g.,* Vincent v. Local 106, Operating Engineers, 207 F. Supp. 414, 417, 50 L.R.R.M. 2879, 2881-2882 (N.D.N.Y. 1962) ; Potter v. Plant Guard

CHANGING CONDITIONS—SALE, LIQUIDATION, OR MERGER OF THE VIOLATOR'S OPERATIONS

Employers have frequently argued that a Board order is mooted, as applicable to them, when the business is sold or dissolved. In *Southport Petroleum Co. v. NLRB*,[87] the Supreme Court was faced with a situation in which, three days after an employer executed a stipulation of obedience to the Board's order, it distributed all of its assets to its four stockholders as a liquidating dividend. Two of the stockholders who received the Texas City refinery (the subject of the Board's order) conveyed their shares to a newly organized Delaware corporation whose remaining stockholders at no time had any interest in the Texas corporation. Implicit in the Board's order, which had provided for reinstatement, was a condition of ongoing operations by the employer. The Court affirmed the Board's order, but held that the offender could present additional evidence to determine whether there was a bona fide discontinuance and true change of ownership, thereby terminating the duty of reinstatement, or whether the liquidation was merely masquerading as a discontinuance.[88] In so holding, the Court rejected the employer's contention that changed conditions—i.e., the liquidation and distribution of the assets—per se rendered the Board's order requiring reinstatement moot.[89]

The courts have held that the fact that a violator has been reorganized in a Chapter XI proceeding, resulting in new man-

---

Workers, 192 F. Supp. 918, 921-922, 47 L.R.R.M. 2804, 2806-2807 (S.D. Tex. 1961); McMahon v. Carpenters, District Council of St. Louis, 35 L.R.R.M. 2067, 2069 (E.D. Mo. 1954). *Cf* Samoff v. Building & Construction Trades Council (Samuel E. Long, Inc.) 475 F.2d 205, 82 L.R.R.M. 2790 (3d Cir. 1973), *vacated and dismissed as moot* in Building & Construction Trades Council v. Samoff, 414 U.S. 808, 84 L.R.R.M. 2421 (1973).

[87] 315 U.S. 100, 103, 9 L.R.R.M. 411, 412 (1942).

[88] *Id.* at 106, 9 L.R.R.M. at 413-414. *Cf.* Regal Knitwear Co., v. NLRB, 324 U.S. 9, 15 L.R.R.M. 882 (1945), wherein the Court held that a successor could be held liable for the acts of his predecessor where there was an identity of interest between the employers.

[89] *See* NLRB v. West Coast Casket Co., 469 F.2d 871, 81 L.R.R.M. 2857, 2859 (9th Cir. 1972); NLRB v. Rosalina Kostilnik, etc. d/b/a Pacific Baking Co., 405 F.2d 733, 70 L.R.R.M. 3102 (3d Cir. 1969) and cases cited therein; NLRB v. Family Heritage Home, Inc. 491 F.2d 347, 350-351, 85 L.R.R.M. 2545, 2546-2547 (7th Cir. 1974); NLRB v. Autotronics, Inc., 434 F.2d 651, 652, 76 L.R.R.M. 2121 (8th Cir. 1970); Cap Santa Vue, Inc. v. NLRB, 424 F.2d 883, 886, 73 L.R.R.M. 2224 (D.C. Cir. 1970); NLRB v. Colonial Knitting Corp., 464 F.2d 949, 80 L.R.R.M. 3164, 3166 n.10 (3d Cir 1972).

agement and ownership,[90] has been placed in receivership,[91] or is insolvent and awaiting liquidation,[92] does not render a Board order moot. Nor does a mere change in the form of ownership bar enforcement.[93] Moreover, even *after* dissolution, state statutes which preserve the corporate entity for a period of years prohibit an offender from urging his changed conditions as a defense to a Board order.[94]

On the other hand, the courts have not ignored the fact that practical problems do exist when an employer has ceased doing business or has become insolvent and is ordered to reinstate discriminatorily discharged employees, pay make-whole orders, or post notices. Under the principle of *Southport Petroleum,* enforcement of the order is granted and the case is then remanded to the Board to consider the possibilities of compliance.[95] Because an employer cannot be forced to do the

---

[90] NLRB v. Autotronics, Inc., 434 F.2d 651, 652, 76 L.R.R.M. 2121, 2122 (8th Cir. 1970) (per curiam).

[91] NLRB v. Coal Creek Coal Co., 204 F.2d 579, 580, 32 L.R.R.M. 2098, 2099 (10th Cir. 1953).

[92] NLRB v. Somerset Classics, Inc., 193 F.2d 613, 616, 29 L.R.R.M. 2331, 2334 (2d Cir. 1952), *cert. denied,* 344 U.S. 816, 30 L.R.R.M. 2711 (1952); NLRB v. Acme Mattress Co., 192 F.2d 524, 528, 29 L.R.R.M. 2079, 2083 (7th Cir. 1951).

[93] *See, e.g.,* De Bardeleben v. NLRB, 135 F.2d 13, 14, 12 L.R.R.M. 685, 686 (5th Cir. 1943), wherein the employer contended that a Board order was invalid as to the corporation when it was rendered after its dissolution, and not applicable to the subsequent partnership since it was based on findings of illegal practices on the part of the corporation. Pointing out that the corporation was still liable pursuant to a state saving statute and that the partnership was clearly a successor, the court held that the changing conditions did not render the order moot.
See also NLRB v. Adel Clay Products Co., 134 F.2d 342, 346, 12 L.R.R.M. 634, 637 (8th Cir. 1943) (partnership took over business and assets of corporation with same management and employees); NLRB v. William Tehel Bottling Co., 129 F.2d 250, 255, 10 L.R.R.M. 791, 796 (8th Cir. 1942) (death of partner of co-partnership where business being carried on by the survivors); *accord,* NLRB v. Colten, d/b/a Kiddie Kover Mfg., Co., 105 F.2d 179, 183, 4 L.R.R.M. 638, 641 (6th Cir. 1939).

[94] NLRB v. Weirton Steel Co., 135 F.2d 494, 498, 12 L.R.R.M. 393, 698 (3d Cir. 1943) (Delaware statute); De Bardeleben v. NLRB, 135 F.2d 13, 14, 12 L.R.R.M. 685, 686 (5th Cir. 1943) (Alabama statute); NLRB v. Timken Silent Automatic Co., 114 F.2d 449, 450, 6 L.R.R.M. 763 764 (2d Cir. 1940) (Michigan statute).

[95] Southport Petroleum Co. v. NLRB, 315 U.S. 100, 106, 9 L.R.R.M. 411, 414 (1942); NLRB v. Autotronics, Inc., 434 F.2d 651, 652, 76 L.R.R.M. 2121,

impossible, the effect of the Board's determination during a subsequent compliance hearing, which overlooks the changed circumstances, may be tested by the court if contempt proceedings are instituted.[96]

Not all courts, however, have been content to enforce Board orders and then allow subsequent Board compliance proceedings to determine whether an employer's sale of equipment and assets renders the order moot and unenforceable. Indeed, the Sixth Circuit views such an approach as "put[ting] the proverbial cart before the horse," [97] and has required the Board itself to determine whether there exists a functioning employer against whom a court decree could in fact be enforced before the Board comes to the court seeking enforcement.[98] The court reasoned that if the necessary privity between the respondents and their successors was lacking, then many issues of fact and law involved in the case would be rendered moot.

2122 (8th Cir. 1970) (per curiam); NLRB v. Kostilnik, d/b/a Pacific Baking Co., 405 F.2d 733, 735, 70 L.R.R.M. 3102, 3103, 3104 (3d Cir. 1969); NLRB v. Ephraim Haspel, 228 F.2d 155, 156, 37 L.R.R.M. 2218, 2219 (2d Cir. 1955); NLRB v. Acme Mattress Co., 192 F.2d 524, 528, 29 L.R.R.M. 2079, 2083 (7th Cir. 1951).

The same rationale has been applied where the changed conditions involved the abolishment of a department within the company. Wallace Corp. v. NLRB, 159 F.2d 952, 19 L.R.R.M. 2311, 2314-2315 (4th Cir. 1947).

[96] NLRB v. West Coast Casket Co., 469 F.2d 871, 873, 81 L.R.R.M. 2857, 2859 (9th Cir. 1972); NLRB v. Somerset Classics, Inc., 193 F.2d 613, 616, 29 L.R.R.M. 2331, 2334 (2d Cir. 1952), *cert. denied,* 344 U.S. 816, 30 L.R.R.M. 2711 (1952); *cf.* NLRB v. New York Merchandise Co., 134 F.2d 949, 12 L.R.R.M. 578 (2d Cir. 1943). *See also* NLRB v. Caroline Mills, Inc., 167 F.2d 212, 214, 21 L.R.R.M. 2542, 2543 (5th Cir. 1948), wherein the court, pointing out that it would not hold the employer in contempt for failing to reinstate an employee when the company had ceased doing business, stated, "The law does not; the Board cannot . . . require that an employer stay in business merely in order to give employment."

But see American Needle & Novelty Co., 206 N.L.R.B. No. 61, 84 L.R.R.M. 1526 (1973), in which the owner of a three-plant operation, who had transferred production work for its Chicago plant to one of its other plants, was ordered to restore the status quo ante by resuming production activities at the Chicago facilities. The Board felt that no undue hardship was involved since the Chicago plant was still in existence, under the same management, and continued to perform much the same functions, with the exception of that of production, that it had done prior to the transfer. *See also* NLRB v. Jackson Farmers, 457 F.2d 516, 79 L.R.R.M. 2909 (10th Cir. 1972).

[97] NLRB v. Schnell Tool & Die Corp., 359 F.2d 39, 62 L.R.R.M. 2091, 2094 (6th Cir. 1966).

[98] NLRB v. Armitage Sand & Gravel, Inc., 495 F.2d 759, 86 L.R.R.M. 2245, 2246 (6th Cir. 1974); NLRB v. Schnell Tool & Die Corp., *supra,* n.97.

Other instances in which changed circumstances have been rejected as a bar to enforcement include: (1) payment of back-pay to a discriminatorily discharged employee who subsequently died; [99] (2) a turnover in Board membership which has resulted in an alleged change of policy; [100] (3) a complete turnover of the supervisory personnel which had engaged in the unlawful conduct; [101] and (4) the completion of a construction project against which the union had engaged in illegal secondary activities.[102] In like fashion, the holding of a rerun election and the certification of a union does not moot the enforcement of a Board order against an employer predicated on findings that the employer engaged in unfair labor practices during the first election campaign.[103]

One possible exception to this line of cases was raised by the Court of Appeals for the Eighth Circuit in *NLRB v. Grace Co.*[104] In *Grace*, the employer contested a Board order directing him to bargain with the union and post notices on the grounds that the employer had permanently closed the plant in question. Objecting to being called upon to "rubber stamp" the Board's order when the facts showed that it was inoperative and impossible to enforce, the court denied enforcement and remanded the case back to the Board to determine whether the plant had

---

[99] NLRB v. Atlantic Towing Co., 179 F.2d 497, 498, 25 L.R.R.M. 2313, 2314 (5th Cir. 1950), *Judgment set aside on other grounds*, 180 F.2d 726, 25 L.R.R.M. 2480 (5th Cir. 1950) (backpay made to employee's estate). *But cf.* Loveman, Joseph & Loeb v. NLRB, 146 F.2d 769, 771, 15 L.R.R.M. 858, 860 (5th Cir. 1945) (order for reinstatement of employee denied where employee was dead). *See also* Estate of Edward Bryan Moritz d/b/a E. B. Moritz Foundry, 220 N.L.R.B. No. 186, —— L.R.R.M. —— (1975) (estate responsible for the unfair labor practices of deceased employer).

[100] NLRB v. Trimfit of California, Inc., 211 F.2d 206, 210, 33 L.R.R.M. 2705, 2707-2708 (9th Cir. 1954).

[101] Dixie Highway Express, Inc., 153 N.L.R.B. 1224 n.2, 59 L.R.R.M. 1624, 1626 (1965).

[102] NLRB v. Local 74, Carpenters (Watson's Specialty Store), 341 U.S. 707, 715, 28 L.R.R.M. 2121, 2124 (1951).

[103] NLRB v. Raytheon, 398 U.S. 25, 27, 74 L.R.R.M. 2177, 2178 (1970); NLRB v. Metalab-Labcraft (Div. Metalab Equip. Co.), 367 F.2d 471, 63 L.R.R.M. 2321, 2322 (4th Cir. 1966); NLRB v. Marsh Supermarkets, Inc., 327 F.2d 109, 55 L.R.R.M. 2017 (7th Cir. 1963), *cert. denied* 377 U.S. 944, 56 L.R.R.M. 2288 (1964); NLRB v. Clark Bros. Co., 163 F.2d 373, 20 L.R.R.M. 2436 (2d Cir. 1947).

[104] 184 F.2d 126, 26 L.R.R.M. 2536 (8th Cir. 1950).

been permanently closed.[105] The court distinguished *Grace* from *Southport* and its progeny on the basis that the instant case did not involve an order which was partially enforceable, nor did it involve a successor employer who could be bound by the Board's order.[106]

CONCLUDING REMARKS TO PART TWO

As we have seen, the *Express Publishing* doctrine, the two-fold test for determining the permissible scope of the Board's order, has been interpreted and misinterpreted, construed both broadly and narrowly, and so riddled with exceptions and qualifications that its straightforward approach has fallen largely to a case-by-case analysis. Moreover, the Board is involved in a serious split of opinion over whether it has the authority to refuse to remedy violations of the Act. Another serious drain on Board resources is found in the tendency of the Board to seek court enforcement of orders governing situations where the violations are minimal or where orders have been rendered moot because of changing conditions, the violator's abandonment, or his attempted compliance with the Board's order.

These problems may be eased, however, through greater Board administrative policy. For example, the vagaries of the *Express Publishing* doctrine might be lessened by using the Board's rule-making authority to set forth definitive guidelines for future reference. Both de minimis violations and moot cases might be better disposed of by employing a more vigorous policy of discretion in prosecuting unfair labor practice charges. It often has been stated that the Board's exclusive authority to prevent

---

[105] *Id.* at 131, 26 L.R.R.M. at 2540. The court also refused to consider the Board's petition for enforcement as withdrawn without prejudice upon the NLRB's report that the employer's plant had indeed been closed. NLRB v. Grace Co., 189 F.2d 258, 28 L.R.R.M. 2320 (8th Cir. 1951).
Cf. NLRB v. U.S. Trailer Mfg. Co., 184 F.2d 521, 523-524, 26 L.R.R.M. 2658, 2660 (8th Cir. 1950) wherein the Eight Circuit distinguished *Grace* from the instant case on the grounds that the rights of employees to reimbursement for lost wages were involved.

[106] NLRB v. Grace Co., 184 F.2d 126, 131, 26 L.R.R.M. 2536, 2540. *See also* NLRB v. Reynolds Corp., 155 F.2d 679, 681-682, 18 L.R.R.M. 2087, 2089 (5th Cir. 1946) (order by Board directing employer to cease and desist interfering with organizational and bargaining rights of its employees denied enforcement where plant in question was only operated by Reynolds as a wartime munitions manufacturer and was turned over to Navy at end of war); Cambridge Dairy Inc., 404 F.2d 866, 70 L.R.R.M. 2218, 2219 (10th Cir. 1968) (order held unwarranted since employer had completely closed his business).

unfair labor practices is a function to be performed in the public interest and not in the vindication of private rights.[107] For this reason the Board has been vested with the discretion to determine if a proceeding, once instituted, may be abandoned. The Board's functions would be better performed adequately only through either a radical or conscious policy of shifting limited resources to those areas which merit most consideration in light of the seriousness of the violation or novelty of the issue.

---

[107] *E.g.*, National Licorice Co. v. NLRB, 309 U.S. 350, 362 6 L.R.R.M. 674, 681-682 (1940).

The Obligation Of A Successor Employer To Remedy His Predecessor's Unfair Labor Practices

We saw in the previous chapter that a change in corporate structure or ownership, liquidation of a business, or distribution of its assets ordinarily will not moot a Board order, and that order will run against a new employer who is "merely a disguised continuance of the old employer." [1] Under our enterprise system there are, of course, a large number of bona fide instances in which one corporation will either purchase, acquire, or merge with another. Often the employer who relinquishes his business (the predecessor) will have an established bargaining relationship or collective-bargaining agreement with a union which represents his employees. When such a relationship exists, questions may arise concerning the responsibility of the acquiring employer (the successor) to recognize or bargain with the union and to remedy unfair labor practices committed by the predecessor.

The Supreme Court recently addressed several issues dealing with the labor relations obligations of successor employers. The Court has held that, where the bargaining unit remains unchanged and a majority of the employees hired by the new employer are represented by a union, the successor employer is required to bargain with the incumbent union. [2] But even though the successor may be bound to recognize and bargain with the union, he is not bound by the substantive provisions of a collective-bargaining agreement negotiated by his predecessor

---

[1] Southport Petroleum Co. v. NLRB, 315 U.S. 100, 106, 9 L.R.R.M. 411 (1942). *See also* NLRB v. Family Heritage Home, Inc., 491 F.2d 347, 85 L.R.R.M. 2545, 2546-2546 (7th Cir. 1974), and cases cited therein.

[2] NLRB v. Burns International Security Services, Inc., 406 U.S. 272, 280-281, 80 L.R.R.M. 2225 (1972).

to which he has not agreed.[3] Additionally, the successor will not be required to fulfill the predecessor's argeement to arbitrate with the union unless there plainly is a substantial continuity of identity in work force hired by the successor and either an expressed or implied assumption of the arbitration agreement.[4]

Once successorship is established under the *Burns* standards, the extent of the successor employer's obligation to remedy unfair labor practices committed by the predecessor remains a relevant issue for this study of NLRB remedies. Following a number of twists and turns, Board holdings in this area were formulated in the now well-established *Perma Vinyl* doctrine.[5] *Perma Vinyl* basically requires the successor to remedy the predecessor's unfair labor practices if he acquires and operates the business in an essentially unchanged form and under circumstances which charge him with the unfair labor practice. The *Perma Vinyl* decision was approved by the Supreme Court in *Golden State Bottling Co. v. NLRB*,[6] in an opinion which disposed of many of the issues that had been generated surrounding the unfair labor practice responsibility of the successor employer.

Early in the administration of the Act, the Board adopted a remedial formula which ordered not only a particular respondent, but also its officers, agents, successors and assigns, to cease and desist from the unfair labor practices found by the Board. The wording of the formula was approved by the Supreme Court in *Regal Knitwear Co. v. NLRB*.[7] The Court, however,

---

[3] *Id.* at 281-291, 80 L.R.R.M. at 2228-2232.

[4] Howard Johnson Co. v. Detroit Local Joint Executive Board, Hotel and Restaurant Employees and Bartenders International Union, AFL-CIO, 417 U.S. 249, 86 L.R.R.M. 2449 (1974); John Wiley & Sons v. Livingston, 376 U.S. 543, 55 L.R.R.M. 2769 (1964); Teamsters, Local 249 v. Bill's Trucking, Inc., 493 F.2d 956, 85 L.R.R.M. 2713 (3d Cir. 1974); The Boeing Company v. Int'l Ass'n of Machinists and Aerospace Workers, AFL-CIO, *et al.*, 504 F.2d 307, 87 L.R.R.M. 2865 (5th Cir. 1974).

[5] Perma Vinyl Corp., 164 N.L.R.B. 968, 65 L.R.R.M. 1168 (1967), *enforced sub nom.* United States Pipe and Foundry Co. v. NLRB, 398 F.2d 544, 68 L.R.R.M. 2913 (5th Cir. 1968).

[6] 414 U.S. 168, 84 L.R.R.M. 2839 (1973). In a recent decision, the Sixth Circuit determined that the Supreme Court decisions in *Wiley*, *Burns*, and *Golden State* should be aplpied on a case-by-case basis to unfair employment practices in violation of Title VII of the U.S. Civil Rights Act of 1964, 42 U.S.C. Sec. 2000 *et seq. See* EEOC v. MacMillan Bloedel Containers, Inc., 503 F.2d 1086, 1090-1091, 8 F.E.P. 897 (6th Cir. 1974).

[7] 324 U.S. 9, 15 L.R.R.M. 882 (1945).

by no means held that such language would have broad application to successor employers; rather, the Court indicated that it was not deciding under what circumstances any kind of successor or assign would be liable for a violation of a Board order.[8] The Court did indicate that the order would bind those who operate as "merely a distinguished continuance of the old employer" and "those to whom the business may have been transferred whether as a means of evading the judgment or *for other reasons*." [9] (emphasis added)

On the other hand, the Court also noted that Rule 65 of the Federal Rules of Civil Procedure provided that "Every order granting an injunction and every restraining order . . . is binding only upon the parties to the action, their officers, agents, servants, employees, and attorneys, and upon those persons in active concert or participation with them who receive actual notice of the order by personal service or otherwise.[10] The Court then approved the application of Board orders to "successors and assigns" because it could not say that under certain circumstances such entities might not be among those reachable by the scope of Rule 65(d). The Court also carefully explained that the case before it involved a sterile, abstract controversy and that future cases involving possible contemptuous conduct of a successor with respect to an enforced Board order would depend upon "an appraisal of his relations and behavior and not upon mere construction of terms of the order." [11]

Perhaps the ambiguity of the guidance contained in *Regal Knitwear* accounts for the tortuous route of the Board's successorship doctrine, the history of which was set forth by the Supreme Court in *Golden State Bottling Co. v. NLRB*.[12]

> The Board has pursued an uneven course in its treatment of a bona fide successor's liability to remedy the unfair labor practices of its predecessor. In 1944 the Board determined that liability

---

[8] *Id.* at 15, 15 L.R.R.M. at 884.

[9] *Id.* at 14, 15 L.R.R.M. at 884, *citing* from Southport Petroleum Co. v. NLRB, 315 U.S. 100, 106, 9 L.R.R.M. 411 (1942) and Walling v. Reuter, 321 U.S. 671, 674, 4 W.H.R. 335 (1944).

[10] For the impact of Rule 65(d) on the scope of Board orders prohibiting a union from engaging in further unfair labor practices against employees of an employer other than that in the immediate case, *see supra*, Chapter III, p. 36.

[11] Regal Knitwear, *supra*, 324 U.S. at 15, 15 L.R.R.M. at 884.

[12] 414 U.S. 168, 174-175, 84 L.R.R.M. 2839, 2841 (1973).

would not be imposed on a bona fide successor, South Carolina Granite Co., 58 NLRB 1448, [15 LRRM 122] enforced sub nom. NLRB v. Blair Quarries, Inc., 152 F.2d 25, [17 LRRM 683] (1945). In 1947 the Board abandoned that view and determined that joint and several remedial responsibility would be imposed upon a bona fide successor who had knowledge of the seller's unfair labor practice at the time of the purchase, Alexander Milburn Co., 78 NLRB 747, [22 LRRM 1249]. When, however, two Courts of Appeals refused to enforce remedial orders against bona fide successors, NLRB v. Birdsall-Stockdale Motor Co., 208 F.2d 234, [33 LRRM 2086] (1953), and NLRB v. Lunder Shoe Corp., 211 F.2d 284, [33 LRRM 2695] (1954), the Board, in 1954 re-examined and over-ruled Alexander Milburn Co., declaring in Symns Grocer Co., 109 NLRB 346, [34 LRRM 1326], that "[n]o provision of the [National Labor Relations] Act authorizes the Board to impose the responsibility for remedying unfair labor practices on persons who did not engage therein." Id., at 348.[13]

In 1967, largely in response to the Supreme Court's decision in *Wiley & Sons*,[14] the Board reversed its decision in *Symns Grocer Co.* and held that in subsequent cases, the successor would be held responsible for remedying the unfair labor practices of the previous employer if the successor acquired and operated the business in basically unchanged form and, under such circumstances, could receive notice of the unfair labor practice charges against the predecessor. Thus, in *Perma Vinyl Corp.*[15] the Board relied on the basic underpinnings of its remedial authority to frame such orders "as will effectuate the policies of the Act" and "achieve the 'objectives of national

---

[13] For a thorough discussion of the development of the various Board doctrines relating to the responsibility of a successor for the predecessor's employees see DuRoss, *Protecting Employee Remedial Rights Under the Perma Vinyl Doctrine*, 39 GEO. WASH. L. REV. 1063 (1971), *cited* with approval in Golden State Bottling Co. v. NLRB, *id.*, 414 U.S. at 178 n. 4, 84 L.R.R.M. at 2842-2843 n. 4.

[14] John Wiley & Sons, Inc. v. Livingston, 376 U.S. 543, 549, 55 L.R.R.M. 2769 (1964) wherein the Court stated:

> Employees . . . ordinarily do not take part in negotiations leading to a change in corporate ownership. The negotiations will ordinarily not concern the well-being of the employees, whose advantage or disadvantage, potentially great, will inevitably be incidental to the main considerations. The objectives of national labor policy, reflected in established principles of federal law, require that the rightful prerogative of owners independently to rearrange their businesses and even eliminate themselves as employers be balanced by some protection to the employees from a sudden change in the employment relationship.

[15] 164 N.L.R.B. 968, 65 L.R.R.M. 1168 (1967).

labor policy.' " [16] The reasoning behind the Board's new change in policy was stated as follows:

> In imposing this responsibility upon a bona fide purchaser, we are not unmindful of the fact that he was not a party to the unfair labor practices and continues to operate the business without any connection with his predecessor. However, in balancing the equities involved there are other significant factors which must be taken into account. Thus, "It is the employing industry that is sought to be regulated and brought within the corrective and remedial provisions of the Act in the interest of industrial peace." When a new employer is substituted in the employing industry there has been no real change in the employing industry insofar as the victims of past unfair labor practices are concerned, or the need for remedying those unfair labor practices. Appropriate steps must still be taken if the effects of the unfair labor practices are to be erased and all employees reassured of their statutory rights. And it is the successor who has taken over control of the business who is generally in the best position to remedy such unfair labor practices most effectively. The imposition of this responsibility upon even the bona fide purchaser does not work an unfair hardship upon him. When he substituted himself in place of the perpetrator of the unfair labor practices, he became the beneficiary of the unremedied unfair labor practices. Also, his potential liability for remedying the unfair labor practices is a matter which can be reflected in the price he pays for the business, or he may secure an indemnity clause in the sales contract which will indemnify him for liability arising from the seller's unfair labor practices.[17]

The Board also held that the bona fide purchaser would be entitled to a full hearing to determine whether he is a successor who is responsible for the predecessor's unfair labor practices. The successor also would be afforded a hearing concerning the enforcement of any order issued against him.[18] The *Perma Vinyl* decision was enforced by the Fifth Circuit in *U.S. Pipe and Foundry Co. v. NLRB*,[19] where the court pointed out that U.S. Pipe had purchased Perma Vinyl with notice of the unfair labor practice proceedings but continued the same operation with regard to the jobs in question. The court saw this

---

[16] *Id.* at 969, 65 L.R.R.M. at 1168-1169. For a further discussion of these principles, see Chapter II, *supra.*

[17] *Id.* at 969, 65 L.R.R.M. at 1169.

[18] *Id.* at 969, 65 L.R.R.M. at 1169.

[19] 398 F.2d 544, 68 L.R.R.M. 2913 (5th Cir. 1968).

as a "sufficient basis for requiring [U.S. Pipe] to offer rein-statement to the employees on the successorship theory." [20]

When the *Perma Vinyl* doctrine reached the Supreme Court in *Golden State Bottling Co. v. NLRB*,[21] the Court adopted it, holding that the bona fide purchaser of a business, who acquires and continues the business with knowledge that his predecessor has committed an unfair labor practice in the discharge of an employee, may be ordered to reinstate the employee with backpay. The Court explained that:

> . . . [w]hen a new employer . . . has acquired substantial assets of its predecessor and continued, without interruption or substantial change, the predecessor's business operations, those employees who have been retained will understandably view their job situations as essentially unaltered. Under these circumstances, the employees may well perceive the successor's failure to remedy the predecessor employer's labor practices arising out of an unlawful discharge as a continuation of the predecessor's labor policies. To the extent that the employees' legitimate expectation is that the unfair labor practices will be remedied, a successor's failure to do so may result in labor unrest as the employees engage in collective activity to force remedial action. Similarly, if the employees identify the new employer's labor policies with those of the predecessor but do not take collective action, the successor may benefit from the unfair labor practices. Moreover, the Board's experience may reasonably lead it to believe that employers intent on suppressing union activity may select for discharge those employees most actively engaged in union affairs, so that a failure to reinstate may result in a leadership vacuum in the bargaining unit. Cf. Phelps Dodge Corp. v. NLRB, 313 U.S. 177, 193, [8 L.R.R.M. 439] (1941). Further, unlike Burns, where an important labor policy opposed saddling the successor employer with the obligations of the collective-bargaining agreement, there is no underlying congressional policy here militating against the imposition of liability.[22]

[20] *Id.,* 398 F.2d at 548, 68 L.R.R.M. at 2915. *But cf.* Wheeler (Northern Virginia Sun, Inc.) v. NLRB, 382 F.2d 172, 65 L.R.R.M. 2921 (D.C. Cir. 1967), where the court held that *Perma Vinyl* did not require the Board to order reinstatement by a second successor employer where that employer did not assume the obligations of the prior employers' unfair labor practices. The two prior employers had settled backpay differences with the employees, and there was no privity between the original employer and the second successor. The continued validity of *Wheeler* is questionable, however, in light of the rationale of the Supreme Court in its *Golden State Bottling Co.* decision set forth *infra,* p. 72. *See also* Ramada Inns, Inc., 171 N.L.R.B. 1060, 68 L.R.R.M. 1209, 1212 (1968) (*Perma Vinyl* not applicable where the successor was a remote purchaser with no knowledge of the unfair labor practices, and there was substantial turnover in the employee complement).

[21] 414 U.S. 168, 84 L.R.R.M. 2839 (1973).

[22] *Id.* at 184-185, 84 L.R.R.M. at 2845.

Section 10(c)'s broad grant of discretion to the Board to fashion relief that would effectuate the policies of the Act was found not to limit the Board's remedial powers to the "actual perpetrator of any unfair labor practice. . . ."[23] The Court also disposed of the ever-lingering Rule 65(d) issue by holding that "a bona fide purchaser, acquiring, with knowledge that the wrong remains unremedied, the employing enterprise which was the locus of the unfair labor practice, may be considered in privity with its predecessor for purposes of Rule 65(d) [F.R.C.P.].[24] This is especially true since the Board's *Perma Vinyl* decision provided the purchaser adequate procedural safeguards of a hearing on the successorship and enforcement issues.[25]

It is apparent, therefore, that under the decisions in *Perma Vinyl* and *Golden State*, a successor employer who knows of pending unfair labor practice charges against the predecessor has a fairly broad responsibility to remedy those violations of the Act. Thus, in both decisions, the successor employers were required to reinstate unlawfully discharged employees and found to be jointly and severally liable for any backpay due the discriminatees.[26] Both the predecessor and successor may be held responsible for backpay; this does not mean, however, that their backpay liabilities will necessarily cover the same time periods. In *Southeastern Envelope Co.*,[27] the predecessor was held responsible for backpay until the discriminatees had secured substantially equivalent employment, while the successor's

---

[23] *Id.* at 176, 84 L.R.R.M. at 2842.

[24] *Id.* at 180, 84 L.R.R.M. at 2842-2844.

[25] *Id.* at 180, 84 L.R.R.M. at 2844. Simply because a predecessor has sold his business does not mean that he then may move to be dismissed from further proceedings, since there may be "tag ends" to the proceeding that would make advisable his continuance as a party, for the order against the original employer may still turn out to be the indispensable basis for imposing liability against successors and assigns. *See* Cap Santa Vue, Inc. v. NLRB, 424 F.2d 883, 73 L.R.R.M. 2224, 2226 (D.C. Cir. 1970). The *Perma Vinyl* decision may not be used by the Board as a justification for adding the dollar volume both of the predecessor and successor in order to satisfy the Board's $500,000 minimum for asserting jurisdiction. Thus, for the Board to assert jurisdiction over either enterprise, each must, on its own, satisfy these dollar volume standards. *See* Martin J. Baker, d/b/a Galaxy Theater, *etc.*, 210 N.L.R.B. No. 118, slip op. p. 5 & n. 8, 86 L.R.R.M. 1191 (1974).

[26] *See also* Riley Aeronautics Corp., 178 N.L.R.B. 495, 499, 74 L.R.R.M. 1543 (1969).

[27] 206 N.L.R.B. 933, 934, 84 L.R.R.M. 1577 (1973).

backpay liability was limited to the period from the date of discrimination until the date of purchase of the enterprise.

As a further limitation on the successor's liability, the Board has held that, where the successor does not have substantially the same work force as the predecessor, the successor will not be required to offer full and immediate reinstatement to the discriminatees. Rather, the successor is obligated merely to place the employees on a preferential hiring list and offer them reemployment as jobs become available, and before other employees are hired for such work.[28] Additionally, where a successor employer unlawfully refused to bargain with the union after hiring a work force made up of a majority of the predecessor's employees, the Board held that employees, who were engaged in an economic strike against the predecessor, did not become unfair labor practice strikers entitled to reinstatement. The Board reasoned that the strikers who were not rehired never became the successor's employees, and there was no evidence that any of these employees ever tendered an unconditional offer to return to work.[29] On the other hand, the Board has required full reinstatement of employees under *Perma Vinyl,* over the objection of a successor who argued that since it had contractually agreed to assume all of its predecessor's financial obligations for Section 8(a)(3) violations, this contract should be construed to limit his remedial obligations to monetary damages, and exclude the reinstatement remedy.[30]

In addition to offering reinstatement and reimbursing backpay, the successor may also be required to post a notice to employees stating that the successor will undertake the remedies previously described.[31] However, as with back pay and reinstatement, the cease and desist and notice requirements placed

---

[28] *Id.* The Ninth Circuit agreed with the Board in one instance that the hiring of 90 out of 125 of the predecessor's employees would not support a finding that the successor had hired "substantially" or "essentially" the same work force. In those circumstances, both the Board and court agreed that it would be inappropriate to order the successor to pay backpay or offer reinstatement to the discriminatees. *See* Thomas Engine Corp., d/b/a Tomadur, Inc., 179 N.L.R.B. 1029 & n. 4, 73 L.R.R.M. 1289 (1969), *enforced sub nom.* UAW v. NLRB, 442 F.2d 1180, 77 L.R.R.M. 2401, 2403 (9th Cir. 1971).

[29] United Maintenance & Mfg. Co., 214 N.L.R.B. No. 31, 87 L.R.R.M. 1469, 1476-1477 (1974).

[30] Emerson Electric Co., 176 N.L.R.B. 744, 71 L.R.R.M. 1297, 1298 (1969).

[31] *See e.g.,* Ocomo Foods Company, 186 N.L.R.B. 697, 702, 75 L.R.R.M. 1537 (1970).

upon a successor employer may differ significantly from those which would be required of the prior owner. Thus, shortly after the *Perma Vinyl* decision the Board in the *Tomadur* case [32] deleted from a notice language which would have required the successor to promise the employees that it would cease and desist from the unfair labor practices committed by his predecessor. Subsequently, in *Golden State,* the Supreme Court noted that as in *Tomadur,* there was no requirement that the bona fide purchaser cease and desist from the illegal activity found.[33] Mr. Justice Brennan noted that this approach seemed conconsistent with the fact that the successor's remedial obligations arise out of another employer's unfair labor practices and not his own.[34] Accordingly, it is now the Board's practice not to enter a cease and desist order which runs against the successor employer, but rather to utilize such orders only against the predecessor.[35]

---

[32] Thomas Engine Corp., d/b/a Tomadur, Inc., 179 N.L.R.B. 1029, 73 L.R.R.M. 1289 & n. 4 (1969), *enforced sub nom.* UAW v. NLRB, 442 F.2d 1180, 77 L.R.R.M. 2401, 2403 (9th Cir. 1971). The Board held that it was significant that the successor's obligation in *Perma Vinyl* was restricted to an affirmative reinstatement order and there was no requirement that he cease and desist from either the 8 (a)(1) or the 8 (a)(3) violations of the predecessor. *Id.,* 2402-2403.

[33] *See* Golden State Bottling Co. v. NLRB, *supra,* 414 U.S. at n. 4, 84 L.R.R.M. at 2842-2843 n. 4.

[34] *Id.*

[35] *See e.g.,* NLRB v. East Side Shopper, Inc., 498 F.2d 1334, 86 L.R.R.M. 2817, 2818 n. 1 (6th Cir. 1974) ; Southeastern Envelope Co., *supra,* 206 N.L.R.B. at 934.

CHAPTER VI

Notification: Disseminating The Board's Order Among The Employees

In addition to the negative, or cease and desist, provisions of an NLRB order in an unfair labor practice case, the Board's remedy will almost always include an affirmative requirement covering the posting of notices. Compliance usually requires that, for a period of sixty days, the respondent employer or union will post, and maintain in a conspicuous location, a signed notice which sets forth the terms and conditions of the cease and desist order.[1] In the case of union-committed unfair labor practices, copies of the order, signed by appropriate union officials, must be furnished to the regional director who will transmit the notice to the employer for posting, if the employer so desires.[2]

At the very least, the notice is a useful means of informing employees that Board action has been taken to remedy activities found to be in violation of employees' rights under the Act.[3] In many cases, however, the notice requirement is especially important because it may be the only affirmative action which the respondent is directed to undertake.[4]

The notice must be both accessible and understandable. Thus, an employer who claimed literal compliance with an order di-

---

[1] The NLRB Field Manual, Sec. 10752.1; *see* NLRB v. Express Publishing Co., 312 U.S. 426, 8 L.R.R.M. 415 (1941), wherein the Supreme Court upheld the power of the Board to require posting of its orders. *See* Chapter III, *supra*, for a discussion of the circumstances in which the Board has ordered that a remedial notice be posted at operations of the respondent other than those directly involved in a particular unfair labor practice case.

[2] Von's Grocery Co., 91 N.L.R.B. 504, 26 L.R.R.M. 1528 (1950).

[3] *Cf.* NLRB v. Douglas & Lomason Co., 443 F.2d 291, 295, 77 L.R.R.M. 2449, 2451 (8th Cir. 1971).

[4] *See e.g.*, National Maritime Union, 78 N.L.R.B. 971, 22 L.R.R.M. 1289 (1948).

recting him to post notices in his plant did not fulfill his obligations when the posting occurred during a time period in which his employees were on strike and, therefore, unable to read the notice.[5] In some instances, the Board has ruled that because a plant employs a bilingual work force, the posted notice must be both in English and the appropriate second language.[6] Also, the courts of appeals have cautioned the Board against the use of superfluous or ambiguous language,[7] or wording that "smacks" of punitive action in the sense that innuendos in the notice suggest that the respondent is basically untrustworthy—reliable only under duress.[8]

Generally, the provisions covering notification simply stipulate that the notice be posted in conspicuous places, such as bulletin boards, time clocks, department entrances, meeting hall entrances, or dues payment windows. Under certain circumstances, however, the Board has fashioned special notification conditions

---

[5] American Newspapers, Inc., 22 N.L.R.B. 899, 6 L.R.R.M. 251 (1940).

[6] John F. Cuneo, 152 N.L.R.B. 929, 59 L.R.R.M. 1226 (1965); Teamsters Local 901 (F. F. Instrument Corp.), 210 N.L.R.B. No. 153, 86 L.R.R.M. 1286 (1974); Pollack Electrical Co., 219 N.L.R.B. No. 195, 90 L.R.R.M. 1335 (1975); *cf.* General Iron Corp., 218 N.L.R.B. No. 109, 89 L.R.R.M. 1783 (1975).

[7] NLRB v. Douglas & Lomason Co., 443 F.2d 291, 295, 77 L.R.R.M. 2449, 2451 (8th Cir. 1971). *Cf.* NLRB v. Priced-Less Discount Foods, Inc. 407 F.2d 1325, 70 L.R.R.M. 2743 (6th Cir. 1969) (Board did not adequately inform employees that they had a right to decertify the union as their representative by bald statement that, pursuant to § 9(c)(1), the employees may petition the NLRB for an election).
See NLRB v. Laney & Duke Storage Warehouse Co., 369 F.2d 859, 63 L.R.R.M. 2552 (5th Cir. 1966), wherein the Board's order against the employer had provided, *inter alia*, that "We [the employer] will not promise to restore the raises which our employees used to get every year before they joined the union." Assuming that the proscription was aimed at unlawful promises of benefit, the court observed that as it stood, it doubted that "the employees will greet this restriction with enthusiasm." *See also* Chapter III, *supra*, for further discussion of ambiguous orders.

[8] *E.g.*, NLRB v. Douglas & Lomason Co., 443 F.2d 291, 77 L.R.R.M. 2449 (8th Cir. 1971) (The court replaced words indicating that the Board had ordered the employer to promise with the words "we promise"); Love Box Co. v. NLRB, 422 F.2d 232, 235, 73 L.R.R.M. 2746, 2749 (10th Cir. 1970) (The court deleted language indicating the Board had ordered the employer to keep its word, and inserted the words "we intend to carry out the order . . . and abide by the following . . ."); Unit Drop Forge Div., Eaton, Yale & Towne Inc. v. NLRB, 412 F.2d 108, 111, 71 L.R.R.M. 2519 (7th Cir. 1969) (same); Amalgamated Local Union 355 (Russell Motors, Inc.) v. NLRB, 481 F.2d 996, 83 L.R.R.M. 2849 (2d Cir. 1973), *enf'g as modified* 198 N.L.R.B. No. 58, 80 L.R.R.M. 1757 (1973) (The court modified the Board's order to read that the union had entered into a "collusive" contract, rather than a "sweetheart" contract.).

which conform to the requirement that the remedy bear some rational relationship to the type of industry involved and to the unfair labor practice which has been committed.

In industries such as construction, where the job site is highly mobile, the Board may require that its notices be posted at the respondent's offices[9] and job sites for sixty days,[10] or at all projects where work is begun by the respondent within a specified period of time commencing from the first date of compliance.[11] For seasonal operations such as the packing or canning industries, the NLRB notice must be posted for 60 days commencing from the date the plant is in full operation—i.e., the so-called peak of the season.[12]

Peculiar or unusual conditions affecting employment may cause the Board to rule that a simple posting is inadequate and that

---

[9] Building & Construction Trades Council (Philadelphia & vicinity) (Fisher Construction Co.), 149 N.L.R.B. 1629, 58 L.R.R.M. 1001 (1964); *cf.* Swinerton and Walberg Co., 94 N.L.R.B. 1079, 28 L.R.R.M. 1148 (1951), *enforced* 202 F.2d 511, 31 L.R.R.M. 2384 (9th Cir. 1953). Reflecting the notion that the scope of the order must bear some relationship to the unfair labor practices committed, the employer in this case was not ordered to post notices in his New York office when the misconduct occurred in San Francisco. The New York office was deemed too far removed from the offending locality and, furthermore, its major operations were confined to manufacturing, whereas the San Francisco operation concerned machinery installation.

[10] Utah Construction Co., 95 N.L.R.B. 196, 28 L.R.R.M. 1300 (1951).

[11] *Compare* J. R. Cantrall Co., 96 N.L.R.B. 786, 28 L.R.R.M. 1588 (1951), *enforced*, 201 F.2d 853, 31 L.R.R.M. 2332 (9th Cir. 1953), *cert. denied*, 345 U.S. 996, 32 L.R.R.M. 2247 (1953) (within six months), *with* Swinerton and Walberg Co., 94 N.L.R.B. 1079, 28 L.R.R.M. 1148 (1951), *enforced*, 202 F.2d 511, 31 L.R.R.M. 2384 (9th Cir. 1953) (within one year). The difference in the time allotted for notification to commence is because of the fact that the *Cantrall* case involved a traditional construction contractor, while the *Swinerton* case involved only isolated instances of machinery installation, the performance of which was dependent upon sales of machinery by the parent company to California purchasers. *See also* Wyoming Valley Bldg. & Construction Trades Council (Altemose Construction Assoc.), 211 N.L.R.B. No. 154, 87 L.R.R.M. 1394 (1974), wherein the Board fashioned several methods of notification in order to reach construction employees who were members of a local which had no regular meeting place.

[12] *See* Wade & Paxton, 96 N.L.R.B. 650, 28 L.R.R.M. 1559 (1951); Charbonneau Packing Corp., 95 N.L.R.B. 1166, 28 L.R.R.M. 1428 (1951); Southern Fruit Distributors, Inc., 81 N.L.R.B. 259 (1949). This particular remedy reflects the Board's overall policy for dealing with seasonal industries in matters which affect the entire bargaining unit at the height of operations. For example, representation elections among employees of seasonal employers are held at the "peak of the season." *See e.g.*, WILLIAMS, JANUS & HUHN, NLRB REGULATION OF ELECTION CONDUCT 402-403 (Lab. Rel. & Pub. Policy Ser., Rep. No. 8, 1974) for an extended discussion of this subject.

additional notification is required. For example, in instances where the plant has closed down, the project has been completed, or the work force has been reduced, the Board has ruled that the respondent must mail a copy of the notice to each employee discriminated against and to each employee employed at the time of the shutdown,[13] completion,[14] or reduction.[15]

The NLRB has also found that "flagrant and gross" unfair labor practices may warrant extraordinary notification provisions in addition to the normal posting requirements. In an attempt to neutralize the effect of aggravated unfair labor practice conduct, the Board may rule that the respondent must mail a copy of the notice to each employee.[16] In a case of unfair labor practices by an employer, the Board may require his bulletin boards be made available to the union for a specified period of time [17] and the union be allowed company time to present its position.[18] Similar provisions may be ordered in cases in which the unlawful conduct involved individual contact between the respondent and the employee.[19]

---

[13] Southland Manufacturing Corp., 157 N.L.R.B. 1356, 61 L.R.R.M. 1552 (1966).

[14] Interboro Contractors, Inc., 157 N.L.R.B. 1295, 61 L.R.R.M. 1537 (1966).

[15] Clement Bros., Inc., 170 N.L.R.B. 1327, 68 L.R.R.M. 1086 (1968).

[16] H. W. Elson Bottling Co., 155 N.L.R.B. 714, 60 L.R.R.M. 1381 (1965), *enf'd on this ground* in NLRB v. H. W. Elson Bottling Co., 379 F.2d 223, 65 L.R.R.M. 2673 (6th Cir. 1967); NLRB v. Teamsters Local 294 (August Bohl Contracting Co. and Cooley Contracting Co.), 470 F.2d 57, 81 L.R.R.M. 2920 (2d Cir. 1972), *enforcing* 193 N.L.R.B. 920, 78 L.R.R.M. 1479 (1971).

[17] Great Lakes Screw Corp., 164 N.L.R.B. 149, 65 L.R.R.M. 1236 (1967); Heck's Inc., 191 N.L.R.B. 886, 77 L.R.R.M. 1513 (1971), *enforced as amended sub nom.* Meat Cutters, Local 347 v. NLRB, 476 F.2d 546, 82 L.R.R.M. 2955 (1973), *cert. denied,* 414 U.S. 1069, 84 L.R.R.M. 2835 (1973); J. P. Stevens and Co., v. NLRB, 461 F.2d 490, 80 L.R.R.M. 2609 (4th Cir. 1972); J. P. Stevens and Co. v. NLRB, 417 F.2d 533, 72 L.R.R.M. 2433 (5th Cir. 1969).

[18] Int'l Union of Electrical Workers (Scott's Inc.) v. NLRB, 383 F.2d 230, 66 L.R.R.M. 2081 (D.C. Cir. 1967); *cf.* Heck's Inc., 191 N.L.R.B. 886, 77 L.R.R.M. 1513 (1971), *enforced as amended sub nom.* Meat Cutters, Local 347 v. NLRB, 476 F.2d 546, 82 L.R.R.M. 2955 (1973), *cert. denied* 414 U.S. 1069, 84 L.R.R.M. 2835 (1973); The Loray Corp., 184 N.L.R.B. 557, 74 L.R.R.M. 1513 (1970). However, on several occasions the Board has refused to grant requests for notice mailing, bulletin board access, or company time to appeal to employees. *See e.g.,* Dee Knitting Mills, 214 N.L.R.B. No. 138, 88 L.R.R.M. 1273 (1974); Moore Mill & Lumber Co., 212 N.L.R.B. No. 27, 86 L.R.R.M. 1545 (1974). For a full treatment of NLRB policies concerning requests for extraordinary remedies to deal with flagrant unfair labor practices see Chapter XIV, *infra.*

[19] *See e.g.,* J. I. Case Co. v. NLRB, 321 U.S. 332, 14 L.R.R.M. 501 (1944) (individual notice to employees who had entered into individual employment

Similarly, where the union's unfair labor practices would tend to impinge upon its members' protected activities, the Board has required that a copy of the remedial notice be mailed to each member of the union.[20] And, in secondary boycott cases, the Board has also ordered that the union mail signed copies of the notice to all employees of the charging party.[21] Also, where the misconduct involved the use of mails in the issuance of coercive statements, such as the sending of letters,[22] leaflets,[23] or postcards,[24] the Board has ordered that notices be mailed to the employees.

If the announcement of a course of action which the Board subsequently finds violative of the Act appears in an employer[25] or union[26] controlled publication, the NLRB has required that a copy of its notice be similarly published.

---

contracts) ; Reed & Prince Mfg. Co., 96 N.L.R.B. 850, 28 L.R.R.M. 1608 (1951), *enforced* 205 F.2d 131, 32 L.R.R.M. 2225 (1st Cir. 1953) (individual notice to each unfair labor practice striker who had been threatened by his employer in soliciting a return to work) ; U.S. Automatic Corp., 57 N.L.R.B. 124, 14 L.R.R.M. 214 (1944) (individual notice to each employee with whom the employer had bargained individually concerning his grievances) ; Atlas Bag and Burlap Co., 1 N.L.R.B. 292, 1 L.R.R.M. 385 (1936) (individual notice to each employee who had entered into unlawful "yellow dog" contract of employment). Significantly, in each of these cases, notices were ordered sent only to those employees who had actual contact with their employer and not to the entire bargaining unit.

[20] *See e.g.*, Int'l Union of Operating Engineers, Local 18, AFL-CIO, 205 N.L.R.B. 901, 84 L.R.R.M. 1349 (1973), enf'd per curiam Docket No. 73-2140 (6th Cir. 1974) ; NLRB v. Local 294, Teamsters, 470 F.2d 57, 64, 81 L.R.R.M. 2920 (2d Cir. 1972), *citing* Philadelphia Moving Picture Machine Operator's Union, Local No. 307, I.A.T.S.E. v. NLRB, 382 F.2d 598, 600, 65 L.R.R.M. 3020, 3022 (3d Cir. 1967).

[21] Teamsters, Local 901 (F. F. Instrument Corp.), 210 N.L.R.B. No. 153, 86 L.R.R.M. 1286, 1288 (1974) *cf.* Union de Tronquistas de Puerto Rico, Local 901 (Lock Joint Pipe & Co. of Puerto Rico), 202 N.L.R.B. 399, 82 L.R.R.M. 1525 (1973) ; Union de Tronquistas de Puerto Rico, Local 901 (Hotel La Concha), 193 N.L.R.B. 591, 78 L.R.R.M. 1377 (1971).

[22] Clark Bros., Inc., 70 N.L.R.B. 802, 18 L.R.R.M. 1360 (1946), *enforced* 163 F.2d 373, 20 L.R.R.M. 2436 (2d Cir 1947)

[23] NLRB v. American Laundry Machine Co., 152 F.2d 400, 17 L.R.R.M. 685 (2d Cir. 1945).

[24] Yoder Co., 47 N.L.R.B. 557, 12 L.R.R.M. 30 (1943).

[25] Meier & Frank Co., 89 N.L.R.B. 1016, 26 L.R.R.M. 1081 (1950) (department store, which had announced invalid no-solicitation rule in company bulletin, ordered to publish notice of its recision and also a facsimile of the Board's order in the same publication).

[26] Typographical Union (American Newspaper Publishers Ass'n), 86 N.L.R.B. 951, 25 L.R.R.M. 1002 (1949) (union, which had announced the

Finally, the Board may order that respondent or an agent of the NLRB read the contents of the notice to the employees if circumstances such as illiteracy [27] or widespread and flagrant violations of the Act [28] deem it necessary. At times some courts have refused to enforce Board orders requiring the employer to read the notice to his employees. These courts have considered that a public reading by the employer would be humiliating and degrading to the employer and would have a lingering effect on future relations between the company and union.[29] Such considerations, however, have been held not to bar a public reading where there are special circumstances, such as a high illiteracy rate among the employees.[30]

On occasion, the Board has also taken the unusual step of requiring a particular agent of the employer to sign the notice because that agent was personally identified with the employer's unlawful conduct. Without that agent's signature, the employees might not recognize that the usual notice contains a bona fide commitment by the employer to refrain from committing similar unfair labor practices in the future.[31]

---

adoption of a bargaining strategy to avoid the impact of the Taft-Hartley restrictions on closed shops and engaged in widespread publication of its policy through its internal bulletins, ordered to publish Board's notice); Variety Artists (Harrah's Club), 195 N.L.R.B. 416, 79 L.R.R.M. 1345 (1972), *supplementing* 176 N.L.R.B. 580, 71 L.R.R.M. 1275 (1969); Musicians Local 368 (Harrah's Club), 195 N.L.R.B. 1104, 79 L.R.R.M. 1650 (1972), *supplementing* 178 N.L.R.B. 707, 72 L.R.R.M. 1284 (1969).

[27] NLRB v. Bush Hog, Inc., 405 F.2d 755, 70 L.R.R.M. 2070, 2072 (5th Cir. 1968); Marine Welding & Repair Works v. NLRB, 439 F.2d 395, 76 L.R.R.M. 2660, 2663 (8th Cir. 1971) and cases there cited.

[28] Sterling Aluminum Co., 163 N.L.R.B. 302, 64 L.R.R.M. 1354 (1967); J. P. Stevens and Co. v. NLRB, 417 F.2d 533, 72 L.R.R.M. 2433 (5th Cir. 1969); Int'l Union of Electrical Workers (Scott's Inc.) v. NLRB, 383 F.2d 230, 66 L.R.R.M. 2081 (D.C. Cir. 1967); Heck's Inc., 191 N.L.R.B. 886, 77 L.R.R.M 1513 (1971), *enf'd as amended sub nom.* Meat Cutters, Local 347 v. NLRB, 476 F.2d 546, 82 L.R.R.M. 2955 (1973), *cert. denied* 414 U.S. 1069, 84 L.R.R.M. 2835 (1973).

[29] *See* Int'l Union of Electrical Workers (Scott's Inc.) v. NLRB, 383 F.2d 230, 66 L.R.R.M. 2081, 2082-2083 (D.C. Cir. 1967), and cases cited therein at n. 5; NLRB v. Laney and Duke Storage Co., 369 F.2d 859, 869, 63 L.R.R.M. 2552 (5th Cir. 1966).

[30] NLRB v. Bush Hog, Inc., 405 F.2d 755, 70 L.R.R.M. 2070, 2072 (5th Cir. 1968), which distinguishes the cases cited *supra*, n. 29.

[31] Southern Athletic Co., 157 N.L.R.B. 1051, 61 L.R.R.M. 1051 (1966); The Paymaster Corp., 162 N.L.R.B. 123, 63 L.R.R.M. 1508, 1509 (1966).

PART THREE

Monetary Remedies

CHAPTER VII

Backpay and Reimbursement

The Board has the statutory power to require the payment of monies to remedy situations in which an employee suffers a loss of earnings because of employment discrimination by an employer, a union, or both, or because of an illegal assessment of union dues, fees, and fines.[1] The purpose of these monetary awards, known as "make-whole" orders, is to restore the discriminatee, as nearly as possible, to the economic position he would have enjoyed without the discrimination.[2] Although the power of the Board to devise such awards is broad and discretionary,[3] it is limited by the stipulation that NLRB orders must be remedial and not punitive in nature.[4]

The NLRB may order an employer or union to reimburse an employee or former employee for a loss of pay resulting from a discriminatory discharge, layoff, or refusal to reinstate. Although primarily used in situations involving loss of work, this backpay remedy may also be ordered following an unlawful change in the employee's job status, such as a discriminatory demotion,[5] transfer,[6] or pay reduction.[7] Reimbursement is directed in instances

---

[1] 29 U.S.C. § 160(c) (1970). Further explanation of the procedural aspects of NLRB backpay procedures can be found in McGuiness, How to take a Case Before the NLRB, Fourth Edition, Chapter 18 (BNA 1976).

[2] Phelps Dodge Corp. v. NLRB, 313 U.S. 177, 8 L.R.R.M. 439, 446 (1941).

[3] NLRB v. Seven-Up Bottling Co., 344 U.S. 344, 31 L.R.R.M. 2237 (1953); NLRB v. J. H. Rutter-Rex Mfg. Co., 396 U.S. 258, 262-263, 72 L.R.R.M. 2881 (1969).

[4] Republic Steel Corp. v. NLRB, 311 U.S. 7, 7 L.R.R.M. 287 (1940), *and see* Chapter II, *supra*, pp. 11-14.

[5] Tan-Tar-A Resort, 198 N.L.R.B. No. 163, 81 L.R.R.M. 1200 (1972); Walker Electric Co., 219 N.L.R.B. No. 52, 90 L.R.R.M. 1171 (1975).

[6] Hall Electric Co., 111 N.L.R.B. No. 5, 35 L.R.R.M. 1414 (1955); M.F.A. Milling Co., 170 N.L.R.B. No. 111, 68 L.R.R.M. 1077 (1968).

[7] Standard Generator Service Co., 186 F.2d 606, 27 L.R.R.M. 2274 (8th Cir. 1951); Cascade Employers Ass'n, 126 N.L.R.B. No. 118, 45 L.R.R.M. 1426

involving union-caused discrimination or situations where employees are found to be subject to an illegal union security clause.[8]

Although the power to devise and compute monetary remedies is primarily a function of the Board and not the courts,[9] both backpay orders and reimbursement remedies are subject to appellate court review. They usually withstand judicial challenge unless it can be shown that the order in question is a "patent attempt to achieve ends other than those which can be fairly said to effectuate the policies of the Act." [10]

Backpay and reinstatement orders arising from the same violation are not necessarily coterminous. The Board has, on occasion, issued remedies that award backpay but not reinstatement to a discharged employee. Thus, if an employee engages in misconduct that would make him an undesirable employee, his reinstatement eligibility may be voided even though the misconduct occurred after he had been discriminatorily discharged or had been out on strike. Similarly, if an employer learns of earlier misconduct of which he was previously unaware, reinstatement may not be ordered. In such instances, however, backpay is usually awarded, but the backpay period is tolled * on the date the employer learned of the employee's criminal record [11] or on the date the employee

---

(1960); Zim's Food Liner v. NLRB, —— F.2d ——, 85 L.R.R.M. 3019 (7th Cir. 1974).

[8] *See* this chapter, pages 95 to 100, and Chapter X, entitled *Remedies Designed to Restore the Union's Representational Integrity, infra,* page 154.

[9] NLRB v. Seven-Up Bottling Co., *see* footnote 3, *supra*; NLRB v. J. H. Rutter-Rex Mfg. Co., 393 U.S. 1117, 70 L.R.R.M. 2828 (1969).

[10] Virginia Electric & Power Co. v. NLRB, 319 U.S. 533, 12 L.R.R.M. 739 (1943); NLRB v. Rutter-Rex Mfg. Co., 393 U.S. 1117, 70 L.R.R.M. 2828 (1969), *revs'g* 399 F.2d 356, 68 L.R.R.M. 2916 (1968).

* Toll, as a verb, herein means "to bar, defeat, or take away." BLACK'S LAW DICTIONARY (3d ed. 1933).

[11] East Island Swiss Products, 220 N.L.R.B. No. 26, 90 L.R.R.M. 1206 (1975) (employer learned of employee's previous discharge and conviction for misappropriating funds). Banker's Club, Inc., 218 N.L.R.B. No. 7, 89 L.R.R.M. 1812 (1975) (employee who would have been replaced because of poor attendance record awarded thirty days backpay but reinstatement denied); Gifford-Hill & Co., 188 N.L.R.B. 337, 76 L.R.R.M. 1349 (1971) (Since Board hearing, employee convicted of five armed robberies and sentenced to serve fifteen years in prison); O. R. Cooper & Son, 220 N.L.R.B. No. 43, 90 L.R.R.M. 1267 (1975) (Employees intentionally destroyed employer's property).

became unavailable for work due to his arrest.[12] Similarly, the Board may order backpay without reinstatement in instances where an employee indicates that he does not want to be reinstated [13] or where the employer is no longer in business, if it can be shown that the operation was discontinued for economic reasons and not to evade remedying an unfair labor practice.[14] The Board, in its discretion, may also order that an employee be reinstated without backpay.[15]

In situations involving bankruptcy, a backpay claim is considered to be a debt founded upon an implied contract under the Bankruptcy Act and is not entitled to priority treatment. In *Nathanson v. NLRB*,[16] the Supreme Court noted that Congress limited the priority of such claims to $600 for each claimant only in regard to wages earned within three months prior to commencement of the proceedings. Subsequent to *Nathanson*, a district court ruled that backpay claims, although possibly legitimate expenses of administration, do not take precedence over valid liens against the Trustee, such as liens of a secured creditor.[17] Furthermore, in both cases the courts held that neither the Board nor its agent could set aside funds to ensure payment of backpay claims.

The amount of the backpay award is the sum of the wages, benefits, and overtime pay the employee would have earned without the discriminatory discharge, less the amount earned by the employee in the interval.[18] Known as the *Woolworth* formula, this method of computation corresponds to the four quarters of the calendar year. Backpay is computed for each quarter individ-

---

[12] East Island Swiss Products, *see* footnote 11, *supra*.

[13] Phelps Dodge, *see* footnote 2, *supra*.

[14] Riley Aeronautics Corp., 178 N.L.R.B. No. 76, 74 L.R.R.M. 1543 (1969); Arnold Graphics v. NLRB, —— F.2d ——, 87 L.R.R.M. 2753, 2756 (6th Cir. 1974) (no backpay where employer lawfully shut down operation at one location and transferred to another.)

[15] Republican Publishing Co., 174 F.2d 474, 24 L.R.R.M. 2052 (1st Cir. 1949), *adj'g in contempt* 180 F.2d 437, 25 L.R.R.M. 2559 (1st Cir. 1950).

[16] 344 U.S. 25, 31 L.R.R.M. 2036 (1952).

[17] Durand v. NLRB, 296 F. Supp. 1049, 70 L.R.R.M. 2651 (W.D. Ark. 1969).

[18] F. W. Woolworth Co., 90 N.L.R.B. 289, 26 L.R.R.M. 1185 (1950); NLRB v. Seven-Up Bottling Co., 344 U.S. 344, 31 L.R.R.M. 2237 (1953).

ually, and the applicable sum found due does not affect, nor is it affected by, the comparable amounts found in other quarters.[19]

Prior to adopting the *Woolworth* formula, the Board had computed backpay on the basis of the amount accumulated during the entire backpay period minus the employee's interim earnings.[20] Upon reconsideration, however, the NLRB determined that this form of computation had an adverse affect on the companion remedy of reinstatement. For example, if an employee, following his discriminatory discharge, obtained a better paying job, it would be profitable for the employer to delay an offer of reinstatement as long as possible. Each day the employee worked on his new job reduced the employer's backpay liability. In addition, the old formula encouraged the employee to waive his right to reinstatement, since such action would prevent further reduction of the sum of the backpay award.[21]

In many cases it may be difficult to determine precisely the amount of backpay due. Where such difficulty arises, the Board will approximate the amount due and may adopt reasonable formulae designed to achieve that end. The judiciary will not interfere with such formulae unless it can be shown that they are arbitrary or unreasonable in the circumstances of the particular case.[22]

ELIGIBILITY AND THE MITIGATION DOCTRINE

Although the finding of an unfair labor practice and discriminatory discharge is presumptive proof that some backpay is owed,[23] an employee who claims backpay must make a reasonable effort to secure employment substantially equivalent to the lost work.[24] If he fails to do so, the Board will deduct from the back-

---

[19] NLRB Field Manual, Sec. 10530.2.

[20] NLRB v. Pennsylvania Greyhound Lines, Inc., 1 N.L.R.B. 1, 51, 1 L.R.R.M. 303 (1935) *enf'd* 303 U.S. 261, 2 L.R.R.M. 599 (1938).

[21] *See* Footnote 3, *supra.*

[22] NLRB v. Brown & Root, Inc., 311 F.2d 447, 452, 52 L.R.R.M. 2115 (8th Cir. 1963); NLRB v. Charley Toppino & Sons, Inc., 358 F.2d 94, 97, 61 L.R.R.M. 2655 (5th Cir. 1966); NLRB v. Carpenters Union, Local 180, 433 F.2d 934, 935, 75 L.R.R.M. 2560 (9th Cir. 1970).

[23] NLRB v. Mastro Plastics Corp., 354 F.2d 170, 178, 60 L.R.R.M. 2578 (2d Cir. 1966), *cert. denied,* 384 U.S. 972, 62 L.R.R.M. 2292 (1966).

[24] Phelps Dodge Corp. v. NLRB, 313 U.S. 177, 8 L.R.R.M. 439 (1941), Madison Courier, Inc., 162 N.L.R.B. No. 51, 64 L.R.R.M. 1148 (1967) *enforced,*

pay award the amount of wage losses it considers willfully incurred.[25] Prior to 1956, registration with a government employment service constituted "conclusive proof" that a reasonable search had been made.[26] In subsequent decisions, however, the Board has held that sufficiency of effort would be determined in light of all of the circumstances particular to the case and the individual's experience.[27]

To advance "the healthy policy of promoting production and employment," the Supreme Court, in 1941, established the mitigation (or willful idleness) doctrine.[28] This rule stipulates that in order to be eligible for backpay, an employee must remain in the labor market, accept substantially equivalent employment, diligently search for alternative work, and not voluntarily quit alternative employment without good cause.[29] On the other hand, a discriminatorily discharged employee who makes a reasonable effort to secure substantially equivalent work but is unsuccessful in his efforts remains entitled to backpay.[30]

Self-employment is treated as a new job and the profits incurred are viewed as earnings.[31] Also, if the employee leaves his new job because of reasons for which he would have left his old position, or if he would have left his original job in order to take the new position, his claim for backpay will be valid up to the

------

—— F.2d ——, 67 L.R.R.M. 2462 (D.C. Cir. 1967), *suppl'g* 82 L.R.R.M. 1667 (1973); Avon Convalescent Home, 219 N.L.R.B. No. 191, 90 L.R.R.M. 1265 (1975).

[25] Phelps Dodge Corp. v. NLRB, *see* footnote 2, *supra.* NHE/Freeway, Inc., 218 N.L.R.B. No. 41, 89 L.R.R.M. 1481 (1975).

[26] Harvest Queen Mill & Elevator Co., 90 N.L.R.B. 320, 26 L.R.R.M. 1189 (1950).

[27] NLRB v. Southern Silk Mills, Inc., 242 F.2d 697, 39 L.R.R.M. 2647 (6th Cir. 1957), *cert. denied*, 355 U.S. 821, 40 L.R.R.M. 2680 (1957).

[28] Phelps Dodge Corp. v. NLRB, 313 U.S. 177, 199-200, 8 L.R.R.M. 439 (1941).

[29] NLRB v. Mastro Plastics Corp., 354 F.2d 170, 174 n. 3, 60 L.R.R.M. 2578 (2d Cir. 1965), *cert. denied*, 384 U.S. 972, 62 L.R.R.M. 2292 (1966); NLRB v. Madison Courier, Inc., 472 F.2d 1307, 80 L.R.R.M. 3377 (D.C. Cir. 1972) and cases cited therein.

[30] NLRB v. Mastro Plastics Corp., *see* footnote 29, *supra.*

[31] Heinrich Motors, Inc. v. NLRB, 403 F.2d 145, 69 L.R.R.M. 2613 (2d Cir. 1965). McCann Steel Co. Inc., 203 N.L.R.B. No. 115, 83 L.R.R.M. 1175 (1973), *enforcement denied pending factual clarification*, McCann Steel Co. v. NLRB, 489 F.2d 1328, 85 L.R.R.M. 2302 (6th Cir. 1974).

time he would have vacated his job.[32] After an employee has unsuccessfully sought equivalent employment for a reasonable period of time,[33] he may be required to look for suitable work at a rate of pay lower than the one he earned before his discharge.[34]

The Board has consistently refused to award backpay to a striking employee, even in instances where the strike was precipitated by an employer's unfair labor practice, or where the strikers are discharged. In *Sea-Way Distributing, Inc.*,[35] the Board held that since the strikers had not abandoned the strike and applied for reinstatement, it could not justify awarding them backpay while they were withholding their services, regardless of the fact that they were discharged. Backpay will be assessed only if the employer, upon receipt of the strikers' unconditional application for reinstatement, refuses to reinstate them because of their union activity.[36] On the other hand, if an employee participates in a strike which began after he was discriminatorily discharged, he is still eligible for backpay.[37]

If the Board finds that an employer has refused the strikers' offer to return to work because of their union activity and that the offer was unconditional, it will award backpay. The backpay period will run from the date five days after the date of the strikers' application for reinstatement to the date of the employer's offer of reinstatement.[38] The Board will allow for reasonable

---

[32] NLRB v. Mastro Plastics Corp., *see* footnote 24, *supra*.

[33] NLRB v. Moss Planning Co., 256 F.2d 653, 42 L.R.R.M. 2393 (4th Cir. 1958) (three months search found reasonable).

[34] NLRB v. Southern Silk Mills, 242 F.2d 697, 39 L.R.R.M. 2647 (6th Cir. 1957); *cert. denied*, 355 U.S. 821, 40 L.R.R.M. 2680 (1957); NLRB v. Madison Courier, Inc., 505 F.2d 391, 87 L.R.R.M. 2440 (D.C. Cir. 1974), and cases cited therein.

[35] Sea-Way Distributing, Inc., 143 N.L.R.B. No. 50, 53 L.R.R.M. 1326 (1963); Volney Felt Mills, 162 F.2d 204, 20 L.R.R.M. 2195 (2d Cir. 1947).

[36] Phelps Dodge Corp. v. NLRB, 313 U.S. 177, 8 L.R.R.M. 439 (1941); NLRB v. Thayer Co., 213 F.2d 748, 34 L.R.R.M. 2250 (1st Cir. 1954), *cert. denied*, 348 U.S. 883, 35 L.R.R.M. 2100 (1954), *suppl'd on remand* 115 N.L.R.B. 1591, 38 L.R.R.M. 1142 (1956).

[37] East Texas Steel Castings Co., 116 N.L.R.B. 1336, 38 L.R.R.M. 1470 (1956), *enf'd* 255 F.2d 284, 42 L.R.R.M. 2109 (5th Cir. 1958).

[38] Sea-Way Distributing Co., *see* footnote 35 *supra*; Roosevelt Roofing & Sheet Metal Works, 204 N.L.R.B. No. 110, 83 L.R.R.M. 1614 (1973), NLRB v. Crosby Chemicals, 188 F.2d 91, 27 L.R.R.M. 2541 (5th Cir. 1951); Artim Transportation Systems, Inc., 166 N.L.R.B. 795, 68 L.R.R.M. 2388 (1967).

delays where the strikers' offer comes at the close of a strike and prestrike operations have not yet been restored. In these circumstances, the backpay period may run from the date that work was available.[39] Furthermore, an employee's participation in union activities, such as picketing or attendance at union-sponsored training sessions does not of itself show insufficient effort on the part of the employee to search for suitable interim employment. The union activity must interfere with an employee's ability to seek alternative employment before the Board will consider such activity as mitigating the respondent's liability.[40]

The Board must consider each employee's claim for backpay separately, taking into account both the record as a whole,[41] and the particular facts concerning the individual.[42] Thus, the NLRB may not consider the strikers as a single group without examining their individual efforts to secure interim or alternative employment.[43]

THE BACKPAY PERIOD

The backpay period runs from the date of the unlawful discharge or refusal by the employer of an unconditional offer to return to work to the date reinstatement is offered.[44] It does not include periods of time in which the employee was unavailable for work, for reasons such as military service,[45] college attendance,[46]

---

[39] Volney Felt Mills v. NLRB, 162 F.2d 204, 20 L.R.R.M. 2195 (2d Cir. 1947), *enf'g* 70 N.L.R.B. 908, 18 L.R.R.M. 1422 (1946).

[40] NLRB v. Madison Courier, Inc., 505 F.2d 391, 87 L.R.R.M. 2440 (D.C. Cir. 1974).

[41] NLRB v. Rice Lake Creamery Co., 365 F.2d 888, 894, 62 L.R.R.M. 2332 (D.C. Cir. 1966).

[42] NLRB v. U.S. Air Conditioning Corp., 336 F.2d 275, 57 L.R.R.M. 2068 (6th Cir. 1964).

[43] NLRB v. Madison Courier, Inc., 472 F.2d 1307, 80 L.R.R.M. 3377 (D.C. Cir. 1972). *And see infra*, p. 132, and n.48.

[44] Richard W. Kaase Co. (Local 219, American Bakery & Confectionery Workers), 141 N.L.R.B. 245, 52 L.R.R.M. 1306 (1963), *enforced in pertinent part* NLRB v. Kaase Co., 364 F.2d 24, 59 L.R.R.M. 2290 (6th Cir. 1965); American Manufacturing Co., 167 N.L.R.B. 520, 66 L.R.R.M. 1122 (1967); Associated Transport Co. of Texas, Inc., 194 N.L.R.B. No. 12, 78 L.R.R.M. 1678 (1971).

[45] NLRB v. Gluek Brewing Co., 144 F.2d 847, 14 L.R.R.M. 912 (8th Cir. 1944).

[46] Two Wheel Corp., 218 N.L.R.B. No. 87, 89 L.R.R.M. 1405 (1975); J. L. Holtzendorff Detective Agency, Inc., 206 N.L.R.B. No. 50, 84 L.R.R.M. 1479 (1973).

pregnancy,[47] or a disability,[48] or times when the backpay claimant would not have worked regardless of discrimination.[49] If, however, the discriminatee's inability to work was due to environmental factors which he would not have encountered absent the discrimination, backpay will be awarded.[50] As shown, the pivotal point of the backpay period is the date of the employer's reinstatement offer. For a more complete and detailed analysis of reinstatement and what constitutes an offer of reinstatement, see Chapter VIII, "Reinstatement of Discriminatorily Discharged Employees," page 103, and Chapter IX, "Reinstatement Rights of Strikers," page 122.

In 1962, the Board established the policy of awarding backpay for the entire period from the discharge to the offer of reinstatement in instances where the Administrative Law Judge's proposed dismissal of the unfair labor practice charge is reversed by the Board. In *A.P.W. Products,*[51] the Board held that unless such action is taken, the respondent benefits at the expense of the discriminatee. Specifically, the discharged employee would not be made whole for the full period of discrimination and to that extent, would be punished because of an erroneous conclusion reached by the Administrative Law Judge. The employer, on the other hand, would be permitted to profit both monetarily and by delaying reinstatement to unwanted employees. Similarly, the backpay period is not tolled where the Board, on remand from an appellate court, reverses a finding of no violation. As before, the backpay period runs the entire period from the discharge to the offer of reinstatement.[52]

---

[47] NLRB v. Mastro Plastics Corp., 354 F.2d 170, 60 L.R.R.M. 2578 (2d Cir. 1965), *cert. denied* 384 U.S. 972, 62 L.R.R.M. 2292 (1966); Avon Convalescent Center, 219 N.L.R.B. No. 191, 90 L.R.R.M. 1264 (1975).

[48] Miller, 204 N.L.R.B. No. 165, 83 L.R.R.M. 1716 (1973), *reh. denied* 87 L.R.R.M. 3276 (7th Cir. 1974).

[49] NLRB v. Carolina Mills, 190 F.2d 675, 28 L.R.R.M. 2323 (4th Cir. 1951).

[50] American Manufacturing Co., 167 N.L.R.B. 520, 66 L.R.R.M. 1123 (1967); Associated Transport Co. of Texas, Inc., 194 N.L.R.B. No. 12, 78 L.R.R.M. 1678 (1971).

[51] NLRB v. A.P.W. Products, 316 F.2d 899, 53 L.R.R.M. 2055 (2d Cir. 1963) *enf'g* 137 N.L.R.B. 25, 50 L.R.R.M. 1042 (1962).

[52] Golay & Company, 447 F.2d 290, 77 L.R.R.M. 3041 (7th Cir. 1971). *And see* Graphic Arts Union, Local 245, 217 N.L.R.B. No. 162, 89 L.R.R.M.

OFFSETS AND ADDITIONS

In the terminology of the backpay hearing, the amount of the backpay award is determined by subtracting the sum of the interim earnings less expenses from the gross backpay. Computation is based on the four quarters of the calendar year, each quarter being computed separately. Known as the *Woolworth* formula,[53] this method of computation is designed only to "make whole" the employee discriminatorily discharged and not to punish the party liable for the discrimination [54] nor reward the individual subjected to the unfair labor practice.[55]

Gross backpay is the amount of money the employee would have earned during the backpay period absent discrimination. It includes not only the wages he would have earned,[56] but also other sums of money or the equivalent he would have received, such as bonuses,[57] raises,[58] overtime pay,[59] vacation pay,[60] and tips.[61] The Board may also order the employer to include in the backpay award contributions the company would have made to pension

1376 (1975) (backpay not tolled from the date the regional director refused to issue complaint until date General Counsel reversed the director and ordered a complaint issued).

[53] F. W. Woolworth Co., 90 N.L.R.B. 289, 26 L.R.R.M. 1185 (1950); *approved in* NLRB v. Seven-Up Bottling Co., 344 U.S. 344, 31 L.R.R.M. 2237 (1953).

[54] NLRB v. Stilley Plywood Co., 199 F.2d 319, 31 L.R.R.M. 2014 (4th Cir. 1952); *cert. denied* 344 U.S. 933, 31 L.R.R.M. 2347 (1953).

[55] Republic Steel v. NLRB, 311 U.S. 7, 7 L.R.R.M. 287 (1940).

[56] In determining the wages the employee would have earned, the Board takes into account such things as the union rate, New England Tank Industries, Inc., 147 N.L.R.B. No. 70, 56 L.R.R.M. 1253 (1964); change of status, Golden State Bottling Co. v. NLRB, 414 U.S. 168, 84 L.R.R.M 2839, 2846 (1973), *aff'g* 467 F.2d 164, 81 L.R.R.M. 2097 (9th Cir. 1972) and the hours the employees' replacement worked, American Casting Service, Inc., 177 N.L.R.B. No. 5, 73 L.R.R.M. 1524 (1969).

[57] Story Oldsmobile, Inc., 145 N.L.R.B. 1647, 55 L.R.R.M. 1217 (1964); Hickman Garment Co., 196 N.L.R.B. No. 51, 80 L.R.R.M. 1684 (1972).

[58] NLRB v. Condensor Corp. of America, 128 F.2d 67, 10 L.R.R.M. 483 (3d Cir. 1942).

[59] Controlled Alloy, Inc., 208 N.L.R.B. No. 140, 85 L.R.R.M. 1494 (1974).

[60] Barberton Plastics Products, Inc., 146 N.L.R.B. No. 54, 55 L.R.R.M. 1337 (1964).

[61] Home Restaurant Drive-In, 127 N.L.R.B. 635, 46 L.R.R.M. 1065 (1960).

plans, insurance programs, or hospitalization policies.[62] From this gross amount, interim earnings are subtracted.

Interim earnings are the wages the backpay claimant actually earned from self or alternative employment during the backpay period. While the Board includes severance pay [63] and money received from government relief projects [64] in this amount, it does not include wages obtained from a second or additional job held prior to the discrimination.[65] Also excluded are expenses relating to all losses the employee incurred in seeking and holding alternative employment which he would not have incurred had he not been discriminated against. Examples of these expenses are employment agency fees, transportation costs, room and board, and family moving costs.[66]

Early retirement benefits that an employee receives as a result of his discharge are considered by the Board to be interim earnings.[67] On the other hand, unemployment compensation and strike or picketing benefits are not.[68] The Board also excludes voluntary contributions from employees who helped their fellow union member.[69] Difficulties occasionally arise over whether to include worker's compensation. In *American Manufacturing Co.*, the Board

---

[62] NLRB v. Rice Lake Creamery Co., 365 F.2d 888, 62 L.R.R.M. 2332 (D.C. Cir. 1966); Shell Oil Co., 218 N.L.R.B. No. 32, 89 L.R.R.M. 1534 (1975); Ace Tank & Heater Co., 167 N.L.R.B. No. 94, 66 L.R.R.M. 1129 (1967) (Board ordered the company to reimburse the employee for a substantial amount of what he would have received under cancelled hospitalization policy.).

[63] NLRB v. United Nuclear Corp., 381 F.2d 972, 66 L.R.R.M. 2101 (10th Cir. 1967), enf'g 156 N.L.R.B. 961, 61 L.R.R.M. 1186 (1966).

[64] Republic Steel Corp. v. NLRB, 311 U.S. 7, 7 L.R.R.M. 287 (1940).

[65] Golay & Company, Inc., 447 F.2d 290, 77 L.R.R.M. 3041 (7th Cir. 1971).

[66] NLRB v. Brown & Root, Inc., 311 F.2d 447, 52 L.R.R.M. 2115 (8th Cir. 1963); Southern Household Products Co., 203 N.L.R.B. No. 138, 83 L.R.R.M. 1247 (1973); Graphic Arts Union, Local 245, 217 N.L.R.B. No. 162, 89 L.R.R.M. 1376 (1975); Harvest Queen Mill & Elevator Co., 90 N.L.R.B. 320, 26 L.R.R.M. 189 (1950).

[67] Shell Oil Co., 218 N.L.R.B. No. 32, 89 L.R.R.M. 1534 (1975).

[68] NLRB v. Gullet Gin Co., 340 U.S. 361, 27 L.R.R.M. 2230 (1951); NLRB v. Laidlaw Corp., 507 F.2d 1381, 87 L.R.R.M. 3216 (7th Cir. 1974), cert. denied —— U.S. ——, —— L.R.R.M. —— (1975).

[69] Hyster Co., 220 N.L.R.B. No. 198, —— L.R.R.M. —— (1975); Although not decided by the Board, an Administrative Law Judge has recently held that Supplemental Unemployment Benefits (SUB) are not considered as interim earnings to offset the backpay due. Rubber Workers Local 374 and Smith, NLRB Case No. 13-CB-4370, decided June 26, 1975, 167 DLR A-4 (BNA, August 27, 1975).

held that only that portion of the compensation which was reparation for physical damage should be excluded from interim earnings. The portion designed to compensate for lost wages should be included.[70] If an employee's alternative work requires him to join a union and pay registration and membership dues, the Board will include in the backpay amount those union expenses.[71] Deductions may be made for employees with a long history of absenteeism. The Board has held that an employer may assume that the absences would have continued if the employee had not been discharged.[72]

Prior to 1962, the Board had refused to add interest to backpay awards, noting that such action would neither effectuate the policies of the Act nor be appropriate.[73] In *Isis Plumbing*,[74] however, the NLRB reversed its position and established the policy of awarding backpay with interest at 6 percent annually on the amount found due for each quarter. Recently, an attempt by a union to obtain a higher rate of interest based on the highest maximum lawful rate under the law of the state of New York was rejected by the Board and Second Circuit.[75]

BURDEN OF PROOF

As noted above, the "finding of an unfair labor practice . . . is presumptive proof that some backpay is owed." [76] The allocation

---

[70] American Manufacturing Co., 167 N.L.R.B. 520, 66 L.R.R.M. 1123 (1967).

[71] NLRB v. Miami Coca-Cola Bottling Co., 360 F.2d 569, 62 L.R.R.M. 2155 (5th Cir. 1966).

[72] Mooney Aircraft, Inc., 164 N.L.R.B. 1102, 65 L.R.R.M. 1349 (1967); *but see* Marine Welding & Repair Works, Inc., *et al.*, 202 N.L.R.B. No. 85, 82 L.R.R.M. 1676 (1973).

[73] Sifers Candy Company, 92 N.L.R.B. 1220, 27 L.R.R.M. 1232 (1951).

[74] Isis Plumbing & Heating Co., 138 N.L.R.B. No. 97, 511 L.R.R.M. 1122 (1962).

[75] Amalgamated Local Union 355 v. NLRB, 481 F.2d 996, 83 L.R.R.M. 2849 (2d Cir. 1973). *See also* United States v. Philmac Mfg. Co., 192 F.2d 517, 519 (3d Cir. 1951); United Steelworkers v. Butler Mfg. Co., 77 L.R.R.M. 2053, 2057 (D.C.W.D. Mo. 1970), *aff'd* 439 F.2d 1110, 77 L.R.R.M. 2057 (8th Cir. 1971).

[76] NLRB v. Mastro Plastics Corp., 354 F.2d 170, 178, 60 L.R.R.M. 2578 (2d Cir. 1966), *cert. denied* 384 U.S. 972, 62 L.R.R.M. 2292 (1966).

of the burden of proof in backpay proceedings was set forth in
NLRB v. Brown & Root, Inc.[77] by the Eighth Circuit:

> . . . in a backpay proceeding the burden is upon the General Counsel
> to show the gross amounts of backpay due. When that has been
> done, however, the burden is upon the employer to establish facts
> which would negative the existence of liability to a given employee
> or which would mitigate that liability.

Under the Board's Rules and Regulations,[78] the General Counsel
will serve the parties with a backpay specification in the name of
the Board and this serves as the basis of the Board's prima facie
case. The specification details for each employee the backpay
periods broken down by calendar quarters, the specific figures and
the basis for computing the gross backpay and interim earnings,
the expenses for each quarter, and any other relevant information. It is also the practice of the General Counsel to include an
approximate net backpay figure which results from a deduction
of mitigating factors discovered through investigation. By including this information, however, the General Counsel does not assume the burden of proving all matters in mitigation. Once the
General Counsel has shown the amount of gross backpay due, the
employer must prove any mitigating factors which would provide
an affirmative defense and permit a deduction from, or offset,
backpay.[79]

Liability of Employers, Unions, and Successor Employers

The Board's backpay order will hold the employer, the union,
or both liable for making whole the discriminatorily discharged
employee. If the employer is the sole respondent, the remedy will
stipulate that in addition to paying the amount of backpay due,

---

[77] 311 F.2d 447, 454, 52 L.R.R.M. 2115 (8th Cir. 1963). *See also* NLRB v.
Ohio Hoist Mfg. Co., 496 F.2d 14, 86 L.R.R.M. 2135, 2136-2137 (6th Cir. 1974).

[78] NLRB RULES AND REGULATIONS, Series 8 (29 C.F.R.), Sections 102.52
and 102.53.

[79] NLRB v. Madison Courier, Inc., 472 F.2d 1307, 80 L.R.R.M. 3377, 3383
(D.C. Cir. 1972) ; NLRB v. Mooney Aircraft, 366 F.2d 809, 813, 63 L.R.R.M.
2208 (5th Cir. 1966).
If an employee dies before the backpay proceeding, backpay dues usually
will be awarded to his estate. The Board is expected to make available for the
employer's cross-examination such evidence as it may reasonably obtain.
Although the evidence submitted might be hearsay in a civil action, it is the
burden of the employer to disprove that a diligent search for alternative employment was made by the dead employee.
NLRB v. Mastro Plastics Corp., 345 F.2d 170, 178, 60 L.R.R.M. 2578 (2d
Cir. 1966) ; *cert. denied* 384 U.S. 972, 62 L.R.R.M. 2292 (1966).

the employer is also responsible for reporting and paying the full tax on the award.[80] The Board's order will usually not hold the president or sole owner of the company personally liable unless there is evidence that the individual had committed some act to justify piercing the corporate veil.[81] The Board, however, did hold an employer association liable for the action of a company which discharged a nonunion employee. Although the company itself was not a member of the association, its president was, and the Board found that membership was maintained through the agency of its president.[82]

If a union is held liable, the Board will require the labor organization to "remove the barrier it has erected" by notifying both the employer and the employee that it no longer has any objection to immediate reinstatement.[83] Compliance with this stipulation will toll the period of the union's liability for the backpay award.[84] Unlike an employer, a union is not required to make social security tax deductions or matching tax payments.[85] In *Teamster Union, Local 249*,[86] the Board noted that the Commission of Internal Revenue has held that backpay awards by a labor organization "cannot legally be treated as wages paid by or on behalf of the employer."

[80] NLRB FIELD MANUAL, Sec. 10694.1.

[81] Chef Nathan Sez Eat Here, 201 N.L.R.B. No. 41, 82 L.R.R.M. 1265 (1973); NLRB v. I.U.O.E., Local 925, AFL-CIO, 460 F.2d 589, 80 L.R.R.M. 2398, 2409 (5th Cir. 1972).

[82] NLRB v. Shuck Construction Co., 243 F.2d 519, 39 L.R.R.M. 2322 (9th Cir. 1957).

[83] Pen and Pencil Workers, Local 19593 (Parker Pen Co.), 91 N.L.R.B. 883, 888-889, 26 L.R.R.M. 1583 (1950). In Radio Officers' Union v. NLRB, 347 U.S. 17, 54-55, 33 L.R.R.M. 2417, 2431-2432 (1954), *Pen and Pencil Workers* was approved in so far as the Board's policy of holding that the absence of the employer in a proceeding against a union for a Section 8(b)(2) violation did not preclude a backpay order running solely against the union. *See also* the discussion in Chapter VIII, *infra*, pages 117 to 118.

[84] Local Union 595, Int'l Ass'n Bridge and Iron Workers (R. Clinton Construction Company) 109 N.L.R.B. No. 12, 34 L.R.R.M. 1285 (1954). Pursuant to current NLRB practice, the union's backpay liability is terminated five days after the receipt by an employer of a notice withdrawing all objection to the reemployment of a discriminatee. *E.g.*, Local 1311, Carpenters (American Riggers, Inc.), 193 N.L.R.B. 995, 78 L.R.R.M. 1450 (1971).

[85] NLRB FIELD MANUAL, Sec. 10694.2.

[86] Teamsters Union, Local 249 (Lancaster Transportation Co.), 116 N.L.R.B. No. 51, 38 L.R.R.M. 1254 (1956).

If both the employer and the union are held liable, the backpay order will direct both parties to remit to the Internal Revenue Service a deduction for income tax and for the employer to make the appropriate deductions and contributions for social security taxes.[87] The order, however, will not stipulate in dollars and cents the portion that each must pay. The fact that Section 10(c) of the Act states that "either one or the other would be responsible for back pay, but not both" does not bar the Board from issuing a remedy that holds both the employer and the union jointly and severally liable. In *Union Starch and Refining Co. v. NLRB*,[88] the court held that Congress manifested no intent to restrict the remedial powers of the Board, but instead sought to preserve its broad authority to dissipate the effects of an unfair labor practice.

In some instances, the Board will distinguish between primary and secondary liability. In *NLRB v. Lexington Electric Products Co.*,[89] the Third Circuit found that it would be "patently inequitable that the employer be more than secondarily responsible for back pay," since the employer had yielded to economic coercion only after unsuccessfully invoking the normal legal remedy against an unfair labor practice strike. The circumstances of the case and the court's subsequent finding of an unfair labor practice on the part of the union did not prevent the employer's coerced action from being another unfair labor practice. The court, however, reasoned that the Act would be fully effectuated "by imposing primary liability to the injured employees upon the union alone, and at the same time holding the employer liable to make the employees whole, should the union fail to do so." [90]

Prior to 1973, the Board pursued a rather uneven course in its treatment of a successor employer's liability to remedy unfair labor practices committed by his predecessor. In *Golden State Bottling Co.*,[91] however, the Supreme Court held that a successor

---

[87] NLRB FIELD MANUAL, Sec. 10692.2 and Sec. 10694.1.

[88] 186 F.2d 1008, 27 L.R.R.M. 2342 (7th Cir. 1951), *cert. denied*, 342 U.S. 815, 28 L.R.R.M. 2625 (1951).

[89] 283 F.2d 54, 46 L.R.R.M. 3028 (3d Cir. 1960), *cert. denied* 315 U.S. 485, 47 L.R.R.M. 2752 (1961).

[90] NLRB v. Lexington Electric Products Co., *supra*, 283 F.2d 54, 46 L.R.R.M. 3028 (1960), *accord*, NLRB v. Bulletin Co., 443 F.2d 863, 77 L.R.R.M. 2599 (3d Cir. 1971), *cert. denied* 404 U.S. 1018, 79 L.R.R.M. 2183 (1972).

[91] Golden State Bottling Co. v. NLRB, 414 U.S. 168, 84 L.R.R.M. 2839 (1973); *Accord* Zim's Foodliner, Inc. v. NLRB, —— F.2d ——, 85 L.R.R.M.

employer who purchases an enterprise with notice of unremedied wrongs may be considered in privity with the former employer. Agreeing with the Board, the Court believed that the public would not benefit by permitting the violator to shed all responsibility simply by disposing of the business. Furthermore, by holding both employers jointly and severally liable, the employee is protected from the possible insolvency either of the predecessor or successor employer.[92]

Effect of Private Settlement Agreements

A private settlement by the parties in an unfair labor practice case does not, of itself, bar the Board from issuing its own backpay order. Instead, the Board looks to see whether the agreement contains provisions that specifically reimburse the employees for monetary losses stemming from the discriminatory action. Thus, in *Great Atlantic & Pacific Tea Co.*,[93] the Board held that it would be inequitable to grant backpay where the parties had explicitly agreed to a salary increase to compensate for the employees' monetary losses resulting from a lockout. On the other hand, where the Board has found that wage increases were not negotiated as compensation for wage losses or that the employees were not fully reimbursed, it has ordered the backpay awards despite the existence of a settlement agreement.[94]

Board Delay Does Not Mitigate Backpay Liability

In *Rutter-Rex Mfg. Co.*,[95] the Supreme Court ruled on the effect that delay on the part of the Board should have on the mitigation of the respondent's liability. Reversing a lower court's decision to toll the backpay period, the Court held that the Fifth Circuit

---

3019, 3028-3029 (7th Cir. 1974). This subject is treated fully in Chapter V, the Obligation of a Successor Employer to Remedy His Predecessor's Unfair Labor Practices, p. 64.

[92] *See also* Gateway Service Co., 209 N.L.R.B. No. 178, 86 L.R.R.M. 1115 (1974).

[93] 145 N.L.R.B. No. 39, 54 L.R.R.M. 1384 (1963).

[94] Safeway Stores, Inc., 148 N.L.R.B. No. 76, 57 L.R.R.M. 1043 (1964); NLRB v. Trinity Valley Iron and Steel Co., 410 F.2d 1161, 71 L.R.R.M. 2067 (5th Cir. 1969); NLRB v. Laidlaw Corp., 507 F.2d 1381, 87 L.R.R.M. 3216 (7th Cir. 1974), *cert. denied,* —— U.S. ——, —— L.R.R.M. —— (1975).

[95] NLRB v. J. H. Rutter-Rex Mfg. Co., 396 U.S. 258, 72 L.R.R.M. 2881 (1969).

exceeded the narrow scope of review provided for the Board's remedial orders when it shifted the cost of the delay from the company to the employees. The lower court argued that the Board had been guilty of "inordinate" delay and was in violation of the Administrative Procedure Act. It concluded that the purpose of the backpay award was to deter unfair labor practices and that a substantial award would be sufficient to achieve this effect. Thus, it tolled the employer's liability on an arbitrary date. The Supreme Court reversed this, basing its holding on its prior decision in *NLRB v. Electric Cleaner Co.*,[96] which held that the Board is not required to place the consequences of its own delay, even if inordinate, on the wronged employees to the benefit of the respondent. Furthermore, it reasoned that even if the delay was in violation of the Administrative Procedure Act, the full backpay remedy was not an abuse of the Board's discretion.[97]

Reimbursement of Illegally Exacted Union Dues, Fees, and Fines

In 1956, the NLRB adopted the *Brown-Olds* remedy [98] in a case where a union violated the Act by maintaining and enforcing an unlawful closed shop agreement, and by incorporating into a collective bargaining agreement work rules and regulations requiring employees to obtain union clearance before seeking employment. The NLRB's broadly conceived order required the union to reimburse employees for dues and assessments collected under the illegal agreement, even though the complaint did not allege that the monies were unlawfully collected. The Board reasoned that the order was necessary to expunge the effects of the unfair labor practice.

The Board's application of the *Brown-Olds* remedy was limited substantially by the Supreme Court in *Local 60, Carpenters v. NLRB.*[99] The Court held that the Board did not have the authority to order a union to reimburse employees for union dues and

---

[96] 315 U.S. 685, 698, 10 L.R.R.M. 501 (1942); NLRB v. Katz, 369 U.S. 736, 748, n. 16, 50 L.R.R.M. 2177 (1962).

[97] Subsequent to the Supreme Court decision, J. H. Rutter-Rex Mfg. Co. filed a suit against the NLRB to recover damages allegedly occasioned by the Board's delay. The Fifth Circuit held that the company could not collect under the Federal Tort Claims Act, J. H. Rutter-Rex Mfg. Co. v. U.S., 515 F.2d 97, 89 L.R.R.M. 2811 (1975).

[98] Plumbing and Pipefitters Local 231 (Brown-Olds Plumbing & Heating Corp.), 115 N.L.R.B. 594, 37 L.R.R.M. 1360 (1956).

[99] 365 U.S. 651, 47 L.R.R.M. 2900 (1961).

fees paid under an unlawful hiring agreement unless there was a showing that specific *individual* employee membership had been induced, obtained, or retained in violation of the Act.[100] If there were no individual coercion, the Court reasoned that the reimbursement order would not be designed to remove the "consequences of the violation"[101] and would then be punitive and beyond the power of the Board.

In accordance with the principles set forth in *Carpenters, Local 60*, the Board has ordered that coerced employees be reimbursed for union dues and fees exacted from them through illegal union security clauses,[102] check-off agreements,[103] and prehire agreements.[104] Where both the employer and union are found to share legal responsibility for the illegal exaction, the Board has ordered they be held jointly and severally liable for reimbursing the employees.[105] Fees and dues will not be reimbursed to members who

---

[100] *Accord*, Local 357, Teamsters v. NLRB, 365 U.S. 667, 47 L.R.R.M. 2906 (1961) which was decided in tandem with *Local 60, Carpenters*, and held that the Board may not order reimbursement of dues and fees under an illegal hiring-hall agreement, where there is no evidence that any employees had been individually coerced.

[101] 365 U.S. 651, 47 L.R.R.M. at 2901.

[102] NLRB v. Booth Services, Inc., —— F.2d ——, 89 L.R.R.M. 3122 (5th Cir. 1975); NLRB v. Hi-Temp, Inc., 503 F.2d 583, 87 L.R.R.M. 2437 (7th Cir. 1974); Crown Cork & Seal Co., 182 N.L.R.B. No. 96, 76 L.R.R.M. 1713 (1970); NLRB v. Jan Power, Inc., —— F.2d ——, 73 L.R.R.M. 2350 (9th Cir. 1970); NLRB v. Midtown Service Co., 425 F.2d 665, 73 L.R.R.M. 2634 (2d Cir. 1970); NLRB v. District 12, United Mine Workers of America, —— F.2d ——, 76 L.R.R.M. 2828 (7th Cir. 1971). Teamsters Local 705 (Gasoline Retailers Ass'n.), 210 N.L.R.B. No. 58, 86 L.R.R.M. 1011 (1974). Further discussion of reimbursement remedies where the employer violates Section 8(a)(2) by illegally dominating or assisting a labor organization can be found in Chapter X, *infra*, pages 154-155.

[103] Paramount Plastic Fabricators, Inc., 190 N.L.R.B. No. 29, 77 L.R.R.M. 1089 (1971) (reimbursement ordered if dues were not otherwise collected by Union); NLRB v. American Beef Packers, Inc., 438 F.2d 331, 76 L.R.R.M. 2530 (10th Cir. 1971); Ogle Protection Service, 183 N.L.R.B. No. 68, 76 L.R.R.M. 1715 (1970), *enforced*, 444 F.2d 502, 77 L.R.R.M. 2832 (6th Cir. 1971).

[104] Luke Construction Co., 211 N.L.R.B. No. 91, 87 L.R.R.M. 1087 (1974).

[105] NLRB v. Hi-Temp, Inc., 503 F.2d 583, 87 L.R.R.M. 2437 (7th Cir. 1974); Sheraton-Kaui Corp. v. NLRB, 429 F.2d 1352, 74 L.R.R.M. 2933 (9th Cir. 1970). *But cf.* Kinney National Maintenance Services v. NLRB, —— F.2d ——, 81 L.R.R.M. 2733 (9th Cir. 1972). Court refused to order employer to reimburse dues from illegal check-off, since that would compel the employer to pay twice. Union which had the money was required to reimburse the employees); and NLRB v. Mears Coal Co., 437 F.2d 502, 76 L.R.R.M.

joined the union voluntarily or who were members of the union when hired.[106]

In cases previously discussed, reimbursement was ordered where employers coerced employees who had actually paid dues to the union through check-off authorizations or otherwise. In the converse situation, where an employer has breached an agreement to check-off employee dues, and the union requests the Board to order the employer to reimburse dues which it has not received from any source, the Board's general rule is that it will order an employer to pay membership dues to the union only if the employees have authorized the employer to deduct dues from their wages and the employer has failed to do so.[107] The purpose of this rule is to protect the employee's right to voluntarily decide for himself whether he wishes to have his dues paid through check-off or by some other manner.

Labor organizations who violate the Act by improper regulation of control of their members will also be ordered to reimburse illegally exacted fines and fees. For example, union fines of members who work behind a union's illegal picket line may be ordered returned to the employees.[108] Similarly, where a union violated Section 8(b)(1)(A) by conditioning the right of the employer's unit employees to obtain picket line passes during a strike upon the payment of one-third of their wages to the union, the Board ordered the union to make the employees whole for the illegal

---

2081 (3d Cir. 1970) (employer not ordered to reimburse dues deductions, since union which had received the money was not a party to the Board's proceedings).

[106] Booth Services, Inc., 206 N.L.R.B. No. 132, 84 L.R.R.M. 1598 (1973); Komatz Construction, Inc. v. NLRB, 458 F.2d 317, 80 L.R.R.M. 2005 (8th Cir. 1972).

[107] Allied Mills, Inc., 218 N.L.R.B. No. 47, —— L.R.R.M. —— (1975), petition for review pending in D.C. Circuit in Case No. 75-1569; Southland Dodge, Inc., 205 N.L.R.B. 276, n. 1, 84 L.R.R.M. 1231 (1973); Ogle Protection Service, Inc., 183 N.L.R.B. 682, 689-690 (1970); *enforced*, 444 F.2d 502, 504, 77 L.R.R.M. 2832 (6th Cir. 1971). Even if backpay is due the employees, the Board will order union dues deducted from the backpay award. Ogle Protection Service, *Id.*

[108] Bricklayers, Local 2 (Weidman Metal Masters), 166 N.L.R.B. No. 26, 65 L.R.R.M. 1433 (1967), Carpenters Local 1620 (David M. Fisher Construction Co.), 208 N.L.R.B. No. 27, 85 L.R.R.M. 1271 (1974). *See generally* NLRB v. Granite State Joint Board, Textile Workers, Local 1029, AFL-CIO (Int'l Paper Box Machine Co.), 409 U.S. 213, 81 L.R.R.M. 2853 (1972); NLRB v. Boeing Co., 412 U.S. 84, 83 L.R.R.M. 2183 (1973).

exaction.[109] Also, a union which runs a hiring hall in an illegal manner by obtaining excessive fees from nonmembers as a condition of referring them for employment will be ordered to reimburse that portion of the fees which is beyond the value of the union's hiring hall services.[110]

Backpay for Wages Lost Due to Union Strike Violence

The Board has consistently held that backpay will not be awarded to employees who are coerced into joining a strike by threats of union violence.[111] The Board has reasoned that other adequate remedies exist which would not interfere with the right to strike; relief from violence can be sought through court injunction under Section (10) (j) of the Act, and if the injunction is ignored, effective contempt action is available. Furthermore, the Board has felt that if all unions were forced to pay back pay awards where a few of its members engaged in misconduct, few unions could afford to establish a picket line. The Board's application of this policy seems calculated to avoid its statutory duties of fashioning remedies which will adequately compensate employees for losses suffered from violations of the Act.

Thus, in a recent case the Board reversed an Administrative Law Judge's recommendation which would have ordered a union to pay backpay awards to employees who were kept from work as a result of the labor organization's picket line violence, threats, and assaults.[112] There, the union not only engaged in threats, criminal assaults, and industrial sabotage, but defied a court injunction and proclaimed that it did "not recognize the authority of the laws or of the Board that administers the law." Thirty-nine employees were trapped inside the plant for a fifteen day period, and attempts by employees who were not engaged in the strike activity to go to work were repulsed by both threats and violence.

---

[109] National Cash Register Co. v. NLRB, 466 F.2d 945, 81 L.R.R.M. 2001 (6th Cir. 1972).

[110] NLRB v. Local 138, Operating Engineers (J. J. Hagerty, Inc.), 385 F.2d 874, 66 L.R.R.M. 2703 (2d Cir. 1967); NLRB v. H. K. Ferguson Co., 337 F.2d 205, 57 L.R.R.M. 2213 (5th Cir. 1964).

[111] *See, e.g.*, Union de Tronquistas De Puerto Rico, Local 901, Teamsters (Lock Joint Pipe & Co. of Puerto Rico), 202 N.L.R.B. 399, 82 L.R.R.M. 1525 (1973).

[112] Union Nacional de Trabajadores, 219 N.L.R.B. No. 157, 90 L.R.R.M. 1023 (1975).

As Member Kennedy noted in his dissent, "It is difficult to conceive of a situation in which backpay orders could be more appropriate," and he went on to say, "We are dealing with a labor organization which denounces the laws applicable to its conduct and which systematically threatens the lives of any and all individuals who dare to act in any manner contrary to its self-interest."

The majority of the Board disagreed, holding that "the only new argument we perceive in our colleague's dissent is that he is shocked by respondent union's expressed contempt for the law and the Board. . . . This argument appears to call not so much for remedy as for punishment. That, of course, is not part of our statutory function."

The Board's holding ignores the settled principle that Board orders are considered punitive only when they go beyond remedying the effects of the particular unfair labor practice found.[113] The remedy advanced by the judge and Member Kennedy is directly related to the loss of work occasioned by the union's unlawful acts, and would be of the same nature as traditional backpay remedies for other violations. The failure of the Board to order backpay here results in innocent employees bearing the burden of the respondent's unlawful acts. After all, this was not a case of a few members engaging in conduct unsanctioned by union leaders. Rather, the union had adopted widespread and repeated violence as its own policy. As in other employee misconduct cases,[114] the Board has misapplied a legal principle designed to deal with lesser instances of misconduct, and has, in effect, sanctioned reprehensible conduct, thereby detracting from the proper exercise of its remedial functions.

---

[113] *See* Chapter II, *supra,* pages 12-14.

[114] *See* Chapter IX, *infra,* pages 135-144.

PART FOUR

Reinstatement Remedies

CHAPTER VIII

Reinstatement of Discriminatorily Discharged Employees

Perhaps more than any other employer unfair labor practice, the discriminatory discharge has caused the most concern among students of the Act. The reason is twofold. Viewing the subject objectively, the discriminatory discharge simply accounts for an extremely high percentage both of unfair labor practices and eventual Board decisions.[1] On the other hand, the discriminatory discharge invites subjective considerations because it arises in an emotionally charged context. Unlike some other types of violations which pit the rights of a labor organization against those of an employer, the mythology of the discharge case may conjure an image of a "David and Goliath" encounter, in which the perceived economic strength of the employer is juxtaposed with the individual employee. Moreover, whenever an issue largely concerns an allocation of an economic loss, there may be a tendency to favor imposing the burden of loss upon the party with the "deeper pockets." While the situation surrounding the individual discharge may be emotionally laden, the rules governing the reinstatement remedy have become fairly well established.

Section 10(c) of the Act empowers the Board "to take such affirmative action including reinstatement of employees . . . as will effectuate the policies of this Act."[2] Reinstatement orders involve determinations concerning workers' reemployment rights, arising in two general contexts: (1) upon the discriminatory discharge or layoff of an employee; and (2) upon the offer of an economic or unfair labor practice striker to return to work.

---

[1] *See* 39 NLRB Ann. Rep. 198 (1974). Approximately 65 percent of all unfair labor practice charges filed against employers contained alleged violations of Section 8(a)(3).

[2] 29 U.S.C. § 160(c) (1970).

The reinstatement rights of discriminatorily discharged employees are usually automatic. The reinstatement rights of strikers, however, do not accrue until an unconditional application for reinstatement has been tendered by them to their employer. Once this has been accomplished, the employees are normally entitled to reinstatement subject to qualifications within the two broad classes of work stoppages; *i.e.,* the employees are categorized as either economic or unfair labor practice strikers.

Although an employee might be otherwise entitled to reinstatement, within certain bounds an employer may properly refuse to reemploy certain individuals because they have engaged in serious misconduct. If, however, the employer is found to have condoned the alleged misbehavior, it no longer serves as a bar to reinstatement.

Discriminatory discharges or layoffs may be attributable either to an employer or a labor organization. When an employer discharges an employee, reinstatement will be ordered if the discharge interferes with, restrains, or coerces the employees in the exercise of their rights under the NLRA or if it was intended to encourage or discourage membership in any labor organization. An employer's obligation to reinstate an employee under such an order will be fulfilled only when he makes an unconditional offer to reinstate the dischargee to his former position or a substantially equivalent one. To be valid, such an offer must not only be unconditional, but it must also be extended for a reasonable period of time and be readily interpretable by the discriminatee as a disavowal of the employer's previous misconduct. Under special circumstances, the Board may order an employer to reinstate supervisory employees, even though they are not defined as employees for purposes of the Act.

When the employee's discharge is initiated by the union, reinstatement will be ordered if both the employer and the labor organization are jointly responsible for the unfair labor practices. When only the union is charged, however, a reinstatement order is not ordinarily issued by the Board. Instead, the offending labor organization need only give notice to the employer and employee that it is no longer opposed to the latter's employment. Whether or not the dischargee is eventually reinstated depends in great measure on the willingness of the employer to resume the employment relationship.

EMPLOYER INITIATED DISCRIMINATORY DISCHARGES

Statutory Background. Since 1935, the Act has made it an unfair labor practice for an employer "by discriminating in regard to *hire or tenure* of employment or any term or condition of employment to encourage or discourage membership in a labor organization."[3] Even where union activities are not involved, an employer may not discriminate in hiring or tenure of employment when such discrimination would interfere with employee rights under Sections 7 and 8(a)(1) to "engage in concerted activities for the purpose of collective bargaining or other mutual aid or protection."[4]

Section 10(c) specifically authorizes the Board to utilize reinstatement as an affirmative remedy.[5] Very early in the history of the NLRB, the Supreme Court, in *Phelps Dodge Corp. v. NLRB*,[6] approved the Board's extension of its reinstatement remedy to the hiring of nonemployee job applicants. The flexibility of the reinstatement remedy as such is almost wholly a matter of adjustments in the accompanying monetary relief.[7] Accordingly, our

---

[3] 29 U.S.C. § 158(a)(3) (1970) (emphasis added). *Cf.* Radio Officers' Union v. NLRB, 347 U.S. 17, 42-43, 33 L.R.R.M. 2417, 2430 (1954).

[4] 29 U.S.C. § 157, 158(a)(1). *See* NLRB v. Washington Aluminum Co., 370 U.S. 2, 12, 50 L.R.R.M. 2235 (1962); Morrison-Knudsen Company v. NLRB, 358 F.2d 411, 61 L.R.R.M. 2625 (9th Cir. 1966); Socony Mobil Oil Co. v. NLRB, 357 F.2d 662, 61 L.R.R.M. 2553 (2d Cir. 1966); Walls Manufacturing Company v. NLRB, 321 F.2d 753, 53 L.R.R.M. 2428 (D.C. Cir. 1963), *cert. denied*, 375 U.S. 923, 54 L.R.R.M. 2576 (1963). The majority of the following material concerns discharges connected with union activities. Of course, Section 7 protection extends to concerted activity unrelated to union activities. *E.g.*, Wall's Mfg. Co. v. NLRB, 321 F.2d 753, 53 L.R.R.M. 2428 (D.C. Cir. 1963), *cert. denied*, 375 U.S. 923, 54 L.R.R.M. 2576 (1963). The language of Section 7 has been broadly construed to protect most types of concerted activities which are in furtherance of a lawful objective. *See e.g.*, NLRB v. Washington Aluminum Co., 370 U.S. 2, 50 L.R.R.M. 2235 (1962). On the other hand, such activity may lose its protection if it is not for mutual aid and protection or if it concerns a matter over which the employer has no control. *See* G&W Electric Specialty Co. v. NLRB, 360 F.2d 873, 62 L.R.R.M. 2085 (7th Cir. 1966); NLRB v. C&I Air Conditioning, 486 F.2d 977, 84 L.R.R.M. 2625 (9th Cir. 1973).

[5] 29 U.S.C. § 160(c) (1970). *See* NLRB v. Republican Publishing Co., 174 F.2d 474, 24 L.R.R.M. 2052 (1st Cir. 1949), wherein the court held that as a proper exercise of discretion, the Board may order an employee reinstated even though it does not authorize an award of backpay.

[6] 313 U.S. 177, 8 L.R.R.M. 439 (1941).

[7] Computation of backpay is discussed at pp. 81-100, *supra*. *See also* Walter S. Johnson Bldg. Co., 209 N.L.R.B. 428, 86 L.R.R.M. 1368 (1974). The

analysis will concern the circumstances in which reinstatement may be granted or denied, *e.g.*, the "for cause" defenses of an employer, terminating reinstatement liability, and special cases of reinstatement.

Suspension or Discharge "for Cause" as a Bar to Reinstatement. Indicative of the strong emotions which had been aroused in Congress prior to the passage of the Taft-Hartley Amendments, the House Report had characterized the "for cause" proviso to Section 10(c) as being:

> . . . intended to put an end to the belief, now widely held and certainly justified by the Board's decisions, that engaging in union activities carries with it a license to loaf, wander about the plants, refuse to work, waste time, break rules, and engage in uncivilities and other disorders and misconduct.[8]

Although these sentiments did not appear so flagrantly in the final Conference Report, there is no doubt that Congress had intended to place some check on the Board. Its authority to direct the reinstatement of employees who had engaged in some form of misconduct was diminished when Congress prohibited the Board from ordering the "reinstatement of any individual as an employee who has been suspended or discharged, . . . for cause." [9]

Essentially, the drafters of the "for cause" limitation codified the sentiments expressed in prior court decisions that had construed the Board's reinstatement authority to be applicable to unfair labor practice situations only. For example, in 1942, the Court of Appeals for the Third Circuit in *NLRB v. Condensor Corp.*[10] had observed that an employee "may be discharged by the employer for a good reason, a poor reason, or no reason at all, so long as the terms of the statute are not violated." [11]

---

discharged employee had worked at a construction project that had been completed prior to the Board's order. Since an order directing the employer to offer the discriminatee reinstatement was considered inappropriate, the Board ordered the employer to notify both the employee and his union that he would be eligible for employment in the future at any of the employer's projects. *Cf.* NLRB v. Interboro Contractors, Inc., 388 F.2d 495, 67 L.R.R.M. 2083 (2d Cir. 1967).

[8] H.R. Rep. No. 245, 80th Cong., 1st Sess. 42 (1947).

[9] 29 U.S.C. § 160(c) (1970). *See also* NLRB v. Electrical Workers, Local No. 1229, 346 U.S. 464, 33 L.R.R.M. 2183 (1953).

[10] 128 F.2d 67, 10 L.R.R.M. 483 (3d Cir. 1942).

[11] *Id.* at 75, 10 L.R.R.M. at 489.

In cases decided subsequent to Taft-Hartley, the courts have indicated that implicit in the statutory amendment is the requirement that the Board's jurisdiction to entertain discharge questions is limited to those situations which involve a violation of the Act.[12] Therefore, the complaint must reflect the results of an investigation which attributes the discharge either to an employer's attempt to discourage or encourage union membership or to an act of reprisal against employees who have engaged in protected concerted activities.[13] Without such evidence, the merit or fairness of a particular discharge is irrelevant.[14]

Many Section 8(a)(3) cases have noted that employee participation in union activity is no bar to his termination so long as the discharge is not predicated upon the employer's desire to encourage or discourage union membership.[15] Nonetheless, when an employer raises just cause as a defense, his motive is put at issue.[16] Even though a colorable claim of just cause may have

---

[12] *Cf.* Radio Officers' Union v. NLRB, 347 U.S. 17, 33 L.R.R.M. 2417 (1954).

[13] Indiana Metal Products Corp. v. NLRB, 202 F.2d 613, 31 L.R.R.M. 2490 (7th Cir. 1953); *cf.* NLRB v. Montgomery Ward & Co., 157 F.2d 486, 19 L.R.R.M. 2009 (8th Cir. 1946).

[14] *See* cases cited at note 13, *supra; see also* NLRB v. McGahey (Columbus Marble Works), 233 F.2d 406, 38 L.R.R.M. 2142 (5th Cir. 1956); NLRB v. Northern Metal Co., 440 F.2d 881, 76 L.R.R.M. 2958 (3d Cir. 1971); Indiana Gear Works v. NLRB, 371 F.2d 273, 64 L.R.R.M. 2253 (7th Cir. 1967); Illinois Ruan Transport Corp. v. NLRB, 404 F.2d 274, 69 L.R.R.M. 2761 (8th Cir. 1968); NLRB v. Commonwealth Foods, 506 F.2d 1065, 87 L.R.R.M. 2609 (4th Cir. 1974) (Despite the coincidence of the discharges and employees union activity, the case was remanded for a determination of whether employees' admissions of thefts were true; if so, reinstatement was to be denied.) For a full examination of an employer's right to deny reinstatement because of employee misconduct, see pages 135-146, *infra*, where the employer's right is discussed along with the analogous issue of striker misconduct.

[15] *E.g.*, Tompkins Motor Lines, Inc. v. NLRB, 337 F.2d 325, 57 L.R.R.M. 2337 (6th Cir. 1964); NLRB v. Williams Lumber Co., 195 F.2d 669, 29 L.R.R.M. 2633 (4th Cir. 1952), *cert. denied*, 344 U.S. 834, 30 L.R.R.M. 2712 (1952).

[16] *Cf.* Laidlaw Corp., 171 N.L.R.B. 1366, 68 L.R.R.M. 1252 (1968), *enforced*, 414 F.2d 99, 71 L.R.R.M. 3054 (7th Cir. 1969), *cert. denied*, 397 U.S. 920, 73 L.R.R.M. 2537 (1970); NLRB v. Great Dane Trailers, Inc., 388 U.S. 26, 65 L.R.R.M. 2465 (1967). *See also*, NLRB v. Hertz Corp., 449 F.2d 711, 715, 78 L.R.R.M. 2569 (5th Cir. 1971), where the court stated:

> Even if Martin's [nonengagement in union activity] were the case, this alone is not decisive of the Company's motivation for the transfer. The motivation and conduct being tested here is the Company's—not Melva Martin's.

While the employer's motivation is important in determining whether Section 8(a)(3) has been violated, no such inquiry is necessary when analyzing a dis-

been established, any hint of employer discrimination will bring the discharge within the ambit of the Act. As the Second Circuit observed:

> The fact that the employer had ample reason for discharging [the employees] is of no moment. It was free to discharge them for any reason good or bad, so long as it did not discharge them for their union activity. And even though the discharges may have been based upon other reasons as well, if the employer was partly motivated by union activity, the discharges were violative of the Act.[17]

Terminating Reinstatement Liability. Unlike the requisite unconditional applications for reinstatement which economic strikers must make,[18] the Board has long held that a discriminatee has no duty to apply for his reemployment in order to protect his reinstatement rights.[19] On the other hand, once an employer makes an unconditional offer of reinstatement to the dischargee, the employer's backpay liability "is tolled (1) on the date of the actual reinstatement, (2) on the date of rejection of the offer, or (3) in the case of discriminatees who did not reply on the date of the last opportunity to accept the offer of reinstatement." [20]

---

charge which has been alleged to violate Section 8(a)(1); that section only requires that the employer's action tends to interfere with, restrain, or coerce employees exercising their Section 7 rights.

[17] NLRB v. Great Eastern Color Lithographic Corp., 309 F.2d 352, 355, 51 L.R.R.M. 2410, 2412 (2d Cir. 1962), *cert. denied*, 373 U.S. 950, 53 L.R.R.M. 2394 (1963). *See also* Wonder State Mfg. Co. v. NLRB, 331 F.2d 737, 55 L.R.R.M. 2814 (6th Cir. 1964); NLRB v. Elias Bros. Big Boy, Inc., 325 F.2d 360, 54 L.R.R.M. 2733 (6th Cir. 1963). *But cf.* NLRB v. Commonwealth Foods, Inc., 506 F.2d 1065, 87 L.R.R.M. 2609 (4th Cir. 1974); NLRB v. Big Three Welding Equipment Co., 359 F.2d 77, 62 L.R.R.M. 2058 (5th Cir. 1966); Barberton Plastic Products, Inc., 141 N.L.R.B. 174, 52 L.R.R.M. 1324 (1963), *enforcement denied in pertinent part*, 354 F.2d 66, 61 L.R.R.M. 2049 (6th Cir. 1965). In the *Barberton* case, the Sixth Circuit strongly disagreed with the Board which had ordered the reinstatement of an employee because of an oblique reference to his union activities made to him by a supervisor. Pointing out that the Board had also found "cause" for his discharge, the court felt that under the particular facts of the case, in which at least 16 adequate grounds for discharge existed—including insubordination, unsafe conduct, a high accident rate, heavy absenteeism, physical violence, and innumerable instances of negligent conduct—the Board could not rely solely upon the self-serving testimony of the dischargee to establish antiunion motivation.

[18] *See* discussion at pp. 131-132, *infra*.

[19] *E.g.*, Morristown Knitting Mills, 80 N.L.R.B. 731, 23 L.R.R.M. 1138 (1948).

[20] American Mfg. Co. of Texas, 167 N.L.R.B. 520, 521, 66 L.R.R.M. 1122 (1967); *accord*, Issac and Vinson Security Services, Inc., 208 N.L.R.B. 47, 85 L.R.R.M. 1517 (1973). *See* Chapter VII, *supra*, pp. 87-89.

Reinstatement is also inappropriate where the employee has refused a prior reinstatement offer.[21]

Timing. Although each of the foregoing conditions may be objectively measured after the fact, the Board does not require that the employees accept or reject an offer of reinstatement within some definite period of time.[22] Instead, the Board has held that the employer's offer must be kept open for a "reasonable" period of time, without defining what constitutes a reasonable time.[23] The courts at times have disagreed with the Board over the duty of the employer to keep his offer open. They have occasionally required that it be incumbent upon the employee, not the employer, to take affirmative action ensuring his prompt response to any employer's offer entailing a specified time limitation.[24] Perhaps the most definitive statement that can be made is that offers which condition reemployment upon a one or two day time limit [25] are much less likely to be viewed as valid offers of reinstatement than those which allow a week or more.[26]

The Offer Must Be Clear and Definite. The employer must make an offer which is bona fide,[27] and it must also be made both

---

[21] NLRB v. Winchester Electronics, Inc., 295 F.2d 288, 292, 49 L.R.R.M. 2013 (2d Cir. 1961).

[22] *See* Ordman, *The National Labor Relations Act: Current Developments,* 24 N.Y.U. Conf. on Lab. 115, 124 (1972) which points out that the situations which give rise to a reinstatement right have been delineated, but, the author admitted, "the outer limits, how long the reinstatement rights continue, remains yet to be defined."

[23] *See* Rafaire Refrigeration Corp., 207 N.L.R.B. 523, 84 L.R.R.M. 1535, (1973); Southern Household Products Co., 203 N.L.R.B. 881, 83 L.R.R.M. 1247 (1973).

[24] *E.g.,* NLRB v. Betts Baking Co., 428 F.2d 156, 74 L.R.R.M. 2714 (10th Cir. 1970); NLRB v. Harrah's Club, 403 F.2d 865, 69 L.R.R.M. 2775 (9th Cir. 1968); NLRB v. Izzi, 395 F.2d 241, 68 L.R.R.M. 2197 (1st Cir. 1968). In each of these cases, the courts of appeals disagreed with the Board's argument that the employer bore sole responsibility of ensuring a reasonable time for consideration of an offer of reinstatement. Instead, the courts observed that in weighing the reasonableness or unreasonableness of any given offer, the responsibility for any alleged lack of time shifts to the employee when the delay is directly attributable to his own actions.

[25] *E.g.,* Rafaire Refrigeration Corp., 207 N.L.R.B. 523, 84 L.R.R.M. 1535 (1973) (one day).

[26] *See* NLRB v. Betts Baking Co., 428 F.2d 156, 74 L.R.R.M. 2714 (10th Cir. 1970) (one week); Southern Household Products Co., 203 N.L.R.B. 881, 83 L.R.R.M. 1247 (1973) (ten days); American Mfg. Co. of Texas, 167 N.L.R.B. 520, 66 L.R.R.M. 1122 (1967) (ten days).

[27] A bona fide offer of reinstatement is one which places the employees within their former or substantially equivalent position, without prejudice

clearly and definitively so that the employees are able to interpret
it as indicative of their employer's willingness to abide by the
provisions of the Act.[28] It follows that when the offer is not
communicated to the employee by his employer, but rather by the
employer's agent, it is invalid unless the employee has knowledge
that the agent possesses the requisite authority to tender the
offer.[29] As long as nothing in the offer suggests a change in
the employee's former rights and privileges, the clear and definite
standard does not require that all the rights and privileges of the
employee be literally specified.[30]

In order to be clear and definite, the reinstatement offer must
be made to the employees in language that is understandable to
them. Thus, in *General Iron Corp.*,[31] the Administrative Law
Judge ruled that English language reinstatement offers mailed to
discriminatorily discharged employees were not bona fide when the
employer knew that the employees spoke only Spanish. The Board
reversed the ALJ and held that the offers were not improper.
The Board's rationale, however, was based on speculative and
unwarranted assumptions. First, the Board assumed that "some"
individuals who cannot readily speak English "often" can read
that language. The Board's reasoning implicitly recognizes the
likelihood that some of the employees might not understand the
offer. Second, the Board assumed that when an "illiterate" person receives a communication which he does not understand, he
"customarily" shows it to a member of the family, "often a child
who is attending public school, a friend, or neighbor who can
read and explain the letter." [32] Besides the obvious possibility
that such persons may not be available to assist any given em-

---

to seniority and other rights and privileges they possessed prior to the discharge. *See* cases cited at note 30, *infra*.

[28] *Compare* B&Z Hosiery Products Co., 85 N.L.R.B. 633, 24 L.R.R.M. 1441
(1949), *enforced*, 180 F.2d 1021, 25 L.R.R.M. 2529 (3d Cir. 1950) (offer must
be made by employer, not fellow employee), *with* Barr Packing Co., 82
N.L.R.B. 1, 23 L.R.R.M. 1527 (1949) (offer must not be posed as hypothetical
question).

[29] Rafaire Refrigeration Corp., 207 N.L.R.B. 523, 84 L.R.R.M. 1535 (1973).

[30] Eastern Die Co., 142 N.L.R.B. 601, 604, 53 L.R.R.M. 1103, 1106 (1963),
enforced, 340 F.2d 607, 58 L.R.R.M. 2255 (1st Cir. 1965), *cert. denied*, 381
U.S. 951, 59 L.R.R.M. 2432 (1965); *cf.* American Enterprises, Inc., 200
N.L.R.B. 114, 81 L.R.R.M. 1491 (1972).

[31] 218 N.L.R.B. No. 109, 89 L.R.R.M. 1788, 1789 (1975).

[32] *Id.* at 1789.

ployee, the Board improperly shifted to the discriminatees the burden of deciphering the employer's letter rather than requiring the employer to remedy properly his unfair labor practice. Finally, the Board stated, without foundation, that "[p]eople do not just ignore or throw away letters written in English, especially where, as here, they come from an employer who has just laid them off." [33] In addition to its questionable factual assumptions, this statement evades the question of whether the employees would understand the letters even if they are retained. Thus, the Board's *General Iron* decision is logically indefensible. Moreover, it is directly contrary to other Board policies which have recognized the needs of non-English speaking employees. For example, the Board will use bilingual ballots in Board-conducted elections if there is an appropriate request.[34] The Board also has required that a notice designed to inform the employees of an employer's unfair labor practice be posted both in English and the appropriate second language.[35] Thus, there is scant justification for permitting an employer to offer reinstatement to discharged employees in a language which the employer knows they are likely not to understand.

The Offer May Not Be Conditional. Aside from the requisite clarity, the key to a valid offer of reinstatement is that it be unconditional.[36] Offers are not unconditional when they contain affirmative or implicit limitations. For example, in *Art Metalcraft Plating Co.,*[37] the Board held that an employer's failure to repudiate his previously announced antiunion policy rendered an other-

---

[33] *Id.*

[34] *E.g.,* NLRB v. Lowell Corrugated Container Corp., 431 F.2d 1196, 75 L.R.R.M. 2346 (1st Cir. 1970); General Dynamics Corp., 187 N.L.R.B. 679, 76 L.R.R.M. 1540 (1971). *See also* WILLIAMS, JANUS, and HUHN, NLRB REGULATION OF ELECTION CONDUCT, 421-425 (Lab. Rel. & Pub. Pol. Ser., Rep. No. 8, 1974).

[35] John F. Cuneo, 152 N.L.R.B. 929, 59 L.R.R.M. 1226 (1965); Teamsters Local 901 (F. F. Instrument Corp.), 210 N.L.R.B. No. 153, 86 L.R.R.M. 1286 (1974); Pollack Electrical Co., 219 N.L.R.B. No. 195, —— L.R.R.M. —— (1975); *See also* Chapter VI, *supra,* p. 73.

[36] *See* NLRB v. Quest-Shon Mark Brassiere Co., 185 F.2d 285, 27 L.R.R.M. 2036 (2d Cir. 1950), *cert. denied,* 342 U.S. 812, 28 L.R.R.M. 2625 (1951) (offer to reinstate employees at another plant without notice that their original jobs no longer existed constituted conditional offer since it was premised on accepting employment at different location).

[37] 133 N.L.R.B. 706, 48 L.R.R.M. 1701 (1961), *enforced,* 303 F.2d 478, 50 L.R.R.M. 2254 (3d Cir. 1962).

wise valid offer conditional. In the *Art Metalcraft* case, the employer had ordered all of his employees who supported union representation to leave his plant. In response to a subsequent offer of reinstatement, the employees stated they could not accept the offer since they were union mmbers. The Board found that the failure of the employer to respond to the employee's declaration indicated that the offer had been conditional upon abandonment of the union; the employer could have explained that he was disavowing his previous policy against employing union adherents.[38]

The Offer May Be Adjusted to Reflect Changed Circumstances. Under special circumstances, the Board itself has recognized that changed circumstances have rendered impractical the requirement of an unconditional offer.[39] For example, where subsequent economic changes eliminate the former position of a discriminatee, the remedy may be limited to reimbursing backpay until the time that the employee would have been discharged for economic reasons.[40]

Thus, even though the Board may order that illegally discharged employees be reinstated, reinstatement may never occur because their jobs have been eliminated for legitimate economic reasons. An employer will be permitted to show that such permissible economic changes have been made and whether or not the former jobs are available. As stated by the Fifth Circuit, ". . . discrimination by the Employer does not compel it to make work for these persons. Such discrimination does not require the Employer to discharge or layoff others to provide jobs for these discriminatees."[41] This situation often occurs where temporary employees are discriminated against. Where the employer in such cases can show that these temporary employees would not have retained their employment, the Board's remedy will be

---

[38] 133 NL.R.B. at 707-708, 48 L.R.R.M. at 1703-1704.

[39] *See* Walter S. Johnson Building Co., cited at note 7, *supra. See also* Chapter III at p. 58, *supra.*

[40] NLRB v. Transamerican Freight Lines, 275 F.2d 311, 45 L.R.R.M. 2864 (7th Cir. 1960); *cf.* Franklin Homes, Inc., 187 N.L.R.B. 389, 76 L.R.R.M. 1412 (1970), *enforced,* 461 F.2d 847, 80 L.R.R.M. 2932 (5th Cir. 1972).

[41] NLRB v. Biscayne Television Corp., 289 F.2d 338, 48 L.R.R.M. 2021, 2022 (5th Cir. 1961). *Cf.* NLRB v. McMahon, 428 F.2d 1213, 74 L.R.R.M. 2684 (9th Cir. 1970).

limited to backpay.[42] If, however, there is a possibility of future employment, such employees may be placed on a preferential hiring list and be ordered reinstated when jobs become available.[43]

In other instances, when employees have become physically disabled during the period between discharge and the Board's reinstatement order, some form of backpay will be granted.[44] Reinstatement may be offered, although the Board may condition reinstatement upon receipt of a certificate of physical fitness from a physician.[45]

Reinstatement of Supervisory Employees. Despite specific statutory language declaring that supervisory employees are not to be considered as employees for purposes of the Act,[46] an interesting

---

[42] Armstrong Rubber Co. v. NLRB, 511 F.2d 741, 89 L.R.R.M. 2100, 2101-2102 (5th Cir. 1975). NLRB v. Corning Glass Works, 293 F.2d 784, 48 L.R.R.M. 2759, 2760-2761 (1st Cir. 1961); Combustion Engineering, Inc., 130 N.L.R.B. 184, 47 L.R.R.M. 1301 (1961). Two Wheel Corp., 218 N.L.R.B. No. 87, 89 L.R.R.M. 1405 (1975) (no reinstatement of student who planned to return to school).

[43] Waukesha Lime & Stone Co., 145 N.L.R.B. 973, 55 L.R.R.M. 1103 (1964), *enforced*, 343 F.2d 504, 58 L.R.R.M. 2782 (7th Cir. 1955); Myers Ceramic Products Co., 140 N.L.R.B. 232, 51 L.R.R.M. 1605 (1962); Ventre Packing Co., 163 N.L.R.B. 540, 64 L.R.R.M. 1414 (1967).

[44] *See* American Mfg. Co. of Texas, 167 N.L.R.B. 520, 66 L.R.R.M. 1122 (1967). If the discharged employee has become disabled through a job-related injury arising out of interim employment, only the amount of money constituting lost wages received under a subsequent workmen's compensation award may be deducted from the backpay order. *See* Chapter VII, *supra*.

[45] Phelps Dodge Corp., 28 N.L.R.B. 442, 7 L.R.R.M. 138 (1940); *cf.* Shawnee Milling Co., 82 N.L.R.B. 1266, 24 L.R.R.M. 100 (1949), *enforcement denied on other grounds*, 184 F.2d 57, 26 L.R.R.M. 2462 (10th Cir. 1950); Niles Firebrick Co., 30 N.L.R.B. 426, 8 L.R.R.M. 61 (1941), *enforced*, 128 F.2d 258, 10 L.R.R.M. 642 (6th Cir. 1942). *But cf.* Lipman Bros. Inc., 147 N.L.R.B. 1342, 56 L.R.R.M. 1420, 1427 (1964) where the Board ordered the reinstatement of a physically disabled employee whose prior job had been eliminated. The employee, although disabled, had performed that job satisfactorily and the Board reasoned that the employer should be required to reinstate him within the unit to another job suitable to his physical condition.

[46] 29 U.S.C. § 152(3) (1970). Pursuant to the Wagner Act, the Supreme Court had sustained the Board's interpretation of the term employee as including supervisory employees. *See* Packard Motor Car Co. v. NLRB, 330 U.S. 485, 19 L.R.R.M. 2397 (1947). The subsequent Taft-Hartley Amendments, however, expressly excluded supervisors from being considered as employees under the Act. *See also* Section 14(a) of the LMRA, [29 U.S.C. § 164(a) (1970)], which provides, *inter alia*, that "... no employer subject to the Act shall be compelled to deem individuals defined herein as supervisors as employees for the purpose of any law, either national or local, relating to collective bargaining." *Cf.* Beasley v. Food Fair of North Carolina, Inc., 415 U.S. 907, 86 L.R.R.M. 2196 (1974).

body of case law involving the reinstatement of supervisors has arisen. Since supervisory employees clearly do not possess any specific statutory right to reinstatement, the Board's authority to grant relief must constitute a discretionary judgment on the part of the NLRB that the reinstatement of supervisors is necessary to effectuate some fundamental policy of the Act. On occasion, the Board has determined that where a supervisor's discharge effectually intimidates nonsupervisory employees in the exercise of their Section 7 rights, the employer commits a violation of Section 8(a)(1).[47] The ensuing reinstatement order is derived from the Board's authority to protect employees in the exercise of their statutory rights.

Section 8(a)(4) Discrimination. Section 8(a)(4) makes it an unfair labor practice for an employer "to discharge or otherwise discriminate against an employee because he has filed charges or given testimony under this Act."[48] Until 1972, there had been some confusion as to whether the mere presence at a formal Board hearing of an employee who does not testify, although he is prepared to do so, entitles the employee to the protection afforded by Section 8(a)(1).[49] In terms of the actual substantive relief

---

[47] *Compare* NLRB v. Better Monkey Grip Co., 243 F.2d 836, 40 L.R.R.M. 2027 (5th Cir. 1957), *cert. denied*, 355 U.S. 864, 41 L.R.R.M. 2007 (1957), *with* NLRB v. Talladega Cotton Factory, Inc., 213 F.2d 209, 34 L.R.R.M. 2196 (5th Cir. 1954) (discharge of supervisor for giving testimony adverse to employer's position in NLRB proceeding); NLRB v. Electro Motive Mfg. Co., 389 F.2d 61, 67 L.R.R.M. 2513, 2514 (4th Cir. 1968) (reinstatement of a supervisor discharged for giving a Board agent a signed statement admitting that he had unlawfully threatened employees); Gainesville Publishing Co., 150 N.L.R.B. 602, 58 L.R.R.M. 1128 (1964) (violation by reducing foreman's pay rate when he refused to cooperate in antiunion drive); *Cf.* General Engineering, Inc., 131 N.L.R.B. 648, 48 L.R.R.M. 1105 (1961), *enforcement denied on other grounds*, 311 F.2d 570, 52 L.R.R.M. 2277 (9th Cir. 1962) (supervisor had refused to assist in discriminatory discharge of employee); *see also* NLRB v. Dewey Bros., Inc., —— F.2d ——, 80 L.R.R.M. 2112 (4th Cir. 1972). *But cf.* NLRB v. Brookside Industries, Inc., 308 F.2d 224, 51 L.R.R.M. 2148 (4th Cir. 1962), *denying enforcement to* Brookside Industries, Inc., 135 N.L.R.B. 16, 49 L.R.R.M. 1420 (1962) (court refused to reinstate a supervisor who was discharged for refusing to engage in antiunion activities. The court based its decision on the conflict of interest which would result because supervisor was also the wife of a nonsupervisory employee. Backpay was awarded, however.

[48] 29 U.S.C. § 158(a)(4) (1970). *See, e.g.*, Big Three Industrial Gas & Equipment Co., 212 N.L.R.B. No. 115, 87 L.R.R.M. 1543 (1974).

[49] *Compare* Ogle Protection Service, Inc., 149 N.L.R.B. 545, 57 L.R.R.M. 1337 (1964) (planning to file charges or to testify not within 8(a)(4)) *with* Thomas J. Aycock, d/b/a Vita Foods, 135 N.L.R.B. 1357, 49 L.R.R.M. 1723

granted an employee who had been either discharged or discriminated against in retaliation for his participation, the distinction between actual and preparatory participation was virtually meaningless. A reinstatement order in such a case could be issued upon the basis of a Section 8(a)(1) or (a)(3) violation in either circumstance.[50]

Nevertheless, the Supreme Court in *NLRB v. Scrivener, d/b/a AA Electric Co.*,[51] held that an employer also violated Section 8 (a)(4) of the Act, when he discharged employees who had given sworn written statements to NLRB agents during an investigatory stage of an unfair labor practice. The employees involved had neither filed charges with the Board, nor actually given testimony in a Board hearing.[52] Similar to remedies for other violations, reinstatement orders in Section 8(a)(4) cases are not limited to actual discharges, but may encompass refusals to hire applicants who have filed previous charges against the employer.[53]

UNION INITIATED DISCRIMINATORY DISCHARGES

Pursuant to Section 8(b)(2), it is an unfair labor practice for a labor organization, *inter alia*, "to cause or attempt to cause an

---

(1962), *enforced,* 328 F.2d 314, 55 L.R.R.M. 2575 (5th Cir. 1964) (fact that employee who was prepared to testify did not actually do so was immaterial to finding a violation of Section 8(a)(4)).

[50] *See* NLRB v. Ritchie Mfg. Co., 354 F.2d 90, 61 L.R.R.M. 2013 (8th Cir. 1965).

[51] 405 U.S. 117, 79 L.R.R.M. 2587 (1972).

[52] *See also* NLRB v. King Louie Bowling Corp., 472 F.2d 1192, 82 L.R.R.M. 2576 (8th Cir. 1973); Sinclair Glass Co. v. NLRB, 465 F.2d 209, 80 L.R.R.M. 3082 (7th Cir. 1972). *But see* Rock Road Trailer Parts and Sales, 204 N.L.R.B. 1136, 83 L.R.R.M. 1467 (1973) (employee fired immediately after engaging in phone conversation with Board representative was not discriminatorily discharged but was fired for cause, since employee had conducted phone conversation in loud and belligerent voice in front of employer's customers and had threatened to put employer out of business); Nachman Corp. v. NLRB, 337 F.2d 421, 57 L.R.R.M. 2217 (7th Cir. 1964); Beiser Aviation Corp., 135 N.L.R.B. 433, 49 L.R.R.M. 1512 (1962).

[53] Central Rigging & Contracting Corp., 129 N.L.R.B. 342, 46 L.R.R.M. 1548 (1960). *See also* Southern Bleachery & Print Works, Inc., 118 N.L.R.B. 299, 40 L.R.R.M. 1174 (1957), *enforced,* 257 F.2d 235, 42 L.R.R.M. 2533 (4th Cir. 1958), *cert. denied,* 359 U.S. 911, 43 L.R.R.M. 2576 (1959); Underwood Machinery Co., 79 N.L.R.B. 1287, 22 L.R.R.M. 1506 (1948), *enforced,* 179 F.2d 118, 25 L.R.R.M. 2195 (1st Cir. 1949). *Cf.* Phelps Dodge Corp. v. NLRB, 313 U.S. 177, 8 L.R.R.M. 439 (1941) (early Supreme Court approval of Board's remedial policy regarding the extension of reinstatement orders to include job applicants in 8(a)(3) situations).

employer to discriminate against an employee in violation of subsection 8(a)(3). . . ." [54] The Board usually remedies an "attempt" to cause employer discrimination by directing the union to cease and desist and to post a notice of the NLRB order.[55] When the discrimination is carried out—*i.e.*, when an employee is discharged or a job applicant denied hire—a reinstatement and backpay order may issue.[56] Reinstatement, however, will be ordered only if both the union and employer have been jointly charged with violations. If solely the union's discrimination was responsible for the discharge, reinstatement will not usually be ordered. Rather, the union merely will be required to notify both the employer and employee that it has no objection to the employee's immediate reinstatement.[57]

The Board's policy of refusing to order reinstatement where only a labor organization is charged with an unfair labor practice poses serious questions as to the adequacy of the discharged employee's relief. In such cases, the Board's affirmative remedy has been limited to orders directing the union to tender backpay to the employee and notify both the employer and affected employees that it has withdrawn its objections to future employment of the discharged employee.[58] As shown below, as a half measure, this truncated form of relief is unfair not only to the employee, but also to the employer. Since an employee must prove the employer and union have both violated the Act in order to ensure his reinstatement rights,[59] the rule encourages the employee to bring charges against the employer regardless of the circumstances or the employer's culpability. Once the employer is charged with discrimination, he cannot defend his actions as the result of

---

[54] 29 U.S.C. § 158(b)(2) (1970).

[55] *See* MORRIS, THE DEVELOPING LABOR LAW 859 (BNA: Washington, 1971).

[55] *E.g.*, Acme Mattress Co., 91 N.L.R.B. 1010, 26 L.R.R.M. 1611 (1950), *enforced*, 192 F.2d 524, 29 L.R.R.M. 2079 (7th Cir. 1951). Of course, the reinstatement order will also be accompanied by a cease and desist provision and affirmative requirements such as notice posting and backpay.

[57] Pen and Pencil Workers, Local 19593, 91 N.L.R.B. 883, 26 L.R.R.M. 1583 (1950).

[58] UAW, Local 291 (Timken-Detroit Axle Co.), 92 N.L.R.B. 968, 27 L.R.R.M. 1188 (1950), *enforced*, 194 F.2d 698, 29 L.R.R.M. 2433 (7th Cir. 1952); *cf.* NLRB v. Local 57, Operating Engineers, 201 F.2d 771, 31 L.R.R.M. 2344 (1st Cir. 1953).

[59] *See* Union Starch & Refining Co. v. NLRB, 186 F.2d 1008, 27 L.R.R.M. 2342 (7th Cir. 1951), *cert. denied*, 342 U.S. 815, 28 L.R.R.M. 2625 (1951).

union coercion. In the *Acme Mattress Co.*,[60] case, the Board rejected union coercion as an employer defense and held the union and employer jointly and severally liable for a discriminatory discharge. In this case, however, the unlawful discharge had been exacted by the union from the employer as its price for terminating an existing strike. According to the majority, a remedial policy was necessary as a means of introducing an economic incentive to help an employer resist unlawful union demands.[61]

About the same time that *Acme Mattress* had been decided, the Board, in *Pen and Pencil Workers, Local 19593* (Parker Pen Co.),[62] first faced the problem of fashioning an affirmative order where the union alone had been charged with an unfair labor practice. The Board claimed that, in the absence of a charge against the employer, its authority to remedy a discriminatory discharge was limited to a certain degree. The NLRB concluded, therefore, that the most it could do for the dischargee was to direct the union "to remove the barrier which it has erected" to reemployment by requiring the offending labor organization to notify both the employee and his employer that it no longer had any objection to immediate reinstatement.[63] The Board added, however, that "[a]s the employer, who is not a respondent, has sole control over the employment of its employees, we cannot order that the [discriminatee] be reinstated." [64] A few years

---

[60] 91 N.L.R.B. 1010, 26 L.R.R.M. 1611 (1950), *enforced*, 192 F.2d 524, 29 L.R.R.M. 2079 (7th Cir. 1951).

[61] *See* 91 N.L.R.B. at 1015-1016, 26 L.R.R.M. at 1615-1616, for a statement of the majority view:

> Our policy of assessing liability for backpay jointly against both the employer and the union, even where the discrimination would not have been effected but for pressures brought by the union, is founded upon a basic principle well established. . . . Whatever the situation may be, the fact remains that, in the ultimate analysis, it is the employer, and only the employer, who *controls* the hiring and discharge of his employees. Recognizing this, this Board and the courts have frequently held that it is the duty of an employer to resist the usurpation of his control over employment by any group that seeks to utilize such control for or against any labor organization, and that the Act affords no immunity because employer believes that the exigencies of the moment require that he capitulate to the pressures and violate the statute.

Cf. NLRB v. Pinkerton's National Detective Agency, 202 F.2d 230, 31 L.R.R.M. 2336 (9th Cir. 1953).

[62] 91 N.L.R.B. 883, 26 L.R.R.M. 1583 (1950).

[63] *Id.* at 888-889, 26 L.R.R.M. at 1585-1586.

[64] *Id.* at 888, 26 L.R.R.M. at 1585.

later, the Supreme Court, in *Radio Officers' Union v. NLRB*,[65] approved the Board's policy of holding that the absence of joinder of the employer in a proceeding against a union for violation of Section 8(b)(2) does not preclude entry by the Board of a backpay order against the union.

A problem created by the policy of the Board in refusing to order reinstatement in these cases is that potential reemployment of the dischargee hinges upon the willingness of the employer to take him back. Making eventual reinstatement dependent upon the beneficence of the employer in this situation may be detrimental to the discharged employee because of the conditions under which the union-initiated discharge had occurred. Since reemployment is voluntary, the employer still faces the possibility of upsetting his relations with the union should he choose reinstatement. As a result, he might succumb to this pressure and not reinstate the discriminatee. Accordingly, the ultimate effect may be that the union has successfully made a show of strength among the remaining employees at the cost of backpay to a discriminatee—an effective and relatively inexpensive weapon for maintaining and encouraging union membership as well as regulating employee conduct. Ironically, the Supreme Court adopted this very rationale in the *Radio Officers' Union* case as the basis for approving the Board's finding of union discrimination. Quoting directly from the trial examiner's opinion, the Court stated:

> . . . the normal effect of the discrimination against Fowler was to enforce not only his obedience as a member of such rules as the union might prescribe, but also the obedience of all his fellow members. It thereby strengthened the Respondent both in its control of its members for their general, mutual advantage, and in its dealings with their employers as their representative. It thus encouraged non-members to join it as a strong organization whose favor and help was to be sought and whose opposition was to be avoided. In its effect upon non-members alone, it must therefore be regarded as encouraging membership in Respondents. * * * Finally, by its demonstration of the Respondent's strength, the discrimination in the present case also had the normal effect of encouraging Fowler and other members to retain their membership in the Respondent either through fear of the consequences of dropping out of membership or through hope of advantage in staying in.[66]

In effect, a serious dilution of the reinstatement rights of em-

---

[65] 347 U.S. 17, 54-55, 33 L.R.R.M. 2417, 2431-2432 (1954).

[66] *Id.* at 32, 33 L.R.R.M. at 2423.

ployees has been created. As long as the employer is a party to the case, charged with either sole [67] or joint responsibility,[68] a dischargee's right to reinstatement is preserved. But, if only the union is named, affirmative relief is limited to backpay and notification.[69] Yet, in either case, the injury suffered by the discharged employee remains the same. Mindful that the "Act does not create rights for individuals which must be vindicated according to a rigid scheme of remedies" [70] neither should the cost of one party's wrongdoing be borne by innocent employees.[71]

This double standard could be eliminated by directing reinstatement in cases even where only the union has been charged with causing an employer to discriminate against an employee.[72] No backpay would be assessed against the employer, and the union could still limit its own backpay liability by giving notice.[73] The shifting of any possible onus of reinstatement from the employer to the Board would probably cause few objections to this purported imposition on the employer's "sole control over the em-

---

[67] *E.g.,* J. R. Cantrall Co., 96 N.L.R.B. 786, 28 L.R.R.M. 1588 (1951), *enforced,* 201 F.2d 853, 31 L.R.R.M. 2332 (9th Cir. 1953), *cert. denied,* 345 U.S. 996, 32 L.R.R.M. 2247 (1953).

[68] NLRB v. Pinkerton's National Detective Agency, 202 F.2d 230, 31 L.R.R.M. 2336 (9th Cir. 1953); Acme Mattress Co., 91 N.L.R.B. 1010, 26 L.R.R.M. 1611 (1950), *enforced,* 192 F.2d 524, 29 L.R.R.M. 2079 (7th Cir. 1951).

[69] Pen and Pencil Workers, Local 19593, 91 N.L.R.B. 883, 26 L.R.R.M. 1583 (1950).

[70] Phelps Dodge Corp. v. NLRB, 313 U.S. 177, 194, 8 L.R.R.M. 438, 446 (1941).

[71] *Cf.* NLRB v. J. H. Rutter-Rex Mfg. Co., 396 U.S. 258, 265, 72 L.R.R.M. 2881, 2883 (1969).

[72] *See generally* Komatz Construction, Inc. v. NLRB, 458 F.2d 317, 80 L.R.R.M. 2005 (8th Cir. 1972). In the *Komatz* case, the court held that partial responsibility for an unfair labor practice could be shifted to an organization although it had not been made a party to the proceeding on general principles of equity. *Cf.* Ford Motor Co. v. NLRB, 305 U.S. 364, 3 L.R.R.M. 663 (1939); NLRB v. American Dredging Co., 276 F.2d 286, 45 L.R.R.M. 2405 (3d Cir. 1960), *cert. denied,* 366 U.S. 908, 48 L.R.R.M. 2070 (1961). In the case of discriminatorily discharged employees, the failure of the Board to order reinstatement clearly places the employees within the "inadequate remedy at law" principle of equity.

[73] Pursuant to current NLRB practice, the union's backpay liability generally is terminated five days after the receipt by an employer of a notice withdrawing all objections to the reemployment of a discriminatee. *E.g.,* Local 1311, Carpenters (American Riggers, Inc.), 193 N.L.R.B. 995, 79 L.R.R.M. 1450 (1971).

ployment of its employees." [74] It may be assumed that in many Section 8(b)(2) cases the employee was discharged or otherwise discriminated against because of the union's illegal action, and not as a result of any employer dissatisfaction with the employee's work performance.

One anticipated objection to this remedy is that the employer should not be required to comply with a Board order fashioned in a proceeding in which the employer did not participate. Procedural objections, however, do not appear insurmountable. The Board could require that the employer be notified of the proceedings and be permitted to intervene. Even more protection could be afforded by requiring that the employer be joined, not necessarily as a respondent, but rather as a party with an interest limited to the requested remedy. Similar objections have been overcome in cases which now require a successor employer to remedy the unfair labor practices of his predecessor. [75] The Supreme Court has held that the Board's remedial powers are not limited to the "actual perpetrator of any unfair labor practice" [76] as long as appropriate procedural safeguards are provided to assure the successor a full hearing concerning the enforcement of any order issued against him. [77]

A similar position was taken by former NLRB General Counsel Peter G. Nash in a case described in a recent Quarterly Report. [78] In that case, the employer acceded to the union's request to discharge an employee for alleged nonpayment of his union dues. The employee filed Section 8(b)(2) and (1)(A) charges against the union, and a Section 8(a)(3) charge against the employer. The Section 8(a)(3) charge was dismissed since the employer was found to have had no reasonable grounds to believe that the union's request for discharge was for any reason other than for nonpayment of his dues. The General Counsel

---

[74] Pen and Pencil Workers, Local 19593, 91 N.L.R.B. 883, 888, 26 L.R.R.M. 1583, 1585 (1950). The Board's refusal to direct reinstatement in the *Pen and Pencil Workers* case had been premised on the employer's right of hire.

[75] *See* Chapter V, *supra*, The Obligation of a Successor Employer to Remedy His Predecessor's Unfair Labor Practices.

[76] Golden State Bottling Co. v. NLRB, 414 U.S. 168, 176, 84 L.R.R.M. 2839, 2842 (1973).

[77] *Id.* at 180, 84 L.R.R.M. at 2844. *See also* Perma Vinyl Corp., 164 N.L.R.B. 968, 969, 65 L.R.R.M. 1168, 1169 (1967), enf'd sub nom., U.S. Pipe and Foundry Co. v. NLRB, 398 F.2d 544, 68 L.R.R.M. 2913 (5th Cir. 1968).

[78] See the Quarterly Report of the NLRB General Counsel for the First Quarter of 1975, 89 L.R.R. 203-205 (1975).

concluded, however, that the union had violated the Act and ordered that a complaint be issued. Even though the Section 8 (a) (3) charge was dismissed, the General Counsel directed that "the Employer be named as a Party In Interest in the Section 8 (b) (2) complaint and that an order be sought requiring the Employer to reinstate the employee to his former or substantially equivalent position in order to fully effectuate the policies of the Act." [79] The General Counsel explained:

> To correct the violation we sought to fashion a remedy which would fully restore the unlawfully discharged employee to the status he enjoyed before the unfair labor practice occurred. We sought the usual 8(b) (2) order requiring the Union to make the employee whole for any losses resulting from his discharge, and to notify the Employer that it had no objection to the employee's immediate reinstatement to his former or substantially equivalent position without prejudice to his seniority or other rights and privileges. See *Automobile Workers (Wisconsin Axle Division, Timken-Detroit Axle Co.)*, 92 NLRB 968. However, this order against the Union alone was deemed insufficient to assure that the employee would be reinstated to his former position with eleven and one-half years seniority which substantially affected his wages and other rights and privileges associated with seniority. The only assured means of achieving status quo ante and providing a meaningful remedy was to order the Employer to reinstate the employee. As we had determined that the Employer had not violated the Act by discharging the employee, the Employer could not be made a respondent in the 8(b) (2) case in the ordinary sense. Nevertheless the Board possesses power under Section 10(c) of the Act to reach parties whose actions or interests are related to unfair practice proceedings. Under this authority the Board has reached and directed a successor employer to remedy the predecessor's unfair labor practices even though the predecessor had acted wholly independently of the successor. *Golden State Bottling Co.* v. *N.L.R.B.*, 414 U.S. 168. Also, in cases involving violations of Section 8(a) (2) the Board has ordered the offending employer to cease giving effect to the collective bargaining agreement with the assisted union, thereby directly affecting the interests of the union which was not a formal respondent in the proceedings. *IAM* v. *N.L.R.B.*, 311 U.S. 72. [80]

The General Counsel's position is a proper view of the Board's remedial authority and its adoption by the Board would do much to improve the effectiveness of remedies for violations of Section 8(b) (2).

---

[79] *Id.*, 89 L.R.R. at 205.

[80] The Board had no opportunity to rule upon the General Counsel's requested remedy since these cases were settled prior to hearing. (Anheuser Busch, Case No. 14-CA-8179, and Brewers Local No. 6, Case No. 14-CB-2875).

CHAPTER IX

Reinstatement Rights of Strikers

In assessing the duty of an employer to reinstate an employee who has engaged in a work stoppage, and consequently, that employee's correlative right to reinstatement, the threshold question asks whether the employee was engaged in an economic or unfair labor practice strike. Generally, an economic striker's right to immediate reinstatement is conditioned upon job availability— *i.e.*, whether or not the particular employee's job has been filled by a *permanent* replacement. Conversely, the unfair labor practice striker's right to reemployment is absolute [1] if he has not engaged in misconduct which would justify a discharge in any event.

Economic Strikers

In addition to those workers who are actively engaged by the employer, the Act provides that "the term 'employee' . . . shall include any individual whose work has ceased as a consequence of, or in connection with, any current labor dispute . . . and who has not obtained any other regular and substantially equivalent employment. . . ." [2] Thus, the same protection given regularly employed workers is extended to strikers. A striker engaged in a work stoppage premised on economic reasons, however, may lose certain reemployment rights if during his absence he has been permanently replaced by another employee.

---

[1] This absolute right of reinstatment assumes that there is a job available to which the unfair labor practice striker may be reinstated. Because business fluctuations may render a Board's order impossible to implement, reemployment is effectuated under the following set of priorities: (1) all replacements must be discharged, Sunshine Hosiery Mills, 1 N.L.R.B. 664, 1 L.R.R.M. 49 (1936) ; (2) available jobs are to be distributed to those affected on a nondiscriminatory basis such as seniority, Timken Silent Automatic Co., 1 N.L.R.B. 335, 1 L.R.R.M. 30 (1936) ; (3) any remainder are to be placed on a preferential hiring list, Tiny Town Togs, Inc., 7 N.L.R.B. 54, 2 L.R.R.M. 236 (1938).

[2] 29 U.S.C. § 152 (3) (1970).

Under the terms of the Act, the reinstatement rights of economic strikers are not premised on any inherent right which they acquire upon entering into an employment relationship. Instead, the reinstatement remedy afforded strikers is conditioned solely upon the employees' Section 7 right to join and participate in labor organizations and to engage in protected concerted activities in general. Every rule, every standard, and every regulation formulated by the Board must reflect this underlying principle.[3]

Without a legitimate business reason on the part of the employer, a refusal to reinstate economic strikers is presumed to be indicative of unlawful intent to abort Section 7 rights. To assert a legitimate business reason, the employer must show that his refusal to reinstate the economic strikers to substantially equivalent jobs was based on the unavailability of such work, whether due to economic circumstances or the hiring of permanent replacements.[4]

The Use of Permanent Replacements for Economic Strikers. As indicated above, the reinstatement rights of an economic striker are conditional. Thus, the employer has the right to replace such striking employees in order to keep his operation functioning. Furthermore, he is under no obligation to discharge the replacements when a striking employee elects to resume his employment.[5] This limitation was approved by the Supreme Court in one of its first Wagner Act decisions, *NLRB v. Mackay Radio & Telegraph Co.,*[6] on the grounds that:

---

[3] Any other rationale is untenable as the Board's authority to fashion relief is dependent upon the commission of an unfair labor practice. *See* 29 U.S.C. § 160 (1970). Without the necessary unfair labor practice, the Board is without jurisdiction, and an employer's treatment of his employees is entirely his prerogative. *See* pp. 105-108, *supra*.

[4] The participation of employees in a strike which is economically oriented, but conducted by illegal means or for an unlawful objective, is also considered a legitimate business reason excusing the employer of any duty to reemploy such strikers pursuant to the "for cause" proviso of Section 10(c). *E.g.,* Oneita Knitting Mills, Inc. v. NLRB, 375 F.2d 385, 64 L.R.R.M. 2724 (4th Cir. 1967); American News Co., 55 N.L.R.B. 1302, 14 L.R.R.M. 64 (1944). *See also* discussion at pp. 135-146, *infra*.

[5] In hiring permanent replacements, an employer commits an unfair labor practice if he offers inducements which have the effect of discriminating in the terms of employment between strikers and nonstrikers. *See* NLRB v. Erie Resistor Corp., 373 U.S. 221, 53 L.R.R.M. 2121 (1963).

[6] 304 U.S. 333, 2 L.R.R.M. 610 (1938).

... [A]n employer, guilty of no act denounced by the statute, has [not] lost the right to protect and continue his business by supplying places left vacant by strikers. And he is not bound to discharge those hired to fill the places of strikers, upon the election of the latter to resume their employment, in order to create places for them.[7]

Mackay, however, did not resolve the issue of whether economic strikers were entitled to the next available job openings in the absence of any union animus on the part of the employer.

Subsequent to *Mackay,* the Board adopted a policy which required employers to deal with economic strikers on the same, nondiscriminatory basis afforded *new* job applicants. Thus, in *Brown & Root, Inc.,*[8] the issue left open in *Mackay* was presented to the Board when, in the absence of any union animus, several replaced strikers sought backpay retroactive to the date openings first occurred in their job classifications. In denying the backpay, the Board held:

... [W]e reject the theory urged by the General Counsel, to the effect that the 13 strikers were entitled to appropriate vacancies as they arose .... In the circumstances of this case, we hold that Respondents had no obligation to seek out or prefer the 13 IAM strikers for vacancies which opened up after their application.[9]

The Board's *Brown & Root* policy was subsequently rendered untenable by two Supreme Court decisions. In *NLRB v. Great Dane Trailers, Inc.,*[10] the Court held that independent proof of union animus is not always essential to a finding that an employer violate Section 8(a)(3) by failing to reinstate a striking employee. The Court stated that "if it can reasonably be concluded that an employer's discriminatory conduct was inherently destructive of important employee rights," no proof of animus is needed,

---

[7] *Id.* at 345-346, 2 L.R.R.M. at 614. Economic strikers cannot be refused reemployment, however, if their jobs have been filled only on a temporary basis. Cyr Bottle Gas Co. v. NLRB, 497 F.2d 900, 87 L.R.R.M. 2253 (6th Cir. 1974). *Cf.* NLRB v. International Van Lines, 409 U.S. 48, 81 L.R.R.M. 2595 (1972).

[8] 132 N.L.R.B. 486, 48 L.R.R.M. 1391 (1961), *enforced,* 311 F.2d 447, 52 L.R.R.M. 2115 (8th Cir. 1963)

[9] *Id.,* 132 N.L.R.B. at 494, 48 L.R.R.M. at 1394. *Accord* Flint Glass Workers (Bartlett-Collins Co.), 110 N.L.R.B. 395, 35 L.R.R.M. 1006 (1954), *affirmed,* 230 F.2d 212, 37 L.R.R.M. 2409 (D.C. Cir. 1956), *cert. denied,* 351 U.S. 988, 38 L.R.R.M. 2238 (1956). *Cf.,* NLRB v. Plastilite Corp., 375 F.2d 343, 64 L.R.R.M. 2741 (8th Cir. 1967)

[10] 388 U.S. 26, 65 L.R.R.M. 2465 (1967).

and a violation can be found "even if the employer introduces evidence that the conduct was motivated by business considerations." [11] Additionally, even where the harm to employees' rights is "comparatively slight," animus need be proved only "*if* the employer has come forward with evidence of legitimate and substantial business justifications for the conduct." [12] In so holding, the Supreme Court undercut the union animus requirement of *Brown & Root*. *Brown & Root* was further eroded by the Supreme Court in *NLRB v. Fleetwood Trailer Co.*,[13] which held that strikers' reinstatement rights do not depend upon job availability as of the moment when the job applications are made. On the contrary, economic strikers' status as employees and their right to reinstatement continue until they have obtained other regular and substantially equivalent employment.[14] Thus, under *Fleetwood,* if an economic striker makes a proper unconditional application for reinstatement, he is entitled to return to work "[i]f and when a job for which the striker is qualified becomes available. . . ." [15] The *Fleetwood* decision noted that these reinstatement rights are not absolute; an employer will not violate the Act by refusing to reinstate economic strikers if he can show that his action was due to "legitimate and substantial business justifications." Such justification is found when either (1) "the jobs which the strikers claim are occupied by workers hired as permanent replacements during the strike in order to continue operations," or (2) "the strikers' job has been eliminated for substantial and bona fide reasons." [16] *Fleetwood* also emphasized that the burden is not on the NLRB General Counsel to show that the strikers' jobs were still available. Rather, the burden is on the employer to show that they were unavailable.[17]

THE LAIDLAW DOCTRINE

In 1968, the Board reexamined its remedial policy concerning the proper treatment to be accorded replaced economic strikers

---

[11] *Id.,* at 33-34, 65 L.R.R.M. at 2469.

[12] *Id.,* (emphasis in the original).

[13] 389 U.S. 375, 66 L.R.R.M. 2737 (1967).

[14] *Id.* at 381, 66 L.R.R.M. at 2739.

[15] *Id.*

[16] *Id.* at 379, 66 L.R.R.M. at 2738.

[17] *Id.* at 378-379, n. 4, 66 L.R.R.M. at 2738, n. 4.

and in the *Laidlaw Corp.*[18] case, overruled its previous policy. Previously, the Board had required employers to deal with economic strikers on the same, nondiscriminatory basis afforded other, new job applicants. Relying upon the Supreme Court's decision in *NLRB v. Fleetwood Trailer Co.,*[19] the Board reasoned in *Laidlaw* that its prior policy of treating an economic striker:

> . . . as a new employee or an employee with less than rights accorded by full reinstatement (such as denial of seniority) was wholly unrelated to any of [an employer's] economic needs, could only penalize [the employee] for engaging in concerted activities, was inherently destructive of employee interests, and thus was unresponsive to the requirements of the statute . . . .[20]

Accordingly, the Board announced that under its new rule concerning the employer's obligation to rehire economic strikers who have been permanently replaced at the time of their application, such strikers:

> . . . (1) remain employees; and (2) are entitled to full reinstatement upon the departure of replacements unless they have in the meantime acquired regular and substantially equivalent employment, or the employer can sustain his burden of proof that the failure to offer full reinstatement was for legitimate and substantial business reasons.[21]

The Board's *Laidlaw* decision was enforced by the Seventh Circuit,[22] and has received substantial approval in other circuits.[23]

---

[18] 171 N.L.R.B. 1366, 68 L.R.R.M. 1252 (1968), *enforced,* 414 F.2d 99, 71 L.R.R.M. 3054 (7th Cir. 1969), *cert. denied,* 397 U.S. 920, 73 L.R.R.M. 2537 (1970).

[19] 389 U.S. 375, 66 L.R.R.M. 2737 (1967).

[20] 171 N.L.R.B. at 1368, 68 L.R.R.M. at 1256.

[21] *Id.* at 1370, 68 L.R.R.M. at 1258 (enumeration is in original). *See* Colour IV Corp., 202 N.L.R.B. 44, 82 L.R.R.M. 1477 (1973), wherein the Board found that an employer successfully claimed "legitimate and substantial business reasons" for refusing to reemploy an economic striker in circumstances in which the employer had suffered a decline in business and the employee had previously possessed only marginal productivity in comparison to his fellow employees who had been retained.

[22] Laidlaw Corp. v. NLRB, 414 F.2d 99, 71 L.R.R.M. 3054 (7th Cir. 1967), *cert. denied,* 397 U.S. 920, 73 L.R.R.M. 2537 (1970).

[23] H & F Binch Co. v. NLRB, 456 F.2d 357, 79 L.R.R.M. 2692, 2697 (2d Cir. 1972) ; Little Rock Airmotive, Inc., v. NLRB, 455 F.2d 163, 79 L.R.R.M. 2544 (8th Cir. 1972) ; NLRB v. Anvil Products, 496 F.2d 94, 86 L.R.R.M. 2822, 2824 (5th Cir. 1974) ; American Machinery Corp. v. NLRB, 424 F.2d

Administration of Laidlaw Rights. Laidlaw requires an employer to maintain a preferential hiring list of economic strikers entitled to reinstatement and to notify them when substantially equivalent jobs become available. Responding to complaints that this might prove onerous to the employer, the Seventh Circuit in *Laidlaw* stated that:

> We do not view the employer's duty to seek out replaced economic strikers to be a severe burden in practice. "Employers, who presumably retain the addresses and phone numbers of the strikers, should not find it overly burdensome to give them notice that a position has fallen vacant." 82 Harv. L. Rev. 1777, 1779 (1969).[24]

But the Seventh Circuit also noted that one issue was not resolved in *Laidlaw*: "when does a striker's right to reinstatement expire?" [25] After the *Laidlaw* decision, this question arose from additional employer complaints that it would be "unreasonably onerous to require employers to keep records for an indefinite time of strikers who might apply for reinstatement after a strike had ended." [26] For example, in *American Machinery Corp. v. NLRB* [27] the Fifth Circuit enforced a *Laidlaw*-type order in a situation wherein an employer who had maintained a list of the names, addresses, and telephone numbers of all replaced economic strikers, failed to inform such employees when job openings occurred. In granting enforcement to the Board's order, the court rejected the employer's contention that his actions were justified on the grounds that he possessed a "legitimate and substantial business reason" created by the difficulty of actually finding economic strikers who had made unconditional applications for employment after their replacements had departed.[28] Nonetheless, the court indicated that its rejection of the employer's

---

1321, 73 L.R.R.M. 2977 (5th Cir. 1970); NLRB v. Johnson Sheet Metal, Inc., 442 F.2d 1056, 1061, 77 L.R.R.M. 2245 (10th Cir. 1971); NLRB v. Hartmann Luggage Co., 453 F.2d 178, 79 L.R.R.M. 2139 (6th Cir. 1971); C. H. Guenther & Son, Inc. d/b/a Pioneer Flour Mills v. NLRB, 427 F.2d 983, 74 L.R.R.M. 2343 (5th Cir. 1970), *cert. denied*, 400 U.S. 942, 75 L.R.R.M. 2752 (1970); NLRB v. Transport Co. of Texas, 438 F.2d 258, 76 L.R.R.M. 2482 (5th Cir. 1971).

[24] 414 F.2d at 105, 71 L.R.R.M. at 3059, n. 2.

[25] 414 F.2d 105, 71 L.R.R.M. at 3059.

[26] NLRB v. Hartmann Luggage Co., 453 F.2d 178, 79 L.R.R.M. 2139, 2141 (6th Cir. 1971).

[27] 424 F.2d 1321, 73 L.R.R.M. 2977 (5th Cir. 1970).

[28] *Id.* at 1327-1329, 73 L.R.R.M. at 2981-2982.

defense, based upon speculation, did not mean the court was totally unreceptive to some limitation of the *Laidlaw* doctrine. Referring to the open-ended nature of the *Laidlaw* rule, the court suggested that the duration of the employer's duty to extend reinstatement privileges to permanently replaced employees might be regulated by reasonable rules which the Board may devise.[29]

Acting upon the Fifth Circuit's suggestion, the Board has instituted several modifications. For example, in *Brooks Research & Mfg., Inc.,*[30] the Board held that an employer might bring reasonable order to his reinstatement obligation by asking replaced strikers from time to time whether they wished to remain on the employer's preferential hiring list and maintain their recall status. Further spelling out the employer's reinstatement obligations, the Board explained in *Brooks* that:

> Under the agreement reached by the parties herein, the Respondent's burden is slight. Thus, when a vacancy arises recall is to be by telephone with confirmation by letter or telegram. Respondent is required only to use the last known addresses and telephone numbers on file with it. The recalled employee has only three working days to report after being notified to return. If an employee refuses an offer of reinstatement or does not respond, his name may be deleted from the list.
> Therefore, contrary to its contention, Respondent does not have to maintain the entire preferential hiring list indefinitely. In addition, there may be other means by which Respondent can cope with its alleged burden. For example, although we find it unnecessary to consider at this time, we note that the Fifth Circuit suggested in American Machinery, supra:
> "... he might notify the strikers when they request reinstatement of a reasonable time during which their applications will be considered current and at the expiration of which they must take affirmative action to maintain their current status."[31]

In *Brooks*, the employer contended that a contractual provision limiting the recall rights of laid-off employees to a period of six months was also applicable to former strikers awaiting reinstatement. In deciding otherwise, the Board stated:

---

[29] *Id.* at 1328, 73 L.R.R.M. at 2981. The court observed that "a reasonable rule would not contravene *Fleetwood*'s assertion that '[t]he right to reinstatement does not depend upon technicalities relating to application.'" *Accord,* NLRB v. Hartmann Luggage Co., 453 F.2d 178, 79 L.R.R.M. 2139, 2141 (6th Cir. 1971).

[30] 202 N.L.R.B. 634, 82 L.R.R.M. 1599 (1973).

[31] *Id.,* at 636, 82 L.R.R.M. at 1602.

We reject the [employer's] contention that economic strikers should
be equated with laid-off employees. The reinstatement rights of
economic strikers under *Fleetwood Trailer* and *Laidlaw* are statutory as distinguished from the rights of laid-off employees.[32]

Similarly, in *Bio-Science Laboratories*,[33] the Board rejected its
General Counsel's contention that replaced strikers awaiting reinstatement under *Laidlaw* must be recalled to work in the same
order as they would be recalled from a layoff under the terms of
an existing collective bargaining agreement. The Administrative
Law Judge, whose decision the Board adopted, repeated the view
that economic strikers cannot be equated with laid-off employees.
The ALJ concluded that unless the parties have specifically agreed
upon an order of reinstatement, the employer may use any
method of recalling former strikers "as long as it is not shown
to have been unlawfully motivated or inherently destructive of
employee rights."

Agreements to Modify or Waive Laidlaw Reinstatement Rights.
The *Laidlaw* doctrine was explained further in two 1971 cases,
United Aircraft Corp.[34] and *Laher Spring & Electric Car Corp.*,[35]
which were decided in tandem. In *United Aircraft*, the NLRB
first established the principle that the reinstatement rights of
permanently replaced economic strikers, as annunciated in *Laidlaw*, might be terminated upon the basis of a strike settlement
between the employer and the union representing the strikers.
In so deciding, the Board reversed its trial examiner who had
found that, despite the employer-union agreement, the employer
had violated the Act by abandoning his preferential recall list
upon the expiration of a negotiated waiting period. The majority
reasoned that this restraint upon the reinstatement rights of economic strikers did not violate the spirit of the *Laidlaw* doctrine,
nor was it in contravention of the Supreme Court's *Fleetwood*
decision which had expressly reserved the question of whether a
labor organization could waive the right of strikers to reinstate-

[32] *Id.*, 82 L.R.R.M. at 1601.

[33] 209 N.L.R.B. 796, 85 L.R.R.M. 1568 (1974).

[34] 192 N.L.R.B. 382, 77 L.R.R.M. 1785 (1971), *aff'd on other grounds in*
Machinists v. United Aircraft Corp., Lodges 743 and 1746, IAM v. NLRB,
—— F.2d ——, 90 L.R.R.M. 2272 (2d Cir. 1975).

[35] 192 N.L.R.B. 464, 77 L.R.R.M. 1800 (1971).

ment ahead of new employees.[36] In upholding the joint actions of the employer and union, the Board stated that its approval of the settlement accord was based on the following points: (1) the agreement was the product of good faith bargaining;[37] (2) there was no evidence that in entering the pact, the employer had sought to undermine the union's status; (3) the recall period had not been unreasonably short (approximately four and one-half months); and (4) there was no evidence of discriminatory intent or objective on the part of either party, in either the negotiation or implementation of the agreement.[38]

One parameter of the *United Aircraft* rule was immediately established in the companion case, *Laher Spring & Electric Car Corp.*[39] There the Board found that an employer had violated Section 8(a)(3), despite the existence of a strike settlement agreement, on the grounds that the settlement had been discriminatorily manipulated.[40] The Board pointed out that a substantial increase in overtime work was coupled with an unexplained failure to fill certain positions during the preferential recall period and was further compounded by a dramatic increase in new hires immediately thereafter. The Board found that such facts indicated that the employer had entered into the accord as part of a scheme to delay or avoid rehiring the strikers. The principles of both *United Aircraft* and *Laher Spring* indicate that the legality of strike settlement agreements will hinge upon subsequent actions under the pact.

---

[36] 192 N.L.R.B. at 386, 77 L.R.R.M. at 1790-1791. In *Fleetwood*, 389 U.S. at 381, 66 L.R.R.M. at 2739, n. 8, the Court had stated:

> The respondent contends that the Union agreed to a nonpreferential hiring list and thereby waived the rights of the strikers to reinstatement ahead of the new applicants. The Board found that the Union, having lost the strike, merely "bowed to the [respondent's] decision." The Court of Appeals did not rule on this point or on the effect, if any, that its resolution might have upon the outcome of this case. Upon remand, the issue will be open for such consideration as may be appropriate.

[37] The authority vested in the union as a representative of the employee enables a labor organization to bargain for the job rights of the individual employee. The establishment of a negotiated cut-off date for recall is analogous to impact bargaining engaged in by unions and employers when a change in operations necessitates job elimination. See *generally*, pp. 204-216, *infra*, Chapter XIII.

[38] 192 N.L.R.B. at 387-388, 77 L.R.R.M. at 1780, 1793.

[39] 192 N.L.R.B. 464, 77 L.R.R.M. 1800 (1971).

[40] *Id.* at 466, 77 L.R.R.M. 1802.

The Board provided another important amplification of the *Laidlaw* doctrine in *Bio-Science Laboratories*,[41] when it found that the employer had not violated the Act when he unilaterally implemented a preferential reinstatement system, not agreed to by the union, for former economic strikers. In *Bio-Science*, the union had taken a consistent negotiating position, both during and after the strike, that permanent replacements should be terminated and the strikers returned to their old jobs. This position was, as the Board found, directly contrary to the Supreme Court's holding in *Mackay Radio*,[42] and the employer was not required to agree to it. Following the strike, the employer was faced with the problem of deciding which of 199 former strikers were to be placed into the thirty-five available positions. The employer presented the union with a proposed reinstatement plan, but the union continued to insist that seniority should prevail and that former strikers should "bump" the permanent replacements.[43] The employer then implemented his plan, hiring exclusively from among the former strikers. The Board dismissed the complaint against the employer, finding that negotiations were at a "stalemate." The Board noted, however, that, unless the employer devised some sort of system to recall former strikers as vacancies arose, he rank the risk of violating Sections 8(a)(1) and (3) under *Laidlaw* and *Fleetwood*.[44] Accordingly the Board stated that "[t]here is nothing in the statute or the case law which suggests that Respondent was obliged to delay [his] recall of former strikers until the Union retreated from its adamant position. . . ." [45]

Unconditional Applications for Reinstatement. An employer's obligation to reemploy an economic or unfair labor practice striker arises immediately upon the filing of an unconditional application for reinstatement by the striker. By assessing back-

---

[41] *Supra*, 209 N.L.R.B. 796, 85 L.R.R.M. 1568 (1974).

[42] NLRB v. Mackay Radio & Telegraph Co., 304 U.S. 333, 2 L.R.R.M. 610 (1938). The *Mackay* decision is discussed in full, *supra*, pp. 123-124.

[43] 209 N.L.R.B. at 800, 85 L.R.R.M. at 1570.

[44] *Id.* at 802, 85 L.R.R.M. at 1571.

[45] *Id.* The Board also rejected the contention that the employer violated the Act by using "unusual" amounts of overtime work in one section rather than recalling former strikers from that section. The Board found that neither the contract nor bargaining history required the employer to consult about overtime. Also, there was no evidence that the amount of overtime had changed after the strike ended. *Id.* at 1569.

pay liability against an employer from the date upon which such an application is tendered, compliance with the employer's reinstatement duty is encouraged.

Just as the employer must make an unconditional offer of reinstatement to discriminatorily discharged employees,[46] the striker's reinstatement application may not attach conditions other than requesting the employer to offer reemployment in the employee's former position or one which is substantially equivalent.[47] It is not necessary that the strikers' applications for reinstatement be made on an individual basis. An offer by the employees to return as a group is treated as an unconditional application.[48] It follows that the employees may designate a labor organization to act as their spokesman, as long as the chosen union represents a majority of the employees in the bargaining unit.[49]

UNFAIR LABOR PRACTICE STRIKERS

A work stoppage that has been initiated or prolonged, in whole or part, by the statutory misconduct of an employer is deemed an unfair labor practice strike.[50] In terms of the relief

---

[46] *See* pp. 111-112, *supra.*

[47] *Cf.* NLRB v. Textile Machine Works, 214 F.2d 929, 34 L.R.R.M. 2535 (3d Cir. 1954); NLRB v. Pecheur Lozenge Co., 209 F.2d 393, 33 L.R.R.M. 2324 (2d Cir. 1953) *cert. denied*, 347 U.S. 953, 34 L.R.R.M. 2027 (1954).

[48] *See* Draper Corp., 52 N.L.R.B. 1477, 13 L.R.R.M. 88 (1943), *enforcement denied on other grounds*, 145 F.2d 199, 15 L.R.R.M. 580 (4th Cir. 1944). *But cf.* Southwestern Pipe, Inc., 179 N.L.R.B. 364, 72 L.R.R.M. 1377 (1969), *enforced in part*, 444 F.2d 340, 77 L.R.R.M. 2317 (5th Cir. 1971). In the *Southwestern Pipe* case, the Board reversed its previous policy concerning the backpay liability incurred by employers who refuse to reinstate unfair labor practice strikers as a body upon the receipt of a group application. Although the reinstatement rights of such individuals remain intact, the backpay liability is terminated for those employees who refuse reinstatement. *See* pp. 87-88, *supra*, for a discussion of the backpay implications of *Southwestern Pipe.*

[49] Electric Auto-Lite Co., 80 N.L.R.B. 1601, 23 L.R.R.M. 1268 (1948).

[50] *See* NLRB v. Mackay Radio & Telegraph Co., 304 U.S. 333, 2 L.R.R.M. 610 (1938). *But cf.* Southwestern Pipe, Inc. v. NLRB, 444 F.2d 340, 77 L.R.R.M. 2317 (5th Cir. 1971); Clinton Foods, Inc., 112 N.L.R.B. 239, 36 L.R.R.M. 1006 (1955). In order to be considered an unfair labor practice strike, a causal relationship must be shown between the work stoppage or prolongation of an existing strike and the employer's violations of the Act. Allied Industrial Workers, Local 289 (Cavalier Div. of Seeburg Corp.) v. NLRB, 476 F.2d 868, 883, 82 L.R.R.M. 2225 (D.C. Cir. 1973), and cases cited

granted, whether the strike is triggered directly by an unfair labor practice or is merely prolonged by one—*i.e.*, initially an economic strike, subsequently converted into an unfair labor practice strike [51]—is irrelevant. In either case, an employer is under an absolute duty to reemploy unfair labor practice strikers in their former jobs,[52] even though the employer may be forced to fire replacements to make room for them once the strike ends.[53] Nevertheless, as in the case of the majority of NLRB "absolute" rules, an employer's obligation to reinstate unfair labor practice strikers is subject to certain conditions: (1) the strikers must make an unconditional application for reinstatement; (2) the striker must not have engaged in any misconduct which would provide the employer cause for refusing to reemploy him, and (3) the strike itself must not be conducted by illegal means or in pursuit of an unlawful end.

Conversion of an Economic Strike into an Unfair Labor Practice Strike. An economic strike may be converted into an unfair labor practice strike if the employer engages in violations of the Act which prolong a work stoppage.[54] Should this occur, the employer is obligated to reinstate the strikers and, if necessary, discharge replacements hired *after* the date of conversion.[55] The rationale underlying the conversion doctrine is that any reinstatement relief afforded unfair labor practice strikers may also justifiably be granted to economic strikers where the employer's

---

therein. (The unfair labor practices must be shown to be a "sole or substantial contributing cause" of the strike's continuation.) General Drivers and Helpers, Local 662 v. NLRB, 302 F.2d 908, 911, 50 L.R.R.M. 2243 (D.C. Cir. 1962), *cert. denied*, 371 U.S. 827, 61 L.R.R.M. 2222 (1962).

[51] *See* 133-135, *infra*, for a discussion of the conversion doctrine.

[52] NLRB v. Fotochrome, 343 F.2d 631, 58 L.R.R.M. 2844 (2d Cir. 1965), *cert. denied*, 382 U.S. 833, 60 L.R.R.M. 2234 (1965); Kitty Clover, Inc. v. NLRB, 208 F.2d 212, 33 L.R.R.M. 2177 (8th Cir. 1953).

[53] Mastro Plastics Corp. v. NLRB, 350 U.S. 270, 37 L.R.R.M. 2587 (1956); NLRB v. Jones & Laughlin Steel Corp., 301 U.S. 1, 1 L.R.R.M. 703 (1937); NLRB v. Sunrise Lumber and Trim Corp., 241 F.2d 620, 625, 39 L.R.R.M. 2441 (2d Cir. 1957) *cert. denied*, 355 U.S. 818, 40 L.R.R.M. 2680 (1957); Colecraft Mfg. Co. v. NLRB, 385 F.2d 998, 1004-1005, 66 L.R.R.M. 2677 (2d Cir. 1967). (Although unfair labor practice strikers may not be permanently replaced, an employer may use temporary replacements during the strike.)

[54] *See* NLRB v. Pecheur Lozenge Co., 209 F.2d 393, 33 L.R.R.M. 2324 (2d Cir. 1953), *cert. denied*, 347 U.S. 953, 34 L.R.R.M. 2027 (1954).

[55] *Id.* at 404-405, 33 L.R.R.M. at 2333. *See also* NLRB v. Remington Rand, Inc., 130 F.2d 919, 11 L.R.R.M. 575 (2d Cir. 1942).

wrongdoing has served to prolong the strike.[56] This nexus between the violation and the strike prolongation is especially evident when the employer's illegal activity takes the form of initiating a back-to-work movement among his striking employees.[57] For example, a conversion to an unfair labor practice strike has been found when the employer bypassed a certified bargaining representative and dealt with the employees directly.[58] The employer is even likelier to be found prolonging the strike when he conditions a reemployment offer on abandonment of the employees' union activities.[59]

In *NLRB v. International Van Lines*,[60] the Supreme Court found the conversion issue irrelevant and ordered the unconditional reinstatement of employees regardless of whether they were economic strikers or unfair labor practice strikers. The employees had refused to cross a union's organizational picket line. The employer informed the employees that because they had failed to work, they were permanently replaced. At the time of the dis-

---

[56] *Eg.*, Coast Radio Broadcast Corp. d/b/a Radio Station KPOL, 166 N.L.R.B. 359, 65 L.R.R.M. 1538 (1967).

[57] *E.g.*, Great Western Mushroom Co., 27 N.L.R.B. 352, 7 L.R.R.M. 72 (1940) (forcing employees to sign no-strike pledges). Coercive strike preparation may also provide the catalyst in applying the conversion doctrine. *See* Southland Cork Co., 146 N.L.R.B. 906, 55 L.R.R.M. 1426 (1964), *modified*, 342 F.2d 702, 58 L.R.R.M. 2555 (4th Cir. 1965). In *Southland*, the employer had "far exceeded the reasonable necessities of the situation"—preparing to hire replacements in anticipation of a strike—when he conspicuously canvassed the local plant neighborhood for job applicants, who were then paraded through the plant while the original employees were still there. The Board held that because the employer's actions were the immediate cause of the strike, the displaced employees would be treated as unfair labor practice strikers in determining their reinstatement rights. *But see* Hot Shoppes, Inc., 146 N.L.R.B. 802, 55 L.R.R.M. 1419 (1964). In *Hot Shoppes*, a companion case of *Southland Cork*, no violation or conversion occurred where the management used standard procedures in attempting to locate job replacements prior to an impending strike. Consequently, it is not preparation which is forbidden, but the use of preparation to coerce employees from exercising their rights that constitutes a violation.

[58] *Compare* W. T. Rawleigh Co., 90 N.L.R.B. 1924, 26 L.R.R.M. 1421 (1950) (employer solicitation followed by refusal to reinstate although vacancies existed), *with* Samuel Bingham's Son Mfg. Co., 80 N.L.R.B. 1612, 23 L.R.R.M. 1266 (1948) (employer told solicited employees that it would not meet with union "until Hell freezes over"). *But see* American Steel & Pump Corp., 121 N.L.R.B. 1410, 42 L.R.R.M. 1564 (1958).

[59] *See* cases cited at note 58, *supra*.

[60] 409 U.S. 48, 81 L.R.R.M. 2595 (1971); *see also* NLRB v. United States Cold Storage Corp., 203 F.2d 924, 32 L.R.R.M. 2024 (5th Cir. 1953), *cert. denied*, 346 U.S. 818, 32 L.R.R.M. 2750 (1953).

charge, however, the employees had not been replaced. The court of appeals ruled that they were economic strikers and not entitled to unconditional reinstatement. The Supreme Court reversed the lower court, holding that the initial discharges were illegal, and reinstatement was required regardless of the nature of the strike.[61] The Court reasoned that the timing of the notice implicitly proved the employer's intent to discriminate against employees for engaging in protected activity.[62]

EMPLOYEE MISCONDUCT AS A BAR TO REINSTATEMENT

As previously indicated in Chapter VIII, Section 10(c) of the Act prohibits the Board from ordering the "reinstatement of any individual as an employee who has been suspended or discharged, . . . *for cause*." [63] The right of employers to refuse to reinstate *economic* strikers who have participated in strike misconduct or have been discharged for cause was recognized by the Supreme Court, over the objections of the Board, in the *NLRB v. Fansteel Metallurgical Corp.*[64] case. In brief, the *Fansteel* case involved employer discharges of employees who participated in the seizure and retention of the company's buildings during the course of a sitdown strike. Brought before the Board on unfair labor practice charges, the employer had been ordered to reinstate the employees who had engaged in the sitdown strike. In the Supreme Court, the Board defended its order as a function of the NLRB's discretionary remedial authority to grant such relief whenever the proposed remedy could be shown to effectuate the policies of the Act.[65]

In issuing its decision, the Supreme Court was unwilling to construe the statutory powers of relief as broadly as the Board had urged. Recalling the intent of Congress, the Court was unable to conclude that the NLRB's remedial authority could be utilized to compel employers to retain persons in their employ regardless

---

[61] 409 U.S. at 53, 81 L.R.R.M. at 2596-2597.

[62] *Id.*

[63] 29 U.S.C. § 160(c) (1970). *See supra*, pp. 106-108. *See also* NLRB v. Electrical Workers, Local No. 1229, 346 U.S. 464, 33 L.R.R.M. 2183 (1953).

[64] 306 U.S. 240, 4 L.R.R.M. 515 (1939).

[65] *Id.* at 253, 4 L.R.R.M. at 519.

of their unlawful conduct.[66] Instead, the Court noted that such a remedial policy would tend to insulate employees engaged in unlawful acts from discharge merely because their illegal conduct occurred within the context of a labor dispute.[67] Finally, the Court chided the Board for defending its order as necessary to effectuate the policies of the Act, concluding that the Board's position could be regarded as counter-productive to those very policies which it seeks to invoke:

> There is not a line in the statute to warrant the conclusion that it is any part of the policies of the Act to encourage employees to resort to force and violence in defiance of the law of the land. On the contrary, the purpose of the Act is to promote peaceful settlements of disputes by providing legal remedies for the invasion of the employees' rights. . . . We are of the opinion that to provide for the reinstatement or reemployment of employees guilty of the acts [plant seizure] which the Board finds to have been committed . . . would not only not effectuate any policy of the Act but would directly tend to make abortive its plan for peaceable procedure.[68]

To determine whether misconduct of *unfair labor practice* strikers should bar their reinstatement, additional analysis is required. Thus, the Board must also consider the impact of the employer's unfair labor practice. Under the *Thayer Doctrine*,[69] the misconduct of both employer and employee must be balanced against one another to determine if the employer has just cause for refusing to reinstate the employee. As stated by the *Thayer* court:

> On the other hand where, as in the instant case, the strike was caused by an unfair labor practice, the power of the Board to order reinstatement is not necessarily dependent upon a determi-

---

[66] *Id.* at 255, 4 L.R.R.M. at 519.

[67] *Id.* at 256, 4 L.R.R.M. at 519. *Fansteel* is not the only case in which the Court has exhibited concern about the exercise of the Board's remedial powers where discharged employees were fortunate enough to be fired during the pendency of a labor dispute. *See,* NLRB v. Local 1229, IBEW (Jefferson Std. Broadcasting Co.), 346 U.S. 464, 33 L.R.R.M. 2183 (1953).

[68] 306 U.S. at 257-258, 4 L.R.R.M. at 520.

[69] *See* NLRB v. H. N. Thayer Co., 213 F.2d 748, 34 L.R.R.M. 2250 (1st Cir. 1954), *cert. denied,* 348 U.S. 883, 35 L.R.R.M. 2100 (1954); Blades Mfg. Corp., 144 N.L.R.B. 561, 54 L.R.R.M. 1087 (1963), *enforcement denied,* 344 F.2d 998, 59 L.R.R.M. 2210 (8th Cir. 1965); Fairview Nursing Home, 202 N.L.R.B. 318, 82 L.R.R.M. 1566 (1973), *enforced* 486 F.2d 1400, 84 L.R.R.M. 3010 (5th Cir. 1973); Local 833, UAW v. NLRB (Kohler Co.), 300 F.2d 699, 49 L.R.R.M. 2485 (D.C. Cir. 1962), *cert. denied* 370 U.S. 911, 50 L.R.R.M. 2326 (1962); Golay & Co. v. NLRB, 447 F.2d 290, 77 L.R.R.M. 3041, 3043 (7th Cir. 1971).

nation that the strike activity was a "concerted activity" within the protection of § 7. Even if it was not, the National Labor Relations Board has power under § 10(c) to order reinstatement if the discharges were not "for cause" and if such an order would effectuate the policies of the Act. Of course the discharge of strikers engaged in non-Section 7 activities often may be for cause, or their reinstatement may not effectuate the policies of the Act, but in certain circumstances it may. The point is that where collective action is precipitated by an unfair labor practice, a finding that that action is not protected under § 7 does not, *ipso facto*, preclude an order reinstating employees who have been discharged because of their participation in the unprotected activity.[70]

Fansteel and *Thayer* recognize one basic fact in labor-management relations: emotions run high during a strike. As a result, the Board is often required to judge the propriety of an employer's refusal to reinstate strikers who engage in illegal or highly questionable conduct during the course of a strike. When employee misconduct is obviously extreme, the Board will often determine that the offending employee has forfeited his protection under the Act and should not be returned to his job. For example, the right of an employer to refuse to reinstate a worker who has engaged in property destruction,[71] misconduct on the picket line,[72] or other types of physical violence,[73] or even threats of physical violence [74] has been upheld in numerous Board and court cases.

---

[70] NLRB v. H. N. Thayer Co., 213 F.2d 748, 757, 34 L.R.R.M. 2250, 2253 (1st Cir. 1954).

[71] NLRB v. Mt. Clemens Pottery Co., 147 F.2d 262, 16 L.R.R.M. 501 (6th Cir. 1945).

[72] NLRB v. Perfect Circle Co., 162 F.2d 566, 20 L.R.R.M. 2558 (7th Cir. 1947) (barring supervisor entrance to plant); Talladega Foundry & Machine Co., 122 N.L.R.B. 125, 43 L.R.R.M. 1073 (1958) (preventing loading and unloading operations by threat of physical presence).

[73] Standard Lime and Stone Co. v. NLRB, 97 F.2d 531, 2 L.R.R.M. 674 (4th Cir. 1938) (employee convicted for assault and battery upon fellow employee); Revere Metal Art Co., 127 N.L.R.B. 1028, 46 L.R.R.M. 1448 (1960), *enforced*, 287 F.2d 632, 47 L.R.R.M. 2635 (2d Cir. 1961) (beating nonstriker); Farah Mfg. Co., 202 N.L.R.B. 666, 82 L.R.R.M. 1623 (1973) (assault on supervisor); Ohio Power Co., 215 N.L.R.B. No. 13, 88 L.R.R.M. 1007 (1974).

[74] *See, e.g.*, Brookville Glove Co., 114 N.L.R.B. 213, 36 L.R.R.M. 1548 (1955), *enforced sub nom.*, NLRB v. Leach, 234 F.2d 400, 38 L.R.R.M. 2252 (3d Cir. 1956); Socony Vacuum Oil Co., 78 N.L.R.B. 1185, 22 L.R.R.M. 1321 (1948). In both cases, striking employees had threatened nonstrikers with bodily harm should they enter or attempt to enter the struck plant. *See also* Ohio Power Co., 216 N.L.R.B. No. 70, 89 L.R.R.M. 1239 (1975).

Violence or the threat of violence is not required before an employee will lose his statutory protection as a result of misconduct. An employee's verbal attack on the quality of the employer's product has been considered improper disloyalty justifying the discharge of the offending employee.[75] Another type of verbal misconduct may justify an employer's refusal of reinstatement. Although in *Milk Wagon Drivers' Union v. Meadowmoor Dairies, Inc.,*[76] the Supreme Court held that a striker's use of unseemly language on the picket line "in a moment of animal exuberance" does not deprive him of the right to reinstatement.[77] In *Montgomery Ward & Co. v. NLRB,*[78] the Tenth Circuit refused to enforce the Board's reinstatement order of an employee who had cursed at a customer when the customer crossed the picket line. The court reasoned that although name calling has generally been excused when directed at nonstrikers and members of management, the striking employee must exercise a greater degree of self-control with regard to the employer's customers and other members of the general public.[79] This decision reflects the principle of the *Fansteel* case which held that the benefits of the Act extended only to protected activities guaranteed by the Act.

Proof of direct participation in the misconduct is not always required. Striking employees who ratify or authorize [80] strike misconduct are treated similarly to those who have actually engaged in the misconduct. Conversely, strikers have no duty to

---

[75] NLRB v. Local 1229, IBEW (Jefferson Std. Broadcasting Co.), 346 U.S. 464, 33 L.R.R.M. 2183 (1953), *aff'g* 94 N.L.R.B. 1507, 28 L.R.R.M. 1215 (1951). *See also,* Boeing Airplane Co. v. NLRB, 238 F.2d 188, 38 L.R.R.M. 2276 (9th Cir. 1956); Hoover Co. v. NLRB, 191 F.2d 380, 28 L.R.R.M. 2353 (6th Cir. 1951); Patterson-Sargent Co., 115 N.L.R.B. 1627, 38 L.R.R.M. 1134 (1956).

[76] 312 U.S. 287, 7 L.R.R.M. 310 (1941).

[77] *Id.* at 293, 7 L.R.R.M. at 312. *Cf.* Longview Furniture Co., 110 N.L.R.B. 1734, 35 L.R.R.M. 1254 (1954).

[78] 374 F.2d 606, 64 L.R.R.M. 2712 (10th Cir. 1967).

[79] *Id.* at 608, 64 L.R.R.M. at 2713. *Cf.* Rock Road Trailer Parts and Sales, 204 N.L.R.B. 1136, 83 L.R.R.M. 1467 (1973) (loud and belligerent remarks which threaten to put employer out of business and which are made in front of customers are not protected).

[80] *E.g.,* Revere Metal Art Co., 127 N.L.R.B. 1078, 46 L.R.R.M. 1448 (1960), *enforced,* 287 F.2d 632, 47 L.R.R.M. 2635 (2d Cir. 1961); Marathon Electric Mfg. Co., 106 N.L.R.B. 1171, 32 L.R.R.M. 1645 (1953), *affirmed sub nom.,* U.E. Local 1113 v. NLRB, 223 F.2d 338, 36 L.R.R.M. 2175 (D.C. Cir. 1955), *cert. denied,* 350 U.S. 981, 37 L.R.R.M. 2639 (1956).

disavow misconduct which they did not initiate and with which they are not connected, either directly or indirectly.[81]

Even though an employee who has been on strike or discriminatorily discharged may be eligible for reinstatement because of protected activities, that eligibility may be voided if he thereafter engages in misconduct that would make him an undesirable employee. Similarly, reinstatement will not be ordered if the employer learns of earlier misconduct of which he was previously unaware. In either situation, the employee will be paid the requisite amount of backpay, but will not be returned to his job.[82]

As the above discussion indicates, in exercising its remedial powers under the Act, the Board traditionally takes care not to fashion orders which will give the appearance of condoning serious misconduct or acts of violence.[83] The criterion used in these judgments, however, is not whether at any particular point there has been a departure from impeccable behavior. Rather, "A distinction is to be drawn between cases where employees engaged in concerted activities exceed the bounds of lawful conduct 'in a moment of animal exuberance' "[84] or in a manner not activated by improper motives, and those flagrant cases in which the misconduct is so violent or of such serious character that it negates the employee's right to reinstatement.[85] The rationale

---

[81] ILGWU v. NLRB (BVD Co.), 237 F.2d 545, 38 L.R.R.M. 2061 (D.C. Cir. 1956).

[82] East Island Swiss Products, 220 N.L.R.B. No. 26, 90 L.R.R.M. 1206 (1975) (employer learned of employee's previous discharge and conviction for misappropriating funds). Banker's Club, Inc., 218 N.L.R.B. No. 7, 89 L.R.R.M. 1812 (1975) (employee who would have been replaced because of poor attendance record awarded 30 days backpay but reinstatement denied); Gifford-Hill & Co., 188 N.L.R.B. 337, 76 L.R.R.M. 1349 (1971) (Since Board hearing, employee convicted of five armed robberies and sentenced to serve fifteen years in prison); NLRB v. Magnuson, —— F.2d ——, 90 L.R.R.M. 3330, 3332-3333 (9th Cir. 1975) and cases there cited.

[83] *See, e.g.,* Quality and Service Laundry, Inc., 39 N.L.R.B. 970, 10 L.R.R.M. 33 (1942), *enforced,* 131 F.2d 182, 11 L.R.R.M. 621 (4th Cir. 1942) *cert. denied,* 318 U.S. 775, 12 L.R.R.M. 890 (1943); Kentucky Fire Brick Co., 3 N.L.R.B. 455, 465-466, 1-A L.R.R.M. 146 (1938), *enforced,* 99 F.2d 89, 2 L.R.R.M. 722 (6th Cir. 1938); Republic Steel Corp., 9 N.L.R.B. 219, 289-391, 3 L.R.R.M. 261 1939), *enforced,* 107 F.2d 472, 5 L.R.R.M. 74 (3d Cir. 1939), *cert. denied on this point,* 309 U.S. 684, 6 L.R.R.M. 708 (1940).

[84] Milk Wagon Drivers Union v. Meadowmoor Dairies, Inc., 312 U.S. 287, 293, 7 L.R.R.M. 310 (1941).

[85] NLRB v. Illinois Tool Works, 153 F.2d 811, 815, 17 L.R.R.M. 841 (7th Cir. 1946).

for this rule was set forth early in the history of the Act by the Third Circuit in *Republic Steel Corp. v. NLRB*,[86] wherein the Court stated:

> . . . some disorder is unfortunately quite usual in any extensive or long drawn out strike. . . . Engaged in it are human beings whose feelings are stirred to depths. Rising passions call forth hot words. Hot words lead to blows on the picket line. The transformation from economic to physical combat by those engaged in the contest is difficult to prevent even when cool heads direct the fight. Violence of this nature, however much it is to be regretted, must have been in the contemplation of the Congress when it provided in Sec. 13 of the Act . . . that nothing therein should be construed so as to interfere with or impede or diminish in any way the right to strike. If this were not so the rights afforded to employees by the Act would be indeed illusory.

Accordingly, in cases decided subsequent to *Republic Steel*, the Board and courts have held that: "not every impropriety committed during [Section 7] activity places the employee beyond the protective shield of the act. The employee's right to engage in concerted activity may permit some leeway for impulsive behavior, which must be balanced against the employer's right to maintain order and respect." [87]

---

[86] 107 F.2d 472, 479, 5 L.R.R.M. 740 (3d Cir. 1939), *cert. denied on this point*, 309 U.S. 684, 6 L.R.R.M. 708 (1940).

[87] NLRB v. Thor Power Tool Co., 351 F.2d 584, 587, 60 L.R.R.M. 2237 (7th Cir. 1965) (obscene remark to supervisor); NLRB v. Hartmann Luggage Co., 453 F.2d 178, 79 L.R.R.M. 2139, 2142 (6th Cir. 1971) (threat to "kill" a strike breaker); NLRB v. Wichita Television Corp., 277 F.2d 579, 585, 45 L.R.R.M. 3096, 3100 (10th Cir. 1960) (strikers carried large obstructive umbrellas on picket line, heckled nonstrikers, and obstructed doorway); NLRB v. Brookside Industries, Inc., 308 F.2d 224, 227, 51 L.R.R.M. 2148 (4th Cir. 1962) (threats of physical harm); NLRB v. Zelrich Co., 334 F.2d 1011, 1014, 59 L.R.R.M. 2225 (5th Cir. 1965) (threats); NLRB v. Big Ben Department Stores, Inc., 396 F.2d 78, 81, 68 L.R.R.M. 2311 (2d Cir. 1968) (obnoxious and overbearing employee found to have been discharged because of his union activities, and not his shortcomings); NLRB v. Terry Coach Industries, Inc., 411 F.2d 612, 71 L.R.R.M. 2287, 2288 (9th Cir. 1969), *enf'g* 166 N.L.R.B. 560, 65 L.R.R.M. 1583 (1967) (blocked entrance to plant with truck and directed profanity toward nonstriking employees); Richlands Textile Inc., 220 N.L.R.B. No. 83, —— L.R.R.M. —— (1975) (threat to burn down employee's house if he did not join the union); Asplundh Tree Expert Co., 220 N.L.R.B. No. 59, —— L.R.R.M. —— (1975) (alleged threat to supervisor where there was nothing to suggest that the employee intended to engage in violence); Overhead Door Corp., 220 N.L.R.B. No. 68, —— L.R.R.M. —— (1975) (individual instances of strikers aiming a gun at employer's light pole, throwing gravel at nonstriking employee's car, pounding on nonstriker's car, and shaking employer's snowplow).

Although *Republic Steel* and *Thor Power Tool* establish the principle that not all misconduct will deprive an employee of the protection of the Act, those cases do not set forth definitive standards to evaluate the various types of misconduct. Rather, the Board examines the circumstances of each individual case and makes an ad hoc evaluation.[88]

The Board has offered various justifications for ordering the reinstatement of an employee who has misbehaved. For example, the employee may have engaged in similar misconduct at an earlier time without having been punished. The facts may also reveal that the misconduct was minor or momentary, not serious enough to justify discharge. In vindicating the use of threats, the Board has found that those threats should not have been taken seriously when they were not intended to be carried out, were obviously incredible, or occurred in an otherwise casual conversation. Even an unsuccessful assault of one employee by another has been excused where the conduct fell short of actual violence, or where the conduct was uncharacteristic of an employee.[89]

These are some factors relied upon in proper circumstances to determine whether or not an employer violated Section 8(a)(3) in refusing to reinstate a misbehaving striker. In making its evaluation of striker misconduct, however, often the Board simply makes the conclusory statement that one of these factors applies, without also analyzing the detrimental impact of the misconduct on innocent persons, the ongoing employer-employee relationship, or the employer's business.

Unfortunately, the courts too often have been required to emphasize that the Board must make a serious and open-minded analysis of the propriety of reinstating strikers who have engaged in dangerous or illegal conduct, harmful to nonstrikers, customers, or the employer's business operations.

The Board has been chastised by the courts for improperly applying decisions such as *Terry Coach* [90] to cases involving more

---

[88] Oneita Knitting Mills v. NLRB, 375 F.2d 385, 64 L.R.R.M. 2724, 2728 (4th Cir. 1967).

[89] *See* the cases cited in footnote 87, *supra.*

[90] NLRB v. Terry Coach Industries, Inc., 411 F.2d 612, 71 L.R.R.M. 2287, 2288 (9th Cir. 1969), *enf'g* 166 N.L.R.B. 562, 65 L.R.R.M. 1583 (1967). *See* NLRB v. Community Motor Bus Co., 439 F.2d 965, 76 L.R.R.M. 2844, 2846 (4th Cir. 1971) (the trivial truck blocking incidents of *Terry Coach* found not applicable to mass picketing).

serious and dangerous misconduct. In some cases the Board has ordered the reinstatement of employees who engaged in conduct which exceeded mere exuberance, impulsiveness or persuasion, and entailed violence, serious threats, intimidation or property damage.

In *Oneita Knitting Mills v. NLRB*,[91] for example, the court reversed the Board's finding that the employer had violated Section 8(a)(3) by refusing to reinstate employees who had engaged in incidents including following cars, throwing objects at nonstrikers' moving vehicles, repeatedly driving a car in front of a nonstriker's car, and blocking plant access by mass picketing. The court explained that under the *Thayer* decision:

> ... violent activity which has as its purpose the intimidation of nonstriking employees or which creates situations fraught with danger to them or to the general public can serve as the basis for an unfair labor practice employer's refusal of reinstatement. The vital policy underlying the Act does not contemplate the protection of such employees and nothing in Thayer supports a contrary view. The court in Thayer simply decided that if employee activity is otherwise unprotected under the Act the Board should balance the unfair labor practice of the employer against the misconduct of the employee. It clearly recognized that certain activity *could* justify a denial of reinstatement and pointed out that Board determinations with respect to such activity were always subject to judicial review. 213 F.2d at 755 n. 14, [34 LRRM 2250].[92]

Similarly, the Board has been prevented from ordering the reinstatement of employees who have engaged in mass picketing involving entrance blocking and violence,[93] serious threat and

---

[91] 375 F.2d 385, 64 L.R.R.M. 2724 (4th Cir. 1967).

[92] *Id.*, 375 F.2d at 390, 64 L.R.R.M. at 2728. The court also expressed its displeasure that the trial examiner appeared to have applied an "inflexible standard, *i.e.*, conduct short of aggravated assault would not result in a forfeiture of the right to reinstatement," *Id.*

[93] NLRB v. Community Motor Bus Co., 335 F.2d 120, 76 L.R.R.M. 2844, 2846 (4th Cir. 1971) (mass picketing and entrance blocking requiring the presence of police escorts for nonstrikers) ; Ruscoe Co. v. NLRB 406, F.2d 725, 70 L.R.R.M. 2566 (6th Cir. 1969) (blocking ingress and egress in violation of state court injunction, rocking a car, pulling a truck driver from his truck and throwing a bottle which shattered the truck's window, and throwing gravel at supervisor). The court noted that there must be reasonable limits to attempts of strikers to persuade others to join the strike. *See also,* Kayser-Roth Hosiery Co. v. NLRB, 447 F.2d 396, 78 L.R.R.M. 2130 (6th Cir. 1971) (blocking ingress and egress in violation of state court injunction; jamming a bus which nonstrikers were then unable to use to continue to work).

intimidation,[94] assaults and fighting,[95] or foul and abusive language to customers.[96]

In sum, the courts will not overturn the Board's misconduct reinstatement unless the Board has acted arbitrarily or illogically.[97] Many of such Board determinations, however, have fallen into the latter category.

Finally, the courts have also ruled that even though the activity which provoked a discharge may have constituted protected activity, reinstatement may not be warranted if a basic antagonism exists between the employer and employee that makes impossible the resumption of a normal employer-employee relationship.[98]

The Burnup and Sims Rule. The *Burnup and Sims* rule governs the employer's mistaken belief that misconduct has occurred. In *NLRB v. Burnup and Sims, Inc.*,[99] the Supreme Court observed that "[u]nion activity often engenders strong emotions and gives rise to active rumors. A protected activity acquires a precarious status if innocent employers can be discharged while engaging in it, even though the employer acts in good faith." Accordingly, the Court stated the rule that ". . . § 8(a)(1) is violated if it is

[94] Federal Prescription Service v. NLRB, 496 F.2d 813, 86 L.R.R.M. 2185 (8th Cir. 1974) *cert. denied*, —— U.S. ——, 87 L.R.R.M. 3035 (1974) (intimidation, verbal assaults, and threats in violation of court order); NLRB v. Pepsi Cola Company, 496 F.2d 226, 86 L.R.R.M. 2251, 2252 (4th Cir. 1974) ("veiled threat" crossed the line from persuasion to threats and intimidation).

[95] Pullman Inc., Trailmobile Division v. NLRB, 407 F.2d 1006, 70 L.R.R.M. 2849 (5th Cir. 1969) (physical attacks on supervisor and another employee in an attempt to persuade them to join strike); Firestone Tire & Rubber Co. v. NLRB, 449 F.2d 511, 78 L.R.R.M. 2591, 2592 (5th Cir. 1971) (threats, forcing a nonstriker to side of the road, attempts to intimidate witnesses in federal injunction proceeding, stopping car of nonstriker and attempting to force him to vacate it).

[96] Montgomery Ward & Co. v. NLRB, 374 F.2d 606, 64 L.R.R.M. 2712 (10th Cir. 1962) (calling a customer who crossed a picket line a "bastard" and a "son-of-a-bitch").

[97] NLRB v. Thor Power Tool Co., 351 F.2d 584, 587, 60 L.R.R.M. 2237 (7th Cir. 1965); NLRB v. Hartmann Luggage Co., 453 F.2d 178, 79 L.R.R.M. 2139, 2142 (6th Cir. 1971).

[98] NLRB v. National Furniture Mfg. Co., 315 F.2d 280, 52 L.R.R.M. 2451, 2456 (7th Cir. 1963); NLRB v. King Louie Bowling Corp., 472 F.2d 1192, 82 L.R.R.M. 2576, 2577 (8th Cir. 1973) (case remanded to the Board for a determination of whether alternative relief such as termination settlement would be appropriate in light of the deteriorated relationship between the employee and manager).

[99] 379 U.S. 21, 23, 57 L.R.R.M. 2385 (1964).

shown that the discharged employee was at the time engaged in a protected activity, that the employer knew it was such, that the basis of the discharge was an alleged act of misconduct in the course of that activity, and that the employee was not, in fact, guilty of that misconduct." [100] Pursuant to *Burnup and Sims*, the burden initially is on the employer to prove his good-faith belief that the employee committed the alleged acts. Thereafter, the burden shifts to the General Counsel to prove the employee was innocent of strike misconduct. [101]

Condonation of the Misconduct by the Employer. The right of an employer to discharge an employee for strike misconduct, which the Supreme Court recognized in the *NLRB v. Fansteel Metallurgical Corp.* [102] case, is limited. If the employer fails to exercise his discharge prerogative promptly, but instead takes action which indicates a willingness to forgive the employee for his misconduct, the Board may infer that the employer has condoned the unprotected acts of the employee. In such circumstances, the employer waives his right to refuse reinstatement. [103] In essence, this concept of employer forgiveness, known as the "condonation doctrine," is an attempt to balance the "for cause" discharge rights of an employer and the statutory protection afforded strikers. This is accomplished by requiring that the discharge be directly related to unforgiven striker misconduct,

---

[100] *Accord*, General Electric Co., Battery Prod., Capacitor Dept. v. NLRB, 400 F.2d 713, 721, 69 L.R.R.M. 2081 (5th Cir. 1968), *cert. denied*, 394 U.S. 904, 70 L.R.R.M. 2828 (1969); NLRB v. Laney & Duke Storage Warehouse Co., 369 F.2d 859, 866, 63 L.R.R.M. 2552 (5th Cir. 1966); Rubin Bros. Footwear, Inc., 99 N.L.R.B. 610, 30 L.R.R.M. 1109 (1952), *set aside on other grounds*, 203 F.2d 486, 31 L.R.R.M. 2614 (5th Cir. 1953). *But cf.*, NLRB v. Community Motor Bus Co., 439 F.2d 965, 76 L.R.R.M. 2844 (4th Cir. 1971) (it was undisputed that the employees engaged in misconduct); Pullman Inc., Trailmobile Div., 407 F.2d 1006, 70 L.R.R.M. 2849, 2855-2856 (5th Cir. 1969) (court disbelieved the employer's alleged "honest belief" that misconduct had occurred).

[101] Auto Workers (Udylite Corp.) v. NLRB, 455 F.2d 1357, 79 L.R.R.M. 2031, 2039 (D.C. Cir. 1971); Dallas General Drivers v. NLRB, 389 F.2d 553, 67 L.R.R.M. 2370, 2371 (D.C. Cir. 1968); NLRB v. Plastic Applicators, Inc., 369 F.2d 495, 63 L.R.R.M. 2510, 2511-2512 (5th Cir. 1966); Rubin Bros. Footwear, Inc., 99 N.L.R.B. 610, 611, 30 L.R.R.M. 1109 (1952). *Cf.* Kayser-Roth Hosiery Co. v. NLRB, 447 F.2d 396, 78 L.R.R.M. 2130, 2133 (6th Cir. 1971).

[102] *Supra*, p. 135, 306 U.S. 240, 4 L.R.R.M. 515 (1939).

[103] *E.g.*, Quality Limestone Products, Inc., 153 N.L.R.B. 1009, 59 L.R.R.M. 1589 (1965).

thereby eliminating potential employer abuses of discharge as an antiunion weapon.

Thus, an employer whose employees engage in unprotected activity has a choice: he may terminate their employment because of the misconduct, or he may instead condone the breach by demonstrating a "willingness to forgive the improper aspect of concerted action, to 'wipe the slate clean.' "[104] Furthermore, as the Sixth Circuit stated in *Plasti-Line Inc. v. NLRB*:[105]

> . . . condonation may not be lightly presumed from mere silence or equivocal statements, but must clearly appear from some positive act by an employer indicating forgiveness and an intention of treating the guilty employees as if their conduct had not occurred.

The failure of an employer to state that he would not reemploy an individual engaged in misconduct does not support a presumption that the employer did, in fact, intend to reinstate the employee. For example, mere silence,[106] an equivocal statement,[107] a shrugging of shoulders,[108] or a reply littered with generalities[109] is not the equivalent of an affirmative act of forgiveness. Thus, in *NLRB v. Colonial Press, Inc.*,[110] the court rejected the Board's condonation finding where company representatives solicited striking employees to come in and talk about reemployment, saying "the door is always open." The court construed the company statements as only preliminary invitations to negotiate reemploy-

---

[104] Confectionery & Tobacco Drivers Union, Local 805 v. NLRB, 312 F.2d 108, 113, 52 L.R.R.M. 2163 (2d Cir. 1963). *See also*, Stewart Die Casting Corp. v. NLRB, 114 F.2d 849, 855-856, 6 L.R.R.M. 907 (7th Cir. 1940), *cert. denied*, 312 U.S. 680, 7 L.R.R.M. 326 (1941); NLRB v. Marshall Car Wheel & Foundry Co., 218 F.2d 409, 413, 35 L.R.R.M. 2320 (5th Cir. 1955); Packers Hide Ass'n v. NLRB, 360 F.2d 59, 62, 62 L.R.R.M. 2115 (8th Cir. 1966); NLRB v. Wallick & Schwalm Co., 198 F.2d 477, 484 (3d Cir. 1952); NLRB v. Community Motor Bus Co., 439 F.2d 965, 76 L.R.R.M. 2844, 2847 (4th Cir. 1971); NLRB v. Cast Optics Corp., 458 F.2d 398, 79 L.R.R.M. 3093, 3097 (3d Cir. 1972).

[105] 278 F.2d 482, 487, 46 L.R.R.M. 2291 (6th Cir. 1960).

[106] Packers Hide Ass'n. v. NLRB, 360 F.2d 59, 62 L.R.R.M. 2115 (8th Cir. 1966).

[107] NLRB v. Marshall Car Wheel & Foundry Co., 218 F.2d 409, 35 L.R.R.M. 2320 (5th Cir. 1955).

[108] Merck & Co., 110 N.L.R.B. 67, 34 L.R.R.M. 1603 (1954).

[109] *Cf.* NLRB v. Dorsey Trailers, Inc., 179 F.2d 589, 25 L.R.R.M. 2333 (5th Cir. 1950).

[110] 509 F.2d 850, 88 L.R.R.M. 2337 (8th Cir. 1975), *rev'g* 207 N.L.R.B. 673, 84 L.R.R.M. 1596 (1973).

ment and not as condonation or unconditional offers of reinstatement.

Once the employer has condoned the unprotected aspects of concerted employee conduct, the customary protections of the Act prevail. The employer may not thereafter rely upon such activity as grounds for reprisal. As the Second Circuit explained, the condonation principle rests upon "a clear public interest in the prompt settlement of labor disputes." [111] Having once waived his privilege to discharge or otherwise to take action against the employees for striking, the employer is bound to his decision. If, however, subsequent to the condonation, the employee repeats the very activity which had been condoned, this action may constitute a breach of the "condonation agreement." The employer may once again be entitled to discharge or discipline the employee.[112]

---

[111] Confectionery & Tobacco Dirvers, *supra*, 312 F.2d 108, 113, 52 L.R.R.M. at 2167.

[112] Poloron Products of Indiana, 177 N.L.R.B. No. 54, 71 L.R.R.M. 1577 (1969). In this same vein, the court in Marshall Car Wheel & Foundry Co., observed that condonation entails "the resumption of the *former* relationship between the strikers and respondent. . . ." *See* 218 F.2d 409, 414, 35 L.R.R.M. 2320, 2323 (5th Cir. 1955). (emphasis added).

PART FIVE

Remedying Illegal Domination of, or Assistance to, Labor Organizations by Employers

CHAPTER X

Remedies Designed to Restore the Union's Representational Integrity

According to Section 8(a)(2) of the National Labor Relations Act, it is unlawful for an employer to "dominate or interfere with the formation or administration of any labor organization or contribute financial or other support to it."[1] The purpose of the provision is twofold; it is designed both to force the employer to "refrain from any action which will place him on both sides of the bargaining table,"[2] and to ensure the employees that those who represent them will not become so subject to employer influence that they are unable to give their devotion to the interests of the group they purport to represent.[3] The Act, however, was also intended to increase industrial stability by encouraging a more cooperative spirit between labor and management.[4] In order to achieve these varied ends, the Board has not looked upon

---

[1] 29 U.S.C. § 158(a)(2) (1970).

[2] NLRB v. Mt. Clemens Metal Products Co., 287 F.2d 790, 791, 47 L.R.R.M. 2771, 2772 (6th Cir. 1961); Nassau and Suffolk Contractors Ass'n, 118 N.L.R.B. 174, 40 L.R.R.M. 1146 (1957).

[3] Holland Mfg. Co., 129 N.L.R.B. 776, 47 L.R.R.M. 1067 (1960), *enforced*, 293 F.2d 187, 48 L.R.R.M. 2743 (3d Cir. 1961). *See also* Bisso Towboat Co., 192 N.L.R.B. 885, 78 L.R.R.M. 1230 (1971); Pangles Master Markets, Inc., 190 N.L.R.B. 332, 77 L.R.R.M. 1596 (1971); Brescome Distributor Corp., 179 N.L.R.B. 787, 72 L.R.R.M. 1590 (1969), *enforced sub nom.* Liquor Salesmen, Local 195 v. NLRB, 452 F.2d 1312, 78 L.R.R.M. 2641 (D.C. Cir. 1971). In each of these cases, the Board found a violation where the presence of a supervisory employee on the union negotiating team cast a doubt upon the independence of the labor organization.

[4] NLRB v. Magic Slacks, Inc., 314 F.2d 844, 52 L.R.R.M. 2641 (7th Cir. 1963); Chicago Rawhide Mfg. Co. v. NLRB, 221 F.2d 165, 35 L.R.R.M. 2665 (7th Cir. 1955). For an extensive treatment of the reluctance of the Board to accept the court's concept of permissible cooperation see *New Standards for Domination and Support Under Section 8(a)(2)*, 82 YALE L.J. 510 (1973). *See also* Hertzka & Knowles v. NLRB, 503 F.2d 625, 87 L.R.R.M. 2503 (9th Cir. 1974), *cert. denied,* —— U.S. ——, 90 L.R.R.M. 2554 (1975), and cases cited therein.

domination, interference, support, or partiality as comparable, but instead, it has viewed these violations as differing in degree of unlawful activity and necessitating different remedies.

Because the statute does not define a dominated labor organization, the Board, through adjudication, has fashioned a test identifying certain characteristics which, when present, confirm the existence of domination. In its most classic form, domination occurs where the employer creates, administrates, and finances the labor organization.[5] Similarly, the Board has found domination in cases in which the employer controlled the meetings of the organization, either directly by presiding over and participating in the decisions of the group,[6] for example, or indirectly through funding,[7] dictation of the agenda,[8] or assuming the responsibility for preparing a report of the meeting for the employees.[9]

---

[5] Wahlgreen Magnetics, 132 N.L.R.B. 1613, 48 L.R.R.M. 1542 (1961); NLRB v. General Shoe Corp., 192 F.2d 504, 29 L.R.R.M. 2112 (6th Cir. 1951), *cert. denied*, 343 U.S. 904, 29 L.R.R.M. 2606 (1952); NLRB v. Clark Phonograph Record Co., 176 F.2d 341, 24 L.R.R.M. 2409 (3d Cir. 1949); Bisso Towboat Co., 192 N.L.R.B. 885, 78 L.R.R.M. 1230 (1971); *cf.* NLRB v. Tappan Stove Co., 174 F.2d 1007, 24 L.R.R.M. 2125 (6th Cir. 1949); Alaska Salmon Industry, Inc., 122 N.L.R.B. 1552, 43 L.R.R.M. 1344 (1959). *But cf.* Wayside Press, Inc. v. NLRB, 206 F.2d 862, 32 L.R.R.M. 2625 (9th Cir. 1953), wherein the court held that the mere employer approval or acquiescence in the formation of an inside union did not constitute a violation.

[6] NLRB v. Stow Manufacturing Co., 217 F.2d 900, 35 L.R.R.M. 2210 (2d Cir. 1954); American Enka Corp. v. NLRB, 119 F.2d 60, 8 L.R.R.M. 632 (4th Cir. 1941). *But cf.* Hertzka & Knowles v. NLRB, 503 F.2d 625, 87 L.R.R.M. 2503 (9th Cir. 1974), *rev'g*, 206 N.L.R.B. 191, 84 L.R.R.M. 1556 (1973), *cert. denied*, —— U.S. ——, 90 L.R.R.M. 2554 (1975), where the court found no interference even though a management representative called and opened the committee meetings and voted to set up the committee. The court reasoned that establishing the committee was the idea of an employee, and the employees could easily outvote the management representative.

[7] Thompson Ramo Wooldridge, Inc., 132 N.L.R.B. 993, 48 L.R.R.M. 1470 (1961), *modified and enforced*, 305 F.2d 807, 50 L.R.R.M. 2759 (7th Cir. 1962); NLRB v. Cabot Carbon Co., 360 U.S. 203, 44 L.R.R.M. 2204, 2207 (1959), and cases there cited at n. 14.

[8] NLRB v. Reed Rolled Thread Die Co., 432 F.2d 70, 75 L.R.R.M. 2344 (1st Cir. 1970).

[9] *Id.*, 75 L.R.R.M. at 2344. *See also* Leslie Metal Arts Co., 194 N.L.R.B. 137, 78 L.R.R.M. 1567 (1971), *enforced in part*, 472 F.2d 584, 82 L.R.R.M. 2002 (6th Cir. 1972); City Welding & Mfg. Co., 191 N.L.R.B. 124, 77 L.R.R.M. 1901 (1971), *enforced*, 463 F.2d 254, 80 L.R.R.M. 3057 (3d Cir. 1972), *cert. denied*, 410 U.S. 927, 82 L.R.R.M. 2597 (1973).

Neither the existence of one or more of these conditions, nor an employer's unexercised potential to dominate a labor organization[10] will be found to constitute a violation, per se, of Section 8(a)(2).[11] Rather, the Board will apply a subjective test and look at all the circumstances in order to determine:

> . . . whether the organization exists as the result of a choice freely made by the employees, in their own interests, and without regard to the desires of their employer, or whether the employees formed and supported the organization, rather than some other, because they knew their employer desired it, and feared the consequences if they did not.[12]

The extent of the employer's involvement in the affairs of the union differentiates interference from domination; interference implies that the involvement is not so great as to subject the labor organization to the will of the employer.[13] Interference violations usually involve employer intrusion upon the administration and maintenance of the labor union, not upon its conception. As an example, the Board has found that an employer interfered with the union when company executives and supervisors had retained their union memberships and participated in union affairs despite their promotions from the rank and file.[14]

Section 8(a)(2) of the Act also prohibits an employer from contributing "financial or other support" to a labor organization. Support or assistance has been found in cases in which an employer has granted a union favors such as access to company bul-

---

[10] *See* NLRB v. Wemyss, 212 F.2d 465, 34 L.R.R.M. 2124 (9th Cir. 1954); NLRB v. Sharples Chemicals, Inc., 209 F.2d 645, 33 L.R.R.M. 2438 (6th Cir. 1954).

[11] Coppus Engineering Corp. v. NLRB, 240 F.2d 564, 39 L.R.R.M. 2315 (1st Cir. 1957); Chicago Rawhide Mfg. Co. v. NLRB, 221 F.2d 165, 35 L.R.R.M. 2665 (7th Cir. 1955); *See* Duquesne University of the Holy Ghost, 198 N.L.R.B. No. 117, 81 L.R.R.M. 1091 (1972), for an extensive Board discussion concerning *actual* versus *potential* domination.

[12] NLRB v. Wemyss, 212 F.2d 465, 34 L.R.R.M. 2124 (9th Cir. 1954) and cases cited therein. *Accord* NLRB v. Sharples Chemicals, Inc., 209 F.2d 645, 33 L.R.R.M. 2438 (6th Cir. 1954).

[13] Duquesne University of the Holy Ghost, 198 N.L.R.B. No. 117, 81 L.R.R.M. 1091, 1093-94 (1972).

[14] Nassau and Suffolk Contractors Ass'n, 118 N.L.R.B. 174, 40 L.R.R.M. 1146 (1957).

letin boards and meeting rooms,[15] or the agreement to pay for union administrative and organizational work.[16]

In *Midwest Piping,* the Board established the doctrine that an employer, faced with conflicting legitimate claims of two or more rival unions, violates Section 8(a)(2) if he recognizes or enters into a contract with one of those unions before its right to be recognized has been finally determined under the special election procedures provided by the Act.[17]

Disestablishment and Withdrawal of Recognition Remedies. In order to effectuate the purposes of Section 8(a)(2) and restore the status quo appropriately, the Board has adopted remedies that directly relate to the seriousness of the violation. If the employer's unlawful practices are proven to be so extensive that they constitute domination of a labor organization, the Board will issue an order directing the disestablishment of the dominated union.[18] Compliance to this remedy may require "absolute and public cleavage" between the dominated organization and any successor to it,[19] and that the employer publicly announce

---

[15] Webb Mfg., Inc., 154 N.L.R.B. 827, 60 L.R.R.M. 1041 (1965); Farrington Mfg. Co., 93 N.L.R.B. 1416, 27 L.R.R.M. 1598 (1951); Merrill Transport Co., 141 N.L.R.B. 1089, 52 L.R.R.M. 1452 (1963).

[16] Coppus Engineering Corp. v. NLRB, 240 F.2d 564, 39 L.R.R.M. 2315 (1st Cir. 1957). The 1959 Landrum-Griffin amendments to the National Labor Relations Act also contain several restrictions on employer payments to employee representatives. *See* Section 302 of the Act (29 U.S.C. § 302).

[17] 63 N.L.R.B. 1060, 1071, 17 L.R.R.M. 40 (1945). *See also* Empire State Sugar Co. v. NLRB, 401 F.2d 559, 69 L.R.R.M. 2359 (2d Cir. 1968); NLRB v. National Container Corp., 211 F.2d 525, 536, 33 L.R.R.M. 2661 (2d Cir. 1954); Iowa Beef Packers, Inc. v. NLRB, 331 F.2d 176, 182-183, 56 L.R.R.M. 2071 (8th Cir. 1964); NLRB v. Signal Oil & Gas Co., 304 F.2d 785, 786-787, 50 L.R.R.M. 2505 (5th Cir. 1962). *See generally* Local Lodge, 1424, I.A.M. v. NLRB, 362 U.S. 411, 412-424, 45 L.R.R.M. 3212 (1960); Int'l Ladies Garment Workers Union v. NLRB (Bernhard-Altman Texas Corp.), 366 U.S. 731, 737-739, 48 L.R.R.M. 2251 (1961); Playskool Inc. v. NLRB, 477 F.2d 66, 82 L.R.R.M. 2916 (7th Cir. 1973).

[18] Carpenter Steel Co., 76 N.L.R.B. 670, 671-672, 21 L.R.R.M. 1232, 1234 (1948); *But cf.* NLRB v. Mt. Clemens Metal Products Co., 287 F.2d 790, 791, 47 L.R.R.M. 2771, 2772 (6th Cir. 1961); *See* NLRB v. District 50, United Mine Workers (Bowman Transportation, Inc.) 355 U.S. 453, 41 L.R.R.M. 2449 (1958), in which a Board order directing the employer not to recognize the union until certified was set aside by the court because the noncomplying assisted union was not eligible for a Board certification and, therefore, the Board order denied the employees the opportunity ever to select the union as their representative.

[19] Dade Drydock Corp., 58 N.L.R.B. 833, 15 L.R.R.M. 67 (1944); Western Union v. NLRB, 113 F.2d 992, 6 L.R.R.M. 753, 757 (2d Cir. 1940), *modif'g and enf'g,* 17 N.L.R.B. 34, 5 L.R.R.M. 292 (1939).

his intention to cease bargaining with the union.[20] When the misconduct involves either widespread interference or support, but falls short of actual domination, the Board has ordered the employer to withdraw recognition unless or until the union has been certified by the Board and to cease effectuating any contract with the union,[21] if the violation has tainted the contract.

When *Midwest Piping* violations have occurred, the Board usually will order the employer to cease recognizing the union until it is certified. Administrative Law Judges have also recommended that the Board mandate an additional remedy which would prohibit a union with an extensive history of Section 8(b)(2) and (1)(A) violations from representing *any* employee not already represented by it for a period of three years, unless and until it is certified by the Board. Further recommendations suggest that the union be required to cease from soliciting membership application cards unless they contain statements acknowledging the union's former violation of employees' statutory rights.[22] The Board, however, has refused to grant the expanded remedies recommended in those cases. Thus, in *Amalgamated Local Union 355 (Russell Motors),*[23] the Board, with court approval, ruled that such remedies were punitive, exceeding the purely remedial nature of proper Board remedies, in that their provisions were not designed solely to remedy the particular unfair labor practices committed in the instant case. In this case, the Board was found to have contemplated future violations of the Act by including among its remedies a broad order to Local 355 not to cause any employer to restrain or coerce any em-

---

[20] Kansas City Power & Light Co. v. NLRB, 111 F.2d 340, 6 L.R.R.M. 938 (8th Cir. 1940); NLRB v. Tappan Stove Co., 174 F.2d 1007, 24 L.R.R.M. 2125 (6th Cir. 1949).

[21] *See e.g.,* Wyco Metal Products Co., 183 N.L.R.B. 901, 74 L.R.R.M. 1411 (1970); Webb Mfg., Inc., 154 N.L.R.B. 827, 60 L.R.R.M. 1041 (1965); Sears, Roebuck & Co., 110 N.L.R.B. 226, 34 L.R.R.M. 1630 (1954). NLRB v. Revere Metal Art Co., 280 F.2d 96, 100, 46 L.R.R.M. 2452 (2d Cir. 1960); NLRB v. Sunset House, 415 F.2d 545, 547, 72 L.R.R.M. 2283 (9th Cir. 1969).

[22] *See* Raymond Buick, Inc., 173 N.L.R.B. 1292, 70 L.R.R.M. 1106 (1968), *as modified,* 182 N.L.R.B. 504, 74 L.R.R.M. 1137 (1970); Vanella Buick Opel, Inc., 194 N.L.R.B. 744, 79 L.R.R.M. 1090 (1971); Amalgamated Local Union 355 (Russell Motors, Inc.), 198 N.L.R.B. No. 58, 80 L.R.R.M. 1757 (1972). *Cf.* Teamster Local 901 (F.F. Instrument Corp.), 210 N.L.R.B. No. 153, 86 L.R.R.M. 1286, 1288 (1974).

[23] 198 N.L.R.B. No. 58, 80 L.R.R.M. 1757 (1972), *enf'd* 481 F.2d 966, 83 L.R.R.M. 2849 (2d Cir. 1973).

ployee in the exercise of his Section 7 rights. Under the broad
order, future violations would be subject to contempt of court
proceedings and make available powerful judicial remedies
which are beyond the purely remedial nature of Board orders.

Monetary and Reimbursement Remedies. When the Board
finds, in the context of Section 8(a)(2) violation, that the employees have paid initiation fees, dues, or other financial obligations related to union membership, it will order that the
employer [24] or the union,[25] or both jointly and severally,[26] must
reimburse the employees for such payments.[27] Similarly, where
the employees have been subject to an illegal union security
agreement with a check-off clause, reimbursement of such dues
will also be ordered,[28] when, in accordance with such a provision,
the employees were forced to support and contribute to that union
to retain their jobs.[29] Where, however, employees are not bound
by any mandatory union membership clause, and willingly
consent to pay their union dues, the Board and courts have

---

[24] NLRB v. Revere Metal Art Co., 280 F.2d 96, 46 L.R.R.M. 2452 (2d Cir.
1960); NLRB v. Hi-Temp, Inc., 503 F.2d 583, 87 L.R.R.M. 2437 (7th Cir.
1974). Virginia Electric & Power Co., v. NLRB, 319 U.S. 533, 12 L.R.R.M.
739 (1943); Bernhardt Bros. Tugboat Service, Inc. v. NLRB, 328 F.2d 757, 55
L.R.R.M. 2550 (7th Cir. 1964); NLRB v. Raymond Buick, Inc., 445 F.2d 644,
77 L.R.R.M. 2728 (2d Cir. 1971), NLRB v. Cadillac Wire Corp., 290 F.2d
261, 48 L.R.R.M. 2149 (2d Cir. 1961).

[25] The reimbursement remedy is also known as the *Brown-Olds Remedy*. See
Plumbing and Pipefitters' Local 231 (Brown-Olds Plumbing & Heating Corp.),
115 N.L.R.B. 594, 37 L.R.R.M. 1360 (1956); NLRB v. Carpenters Local 111,
278 F.2d 823, 46 L.R.R.M. 2253 (1st Cir. 1960); Gasoline Retailers Ass'n of
Metropolitan Chicago, 210 N.L.R.B. No. 58, 86 L.R.R.M. 1011 (1974). *But
cf.* Local 60, Carpenters v. NLRB, 365 U.S. 651, 47 L.R.R.M. 2900 (1961)
which held the *Brown-Olds Remedy* inapplicable to dues which were paid
willingly. For a further discussion of NLRB orders to reimburse illegally
exacted union dues, fees and fines, see Chapter VII, *supra*, pp. 96-100.

[26] NLRB v. Cadillac Wire Corp., 290 F.2d 261, 48 L.R.R.M. 2149 (2d
Cir. 1961); NLRB v. Hi-Temp, Inc., 503 F.2d 583, 87 L.R.R.M. 2437 (7th Cir.
1974).

[27] Rival union requests for organizing expenses incurred as a result of
employer violations of Section 8(a)(2) have been denied by the Board. See
Amalgamated Local Union 355 (Russell Motors), 198 N.L.R.B. No. 58, 80
L.R.R.M. 1757 (1972), *enf'd*, 481 F.2d 996, 83 L.R.R.M. 2849 (2d Cir. 1973).

[28] *See* the cases cited, *supra*, footnote 24.

[29] Local 60, Carpenters v. NLRB, 365 U.S. 651, 47 L.R.R.M. 2900 (1961);
NLRB v. Hi-Temp, Inc., 503 F.2d 583, 87 L.R.R.M. 2437, 2439 (7th Cir.
1974); Virginia Electric & Power Co. v. NLRB, 319 U.S. 533, 540, 12 L.R.R.M.
739 (1943).

refused to order reimbursement.[30] Reimbursement has been limited to those employees who were coerced into signing check-off authorizations, and employees who freely consented to check-off were not compensated for dues paid to the union.[31] At least one court has ruled that reimbursement of illegally checked-off dues would not be ordered where the Board had subsequently certified the union as the employees' representative.[32]

CONCLUDING REMARKS

Illegal employer domination of, or interference with, a labor organization may entail various degrees of improper involvement. NLRB remedies for such violations are graduated to reflect differing degrees of employer interference. Such remedies are designed to ensure that labor organizations properly reflect the needs and desires of their members, and not those of the employer. Where necessary, NLRB remedies will also make union members whole for dues or fees which were unwillingly paid to an improperly dominated or assisted labor organization. Clearly, then, the remedies described in this chapter are designed to carry out the objectives of Section 1 of the National Labor Relations Act which gives employees the right to a "free" choice in selecting their bargaining representatives.

---

[30] NLRB v. Shedd-Brown Mfg. Co., 213 F.2d 163, 34 L.R.R.M. 2278 (7th Cir. 1954) ; *cf.* Remington Arms Co., 62 N.L.R.B. 611, 16 L.R.R.M. 199 (1945).

[31] Clement Bros. Co., 165 N.L.R.B. 698, 65 L.R.R.M. 1437 (1967), *enf'd,* NLRB v. Clement Bros., 407 F.2d 1027, 70 L.R.R.M. 2721 (5th Cir. 1969).

[32] *See* NLRB v. Englander Co., 237 F.2d 599, 38 L.R.R.M. 2765 (3d Cir. 1956).

PART SIX

Remedies Involving the Establishment and Breach of the Good Faith Bargaining Obligation

Bargaining Orders to Remedy Employer Unfair Labor Practices— The Gissel Decision

Section 9(a) of the National Labor Relations Act [1] states that:

> Representatives designated or selected for the purposes of collective bargaining by the majority of the employees in a unit appropriate for such purposes, shall be the exclusive representative of all the employees in such unit for the purposes of collective bargaining in respect to rates of pay, wages, hours of employment or other conditions of employment. [2]

The Act, furthermore, makes it an unfair labor practice for an employer "to refuse to bargain collectively with the representatives of his employees. . . ." [3] Under the circumstances of an unlawful refusal to bargain, the NLRB is empowered to issue "an order requiring such person to cease and desist from such unfair labor practice, and to take such affirmative action . . . as will effectuate the policies of this Act." [4] Frequently the Board has issued bargaining orders against employers in seeking to remedy such violations.

A critical and controversial area involving the application of the NLRB's bargaining order remedy lies in the establishment of a bargaining relationship between an employer and union. Specifically, there is continuing litigation and concern over the circumstances under which an employer may be ordered to *recognize and bargain with* a labor organization claiming representation of the majority work force. The controversy stems largely from the

---

[1] 49 Stat. 449 (1935), *as amended*, 29 U.S.C. §§ 151-168 (1970).

[2] *Id.* at § 159(a).

[3] *Id.* at § 158(a)(5).

[4] *Id.* at § 160(c).

process by which a union has been "designated or selected" as the collective bargaining representative for the employees.

Board certification of a union based upon the results of a representation election [5] historically has been the preferred method for determining the exclusive bargaining agent,[6] resulting in the employer's obligation to extend recognition to the union for collective bargaining purposes. Clearly, however, other procedures are available to establish the bargaining relationship.[7] Efforts by the NLRB to enforce the right of workers to select union representation have been challenged when union majority status evolved by means other than the formal certification process.

The Supreme Court in *NLRB v. Gissel Packing Co.*[8] affirmed Board use of the bargaining order as an authorized remedy in situations where employer unfair labor practices have undermined the union's majority status and have made a fair representation election improbable. In addition, the Court resolved two other basic issues: (1) the duty to bargain can arise without a Board-conducted election; (2) union authorization cards, when obtained from a majority of employees without misrepresentation or coercion, are sufficiently reliable to provide a valid alternate route to obtaining majority status. *Gissel* established certain criteria to determine the appropriateness of the bargaining order based on an appraisal of the effects of various unfair labor practices on the election "laboratory conditions." [9] *Gissel* also charges the NLRB with issuing remedial orders consistent with these criteria.

The purpose of Chapters XI and XII is to evaluate the use of the bargaining order remedy under the framework of the *Gissel* principles as they have been interpreted and amended. Specific considerations in this analysis include: the issuance of a bargaining order based solely upon the showing of a card majority; the validity of the Board's analysis of the causal relationship between employer misconduct and the election process; the retroactive effect of *Gissel* bargaining orders; union misconduct as grounds for denial of a bargaining order; and the impact of changed circumstances upon the order.

---

[5] *Id.* at § 159.

[6] NLRB v. Gissel Packing Co., 395 U.S. 575, 596, 71 L.R.R.M. 2481 (1969); Aaron Bros., 158 N.L.R.B. 1077, 62 L.R.R.M. 1160 (1966).

[7] United Mines Workers v. Arkansas Oak Flooring, 351 U.S. 62, 37 L.R.R.M. 2828 (1956); Franks Bros. v. NLRB, 321 U.S. 702, 14 L.R.R.M. 591 (1944).

[8] 395 U.S. 575, 71 L.R.R.M. 2481 (1969).

[9] General Shoe Corp., 77 N.L.R.B. 124, 21 L.R.R.M. 1337 (1948).

ESTABLISHING A BARGAININ RELATIONSHIP ABSENT EMPLOYER UNFAIR LABOR PRACTICES

Several options exist for an employer when a union demands recognition and bargaining in its effort to organize a particular unit of employees. The company may extend voluntary recognition to the union solely on the basis of a majority strength shown by signed authorization cards,[10] polling of employee sentiment,[11] or other evidence. In such situations, reliance upon the Board's election machinery is not necessary. The parties are free to bargain, and the union obtains status as the uncertified agent of the employees.

Without a willingness by the employer to offer voluntary recognition to the union, either party may petition the NLRB for an election.[12] From the employer's standpoint, this option provides the opportunity to test the measure of pro-union sentiment and to prepare a campaign of argument and persuasion against unionization. If a majority of the eligible workers in the unit vote affirmatively for representation in a fair and free election, the Board then will certify the union as the exclusive bargaining representative. Under the Wagner Act,[13] the NLRB was enabled to certify a union on the basis of secret ballot elections or "any other suitable method." The Taft-Hartley Amendments in 1947 provided, under Section 9, that certification could be obtained only by a representation election.

Once the union has become voluntarily recognized or Board certified, the employer is then obligated to maintain recognition and to bargain with the union. The failure to do so may lead to a Section 8(a)(5) violation. It is important to note briefly certain privileges that certification allows the union.[14] A certified union is protected for a reasonable period of time, usually at least one year, from the claim that it no longer represents a majority of the employees.[15] Similarly, the Act provides that for a period of twelve

---

[10] Extending recognition to a union which in fact lacked majority status despite apparent evidence of support would constitute a violation of Sections 8(a)(1) and 8(a)(2) of the Act. *See e.g.,* Int'l Ladies Garment Workers v. NLRB, 366 U.S. 731, 48 L.R.R.M. 2251 (1961). *See also* Chapter X, *supra.*

[11] Struksnes Construction Co., 165 N.L.R.B. 1062, 65 L.R.R.M. 1385 (1967).

[12] *See* 29 U.S.C. §§ 159(c)(1)(A) and (B).

[13] 49 Stat. 449 (1935).

[14] *See* General Box Co., 82 N.L.R.B. 678, 23 L.R.R.M. 1589, 1590 (1949).

[15] Brooks v. NLRB, 348 U.S. 96, 35 L.R.R.M. 2158 (1954).

months following a valid election, no other election may be held.[16] The Act protects a certified union against recognitional or organizational picketing by a rival union.[17] Also, a certified union, under Section 8(b)(4)(D), is free from certain restrictions placed on concerted activity during work assignment disputes.[18]

GISSEL BARGAINING ORDERS TO ESTABLISH BARGAINING RELATIONSHIPS

Under the conditions either of voluntary recognition or certification, a bargaining relationship is formed and the parties become subject to the provisions of the Act and to the remedial powers of the Board. Different issues arise, however, concerning the use of the bargaining order where initial recognition of the union, absent an election, is ordered by the Board. In appropriate circumstances, such orders are issued to remedy employer unfair labor practices which have destroyed the possibility of holding a fair election. A bargaining order, however, is never preferable to a fair election:

> Since a bargaining order dispenses with the necessity of a prior secret election, there is a possibility that the imposition of such an order may unnecessarily undermine the freedom of choice that Congress wanted to guarantee to the employees, and thus frustrate rather than effectuate the policies of the Act.[19]

The Supreme Court's *Gissel* decision [20] clarified the question of the appropriateness of an NLRB-issued bargaining order where majority support for the union has been shown by means other than a Board-conducted election, but where employer unfair labor practices have prevented a fair election. The Court outlined the situations under which union authorization cards would serve as the basis for establishing majority status and thereby bind an employer to recognize and bargain with the union. Thus, *Gissel* approved an NLRB remedy designed to permit employees to select a collective bargaining representative when employer conduct taints the election atmosphere. Of course, the unfair labor prac-

---

[16] 29 U.S.C. § 159(c)(3).

[17] 29 U.S.C. § 158(b)(7)(C). However, § 158(b)(7)(A) extends similar protection to a noncertified union lawfully recognized by the employer, as long as "a question concerning representation may not appropriately be raised under Section 9(c) of this Act...."

[18] General Box Co., 82 N.L.R.B. 678, 23 L.R.R.M. 1589, 1590 (1949).

[19] NLRB v. Flomatic Corp., 347 F.2d 74, 78, 59 L.R.R.M. 2535, 2538 (2d Cir. 1965).

[20] NLRB v. Gissel Packing Co., 395 U.S. 575, 71 L.R.R.M. 2481 (1969).

tices committed by the employer, such as discriminatory discharges, coercive conduct, and improper threats, are also still remedied traditionally by backpay awards, reinstatement, and notice posting.

The *Gissel* decision approved an approach which the Board had adopted to replace the "good faith doubt" test, found unworkable. Cases prior to *Gissel* dealing with the issuance of bargaining order remedies evolved from the *Joy Silk* doctrine which stated, in effect, that an employer could refuse to bargain with a union if he had "good faith doubt" of its majority status, and that he could insist upon an election.[21] A bargaining order would issue upon the finding of a lack of good faith doubt, as shown by employer unfair labor practices designed to undermine the union's majority strength. In the *Aaron Brothers*[22] decision the Board modified *Joy Silk* to provide that the burden of proving bad faith lay with the General Counsel. The employer did not have to provide a reason for rejecting the union's majority claim, and he "will not be held to have violated his bargaining obligation . . . simply because he refuses to rely upon cards, rather than an election, as the method for determining the union's majority."[23]

The Board's brief to the Supreme Court in *Gissel* was based generally on the *Aaron Brothers* approach.[24] But at the *Gissel* oral argument, counsel for the Board announced that the *Joy Silk* doctrine had been abandoned, that the employer's good faith was now largely "irrelevant," and that the "key to the issuance of a bargaining order is the commission of serious unfair labor practices that interfere with the election processes and tend to preclude the holding of a fair election."[25]

The Supreme Court formulated criteria for issuing bargaining orders which vary according to the scope and degree of employer unlawful conduct. First, *Gissel* identified the "exceptional" case, characterized by "outrageous" and "pervasive" unfair labor practices with coercive effects that cannot be eliminated by traditional remedies, thereby destroying the possibility of a fair election.[26]

---

[21] Joy Silk Mills, Inc., 85 N.L.R.B. 1263, 24 L.R.R.M. 1548 (1949), *enf'd*, 185 F.2d 732, 27 L.R.R.M. 2012 (D.C. Cir. 1950), *cert. denied*, 341 U.S. 914, 27 L.R.R.M. 2633 (1951).

[22] 158 N.L.R.B. 1077, 62 L.R.R.M. 1160 (1966).

[23] *Id.* at 1078.

[24] 395 U.S. at 594.

[25] *Id.*

[26] 395 U.S. at 613-614.

In such a case the remedy could be issued without proof that the
employer had violated Section 8(a)(5) or that a bargaining demand had been made and unlawfully rejected.[27]

The second situation found appropriate for a bargaining order
was in "less extraordinary cases marked by less pervasive practices which nonetheless still have the tendency to undermine
majority strength and impede the election process." [28] The Court
emphasized that in fashioning an appropriate remedy for less than
outrageous violations, the Board should consider that ascertaining
employee choice is as important as deterring employer misbehavior.[29] The Court stated that the Board could take into consideration:

> . . . the extensiveness of an employer's unfair practices in terms of
> their past effect on election conditions and the likelihood of their
> recurrence in the future. If the Board finds that the possibility of
> erasing the effects of past practices and of ensuring a fair election
> (or a fair rerun) by the use of traditional remedies, though present,
> is slight and that employee sentiment once expressed through cards
> would, on balance, be better protected by a bargaining order, then
> such an order should issue.[30]

To fulfill this second *Gissel* category, proof that at some point in
time the union possessed majority status is generally required. The
Board, however, may issue the bargaining order without proof that
the union has been able to maintain its majority status,[31] or even
in cases where the evidence clearly shows that the union, "which
once had possession of cards from a majority of the employees,
represents only a minority when the bargaining order is entered." [32]

---

[27] *Id.* As the Board stated recently, there is nothing in *Gissel* which conditions a bargaining order remedy upon a demand for bargaining of the union.
Ludwig Fish & Produce, Inc., 220 N.L.R.B. No. 160, 90 L.R.R.M. 1348, 1349
(1975).

[28] 395 U.S. at 614.

[29] 395 U.S. at 613-614.

[30] *Id.*

[31] 395 U.S. at 614. *See e.g.*, Grismac Corp., 205 N.L.R.B. 1108, 84 L.R.R.M.
1256 (1973), where a bargaining order was denied because the authorization
card count indicated less than a majority of the unit.

[32] 395 U.S. at 610. *See also*, Peerless of America, Inc. v. NLRB, 484 F.2d
1108, 1116, 83 L.R.R.M. 3000, 3006 (7th Cir. 1974), where it was held sufficient for the union to have had a card majority on the date it sought recognition. It was not necessary for the union to retain the majority support up to
the time of the scheduled election.

In a third class of cases, characterized by "minor or less extensive" violations and minimal interference with election conditions, the Board may not use the bargaining order remedy to establish the bargaining relationship.[33]

Application of the criteria established in *Gissel* was left to the Board. Certain questions related to the use of the bargaining order were not resolved, as exemplified in the following sections. In addition, the Court seemed to acknowledge the potential difficulty in dealing with graduated unfair labor practices necessitating different Board-ordered remedies.[34] The following sections analyze these *Gissel*-related issues.

Employer Insistence that the Union Prove its Majority in an Election—The Linden Lumber Decision.

The Court in *Gissel* failed to deal with the appropriateness of a bargaining order in circumstances where there had been no impairment of election "laboratory conditions" by the employer. It specifically declined a ruling upon the issue of:

> . . . whether, absent election interference by an employer's unfair labor practices, he may obtain an election only if he petitions for one himself; *whether, if he does not, he must bargain with a card majority if the Union chooses not to seek an election. . . .*[35]

In *Gissel,* the union had urged the position that:

> If the employer does not himself petition for an election . . . he must recognize the Union regardless of his good or bad faith and regardless of his other unfair labor practices, and should be ordered to bargain if the cards were in fact validly obtained.[36]

In effect, the union was seeking to establish authorization cards as a "freely interchangeable substitute for elections." [37] The Court properly declined to rule on this broader question since the facts in *Gissel* involved employer unfair labor practices prohibiting an election order.

Nearly six years later, in *Linden Lumber v. NLRB,*[38] the Supreme Court addressed the issue of whether proof of majority status as

---

[33] 395 U.S. at 615.

[34] *Id.* at 616-617.

[35] *Id.* at 601, n.18. (emphasis added).

[36] *Id.* at 595.

[37] *Id.* at 601, n. 18.

[38] 419 U.S. 301, 87 L.R.R.M. 3236 (1974).

established, for example, by signed authorization cards will warrant use of the bargaining order against an employer who has declined recognition to the union, has refused to petition for an election, but has committed no unfair labor practices dissipating the union's status or preventing an election. In *Linden Lumber,* "the issue thus presented [was] whether cards provide a test of employee sentiment so objective and workable that a card majority requires a bargaining order when neither the employer nor the union has petitioned for an election." [39] The Court held that under such circumstances the union has the burden of filing for an election, and an employer does not violate Section 8(a)(5) by refusing to recognize the union on the basis of a card majority.

The appeals to the Supreme Court originated from the Board cases, *Linden Lumber Co.* and *Wilder Mfg. Co.,*[40] in which unions demanded employer recognition. The companys' refusals were unaccompanied by independent unfair labor practices that may have interfered with representation election proceedings. The unions filed Section 8(a)(5) violation charges and sought Board-ordered recognition as part of the remedy. The NLRB declared that refusal to accept evidence of employee majority support, other than the certified results of an election, did not constitute an unlawful refusal to bargain.

These Board decisions represented a reassessment of prior policy which provided that a bargaining obligation arose without an election where the employer through convincing evidence had "independent knowledge" of a union's majority status.[41] The Supreme Court in *Gissel* had indicated that examples of "convincing evidence" of majority support might come from "a union-called strike or strike vote, or possession of cards signed by a majority of the employees." [42] The NLRB now sought to limit the

---

[39] 83 YALE L.J. 1689, 1695-96 (1974).

[40] Linden Lumber Div., Summer & Co., 190 N.L.R.B. 718, 77 L.R.R.M. 1305 (1971) and Wilder Manufacturing Co., 198 N.L.R.B. No. 123, 81 L.R.R.M. 1039 (1972). (Second Supplemental Decision and Order).

[41] The "independent knowledge" doctrine was discussed in the *Gissel* case: "When confronted by a recognition demand based on possession of cards allegedly signed by a majority of his employees, an employer need not grant recognition immediately, but may, *unless he has knowledge independently* of the cards that *the union has a majority,* decline the union's request and insist on an election, either by requesting the union to file an election petition or by filing such a petition himself under §9(c)(1)(B)." 395 U.S. at 591 (emphasis added.) *See also* pp. 169-171, *infra.*

[42] 395 U.S. at 597.

"independent knowledge" doctrine to situations such as where "the employer having agreed to abide by the results of a private poll of his employees, subsequently reneged on that agreement when the poll confirmed the union's claim of majority." [43] In all other situations, the Board felt forced to assess subjective factors such as intent and the state of employer "independent knowledge." This was deemed inconsistent with *Gissel's* abandonment of the "good faith doubt of majority status" test.

The District of Columbia Court of Appeals in review reversed and remanded [44] the Board's decision. In sum, the D.C. Circuit held that "if 'independent knowledge' is to be restricted, some alternative must be put in its place to prevent an employer's deliberate flouting and disregard of union cards without rhyme or reason." [45] Despite any inherent difficulties the Board faced in divining employer independent knowledge, the court was unwilling, in effect, to force the union to file a petition for an election in order to obtain recognition.

As an alternative to the independent knowledge test, the court of appeals, advocated gauging the employer's willingness to file for an election. Prior to the policy shift in *Linden Lumber,* when investigating Section 8(a)(5) violations, the Board had used the employer's willingness as a test of his good faith doubt of the union's majority status.[46] The Board later abandoned this approach because of the difficulty in judging the employer's willingness; the problems generated by the good faith test were simply renewed.[47] The court, on the other hand, stated that "[i]t is conceivable that a restriction of 'independent knowledge' to an agreement to abide by an authentication would be acceptable, if the employer was required to evidence his good faith doubt as to majority status, by petitioning for an election." [48] The court bolstered its view by

---

[43] Wilder Mfg. Co., 198 N.L.R.B. No. 123, ——, 81 L.R.R.M. 1039, —— (1972).

[44] Truck Drivers Local 413 v. NLRB, 487 F.2d 1099, 84 L.R.R.M. 2177 (D.C. Cir. 1973).

[45] *Id.* at 1113, 84 L.R.R.M. 2177, 2187.

[46] Wilder Mfg. Co., 185 N.L.R.B. 175, 75 L.R.R.M. 1023 (1970). The factors were: the employer did not file a petition; he did not urge or suggest that the employees or the union do so; and he did not indicate a *willingness* to participate in a representation election.

[47] 198 N.L.R.B. No. 123, 81 L.R.R.M. 1039, 1040 (1972).

[48] Truck Drivers Local 413 v. NLRB, 487 F.2d 1099, 1111, 84 L.R.R.M. 2177, 2186 (D.C. Cir. 1973).

saying that authorization cards create "sufficient probability" of union majority status that an employer who doubts the union's status is obligated to petition for an election in order to avoid a violation of the Act.[49]

The Supreme Court, by a 5-4 vote, narrowly overruled the court of appeals and endorsed the Board's rule. The Court could find no basis for placing the burden of petitioning for an election on the employer who is unwilling to accept authorization cards as evidence of majority status. Furthermore, the Court found merit in the Board's contention that it was assessing subjective factors when examining an employer's reasons for rejecting the union's request for recognition. While the majority did not rule that authorization cards "are wholly unreliable as an indication of employee support of the union," it acknowledged that sufficient factors existed to undermine card use as "convincing evidence" of majority status.[50] The Supreme Court agreed that the union must initiate the election procedure when its demands for recognition are rejected. The majority did not rule upon whether or not a union could establish a bargaining obligation where an employer failed to honor an agreement to determine majority status by means of a poll, card check, or other legally appropriate method.[51]

The four dissenting justices in *Linden Lumber* argued that legislative history, together with appropriate sections of the Act, required an employer, when approached by a union possessing convincing evidence of majority support, to take some affirmative action. It listed four alternatives available to the employer: immediately recognizing the union; filing an election petition; agreeing to an expedited consent election upon the filing of a union petition; or refusing to recognize the union at the risk of committing an unfair labor practice.[52] The majority and the dissenting minority critically departed upon the issue of developing a workable measurement of majority support to trigger an employer's obligation to recognize and bargain with the union. There was no dispute that the duty to bargain may arise in instances where there has been no certification.

The dissenting opinion emphasized that the Board was obligated to outline certain standards which would define such "convincing

---

[49] *Id.*

[50] 419 U.S. 301, 306, 87 L.R.R.M. 3236, 3237-3238.

[51] *Id.* at 310, 87 L.R.R.M. 3236, 3239, n. 10. In both *Linden Lumber* and *Wilder*, the Board found that no such voluntary agreement had been entered.

[52] *Id.* at 312-313, 87 L.R.R.M. 3236, 3240.

evidence." The dissent declined to suggest any factors that might apply, stipulating that the Board was best qualified to do this.[53] The Board in *Linden Lumber,* however, essentially determined that its administrative expertise did not enable it "to determine the circumstances under which an employer must take evidence of majority support as 'convincing.' "[54]

Employer Independent Knowledge of the Union's Majority

As shown in *Linden Lumber,* the Supreme Court majority developed the rule that "unless an employer has engaged in an unfair labor practice that impairs the electoral process, a union with authorization cards purporting to represent a majority of the employees which is refused recognition, has the burden of taking the next step in invoking the Board's procedure."[55] The Court specifically noted that a union would not be under the same burden to file for an election if an employer were to breach an agreement permitting the determination of majority status in some way other than by a Board-conducted election,[56] and cited as an example the Board's *Snow & Sons* decision,[57] discussed below. Also not addressed in *Linden Lumber* is the obligation of an employer to bargain with a union where the employer has initiated his own means of verifying the union's majority status. Such independent knowledge may be gained through methods such as unilateral polling, interrogation, or card checks.[58] The following discussion deals with the Board's present policy of requiring an employer with such independent knowledge to bargain with the labor organization claiming to represent his employees.

In *Snow & Sons,* the Board held that an employer who had agreed to, and did not question the accuracy of, a check of employee union authorization cards could not thereafter insist upon an election. The employer reneged on his agreement after a card check by an impartial party established the validity of the union's

---

[53] *Id.* at 314, 87 L.R.R.M. at 3241, n. 5.

[54] *Id.* at 314, 87 L.R.R.M. at 3241.

[55] 419 U.S. at 310, 87 L.R.R.M. at 3239.

[56] *Id.* at 310, n. 10.

[57] 134 N.L.R.B. 709, 49 L.R.R.M. 1228 (1961), *enf'd,* 308 F.2d 687, 51 L.R.R.M. 2199 (9th Cir. 1962).

[58] *See e.g.,* R & M Electric Supply Co., 200 N.L.R.B. 603, 81 L.R.R.M. 1553 (1972).

claim.[59] The result was similar in *Redmond Plastics, Inc.*[60] where the employer made his own validation of the signatures on the cards and acknowledged that the union represented a clear majority. The company afterwards attempted to argue that it sought advice of labor counsel prior to executing a recognition agreement. Based upon that advice, the company then insisted on an election. The Board, however, felt that the employer's initial willingness to accept the cards as proof of the majority and to recognize the union could not be overlooked because of his intervening doubt. More recently, the employer in *Harding Glass Industries, Inc.*[61] argued that although he had agreed to a card check at the insistence of the union's representative, he had understood that the results would not be binding before he could reach his attorney for advice. The Board rejected this contention. It found that the company had eliminated any doubt it may have had regarding the union's strength by sending a representative to participate in the card checks.

In determining that the obligation to bargain exists, the Board need not find that the employer has expressly agreed with the union to resolve the issue of representation. The Board attempts to determine if the employer has obtained independent confirmation of the union's majority position. In *Nation-Wide Plastics Co.*,[62] the company held a secret ballot election to ascertain if the employees wanted a union—the result was eight to three for the union. The employer then requested an NLRB election, claiming doubt of the union's status. The Board found its *Linden Lumber* decision inapplicable and stated:

> An employer cannot disclaim the results simply because it finds them distasteful. Having undertaken a determination which he could, under proper circumstances, insist be made by the Board, he may not thereafter repudiate the route he himself chose.[63]

The NLRB reached a similar result in *Sullivan Electric Co.*,[64] where the employer asked the workers individually if they had

---

[59] *See also*, Summersville Industrial Equip. Co., 197 N.L.R.B. 731, 80 L.R.R.M. 1664 (1972).

[60] 187 N.L.R.B. 487, 76 L.R.R.M. 1035 (1970).

[61] 216 N.L.R.B. No. 52, 88 L.R.R.M. 1506 (1975).

[62] 197 N.L.R.B. 996, 81 L.R.R.M. 1036 (1972).

[63] *Id.* at 996, 81 L.R.R.M. 1036, 1038.

[64] 199 N.L.R.B. 809, 81 L.R.R.M. 1313 (1972), *enf'd* in Sullivan Electric Co. v. NLRB, 479 F.2d 1270, 83 L.R.R.M. 2513 (6th Cir. 1973).

signed authorization cards. The employer was held to be bound by the results of that poll which showed a union majority and, therefore, he could not decline the union's request to bargain.[65] Thus, a unilateral undertaking by the employer to test the extent of union support can result in the same employer bargaining obligation as can an agreement for resolving the question of majority status made by both parties.

Application of the Gissel Criteria to Determine the Impact of Employer Misconduct on the Election Atmosphere

Since the Supreme Court's *Gissel* decision, there has been a profusion of NLRB and court decisions covering myriad factual situations. Although an exhaustive analysis of the Board's application of the *Gissel* doctrine would be inappropriate here, given the introductory nature of this study, the following discussion provides examples of the Board's handling of *Gissel* issues in typical factual contexts. Where employer violations are egregious, the Board has issued bargaining orders without noticeable court interference. In cases involving less serious unfair labor practices, however (i.e., *Gissel* category two), the Board has been cautioned several times by the courts that it must thoroughly analyze the impact of the employer's violations on the chance of holding a fair election. Without such an analysis, the courts quite properly have denied enforcement of the bargaining order, remanded the case to the Board for further consideration, or substituted their own analyses in order to save the time lost by a remand to the Board.

Gissel Category One: "Outrageous" and "Pervasive" violations

In *Gissel*, the Court decribed a category of "exceptional" cases which are marked by "outrageous" and "pervasive" unfair labor practices, and stated that a bargaining order would be appropriate if these violations are of:

---

[65] *See also,* E. S. Merriman & Sons, 219 N.L.R.B. No. 117, 90 L.R.R.M. 1161 (1975) (interrogation) ; Schreiber Freight Lines, Inc., 204 N.L.R.B. 1162, 83 L.R.R.M. 1612 (1973). *Cf.* R & M Electric Supply Co., 200 N.L.R.B. 603 81 L.R.R.M. 1553 (1972). (The Board determined that the fact that the employer asked two workers about their card signing did not constitute a poll revealing majority status.) *And see* Tennessee Shell Co., 212 N.L.R.B. No. 24, 86 L.R.R.M. 1704 (1974) (no violation because employer's knowledge of union's majority was not obtained solely from employer's interrogation of employees).

. . . such a nature that their coercive effects cannot be eliminated by the application of traditional remedies with the result that a fair and reliable election cannot be had.[66]

The Supreme Court also indicated that the lower court had left open the possibility that in category one cases, a bargaining order might be imposed "without need of inquiry into majority status on the basis of cards or otherwise." [67] The Board, however, has not followed this Court dictum and has consistently required that before a bargaining order is issued, there must be a showing that the union, *at one point,* had enjoyed majority status among the bargaining unit employees.[68] Once there has been a showing of union majority,[69] the Board will determine whether a category one unfair labor practice has occurred. If so, a bargaining order is considered appropriate and the Board is not required to make the determination called for in the intermediate situation [i.e., category two] that a fair rerun election might not be possible.[70]

Examples of violations which fulfill category one criteria can be found in *Gissel* itself, where such violations involved discharges of

---

[66] 395 U.S. at 614, 71 L.R.R.M. at 2495.

[67] *Id.* at 613.

[68] Meat Cutters Local 576 (Wilson Wholesale Meat Co.) v. NLRB, —— F.2d ——, 89 L.R.R.M. 3124 (D.C. Cir. 1975). *And see e.g.,* Loray Corp., 184 N.L.R.B. 557, 74 L.R.R.M. 1513 (1970). *See also,* Fuqua Homes Missouri, Inc., 201 N.L.R.B. 147, 82 L.R.R.M. 1142 (1973). In *Loray,* even though a bargaining order was not issued, the employer was required to send individual notices to employees, and to read the same notice to the employees. The employer also was ordered to give the union access to company bulletin boards for three months. The Board ordered that an election be held upon the union's request with no required showing that 30 percent of the employees desired an election. The employer, the Board believed, had made it impossible for the union to solicit further signatures. In *Fuqua Homes,* however, the union's request for extraordinary remedies was denied.

[69] In recent Board action it was held that pursuant to an accretion or "additional store" clause in a collective bargaining agreement, the employer may become obligated to extend recognition to the union when it can demonstrate a majority through authorization cards. Under such clauses, the employer voluntarily agrees to recognize the union as the bargaining agent in any additions to the original bargaining unit. *See* Houston Division of the Kroger Co., 219 N.L.R.B. No. 43, 89 L.R.R.M. 1641 (1975). *But see* Local 455, Retail Clerks (Kroger Co.) v. NLRB, 510 F.2d 802, 88 L.R.R.M. 2592 (D.C. Cir. 1975) in which the court had reversed and remanded the Board's earlier finding of a violation in the *Kroger* case. *And see* Smith's Management Corp., 219 N.L.R.B. No. 45, 89 L.R.R.M. 1646 (1975).

[70] 395 U.S. at 615, 71 L.R.R.M. at 2496.

several employees and employer threats that unionization could result in his going out of business and closing the plant.[71]

NLRB and circuit court decisions have provided some means of identifying the types of unlawful conduct considered "outrageous and pervasive." In one instance, the discriminatory layoff of 50 percent of the bargaining unit merited a bargaining order.[72] In *Mallow Plating Works, Inc.*,[73] employer conduct of like impact included unlawful interrogation, solicitation rules, threats of reprisal, inducements, and discriminatory layoffs.

One of the strongest affirmations of the use of the bargaining order under the special circumstances outlined in *Gissel* was made in *J. P. Stevens & Co. v. NLRB*.[74] The violations included surveillance, interrogation, threats, promises of benefits, enforcement of dormant no-solicitation rules, and employee discharges. The decision stated the remedy was justified under both *Gissel* criteria. Thus, *Gissel* approved the Board's longstanding policy of issuing a bargaining order when such an order is the only effective remedy for egregious employer violations.[75] But as the following discussion indicates, the line between category one and category two violations is not easily drawn.

Gissel Category Two: "Less Pervasive" Violations

In *Gissel,* the Court noted that the core of its holding was its approval of "the Board's use of the bargaining order in cases marked by less pervasive practices which nonetheless still have the tendency to undermine majority strength and impede the elction

---

[71] *Id.* at 588, 616-620. The *Gissel* decision involved four consolidated petitions for certiorari. In one (*Sinclair*), discussed in the text, the Court found a category one violation and issued a bargaining order. The other three cases (*Gissel, Heck's,* and *General Steel*) were remanded for further consideration by the Board.

[72] Welcome-American Fertilizer Co., 179 N.L.R.B. 217, 72 L.R.R.M. 1295 (1969), *supplementing* 169 N.L.R.B. 862, 67 L.R.R.M. 1484 (1968); NLRB v. Sitton Tank Co., 467 F.2d 1371, 81 L.R.R.M. 2491 (8th Cir. 1972) ("The surest method of undermining 'a union's majority or impeding an election process' is to discharge all the pro-union employees.") NLRB v. Lou DeYoung's Market Basket, Inc., 430 F.2d 912, 915, 75 L.R.R.M. 2129 (6th Cir. 1970).

[73] 193 N.L.R.B. 600, 78 L.R.R.M. 1329 (1971). *See also* Justus Co., 199 N.L.R.B. 422, 81 L.R.R.M. 1517 (1972), Elm Hill Meats, 205 N.L.R.B. 285, 84 L.R.R.M. 1089 (1973).

[74] 441 F.2d 514, 76 L.R.R.M. 2817 (5th Cir. 1971).

[75] Gissel, *supra*, 395 U.S. at 614, 71 L.R.R.M. at 2495.

process." [76] In order for a bargaining order to be issued for such "category two" violations, there must be evidence that at one point the union had majority support and an analysis of the impact of the unfair labor practices upon the election atmosphere. [77] In delegating this task to the Board, the Court promulgated an analytical framework:

> In fashioning a remedy in the exercise of its discretion, then, the Board can properly take into consideration the extensiveness of an employer's unfair practices in terms of their past effect on election conditions and the likelihood of their recurrence in the future. If the Board finds that the possibility of erasing the effects of past practices and of enduring a fair election (or a fair rerun) by the use of traditional remedies, though present, is slight and that the employee sentiment once expressed through cards would, on balance, be better protected by a bargaining order, then such an order should issue. [78]

Cases in this area do not always clarify the degree of seriousness necessary to support a bargaining order. The Board's case-by-case approach has generated controversy, especially at the circuit court level where enforcement of an order is sought. [79] Thus, the Board has not always provided a clear distinction between the types of unfair labor practices required to satisfy each category. Two commentators have pointed out that:

> ... the Board has attempted no real demarcation between the Court's two categories of employer response to a demand for recognition that will warrant a bargaining order. The Board has instead tended to merge the Court's criteria for both categories, adding in some cases the ultimate footnote that in any event the employer conduct was so pervasive and coercive as to warrant a bargaining order even in the absence of an 8(a)(5) violation. [80]

In the following discussion we have extracted a few cases from the large volume of the Board's *Gissel* bargaining order decisions

---

[76] *Id.*, 71 L.R.R.M. at 2495.

[77] *Id.*, 71 L.R.R.M. at 2495.

[78] *Id.*

[79] *See generally,* WILLIAMS, JANUS, AND HUHN, NLRB REGULATION OF ELECTION CONDUCT, for analysis of Board policy in regulating conduct by both parties after postelection objections.

[80] Christensen & Christensen, *Gissel Packing and "Good Faith Doubt" The Gestalt of Required Recognition of Unions under the NLRA*, 37 U. CHI. L. REV. 411, 495-496 (1970). *See also* Carson, *The Gissel Doctrine: When a Bargaining Order Will Issue*, 411 FORDHAM L. REV. 85, 113 (1972).

in order to provide examples of employer violations found to fall within category two.[81]

There are some classes of unlawful conduct to which the Board seems to apply an approximate per se rule that a bargaining order is warranted. In *General Stencils, Inc.* the Board stated:

> A direct threat of loss of employment, whether through plant closure, discharge, or layoff, is one of the most flagrant means by which an employer can hope to dissuade employees from selecting a bargaining representative. . . . Such threats can only have one purpose, to deprive employees of their right freely to select or reject a bargaining representative.[82]

The fact that the threat of closure in this case had been made to only one employee out of a work force of thirty-two was not seen by the Board as determinative. The Board's finding was reversed by the Second Circuit, however.[83] In *The Great Atlantic & Pacific Tea Company*,[84] it was suggested that the threat to shut down was more serious than a threatened discharge since it affected the "overall continuity of employment." [85]

The actual discharge of employees because of their pro-union activities, or other discriminatory action against union adherents usually prompts a bargaining order.[86] In *D. M. Rotary Press*,[87]

---

[81] For a detailed yearly breakdown of NLRB *Gissel* decisions organized by the type of unfair labor practice committed, see the 1971-1974 annual supplements to MORRIS, THE DEVELOPING LABOR LAW, B.N.A., Washington (1971), Chapter 10.

[82] 195 N.L.R.B. 1107, 79 L.R.R.M. 1608 (1972), *on remand from* 438 F.2d 894, 76 L.R.R.M. 2288 (2d Cir. 1971), *and reversed in* 472 F.2d 170, 82 L.R.R.M. 2081 (2d Cir. 1972).

[83] *See* NLRB v. General Stencils, *supra*, 472 F.2d 170, 82 L.R.R.M. 208 (2d Cir. 1972).

[84] 210 N.L.R.B. No. 89, 86 L.R.R.M. 1444 (1974).

[85] *Id.* (Administrative Law Judge's opinion). For other cases involving threats affecting job security, *see also*, Tri-City Paving, Inc., 205 N.L.R.B. 174, 84 L.R.R.M. 1086 (1973); Milgo Industrial, Inc., 203 N.L.R.B. 1196, 83 L.R.R.M. 1280 (1973) *enf'd*, 497 F.2d 919, 87 L.R.R.M. 3274 (2d Cir. 1974); Oahu Refuse Collection Co., 212 N.L.R.B. No. 51, 86 L.R.R.M. 1719 (1974).

[86] *See* Fotomat Corp., 202 N.L.R.B. No. 3, 82 L.R.R.M. 1475 (1973), *enforced in an unpublished opinion*, 489 F.2d 752, 85 L.R.R.M. 2768 (2d Cir. 1974); Vangas Inc., 209 N.L.R.B. 961, 86 L.R.R.M. 1230 (1974) *enf'd*, —— F.2d ——, 89 L.R.R.M. 2508 (9th Cir. 1975).

[87] 208 N.L.R.B. 366, 85 L.R.R.M. 1477 (1974). *But cf.* MPC Restaurant Corp. v. NLRB, 481 F.2d 75, 83 L.R.R.M. 2769 (2d Cir. 1973), where the bargaining order was based on the discharge of a union organizer, even though he represented a different local of the union seeking representation. The court wrote, "The discharge of a Local 1 union organizer certainly could be thought

the employer discharged 80 percent of the work force after the union requested recognition. The Board held this had "decimated" the union and rendered any future election impossible. In this case, if only one employee had been discharged in violation of Section 8(a)(3), the discharge might have been deemed insufficient to warrant a bargaining order.[88] In another case, however, where one individual from a unit of five employees was fired, the Board was persuaded that the effect of the employer's conduct could not be remedied by normal means.[89]

Thus, the size of the work force is a key consideration in determining the proper remedy. The Board, in *Joseph J. Lachniet*,[90] noted that employer unfair labor practices would tend to be "pervasive" in a small unit since they would come to the attention of virtually every employee. In a similar case, reprisal and promises of benefits occurring in a five-man unit resulted in an order to bargain.[91] The "lingering effect" of unlawful inducements is likely to be found in cases where a substantial segment of the work force is affected.[92]

In a number of instances, the Board has held that unlawful employer promises and grants of benefits greatly undermine union support and have a lasting impact on election conditions.[93] The Board expressed the rationale, in *Teledyne Dental Products*,[94] that

---

to have an adverse effect on the rights of other employees of the same establishment although these others were subject to the potential jurisdiction of another local." 481 F.2d at 79, 83 L.R.R.M. 2769, 2772.

[88] Munro Enterprises, Inc., 210 N.L.R.B. 403, 86 L.R.R.M. 1620 (1974).

[89] Cornelius American, Inc., 194 N.L.R.B. 909, 79 L.R.R.M. 1206 (1972).

[90] 201 N.L.R.B. 855, 82 L.R.R.M. 1402 (1973). The violations included unlawful threats and promises and discriminatory layoffs of two employees.

[91] Colonial Knitting Corp., 187 N.L.R.B. 980, 76 L.R.R.M. 1244 (1971), *enf'd*, 464 F.2d 949, 80 L.R.R.M. 3164 (3d Cir. 1972). *See also*, Felsa Knitting Mills, 208 N.L.R.B. 508, 85 L.R.R.M. 1319 (1974) (involving six employees).

[92] C & G Electric, 180 N.L.R.B. 427, 73 L.R.R.M. 1041 (1969), Gruber's Super Market, 201 N.L.R.B. 612, 82 L.R.R.M. 1495 (1973), *reversed*, 501 F.2d 697, 87 L.R.R.M. 2037 (7th Cir. 1974); Royal Aluminum Foundry, 208 N.L.R.B. 102, 85 L.R.R.M. 1056 (1974).

[93] Skaggs Drug Centers, Inc., 197 N.L.R.B. 1240, 80 L.R.R.M. 1505 (1972), *enf'd*, —— F.2d ——, 84 L.R.R.M. 2384 (9th Cir. 1973). The Board and court noted the size of the wage increases given by the employer. *See also* NLRB v. Tower Records, —— F.2d ——, 79 L.R.R.M. 2736 (9th Cir. 1972).

[94] 210 N.L.R.B. 435, 86 L.R.R.M. 1134 (1974).

the inducements promoted direct dealing with the employer rather than through a union representative, and therefore:

> such conduct by its very nature, has a long-lasting, if not permanent, effect on the employees' freedom of choice in selecting or rejecting a bargaining representative.[95]

In this case, however, the employer had solicited grievances with promises of rectification and had provided the added benefit of a coffee break. The Board reversed the Administrative Law Judge who was of the opinion that the violations generated minimal impact upon chances for a fair election. By comparison, the employer in *California Pellet Mill Co.*[96] made several promises of benefits, the lack of which had been a direct issue in the union's campaign. The Board denied a bargaining order request, even though it stated it did not condone the "serious" unfair labor practices.

Incidents of interrogation and surveillance are often noted by the Board as contributing factors to the decision to require the employer to bargain with the union.[97] Usually, such violations are one element of the employer's overall course of conduct in response to a unionization attempt.[98] In *Tennessee Shell Co.,*[99] the questioning of a number of employees was considered a less serious violation since it was not accompanied by employer threats. Limited instances of unlawful interrogation also are treated as minor unfair labor practices.[100] An employer poll which did not conform to the *Struksnes* [101] guidelines, thereby constituting an unfair labor practice, was insufficient to warrant a bargaining order [102] where the employer's purpose had been to determine the extent of union support.

---

[95] *Id.* at 436, 86 L.R.R.M. at 1135.

[96] 219 N.L.R.B. No. 77, 89 L.R.R.M. 1669 (1975). *See also* Restaurant Associates Industries, 194 N.L.R.B. 1066, 79 L.R.R.M 1145 (1972).

[97] *See e.g.,* Empire Corp., 212 N.L.R.B. No. 81, 86 L.R.R.M. 1659 (1974).

[98] Felsa Knitting Mills, *supra* at note 91, Colonial Knitting Corp., *supra* at note 91, D. M. Rotary Press, *supra* at note 87. *See also,* The Great Atlantic & Pacific Tea Co., 194 N.L.R.B. 774, 79 L.R.R.M. 1087 (1971).

[99] 212 N.L.R.B. No. 24, 86 L.R.R.M. 1704 (1974).

[100] Kimmel's Shop Rite, 213 N.L.R.B. No. 69, 87 L.R.R.M. 1193 (1974), Ring Metals Company, 198 N.L.R.B. No. 143, 81 L.R.R.M. 1001 (1972), Action Advertising Co., 195 N.L.R.B. 629, 79 L.R.R.M. 1455 (1972).

[101] 165 N.L.R.B. 1062, 65 L.R.R.M. 1385 (1967).

[102] Northeastern Dye Works, 203 N.L.R.B. No. 159, 83 L.R.R.M. 1225 (1973).

Despite some forceful statements by the Board concerning the impact of certain employee conduct upon the union's status and the election "laboratory conditions," meaningful guidelines to evaluate the circumstances necessitating bargaining orders are lacking. Former NLRB Chairman Miller attempted in his dissent in *General Stencils, Inc.*[103] to initiate certain principles that would apply in *Gissel* cases.

He made the initial distinction between employer *action* and employer *speech*. On the former he noted:

> The employer who identifies the sources of employee discontent and remedies them, or identifies the principal union adherents and removes them, demonstrates *by his actions* that he will oppose the union by unlawful means and that employees who support it do so at their own grave peril. The message is communicated to all by means which will be clear to all. In the matter of employer resistance to employee rights, actions do indeed speak louder than words.[104]

With respect to the latter area of conduct, he added:

> Once we depart the realm of action . . . and enter the world of speech divorced from action, our decisions under Gissel appear at first blush to be so diverse that no rules can be discerned.[105]

Because of this distinction and the problems emanating from it, he would assess employer speech by a threefold approach:

1) What actions were threatened?

2) Were the threats, considering their source, their deliberateness and their specificity, likely to be seriously regarded by the employees?

3) How widely were the threats disseminated among the employees?[106]

Appellate Court Comments on and Criticisms of the Board's Application of Gissel.

Because of the large number of *Gissel* bargaining order cases decided by the Board, many of these cases are taken before the United States Courts of Appeals on petitions for review or applica-

---

[103] General Stencils, Inc., 195 N.L.R.B. 1109, 79 L.R.R.M. 1609 (1972), *rev'd*, 472 F.2d 170, 82 L.R.R.M. 2081 (2d Cir. 1972).

[104] *Id.* at 1112-1113, 79 L.R.R.M. 1609, 1612.

[105] 195 N.L.R.B. 1109, 1113, 79 L.R.R.M. 1609, 1612.

[106] *See also* Lawrence Rigging, Inc., 202 N.L.R.B. 1094, 1096, n. 11, 82 L.R.R.M. 1784, 1787 (1973).

tions for enforcement. Although the Board's bargaining orders are often enforced, on several occasions the judiciary has felt compelled to emphasize to the Board the importance of establishing, in each case, a causal connection between employer unfair labor practices and the detrimental impact of those violations on the future chance for a fair election. For example, in *NLRB v. Drives, Inc.*[107] the court emphasized the requirement under *Gissel* to weigh the impact of violations on the *continuing* possibility of determining employee choice. This question is distinguished from that of determining whether the employer's actions led to the union's election defeat. The court believed the Board had been deficient in this regard. Relying on its own analysis, the court enforced the bargaining order after finding that specific *post-election* unfair labor practices prejudiced the likelihood of a rerun election. It rejected a number of pre-election violations which the Board had found, and it completely disregarded the 8(a)(5) unfair labor practice charge in its consideration of the bargaining order remedy.[108]

The Second Circuit in *NLRB v. General Stencils, Inc.*[109] issued a strong criticism of the Board's procedure and policies in formulating remedies. It denied enforcement of the order in this instance on the grounds that the NLRB had failed to justify a need for issuing the order.[110] In effect, it accused the agency of inconsistent handling of the complaint because the NLRB had not explained "why, and in what respects the case differs from others when it has reached an opposite conclusion." [111] The court strongly urged that the Board apply its rule-making powers to issue definitive guidelines to benefit unions, employers, and reviewing courts.

---

[107] 440 F.2d 354, 76 L.R.R.M. 2296 (7th Cir. 1971). Similar criticisms of the Board's *Gissel* analysis are found in Peerless of America, Inc. v. NLRB, 484 F.2d 1108, 83 L.R.R.M. 3000 (7th Cir. 1973) and cases cited therein; NLRB v. Gruber's Super Market, Inc., 501 F.2d 697, 87 L.R.R.M. 2037 (7th Cir. 1974); Fremont Newspapers, Inc. v. NLRB, 436 F.2d 665, 76 L.R.R.M. 2049 (8th Cir. 1970); Walgreen Co. v. NLRB, 509 F.2d 1014, 88 L.R.R.M. 2401 (7th Cir. 1975).

[108] NLRB v. Drives, Inc., 440 F.2d 354, 76 L.R.R.M. 2296 (7th Cir. 1971).

[109] 438 F.2d 894, 76 L.R.R.M. 2288 (2d Cir. 1971). After remand to the Board, court repeated substantially the same criticism in NLRB v. General Stencils, 472 F.2d 170, 82 L.R.R.M. 2081 (2d Cir. 1972).

[110] *See also*, NLRB v. Miller Trucking Service, Inc., 445 F.2d 927, 77 L.R.R.M. 2964 (10th Cir. 1971), NLRB v. Essex Wire Corp., 496 F.2d 862, 80 L.R.R.M. 3166 (6th Cir. 1972), NLRB v. Kaiser Agricultural Chemicals, 473 F.2d 374, 82 L.R.R.M. 2455 (5th Cir. 1973).

[111] 438 F.2d at 902, 76 L.R.R.M. 2288, 2294.

The Second Circuit raised the key point that inadequate analysis of the facts and generalized application of the law to the facts seriously hamper the judicial review process:

> Detailed explication of this sort is peculiarly necessary because of the possibility, which has here become an actuality, that a reviewing court will vacate one of the § 8(a)(1) findings on the "totality" of which the Board relied to justify a bargaining order, and the consequent possible need for a remand unless the court can be satisfied that the error did not affect the command to bargain.[112]

In *Peerless of America, Inc. v. NLRB*,[113] the Seventh Circuit again emphasized the need of the NLRB to make "specific findings" on the impact of the violations upon the election and a "detailed analysis" of the probability of a future fair election. By "specific findings," it said:

> We mean only that [the Board] estimate the impact, taking into account the factors in the particular case which are indicative of actual effect or which plausibly, in the light of existing knowledge, would contribute to or detract from an actual impact.[114]

Also, it suggested factors to be considered in measuring the likelihood of a recurrence of employer misconduct: "whether the employer has a history of anti-union animus and Labor Act violations, whether the employer has taken affirmative rectifying measures or otherwise indicated his cooperativeness in assuring a free election, etc." [115] The court then made its own detailed analysis of the impact of the violation on the chance of a fair election and refused to enforce the bargaining order.

The court, in *NLRB v. Kostel Corp.*,[116] mentioned certain criteria that could be applied to measure the probability of a future fair election in the wake of unfair labor practices. It cited the size of the employee unit, the nature of the company's business, the

---

[112] *Id. See also,* NLRB v. Scoler's Inc., 466 F.2d 1289, 81 L.R.R.M. 2299 (2d Cir. 1972), NLRB v. Gibson Products Co., 494 F.2d 762, 86 L.R.R.M. 2636 (5th Cir. 1974).

[113] 484 F.2d 1108, 83 L.R.R.M. 3000 (7th Cir. 1973).

[114] *Id.* at 1118, n. 16, 83 L.R.R.M. 3000, 3008, n. 16.

[115] *Id. See also,* NLRB v. Gruber's Super Market, Inc., 501 F.2d 697, 87 L.R.R.M. 2037 (7th Cir. 1974). In *Gruber's Super Market,* the court stated that the Board's request that the court defer to its administrative expertise was misplaced, since this "presumed expertise 'does not relieve the Board of its responsibility to explain its conclusions in terms reviewing courts can understand.'" *Id.,* at 704, 87 L.R.R.M. at 2042, *citing* Peerless of America, Inc. v. NLRB, 484 F.2d 1108, 1118 n. 16, 83 L.R.R.M. 3000 (7th Cir. 1974).

[116] 440 F.2d 347, 76 L.R.R.M. 2643 (7th Cir. 1971).

type of unfair labor practices, and the size of the surrounding community.[117]

The case-by-case method of enforcing bargaining orders creates pitfalls in the efficacy of the NLRB's administrative process. The drive for clearer policies and rule making has come both from within the Board and from the courts. Until such time as the Board frames guidelines to deal with *Gissel*-type cases, the absence of certainty and uniformity will continue to confound unions, employers, and courts alike.

Retroactive Applicability of the Bargaining Order— The Trading Port Decision

Gissel bargaining order cases involve a union's demand for recognition and an employer who allegedly unfairly undermined the union's majority status. A considerable lapse of time occurs between the union's initial demand for recognition or filing of an election petition, and final Board or appellate court disposition of the case. The Board's position has fluctuated concerning whether such bargaining orders have retroactive effect and apply to unilateral changes made by the employer during this interim period.

In 1975, the Board reversed its *Steel-Fab, Inc.*[118] decision and held in *Trading Port, Inc.*,[119] that a *Gissel*-type bargaining order would henceforth have retroactive effect. The Board stated:

> We find that an *employer's obligation* under a bargaining order remedy *should commence as of the time the employer has embarked on a clear course of unlawful conduct or has engaged in sufficient unfair labor practices to undermine the union's majority status.*

---

[117] In like manner, several recent circuit court decisions have refused to enforce *Gissel* bargaining orders because the Board had applied an improper analysis. These courts also suggested that the Board employ criteria such as those discussed above in order to better carry out its assumed expertise and to be "given [the] special respect by reviewing courts," mentioned in Gissel, *supra*, 395 U.S. at 612, n. 32, 71 L.R.R.M. at 2495. *See e.g.*, NLRB v. Ship Shape Maintenance Co., 474 F.2d 434, 81 L.R.R.M. 2865 (D.C. Cir. 1972); Shulman's Inc. v. NLRB, 519 F.2d 498, 89 L.R.R.M. 2729 (4th Cir. 1975); NLRB v. Anvil Products, Inc., 496 F.2d 94, 86 L.R.R.M. 2822 (5th Cir. 1974); Litton Industries, Inc. (Automated Business Systems) v. NLRB, 497 F.2d 262, 86 L.R.R.M. 2659 (6th Cir. 1974); NLRB v. East Side Shopper, Inc., 86 L.R.R.M. 2817 (6th Cir. 1974); NLRB v. Leslie Metal Arts Co., 472 F.2d 584, 82 L.R.R.M. 2002 (6th Cir. 1972); NLRB v. Urban Telephone Corp., 499 F.2d 239, 86 L.R.R.M. 2704 (7th Cir. 1974); National Cash Register Co., 494 F.2d 189, 85 L.R.R.M. 2657 (8th Cir. 1974); NLRB v. Medical Manors, Inc., 497 F.2d 292, 86 L.R.R.M. 2609 (9th Cir. 1974).

[118] 212 N.L.R.B. No. 25, 86 L.R.R.M. 1474 (1974).

[119] 219 N.L.R.B. No. 76, 89 L.R.R.M. 1565 (1975).

Such a position eliminates the possible ill effects of dating a bargaining order as of the issuance of the Board's decision, which has resulted in unremedied unfair labor practices, while at the same time assuring, as the Supreme Court stressed in Gissel, that bargaining orders, by remedying *all* of an employer's unfair labor practices, will "re-establish the conditions as they existed before the employer's unlawful campaign" and not place a union in a disadvantaged position. Moreover, it seems to accord most closely with what actually happened. An employer, as the Supreme Court has held, has a right to an election so long as he does not fatally impede the election process. Once he has so impeded the process, he has forfeited his right to a Board election, and must bargain with the union on the basis of other clear indications of employees' desires. It is at that point, we believe, the employer's unlawful refusal to bargain has taken place.[120]

The earlier *Steel-Fab* decision, which the Board passed by a 3-2 majority, held the seriousness of the employer's misconduct and its impact upon a fair election as the relevant considerations in deciding whether to order an employer to bargain with a union. The majority (Chairman Miller and Members Kennedy and Penello) argued that no real purpose was served in additionally finding that the employer had violated Section 8(a)(5) by his conduct.[121] Dissenting Members Fanning and Jenkins argued that an additional finding that the employer had violated Section 8(a)(5) was necessary to give retroactive effect to a bargaining order. Otherwise, they argued, the remedy would be inadequate to counter any of the employer's intervening unilateral actions such as changes in employment conditions, refusals to furnish information to the union, or a decision to relocate a plant or to go out of business.[122]

Soon thereafter, another such case came before the Board in *Elm Hill Meats of Owensboro*.[123] In that case, the company rejected the union's initial request for recognition. The union petitioned for an election and, subsequently, filed unfair labor practice charges.

---

[120] *Id.*, 89 L.R.R.M. at 1569 (Emphasis added.) *See also* American Map Co., 219 N.L.R.B. No. 186, 90 L.R.R.M. 1242 (1975); Baker Machine & Gear, Inc., 220 N.L.R.B. No. 40, 90 L.R.R.M. 1454 (1975); Independent Sprinkler & Fire Protection Co., 220 N.L.R.B. No. 140, 90 L.R.R.M. 1564 (1975); Ann Lee Sportswear, Inc., 220 N.L.R.B. No. 153, 90 L.R.R.M. 1352 (1975), Donelson Packing Co., and Riegel Provision Co., 220 N.L.R.B. No. 159, 90 L.R.R.M. 1549 (1975).

[121] Steel-Fab, Inc., 86 L.R.R.M. at 1476. *See also* Chairman Miller's dissent in United Packing Co., 187 N.L.R.B. 878, 880, 76 L.R.R.M. 1156, 1158 (1971).

[122] *Id.* at 1479-1483. *See* pp. 207-210, *infra*, for a discussion of Section 8(a)(5) violations.

[123] 213 N.L.R.B. No. 100, 87 L.R.R.M. 1227 (1974).

During the period between the issuance of the Administrative Law Judge's decision and the Board's order, the employer closed his plant for economic reasons. Relying on *Steel-Fab,* the Board concluded that the bargaining order acted *in futuro,* and since the decision to close down the plant occurred almost two months before the issuance of the bargaining order, no bargaining obligation applied to that decision to close or its effects.[124]

The rationale of the *Steel-Fab* and *Elm Hill Meats* decisions was reconsidered in *Trading Port.* This occurred after the expiration of the term of Chairman Miller and the commencement of the term of the new chairman, Betty Southard Murphy. With only Member Kennedy dissenting, the Board expressed its displeasure with the result in *Elm Hill Meats* on the grounds that "an employer, by committing serious unfair labor practices, could delay the holding of an election indefinitely." Furthermore, an employer could assure himself of a substantial period of time during which he could make unilateral changes after a union had established its majority status.[125]

At least one exception exists to the general rule established in *Trading Port,* that a *Gissel* bargaining order remedy is effective from the time the employer began a clear course of unlawful conduct. If the union does not attain its majority status until after the beginning of employer misconduct, the bargaining order will be effective from the date of union majority. For example, in *Bookland Inc.,*[126] the employer's misconduct began on August 1;

---

[124] *Id.* at 1229.

[125] Trading Port, Inc., 89 L.R.R.M. at 1569. A related issue involves whether a district court should issue a Section 10(j) injunction requiring an employer to bargain with a union pending Board determination of the propriety of a *Gissel* bargaining order. Until recently, the courts had generally refused to grant such injunctions. *See* Boire v. Pilot Freight Carriers, Inc., 515 F.2d 1185, 89 L.R.R.M. 2908 (5th Cir. 1975); *reh. denied,* 521 F.2d 795, 90 L.R.R.M. 3055 (1975) (Fifth Circuit specifically refused to follow the Second Circuit's decision in Seeler v. Trading Port); Kaynard v. Lawrence Rigging, Inc., —— F. Supp. ——, 80 L.R.R.M. 2600 (E.D.N.Y. 1972); Fuchs v. Steel-Fab, Inc., 356 F. Supp. 385, 83 L.R.R.M. 2635 (D. Mass. 1973). However, in Seeler v. Trading Port, Inc., 517 F.2d 33, 89 L.R.R.M. 2513 (2d Cir. 1975), the Second Circuit issued the first appellate court decision requiring a district court to enter such a bargaining order. *See also* Smith v. Old Angus, —— F. Supp. ——, 82 L.R.R.M. 2930 (D.C. Md. 1973). The crucial difference between these two positions is the point at which the courts viewed the status quo ante (which the injunction was intended to restore) as terminating. The Fifth Circuit in *Pilot Freight* viewed the status quo ante as that period prior to the commencement of union activity. The Second Circuit's *Trading Port* decision viewed it as the period prior to the beginning of the employer's unlawful campaign.

[126] 221 N.L.R.B. No. 11, —— L.R.R.M. —— (1975).

the union demanded recognition on August 7, but did not attain majority status until August 11. The Board ordered the respondent employer to bargain as of August 11, and not the date of demand.

After *Trading Port* was decided, the Board explained that its decision was merely a reaffirmation of longstanding legal principles. Thus, the Board urged in *Baker Machine & Gear, Inc.,*:

> No element of retroactivity is present in imposing the bargaining obligation as of the time the employer began his subversion of the statute. No new law or rule is being enacted governing conduct or relations previously not subject to the law. Instead, the remedy we impose does no more than reach all the unlawful actions committed, whether early or late in the course of the misconduct. The only element of retroactivity is that the misconduct being remedied occurred prior to issuance of the complaint and our consideration of the case; but this is the situation in every civil or criminal case where a wrong is remedied, for the remedy can be applied only after the wrong has been committed.[127]

Board remedies traditionally are designed to provide relief for wrongful acts committed prior to the issuance of a complaint. The Board's description of *Trading Port*'s impact, however, is somewhat disingenuous. In deciding the case, the Board had specifically stated that by finding a Section 8(a)(5) violation when issuing a *Gissel* bargaining order, it was reversing *Steel-Fab.* In this way, the Board would be able to remedy unilateral employer actions which occurred after the employer had embarked upon a course of illegal conduct. Thus, when the Board openly disavowed its previous decision in *Elm Hill Meats,* it appeared to notify employees that, thereafter, such unilateral actions would be subject to the Board's remedial process.[128] Therefore, *Trading Port* exceeded a mere reaffirmation of the Board's power to remedy prior violations and established that certain employer conduct, not previously enjoined, would thereafter be subject to remedial action.

The eventual impact of *Trading Port* is not yet clear and awaits further Board decisions. The principles established in that case,

---

[127] 220 N.L.R.B. No. 40, 90 L.R.R.M. 1454, 1456 (1975).

[128] In criticizing *Elm Hill Meats,* the Board did not limit its decision to the situation where unilateral actions were taken only after an Administrative Law Judge had recommended a bargaining order. Rather, *Trading Port* clearly was meant to apply to unilateral actions taken following the commencement of an employer's illegal activities. *See also* the dissenting opinions of Members Fanning and Jenkins in Steel Fab, Inc., 212 N.L.R.B. No. 25, 86 L.R.R.M. 1474, 1478-1483 (1974).

however, present employers with a complex and troublesome legal situation. An employer charged with unfair labor practices in the course of a union-organizing campaign now will confront the problem of running his business on a day-to-day basis, always knowing that unilateral actions he undertakes with respect to mandatory subjects of bargaining may be ordered set aside in order to restore the status quo ante.[129] If *Trading Port* means that no such unilateral changes may be made during this period, important and vital changes in operations motivated by valid business considerations may be delayed or foresaken.

The employer must first anticipate whether or not a bargaining order will issue from the unfair labor practice charge. If an employer commits the "outrageous" and "pervasive" type of unfair labor practices described in *Gissel's* first category, the problem of predicting the outcome is minimal. Our discussion of the practical application of the *Gissel* bargaining order test,[130] however, indicates that an extremely large number of these cases are by no means clear cut. Which combination of unfair labor practices will warrant a bargaining order is unclear, and the courts often disagree with the Board's analysis of the particular case. The issue is even more complicated when the disposition of unfair labor practice allegations requires resolving credibility differences among witnesses. Sometimes, it must be resolved whether the company will be held responsible for improper actions of its supervisory personnel when these actions are isolated instances of misconduct not shown to reflect a company policy.[131]

Now, if an employer facing unfair labor practice charges wishes to act in accordance with *Trading Port* and at the same time make unilateral changes pending resolution of the bargaining order issue, his lawful course of action is unclear. The standard method of avoiding Section 8(a)(5) violations is to bargain with an incumbent union. But in a *Trading Port* situation, no incumbent exists.

---

[129] Situations in which an employer subcontracts work to another, but does not thereby change employment conditions, generally have been remedied by ordering the original employer to rehire his employees and resume work. The *Trading Port* decision has not yet been applied to this situation, however. *See* Fibreboard Paper Products Corp. v. NLRB, 379 U.S. 203, 57 L.R.R.M. 2609 (1964), NLRB v. Florida-Texas Freight, Inc., 203 N.L.R.B. 509, 83 L.R.R.M. 1093 (1973), *enforced*, 489 F.2d 1275, 85 L.R.R.M. 2845 (6th Cir. 1974).

[130] *Supra*, pp. 171-181.

[131] *See e.g.*, NLRB v. General Industries Electronics Co., 401 F.2d 297, 300, 69 L.R.R.M. 2455 (8th Cir. 1968); Metropolitan Life Ins. Co. v. NLRB, 371 F.2d 573, 580, 64 L.R.R.M. 2130 (6th Cir. 1967). *Cf.* Collins & Aikman Corp. v. NLRB, 395 F.2d 277, 281, n. 5, 68 L.R.R.M. 2320 (4th Cir. 1968).

The employer may choose to bargain with the union seeking representation. By anticipating a bargaining order rather than an election order, however, the employer risks bargaining during a lengthy period in which the union represents a minority. Under other circumstances, such dealings with a union found not to represent a majority of the employees have been found to violate Section 8 (a) (2).[132]

Similarly, *Trading Port* does not resolve issues concerning the legality of changes agreed to by a union and employer when the Board later determines that an election should be held to test the union's representative status. Even assuming that the employer may properly deal with a union pending the Board's decision, the situation becomes more complicated if rival unions are seeking to represent the unit employees. In that case, if the employer deals with one of the unions prior to the Board's determination, he also risks committing a *Midwest Piping* violation of Section 8(a) (2).[133] The only safe course for an employer in such a situation is to avoid unilateral changes, at the possible expense of his business.

Thus, *Trading Port* raises many problems which it does not address. These are problems potentially unfair to employers, employees, and unions alike.

---

[132] *See* Int'l Ladies Garment Workers Union (Bernhard-Altmann Texas Corp.) v. NLRB, 366 U.S. 731, 737-738, 48 L.R.R.M. 2251 (1961).

[133] *See* Chapter X, *supra*, pp. 152-153.

CHAPTER XII

Defenses to a Gissel Bargaining Order

On occasion employers have contested enforcement of bargaining orders on the grounds that circumstances have changed since the initial order was issued by the Board, and, therefore, the remedy is no longer appropriate. This issue commonly arises where there has been a substantial delay in time between the Board's original order and the subsequent enforcement proceeding. In effect, the employer posits that conditions now permit a fair election to be held, and since an election is the preferred means of establishing union majority status, the bargaining order should be vacated. In most cases the basis for this claim arises because of substantial employee turnover in the bargaining unit, or a change in management and ownership of the offending company. Commonly, also, the passage of time has dissipated the effects of the employer's unfair labor practices. The NLRB for the most part has refused to reconsider the appropriateness of a bargaining order in light of such altered circumstances, while certain circuit courts have split on the issue.

A number of considerations arise when analyzing changed circumstances and the propriety of a bargaining order. Generally the validity of a lawful Board order, does not diminish because of changed conditions which ordinarily would warrant a lesser remedy.[1] Also, in *Gissel* the Court pointed out that the Board retains its authority to issue a bargaining order "even where it is clear that the union which once has possession of cards from a majority of the employees, represents only a

---

[1] NLRB v. Benne Katz d/b/a Williamsburg Steel Products Co., 369 U.S. 736, 50 L.R.R.M. 2177 (1962) Franks Bros. Co. v. NLRB, 321 U.S. 702, 14 L.R.R.M. 591 (1944) (employer turnover); NLRB v. Pennsylvania Greyhound Lines, Inc., 303 U.S. 261, 2 L.R.R.M. 599 (1938); NLRB v. Staub Cleaners, 418 F.2d 1086, 1089, 72 L.R.R.M. 2755, 2760 (2d Cir. 1969). *See also* Chapter IV, *supra*, pp. 58-63.

minority when the bargaining order is entered." [2] The stated purpose of the Court's decision was to prevent the employer from benefiting from his own unlawful conduct by resorting to delaying tactics during the unfair labor practice proceedings. The Supreme Court in *Gissel* also indicated, however, that the necessity for a bargaining order should be judged in part on the likelihood of future violations interfering with election conditions, since the order is designed to deter future misconduct as well as to remedy past election damage.[3] Thus, the question arises, can a policy of not permitting reconsideration of an NLRB bargaining order be justified where the delay in enforcement and change in circumstances are not attributable to further employer misconduct or interference, and where there exists a claim that a free election can now be conducted?

Two opposing decisions rendered by the circuit courts of appeals established precedents which have been cited in disputes over whether the Board should set aside a bargaining order where conditions may have altered the need for such a remedy. In *NLRB v. L.B. Foster Co.*[4] the Ninth Circuit rejected a reconsideration request of the offending employer in its review of an application to enforce the original order. Because of a delay brought about by litigation and Supreme Court review of the *Gissel* case, nearly three years had transpired since the 8(a)(1) violations had been committed. Two years separated entry of the Board's order and the appeal. One of the company's main arguments was that this delay and substantial employee turnover had greatly altered the need for the remedy. The court, in fact, conceded the possibility that there no longer were any employees who had been involved in the earlier union campaign. Nevertheless, relying upon the *Gissel* case and its own previous decisions, the court granted the Board's application for enforcement of the order.

The court reasoned that only the circumstances which provoked the original Board order should determine the validity of that order. Changes occurring subsequent to the commission of the unfair labor practices are not appropriate bases for denying enforcement, according to the Ninth Circuit. In part, the

---

[2] NLRB v. Gissel Packing Co., 395 U.S. 575, 610, 71 L.R.R.M. 2481 (1969).

[3] *Id.*, at 612.

[4] 418 F.2d 1, 72 L.R.R.M. 2736 (9th Cir. 1969), *cert. denied*, 397 U.S. 990, 73 L.R.R.M. 2791 (1970).

court stated, "There is no hint in the Supreme Court's *Gissel* opinion, either as to *Sinclair* or as to the other cases there decided, that there should be a reconsideration in light of subsequent occurrences." [5] Significantly, the court found it unnecessary to ascribe the enforcement delay to the employer. The employer's circumstances were accepted as an "unfortunate but inevitable" by-product of the administrative process.

The court in *L.B. Foster* also felt that failure to enforce the remedy because of intervening employee turnover would encourage the employer to violate the Act during the course of a union campaign:

> He will have as an ally, in addition to the attrition of union support inevitably springing from delay in accomplishing results, the fact that turnover itself will help him, so that the longer he can hold out the better his chances of victory will be.[6]

Also, the court believed that turnover within the bargaining unit after the union had been denied the opportunity to resolve its claim of majority representation harmed the union's bid for recognition.

> The ability of a union [after certification] to maintain its position, even in an enterprise where turnover is rapid, is vastly different from its ability to do so where it has lost an election, is not recognized, and can do nothing whatever for the employees. To a union, recognition and bargaining are the be-all and end-all of its existence.[7]

In *NLRB v. American Cable System, Inc.,*[8] the Fifth Circuit took a contrary position, finding that a bargaining order should

---

[5] 418 F.2d 1, 5, 72 L.R.R.M. 2736, 2739. *Accord*, NLRB v. Coca-Cola Bottling Co. of San Mateo, 472 F.2d 140, 82 L.R.R.M. 2088 (9th Cir. 1972); NLRB v. Tri-State Stores, Inc., 477 F.2d 204, 81 L.R.R.M. 2419, 2422 (9th Cir. 1972); NLRB v. South Bay Daily Breeze, 415 F.2d 360, 367, 72 L.R.R.M. 2081, 2086 (9th Cir. 1969); *cert. denied*, 397 U.S. 915, 73 L.R.R.M. 2537 (1970) (Passage of time does not make the bargaining order inappropriate). Ex-Cell-O Corp. v. NLRB, 449 F.2d 1058, 77 L.R.R.M. 2547 (D.C. Cir. 1971). Judge Ely, in a concurring opinion in *L. B. Foster* wrote that despite the apparent prohibition by *Gissel* against reconsideration of the appropriateness of a bargaining order, "I would hope that . . . the Board will yet consider itself empowered to determine that the now more desirable course is the conducting of a fair election under the protection of the cease and desist order." *Id.* at 6, 72 L.R.R.M. 2737, 2740.

[6] *Id.*

[7] *Id.*

[8] 427 F.2d 446, 73 L.R.R.M. 2913 (5th Cir. 1970), *cert. denied*, 400 U.S. 957, 75 L.R.R.M. 2810 (1970).

not be issued unless the Board has assessed current conditions affecting the likelihood of a fair rerun election. In this case the bargaining order had been remanded to the Board for additional findings in light of the *Gissel* opinion.[9] Upon review, the NLRB refused to consider evidence of intervening circumstances (*e.g.*, employee turnover and a change in management) and it once again petitioned for enforcement of the bargaining order. The Board relied in part on *L.B. Foster* as the basis for its action.

The court in *American Cable* rejected the NLRB's approach on the grounds that a remand implied a requirement of the Board to evaluate any changes in conditions which had arisen since the occurrence of the unfair labor practices. In addition to distinguishing *American Cable* from the *L.B. Foster* case, the Fifth Circuit believed the salience of *Gissel* required consideration of subsequent circumstances which may alter the initial conclusion that a bargaining order is necessary to remedy the employer's unlawful conduct. In part, the court's concern stemmed from the acknowledged extraordinary nature of the remedy, as representation election is the preferred method of ascertaining employee choice:

> *Gissel* does not apply a nunc pro tunc principle, giving the then sins of the Company a now application. It requires contemporaneity —a present view, albeit with an historical prospective. Industrial democracy should be allowed to work its will if the present conditions are sufficiently antiseptic for an election. On the other hand, if the employer's 1965 violations of § 8(a)(1) and (3) have a 1970 existence, *Gissel* commands the issuance of a bargaining order.[10]

Some of the court's language in *American Cable* suggests support for a general policy of reappraising bargaining orders in the light of changed circumstances. The Fifth Circuit subsequently emphasized, however, that its decision veered from

---

[9] 414 F.2d 661, 71 L.R.R.M. 2979 (5th Cir. 1969), *enforcing in part* 161 N.L.R.B. 332, 63 L.R.R.M. 1296 (1966). In *NLRB v. L. B. Foster Co.* the petition for enforcement arose *after* the *Gissel* decision had been handed down.

[10] 427 F.2d 446, 449, 73 L.R.R.M. 2913, 2914. For cases in accord with *American Cable see*: NLRB v. American Art Industries, Inc., 415 F.2d 1223, 72 L.R.R.M. 2199 (5th Cir. 1969) *cert. denied* 397 U.S. 990, 73 L.R.R.M. 2791 (1970), NLRB v. Canton Sign Co., 457 F.2d 832, 79 L.R.R.M. 2972, 2978-2979 (6th Cir. 1972). *And see* NLRB v. Hood, Inc., 496 F.2d 515, 86 L.R.R.M. 2129, 2132-2133 (1st Cir. 1974) where the court remanded the case for the Board to reconsider the bargaining order in light of a five and one-half year delay which was not attributed to the employer. *Cf.* NLRB v. Ben Duthler, 395 F.2d 28, 35, 68 L.R.R.M. 2324 (6th Cir. 1968); C-B Buick, Inc., 506 F.2d 1086, 87 L.R.R.M. 2878 (3d Cir. 1974) (bargaining order denied because of the passage of time and execution of collective bargaining agreement).

L.B. Foster because the remand to the Board required consideration of additional findings.[11] In *NLRB v. Gibson Products Co.*[12]
the Fifth Circuit added that *American Cable* applied only to the
second category of *Gissel*-type violations.[13] The Seventh Circuit
openly rejected *American Cable* stating that *L.B. Foster* is the
better rule since it does not encourage continued employer unfair
labor practices.[14] In *NLRB v. Copps Corp.*,[15] however, the same
court expressed a concern over the two-year delay since issuance of the order. Although the court indicated that it still followed the rule of *L.B. Foster,* it modified the Board's order to
include the provision that employees be notified of their right to
petition for an NLRB election after a reasonable period of time.[16]

In *General Steel Products, Inc. v. NLRB*,[17] the Fourth Circuit
reviewed one of the cases the Supreme Court consolidated, in
Gissel and which had been remanded to the Board for additional
findings. On remand, the company sought to introduce evidence
that its change in ownership and management would eradicate
the effects of its past practices and ensure against a repetition of
its unlawful opposition to the union. The NLRB refused to allow
a hearing for this purpose and simply decided the case on the
basis of the original evidence. Citing the decision in *American
Cable*, the court, on review, held that under the circumstances of
the remand, the Board was required to consider the evidence

---

[11] J.P. Stevens & Co. v. NLRB, 441 F.2d 514, 76 L.R.R.M. 2817 (5th Cir.
1971). *See also* General Steel Products, Inc. v. NLRB, 445 F.2d 1350, 77
L.R.R.M. 2801 (4th Cir. 1971).

[12] 494 F.2d 762, 86 L.R.R.M. 2636 (5th Cir. 1974).

[13] This would follow from the requirement under *Gissel* that in first category offenses the Board find "that a fair and reliable election cannot be had."
395 U.S. 575, 614.

[14] New Alaska Development Corp. v. NLRB, 441 F.2d 491, 76 L.R.R.M. 2689
(7th Cir. 1971) *and cases cited therein*; NLRB v. Henry Colder Co., 447 F.2d
629, 77 L.R.R.M. 3153 (7th Cir. 1971), NLRB v. Kostel Corp., 440 F.2d 347,
76 L.R.R.M. 2643 (7th Cir. 1971).

[15] 458 F.2d 1227, 80 L.R.R.M. 2054 (7th Cir. 1972).

[16] This same approach had been suggested by the Supreme Court in *Gissel*.
See, 395 U.S. at 613. *Accord*, NLRB v. Henry Colder Co., 447 F.2d 629, 631,
77 L.R.R.M. 3153, —— (7th Cir. 1971), and cases there cited; NLRB v. Priced-
Less Discount Foods, Inc., 407 F.2d 1325, 70 L.R.R.M. 2743 (6th Cir. 1969);
NLRB v. Triangle Plastics, Inc., 406 F.2d 1100, 70 L.R.R.M. 2702 (6th Cir.
1969). *But compare* Inter-Polymer Industries, Inc. v. NLRB, 480 F.2d 631,
83 L.R.R.M. 2735, 2737 (9th Cir. 1973) (no "unusual circumstances" exist to
require the requested provision.)

[17] 445 F.2d 1350, 77 L.R.R.M. 2801 (4th Cir. 1971).

offered by General Steel. Subsequently, the Board vacated its bargaining order and directed a second election on the basis that the turnover in management reestablished the requisite laboratory conditions.[18]

Judge Haynsworth's concurring opinion in *General Steel* suggested the broader position that conditions caused by a change in ownership or the company's management should be accorded greater significance when evaluating the appropriateness of bargaining orders.

> When the Board considers, as it must under *Gissel*, the likelihood of further unfair labor practices, there hardly could be anything of greater significance than the departure of the old oppressive management and the substitution of new management and supervisory staff with a very different history in dealing with labor organizations.[19]

The Second Circuit in *NLRB v. General Stencils, Inc.*,[20] after vacating and remanding a bargaining order for further findings, *suggested* that the NLRB consider the issue of employee turnover. In *NLRB v. Ship Shape Maintenance Co.*,[21] the District of Columbia Court of Appeals went a step further when it denied enforcement to a bargaining order because it believed high employee turnover diminished the effect of the employer's violations:

> Although normal employee turnover in a proposed bargaining unit is not generally sufficient ground for refusing to enforce an otherwise valid bargaining order, we believe that the extraordinary rate of turnover indigenous to the Company's . . . operations greatly strengthens our conclusion that the adverse effects of the Company's unfair labor practice violation . . . should be reasonably and ade-

---

[18] General Steel Products, 199 N.L.R.B. No. 121, 81 L.R.R.M. 1513 (1972).

[19] 445 F.2d 1350, 1357, 77 L.R.R.M. 2801, 2806.

[20] 438 F.2d 894, 76 L.R.R.M. 2288 (2d Cir. 1971), *remanding* 178 N.L.R.B. 18, 71 L.R.R.M. 1652 (1969). Subsequently, the Court again was asked to review the Board's order and it denied enforcement because the record as a whole failed to support the bargaining order. The suggestion again was made that employee turnover was relevant to the Board's analysis. *See,* NLRB v. General Stencils, Inc., 472 F.2d 170, 82 L.R.R.M. 2081 (2d Cir. 1972), *denying enforcement to* 195 N.L.R.B. No. 173, 79 L.R.R.M. 1608 (1972). *Accord* NLRB v. Gruber's Mkt., 501 F.2d 697, 87 L.R.R.M. 2037, 2043 (7th Cir. 1974).

[21] 474 F.2d 434, 81 L.R.R.M. 2865, (D.C. Cir. 1972), *denying enf. in part to* 189 N.L.R.B. No. 58, 77 L.R.R.M. 1137 (1971).

quately dissipated, prior to the holding of a new representation election.[22]

After the Fifth Circuit's decision in *American Cable,* the NLRB in *Gibson Products Co.*[23] stated its disagreement with the court's position. In its view, there is no support in *Gissel* or in statutory regulations for a policy of assessing the need for a bargaining order by events occurring subsequent to commission of the unfair labor practices. The Board believed the Supreme Court had considered the potential harshness of imposing a bargaining representative on new employees, but that it had discerned an overriding need to structure the bargaining order as a remedy for past injuries as well as a future deterrent. Additionally, the Board noted that although there often were situations in which changes and intervening circumstances raised the argument that a new fair election could be held:

> [t]he union and the employees then supporting it were entitled to an election at an earlier time, and, if the employer's original unfair labor practices were of such a nature as to deprive them of an election at that time, to permit one now . . . 'would in effect be rewarding the employer.' [24]

The Board's *Gibson Products* decision was reversed by the Fifth Circuit.[25]

Another exception to the courts' basic reluctance to review bargaining orders in the light of changed circumstances has evolved. Where the Board is found to be directly responsible for the delay in enforcement of the bargaining order, the courts have reviewed the current propriety of the order. In *Clark's Gamble Corp. v. NLRB,*[26] the court focused upon the protracted handling of the case by the trial examiner and the Board—over two years—and the substantial employee turnover occurring during this period. It was specifically noted that the employer had

---

[22] 474 F.2d at 443, 81 L.R.R.M. 2865, 2871. The turnover was such that in a six month period approximately 150 persons were employed for an average work force of 35-40.

[23] 185 N.L.R.B. 362, 75 L.R.R.M. 1055 (1970).

[24] *Id.* at 363, 75 L.R.R.M. 1055, 1056. *See also,* Gibson Products, 199 N.L.R.B. No. 115, 81 L.R.R.M. 1499 (1972).

[25] NLRB v. Gibson Products, 494 F.2d 762, 86 L.R.R.M. 2636 (5th Cir. 1974).

[26] 422 F.2d 845, 73 L.R.R.M. 2669 (6th Cir. 1970), *cert. denied,* 400 U.S. 868 (1970).

not engaged in any delaying tactics. Despite Board objections, the court concluded:

> The thrust and philosophy of the Act is that employees be represented by a bargaining agent of their choice and in this situation which fails to reflect the selection of an agent by the employees sought to be affected, and where the period for personnel turnover has been extended by the Board-occasioned delay, we conclude that it would be contrary to the intent of the Act to order enforcement.[27]

The court also expressed the view that *Gissel* did not prevent consideration of employee turnover in the enforcement of bargaining orders. The Sixth Circuit in later cases has emphasized that *Clark's Gamble* was a limited ruling, applicable only to delays caused by Board inaction.[28]

Analysis of these cases demonstrates that narrowly drawn conditions may provide for the reappraisal of mandatory bargaining orders because of subsequent events or circumstances. The Board's basic policy is to reject any such request by the employer. In fact, the NLRB has been unwilling to accept the limited exceptions to the rule which have been formulated by the circuit courts of appeals. These cases also support the conclusion that there is substantial disagreement over the interpretation of the *Gissel* case as it applies to this issue. At the heart of the problem rests a delicate balancing of considerations. On the one hand, a need for finality of Board remedial orders exists so that no "premiums" await those who delay adjudication or continue violating the Act. On the other hand, the Board and the courts must make every effort to ensure that the employees themselves are guaranteed the freedom to accept or reject union representation in the forum designed by Congress under the Act. The Board does not serve this latter goal by its refusal, under any circumstances, to consider changed conditions.

UNION VIOLENCE AS A DEFENSE TO A BARGAINING ORDER

Certain limited grounds for an employer's defense against entry of a bargaining order were established in the *Laura Modes*

---

[27] *Id.* at 847, 73 L.R.R.M. 2669, 2670.

[28] G.P.D., Inc. v. NLRB, 430 F.2d 963, 74 L.R.R.M. 3057 (6th Cir. 1970); NLRB v. Lou De Young's Market, 430 F.2d 912, 75 L.R.R.M. 2129 (6th Cir. 1970).

case.[29] There, the NLRB denied a bargaining order request stemming from employer unfair labor practices because the union, by engaging in acts of physical violence, had demonstrated a "total disinterest" in pursuing its representation rights through the lawful means provided by the Act. The Board deemed it inappropriate under such circumstances to issue the bargaining order.

> Our powers to effectuate the statutory policy need not, we think, be exercised so single-mindedly in aiming for remedial restoration of the *status quo ante,* that we must disregard or sanction thereby union enforcement of an employer's mandatory bargaining duty by unprovoked and irresponsible physical assaults of the nature involved here.[30]

Another representation election was directed in order to preserve the employees' right of free choice.

A key factor in cases where the Board has withheld a bargaining order because of union misconduct has been a determination that the union had demonstrated by its violent conduct, a "plan of intimidation" against the company.[31] This determination has been developed in subsequent cases and has become a primary consideration in the NLRB's review of the propriety of bargaining orders where union misconduct is also at issue. The Board focuses upon the nature and seriousness of the union's actions, and balances these factors against any mitigating employer unfair labor practices.

In *Artcraft Mantel & Fireplace Co.*[32] there was evidence of union violence, threats, intimidation, and blackmail during a strike stemming from the company's refusal to extend recognition to the union. The Board, however, underscored the fact that the violence and unlawful conduct continued after the union had entered into a preliminary consent decree. The NLRB considered this to be a "plan of intimidation" probably more serious than in *Laura Modes,* and consequently it denied the bargaining order request. Furthermore, the employer's conduct in *Artcraft*

---

[29] Laura Modes Co., 144 N.L.R.B. 1592, 54 L.R.R.M. 1299 (1963).

[30] *Id.* at 1596, 54 L.R.R.M. 1299, 1301-1302.

[31] United Mineral & Chemical Corp., 155 N.L.R.B. 1390, 60 L.R.R.M. 1537 (1965) ; Artcraft Mantel & Fireplace Co., 174 N.L.R.B. 737, 70 L.R.R.M. 1294 (1969).

[32] 174 N.L.R.B. 737, 70 L.R.R.M. 1294 (1969).

Mantel and Fireplace was found to be less severely violative of the Act.

The Board reached a similar decision in *Allou Distributors, Inc.*,[33] although the situation arose during a decertification effort rather than a representation election proceeding.[34] Upon discovering that some employees supported a decertification petition, the union initiated threats and acts of violence designed to coerce a withdrawal of the employees' petition. The Board particularly emphasized the union's deliberate attempt to impede the statutory process in order to maintain its majority status.

In other cases, where there is no showing that a labor organization has sought to circumvent the Act by means of violence and intimidation, the NLRB has refused to deny the request for a bargaining order.[35] Instances of minor or infrequent misconduct by the union, especially arising during recognition picketing or unfair labor practices strikes,[36] have offered inadequate proof of an intimidation scheme. In such cases, the Board has refused to deny a bargaining order request.[37]

The Board has taken the position that when weighing the seriousness of the union's misconduct, the employer's violations must be considered on an equal basis in order to determine the propriety of the bargaining order request.[38] The Second Circuit rejected this policy and follows its own course of reasoning.[39]

---

[33] 201 N.L.R.B. 47, 82 L.R.R.M. 1102 (1972).

[34] The Board rejecting the holding by the Administrative Law Judge that *Laura Modes* was limited in its application to situations where a union was seeking initial recognition based on authorization cards. *But cf.* Cascade Corp., 192 N.L.R.B. 533, 77 L.R.R.M. 1823 (1971) *rev'd on other grounds*, 466 F.2d 748, 81 L.R.R.M. 2123 (6th Cir. 1973) where the Board held that *Laura Modes* must be distinguished in cases where the union is already certified.

[35] *See*, Pacific Abrasive Supply Co., 182 N.L.R.B. 329, 74 L.R.R.M. 113 (1970); New Fairview Hall Convalescent Home, 206 N.L.R.B. 688, 85 L.R.R.M. 1227 (1973), *enforced*, —— F.2d ——, 89 L.R.R.M. 3127 (2d Cir. 1975); Cascade Corp., 192 N.L.R.B. 533, 77 L.R.R.M. 1823 (1971) *rev'd on other grounds*, 466 F.2d 748, 81 L.R.R.M. 2123 (6th Cir. 1973). *Cf.* The Dow Chemical Corp., 216 N.L.R.B. No. 16, —— L.R.R.M. —— (1975).

[36] *E.g.*, Pacific Abrasive Supply Co., *supra* at note 35.

[37] *E.g.*, New Fairview Hall Convalescent Home, *supra* at note 35; Cascade Corp., *supra* at note 7.

[38] United Mineral & Chemical Corp., 155 N.L.R.B. 1390, 60 L.R.R.M. 1537 (1965), *enforcement denied in part*, NLRB v. United Mineral Corp., 391 F.2d 829, 67 L.R.R.M. 2343 (2d Cir. 1968).

[39] *Supra* at note 38.

In *NLRB v. United Mineral Corp.*, referring to the analogy between bargaining orders granted to unions involved in misconduct during bargaining cases and the reinstatement of unfair labor practice strikers who engaged in misconduct during the course of a strike, the court stated:

> However, we are not at all convinced that the standards in the two situations should be the same. In the reinstatement cases balancing is highly appropriate since the employee must either be rehired or not be; in the bargaining situation there is usually a third solution, to wit, an election, certainly the preferred way of testing employer sentiment.[40]

Consequently, the Second Circuit's *United Mineral* standard provides less reason to condone union misconduct even when accompanied by company violations, except in instances where the employer's unfair labor practices prevented an election.

Recently, however, the Second Circuit in *Donovan v. NLRB* [41] affirmed the Board's rejection of the employer's *Laura Modes* defense to the bargaining order. The Court cited its earlier *United Mineral* decision, but here it stated that the Board had applied the proper balance between the union's illegal activities and the company's violation, "[i]n as much as the collective facts when sorted and collated show the Company to be the more guilty party. . . ." [42]

On the whole, it may be said that the Board considers the ruling under *Laura Modes* to be "the extraordinary sanction of withholding an otherwise appropriate remedial bargaining order." [43] Mere instances of misconduct by the union may generate unfair labor practice charges and cease and desist orders, but evidence of deliberate attempts to circumvent the Act by means of violence and coercion is required to warrant refusal of a remedial bargaining order. For example, the NLRB recently revoked its certification of a militant union because of its "brutal and unprovoked physical

---

[40] 391 F.2d at 841, 67 L.R.R.M. 2343, 2351. However the NLRB specifically rejected this test. *See,* World Carpets of New York, Inc., 188 N.L.R.B. 122, 76 L.R.R.M. 1225 (1971), *supplementing,* 163 N.L.R.B. 597, 64 L.R.R.M. 1381 (1967), *enforced in part,* 463 F.2d 57, 80 L.R.R.M. 2712 (2d Cir. 1972).

[41] —— F.2d ——, 89 L.R.R.M. 3127 (2d Cir. 1975) *cert. denied* —— U.S. —— (1975). *See generally* NLRB v. World Carpets, 463 F.2d 57, 80 L.R.R.M. 2712 (2d Cir. 1972).

[42] —— F.2d ——, 89 L.R.R.M. 3127, 3132.

[43] *Id.* at ——, 89 L.R.R.M. 3127, 3131 (1975).

violence and extensive record of similar aggravated misconduct in other contemporaneous cases." [44]

UNION RACIAL AND SEX DISCRIMINATION AS A DEFENSE TO A BARGAINING ORDER

A related issue of somewhat different dimensions was reviewed by the Eighth Circuit in *NLRB v. Mansion House Corp.*,[45] when it ruled that the employer could defend against a bargaining order by showing that the union practiced racial discrimination in its membership. The court held that the NLRB, as a federal agency, was prohibited by the Due Process Clause of the Fifth Amendment of the United States Constitution from requiring an employer to bargain with the union. It stated:

> When a governmental agency recognizes such a union to be the bargaining representative it significantly becomes a willing participant in the union's discriminatory practices.[46]

Accordingly, the court held that "the remedial machinery of the National Labor Relations Act cannot be made available to a union which is unwilling to correct past practices of racial discrimination." [47]

Following *Mansion House,* the Board, in a split decision in *Bekins, Moving and Storage Co. of Florida, Inc.,*[48] held that it could not constitutionally certify a labor organization shown to be engaging in unlawful racial discrimination, but that it would not investigate allegations of racial discrimination until *after* the election had been held and the union involved had received a majority of the votes. Thus, as the Board majority including Chairman Miller and Member Jenkins, explained in *Bekins*:

> Accordingly, a precertification inquiry, in our opinion, need not be made at the original hearing, but may be made after an election has been held and at that time, only if the labor organization involved has received a majority of the valid votes cast and is thus, absent any showing of grounds for disqualification, *prima facie* eligible for certification by this Board as the exclusive agent of all

---

[44] *See*, Union Nacional De Trabajadores (Carborundum Co. of Puerto Rico), 219 N.L.R.B. No. 157, 90 L.R.R.M. 1023 (1975).

[45] 473 F.2d 471, 82 L.R.R.M. 2608 (8th Cir. 1973).

[46] *Id.*, 473, 82 L.R.R.M. at 2610.

[47] *Id.*, 477, 82 L.R.R.M. at 2613.

[48] 211 N.L.R.B. No. 7, 86 L.R.R.M. 1323 (1974).

employees in the unit. The Board has limited resources and an ever-increasing caseload. We attempt to give employees an opportunity to express their representational wishes through a secret ballot election with as little delay as possible. If we were to hold that the inquiry concerning the issue of disqualification was to be made at the original hearing before an election was held, we would be allocating our limited resources and time to determine an issue not yet ripe for consideration, we would significantly delay the holding of elections, and we would thus fail to effectuate the purposes and policies of the Act. Furthermore, under Section 9(c)(1) of the Act, we would be deprived of the often necessary and meaningful recommendations of a Hearing Officer if the inquiry were made in the preelection hearing since that hearing is only a fact finding, nonadversary one. Unlike the original preelection hearing, a post election hearing can, in an appropriate case, culminate in the issuance of a report and recommendations by a Hearing Officer, and affords the parties an opportunity to file exceptions and briefs. Limiting the litigation of the disqualification issue to the post election hearing would thus give us the benefit of credibility resolutions, where needed, and recommendations; and, at the same time, the litigants' rights to procedural due process would be fully protected.[49]

Member Kennedy concurred in the *Bekins* decision, but would limit consideration to the issues of "race, alienage, or national origin." Member Kennedy did not view sex discrimination as raising a constitutional issue and would permit such practices to be raised only in cases alleging a union's breach of its fair representation duty and not as a defense to a union's certification.[50]

Members Fanning and Penello dissented, stating that they would not consider allegations of discriminatory practices by labor orga-

---

[49] *Id.*, 86 L.R.R.M. at 1327 (italics in original). *See also* S. H. Kress & Co., 212 N.L.R.B. No. 12, 86 L.R.R.M. 1508 (1974); Petrie Stores Corp., 212 N.L.R.B. No. 14, 86 L.R.R.M. 1509 (1974); Bell & Howell Co., 213 N.L.R.B. No. 79, 87 L.R.R.M. 1172 (1974); Alden Press Inc., 212 N.L.R.B. No. 91, 86 L.R.R.M. 1605 (1974); Community Service Publishing, Inc., 216 N.L.R.B. No. 180, 89 L.R.R.M. 1261 (1975); Capitol City, Inc., 212 N.L.R.B. No. 52, 86 L.R.R.M. 1497 (1974). In the above cases, the Board ruled that the employer objections to alleged union racial discrimination raised at the pre-election hearing stage were untimely. By the same token, the Board has quashed subpoenas requested in pre-election hearings which related to documents designed to inquire into the union's membership practices. *See* United Construction Contractors Ass'n, 212 N.L.R.B. No. 127, 86 L.R.R.M. 1734 (1974), Alden Press, Inc., 212 N.L.R.B. No. 91, 86 L.R.R.M. 1605 (1974); Union Carbide Corp., 86 L.R.R.M. 1606 (1974) (decision of the Regional Director regarding subpoena pursuant to allegations of sex discrimination). *See also* Williams Enterprises, Inc., 212 N.L.R.B. No. 132, 87 L.R.R.M. 1044 (1974), where a bargaining order issued despite an employer's post-election *Bekins* objections. The Board found that the facts presented did not support the allegations of discrimination.

[50] *Id.*, 86 L.R.R.M. at 1329, 1330 n. 29, 1331.

nizations in a precertification proceeding but would "leave such questions as they may raise, with respect to the Petitioner's willingness or capacity to represent fairly all employees in the bargaining unit, to be resolved in other proceedings under the Act." [51] The dissent argued that the certification of a union as an exclusive representative operates to create the "necessary condition" for permitting the sanction of law and government to run against the offending practices.[52] Members Fanning and Penello stated further that the language of Section 9(c)(1) mandated [53] the Board to certify a union which had won an election that was proper except for the alleged discriminatory practices.[54]

In *Plastiline, Inc. v. Johansen,*[55] an employer who wished to advance a *Bekins* discrimination objection to an election proceeding requested the U.S. district court to require the Board to test the alleged discrimination *before* proceeding with an election to determine the union's majority status. Both parties agreed that the Board was required to consider the discrimination charges, which, if sustained, would justify the Board's refusing to issue a bargaining order. The district court refused to grant the requested relief, and was upheld by the Ninth Circuit which stated:

> Appellant wants us to hold that the district court should require the labor board to fully explore discrimination charges as the first step in resolving the right to represent.
> We hold that this is an area where the board may exercise its discretion in the sequence in which it does justice.

The *Bekins* issue was also raised before the Fifth Circuit in *NLRB v. Bancroft Mfg. Co.*[56]—a postelection refusal to bargain case. The employer had requested leave of the Administrative Law Judge to amend his answer to include a *Mansion House* defense, and enforcement of a subpoena *duces tecum* for statistical data concerning the union's racial discrimination. Both motions were denied by the board. The court ruled that both *Mansion House* and *Bekins* dealt with union discrimination at the "local level only,"

---

51 *Id.,* 86 L.R.R.M. at 1335.

52 86 L.R.R.M. at 1333.

53 29 U.S.C. § 158(c)(1) provides in part that the Board "*shall* direct an election by secret ballot and *shall* certify the results thereof . . . ." (Emphasis added.) *But see, supra* p. 45 n. 28.

54 *Id.,* 86 L.R.R.M. 1333-1334.

55 —— F.2d ——, 88 L.R.R.M. 3183 (9th Cir. 1975).

56 516 F.2d 436, 89 L.R.R.M. 3105 (5th Cir. 1975).

since it is the local which usually bargains with employers and is charged with fair representation of its members.[57] The company had argued that the local union was a branch of a national union allegedly notorious for its discriminatory membership policies, and therefore the local's certification should be revoked. The court found that the company had failed to show any nexus between the policies of the national and local unions, and therefore, the Board did not abuse its discretion in refusing to enforce the subpoena or to allow the amendment to the employer's answer.

The issue of a *Bekins* defense in the context of sex discrimination came before the Board in several cases.[58] The Board, however, found that sex discrimination would not justify withholding a bargaining order from a union. This result arose from the pivotal position of Member Kennedy who, although concurring in the original *Bekins* decision, had stated that employer allegations of sex discrimination were not constitutionally based, unlike race discrimination charges. Thus, Members Kennedy, Fanning and Penello all agreed in *Bell & Howell* that an allegation of unlawful sex discrimination could not be raised in a pre-election proceeding. Even though all three viewed sex discrimination as prohibited by the National Labor Relations Act, they required the matter to be raised after certification, in an unfair labor practice proceeding based on an allegation that the union had breached its duty of fair representation. Chairman Miller and Member Jenkins, in dissent, argued that sex discrimination charges could be considered in precertification proceedings in order to determine if such discrimination disqualified the union from NLRB certification.

From the above discussion, it can be seen that the positions of the "Miller Board" on the *Bekins* issue were fairly well defined. In future cases involving allegations of union racial or sex discrimination, it should be remembered that the terms of Chairman Miller and Member Kennedy have expired. Chairman Miller's successor, Chairman Murphy, has not yet expressed an opinion on the *Bekins* issue;[59] neither has Member Kennedy's replacement, Peter

---

[57] *Id.*, 516 F.2d 436, 89 L.R.R.M. at 3112, citing Grant's Furniture Plaza, Inc., 213 N.L.R.B. No. 80, 87 L.R.R.M. 1175 (1974), and Williams Enterprises Inc., 212 N.L.R.B. No. 132, 87 L.R.R.M. 1044 (1974).

[58] Bell & Howell Co., 213 N.L.R.B. No. 79, 87 L.R.R.M. 1172, 1174-1175 (1974), 220 N.L.R.B. No. 147, —— L.R.R.M. —— (1975); Grants Furniture Plaza, Inc., 213 N.L.R.B. No. 80, 87 L.R.R.M. 1177 (1974).

[59] In Ploof Transfer Co., 220 N.L.R.B. No. 110, —— L.R.R.M. —— (1975), the *Bekins* issue was raised in a case before Chairman Murphy, who con-

Walther. Until future such cases come before the Board, the Board's policy apparently has temporarily been placed in limbo.

Concluding Remarks

Empirical data suggest that the NLRB has issued *Gissel* bargaining orders based on authorization cards in only a small number of cases, when compared to the total number of certifications.[60] During the period 1962-1975 there were 114,301 representation elections held, 63,185 certifications issued, and 1405 instances where cards were used to order an employer to bargain. Therefore, based on statistics, the *Gissel* remedy accounted for only 2.2 percent of the total number of bargaining relationships established by the Board. As summarized by Chairman Murphy.

> [O]n both an absolute and a relative basis, requiring an employer to bargain based on authorization cards is the exception rather than the rule and in the overwhelming majority of instances, union bargaining rights are established pursuant to secret-ballot elections conducted by the Board.[61]

Despite such statistical evidence, however, the bargaining order remedy retains substantial importance in cases in which it is alleged that an employer responded to a union organizing campaign with widespread unfair labor practices. Our discussion has shown that the Board's application of the *Gissel* criteria in specific cases has not been immune from criticism by the parties involved in the representation election process, the judiciary and the bar. One commentator noted:

> One thing is clear. Law reform is needed in the United States with respect to the issuance of bargaining orders. Procedures must be devised to preclude employers from engaging in delaying tactics and precipitating costly frivolous litigation to evade their duty to bargain. Nor may unions be permitted to foist themselves on a non-consenting majority. Employees should not continue to be the stakes in the floating card game between employers and unions.[62]

---

curred in the Board's rejection of a *Bekins* defense "inasmuch as the same conclusion is reached under any view of the holding" in *Bekins*.

[60] *See,* DAILY LABOR REPORT, No. 206, E-1 (October 23, 1975), Statement of NLRB Chairman Murphy During Oversight Hearings Before the House Labor Subcommittee on Labor-Management Relations.

[61] *Id.*

[62] Address by Florian Bartosic, Secretary, ABA Section of Labor Relations Law, to the annual American Bar Association meeting, August 12, 1975, *see,* DLR, No. 157, D-1, D-11 (August 13, 1975).

The purpose of Chapters XI and XII has been to evaluate whether the Board's exercise of its remedial powers has best effectuated the policies of the Act. Although the Supreme Court in *Gissel* sought to clarify and simplify the procedure for issuing bargaining orders, it established criteria which the Board has had difficulty administering on a case-by-case basis. As a result, there have been conflicts between the NLRB and the judiciary in the enforcement process.

The Board often has demonstrated a failure to analyze properly whether there is a causal relationship between employer misconduct and the representation election process. In certain cases there has been an incomplete assessment of the seriousness of the employer's violations. No doubt this problem stems, in part, from the difficulty in dealing with the Supreme Court's test which anticipates that various unfair labor practices will carry differing remedial consequences, depending upon the circumstances of the individual case. However, the Board is compelled to undertake the task and should do so with renewed diligence.

CHAPTER XIII

Remedying Breaches of the Bargaining Obligation

Upon voluntary recognition, certification, or the issuance of a *Gissel* bargaining order,[1] the statutory bargaining provisions oblige the employer to bargain with the union as the exclusive representative of the employees in the appropriate bargaining unit. Once this bargaining obligation is established, Sections 8(a)(5) [2] and 8(b)(2) [3] make it an unfair labor practice for the employer and union, respectively, to refuse to bargain collectively. Section 8(d) [4] requires this bargaining obligation to entail that the employer and union "confer in *good faith* with respect to wages, hours, and other terms and conditions of employment . . . ." (emphasis added).

In the absence of unusual circumstances, the union's majority is irrebuttably presumed for a reasonable period, normally one year, after the establishment of the bargaining obligation.[5]

---

[1] *See* Chapters XI and XII, *supra.*

[2] 29 U.S.C. § 158(a)(5) (1970).

[3] 29 U.S.C. § 158(b)(2) (1970).

[4] 29 U.S.C. § 158(d) (1970) provides in relevant part that:

> For the purposes of this section, to bargain collectively is the performance of the mutual obligation of the employer and the representative of the employees to meet at reasonable times and confer in good faith with respect to wages, hours, and other terms and conditions of employment, or the negotiation of an agreement, or any question arising thereunder, and the execution of a written contract incorporating any agreement reached if requested by either party, but such obligation does not compel either party to agree to a proposal or require the making of a concession . . . .

[5] Brooks v. NLRB, 348 U.S. 96, 98, 35 L.R.R.M. 2158 (1954); Armco Drainage & Metal Products, 116 N.L.R.B. 1260, 38 L.R.R.M. 1457 (1956).

The bargaining obligation requires that there be "at least one year of *actual* bargaining" between the parties.[6]

REMEDIES FOR IMPROPER WITHDRAWAL OF RECOGNITION

After the initial year, the presumption of the union's majority status continues, but may be rebutted by a showing that the union no longer commands a majority, or by objective evidence of the employer's good faith doubt of the union's majority status.[7] To justify withdrawal of union recognition in the light of its presumptive representative status, the employer must affirmatively show either "that the union in fact no longer enjoyed majority support on the date of the refusal to bargain, or that the refusal to bargain was predicated upon a reasonably grounded good-faith doubt of majority support."[8] Where, however, the union's loss of majority or the employer's doubt of majority is caused by employer unfair labor practices, the employer is precluded from asserting the union's changed status as a defense to a refusal-to-bargain charge.[9] An employer found to have violated the Act by improperly withdrawing recognition from the union generally will be required to "cease and desist" from the refusal to bargain, and from further similar violations. The employer will also be ordered to recognize and bargain with the union upon request, and to post the appropriate notices.[10]

---

[6] Mar-Jac Poultry Co., 136 N.L.R.B. 785, 49 L.R.R.M. 1854 (1962) (emphasis added). *Cf.* Groendyke Transport Inc., 207 N.L.R.B. 381, 84 L.R.R.M. 1458 (1973).

[7] NLRB v. Little Rock Downtowner, 414 F.2d 1084, 1091, 72 L.R.R.M. 2044 (8th Cir. 1969); Celanese Corp. of America, 95 N.L.R.B. 664, 672, 28 L.R.R.M. 1362 (1951), *cited with approval* in NLRB v. Burns Security Services, 406 U.S. 272, 279, n. 3, 80 L.R.R.M. 2225 (1972); NLRB v. Cayuga Crushed Stone, Inc., 474 F.2d 1380, 1383, 82 L.R.R.M. 2951 (2d Cir. 1973).

[8] Terrell Machine Co. v. NLRB, 427 F.2d 1088, 1090, 73 L.R.R.M. 2381 (4th Cir. 1970), *cert. denied*, 398 U.S. 929, 74 L.R.R.M. 2240 (1970).

[9] Franks Bros. Co. v. NLRB, 321 U.S. 702, 14 L.R.R.M. 591 (1944); NLRB v. Sky Wolf Sales, 470 F.2d 827, 830, 82 L.R.R.M. 2050 (9th Cir. 1972); C&C Plywood Corp., 163 N.L.R.B. 1022, 64 L.R.R.M. 2065 (1967), *enforced*, 413 F.2d 112, 71 L.R.R.M. 2796 (9th Cir. 1969); NLRB v. Parma Water Lifter Co., 211 F.2d 258, 33 L.R.R.M. 2810 (1954) (9th Cir. 1954), *cert. denied* 348 U.S. 829, 34 L.R.R.M. 2898 (1954).

[10] *See e.g.*, NLRB v. Leatherwood Drilling, 513 F.2d 270, 89 L.R.R.M. 2460 (5th Cir. 1975) and cases there cited.

If an employer who illegally withdraws recognition from the union also abrogates a collective bargaining agreement, the Board can "enforce" the agreement by ordering the employer to reactivate and abide by it and pay, with interest, lost monetary benefits to the employees.[11]

MANDATORY SUBJECTS OF BARGAINING

The Act also mandates that the employer bargain only with regard to subjects which fall within the statutory language.[12] The difference between mandatory and permissive subjects of bargaining was explained by Chief Justice Warren in his majority opinion in *Fibreboard Corp. v. NLRB*: [13]

> Section 8(a)(5) of the National Labor Relations Act provides that it shall be an unfair labor practice for an employer "to refuse to bargain collectively with the representatives of his employees." Collective bargaining is defined in § 8(d) as
>
>> "the performance of the mutual obligation of the employer and the representative of the employees to meet at reasonable times and confer in good faith with respect to wages, hours, and other terms and conditions of employment."
>
> Read together, these provisions establish the obligation of the employer and the representative of its employees to bargain with each other in good faith with respect to "wages, hours, and other terms and conditions of employment . . . ." The duty is limited to those subjects, and within that area neither party is legally obligated to yield. *Labor Board v. American Ins. Co.*, 343 U.S. 395.
>
> Mr. Justice Stewart, concurring, further explained: [57 LRRM 2617] decisions concerning the volume and kind of advertising expenditures, product design, the manner of financing, and sales, all may bear upon the security of the workers' jobs. Yet it is hardly conceivable that such decisions so involve "conditions of employment" that they must be negotiated with the employees' bargaining representative.
>
> In many of these areas the impact of a particular management decision upon job security may be extremely indirect and uncertain, and this alone may be sufficient reason to conclude that such decisions are not "with respect to * * * conditions of employment." Yet

---

[11] NLRB v. George E. Light, Boat Storage, Inc., 373 F.2d 762, 64 L.R.R.M. 2457 (5th Cir. 1967), *modif'd* 382 F.2d 577, 66 L.R.R.M. 2384 (5th Cir. 1967); NLRB v. Huttig Sash & Door Co., 362 F.2d 217, 62 L.R.R.M. 2271 (4th Cir. 1966).

[12] *See e.g.*, NLRB v. Wooster Div. of Borg-Warner Corp., 356 U.S. 342, 349, 42 L.R.R.M. 2034 (1958).

[13] Fibreboard Paper Products Corp. v. NLRB, 379 U.S. 203, 209-210, 57 L.R.R.M. 2609, 2611 (1964).

there are other areas where decisions by management may quite clearly imperil job security, or indeed terminate employment entirely. An enterprise may decide to invest in labor-saving machinery. Another may resolve to liquidate its assets and go out of business. Nothing the Court holds today should be understood as imposing a duty to bargain collectively regarding such managerial decisions, which lie at the core of entrepreneurial control. Decisions concerning the commitment of investment capital and the basic scope of the enterprise are not in themselves primarily about conditions of employment, though the effect of the decision may be necessarily to terminate employment. If, as I think clear, the purpose of § 8(d) is to describe a limited area subject to the duty of collective bargaining, those management decisions which are fundamental to the basic direction of a corporate enterprise or which impinge only indirectly upon employment security should be excluded from that area.

A union may waive its right to consult about employer changes within mandatory subjects of bargaining, if such a waiver is "clear and unmistakable." [14] Thus, an employer who has bargained for and won the right to make particular kinds of unilateral changes in wages, hours, or working conditions need not bargain again during the life of the contract in order to exercise those rights.[15]

REMEDIES FOR ILLEGAL UNILATERAL CHANGES

The employer's bargaining obligation continues during the life of the contract and as long thereafter as the union retains its majority status. While the contract is in effect, the employer must bargain not only over questions arising from alleged breaches of the contract,[16] but also over other mandatory bar-

---

[14] NLRB v. Perkins Machine Co., 326 F.2d 488, 55 L.R.R.M. 2204 (1st Cir. 1964), *accord* NLRB v. C&C Plywood Corp., 385 U.S. 421, 430-431, 64 L.R.R.M. 2065 (1967), *affirming* 148 N.L.R.B. 414 (1967); Timken Roller Bearing Co. v. NLRB, 325 F.2d 746, 751, 54 L.R.R.M. 2785 (6th Cir. 1963), *cert. denied,* 376 U.S. 971, 55 L.R.R.M. 2878 (1964); Beacon Journal Pub. Co. v. NLRB, 401 F.2d 366, 367-368, 69 L.R.R.M. 2232 (6th Cir. 1968); NLRB v. Item Co., 220 F.2d 956, 35 L.R.R.M. 2709 (5th Cir. 1955), *cert. denied,* 350 U.S. 836, 36 L.R.R.M. 2716 (1955).

[15] *See e.g.,* Ador Corp., 150 N.L.R.B. 1658, 1660, 58 L.R.R.M. 1280, 1281 (1965).

[16] *See* Timken Roller Bearing Co. v. NLRB, 325 F.2d 746, 753, 54 L.R.R.M. 2785 (6th Cir. 1963), *cert. denied* 376 U.S. 971, 55 L.R.R.M. 2878; NLRB v. Goodyear Aerospace Corp., 388 F.2d 673, 674, 67 L.R.R.M. 2447 (6th Cir. 1968).

gaining subjects not included in the existing contract.[17] In
short, Section 8(a)(5) does not permit the employer to make unilateral changes in employment conditions—whether established
by contract or not—unless he first consults with his employees'
bargaining representative.[18]

To determine whether an employer's unilateral action constitutes a breach of his statutory bargaining obligation, and the
appropriate remedy for such violation, "the particular facts of a
particular case must be examined." [19] A few representative cases
will illustrate typical unilateral action refusal to bargain remedies.

An employer who unilaterally implements changes in rates of
pay, wages, hours, or other terms or conditions of employment
will be ordered to reimburse employees if lost wages or other
benefits occur because of these changes.[20] For example, employers who have unilaterally discontinued payment of regularly
scheduled bonuses will be ordered to pay past bonuses and to
bargain in the future about such changes.[21] Where an employer
was found to have violated the Act by unilaterally reducing
employees' hours of work, the employees were reimbursed for
monetary losses.[22] Similarly, an employer who unilaterally
changed work schedules and lunch periods, and who eliminated

---

[17] NLRB v. Jacobs Mfg. Co., 196 F.2d 680, 683-684, 30 L.R.R.M. 2098, (2d
Cir. 1952); Local Union No. 9735, United Mine Workers v. NLRB, 258 F.2d
146, 149, 42 L.R.R.M. 2320 (D.C. Cir. 1958).

[18] NLRB v. C & C Plywood, 385 U.S. 421, 425, 64 L.R.R.M. 2065 (1967);
NLRB v. Katz, 369 U.S. 736, 743, 50 L.R.R.M. 2177, 2180 (1962); NLRB v.
Huttig Sash and Door Co., 377 F.2d 964, 65 L.R.R.M. 2431 (8th Cir. 1967);
Int'l Woodworkers of America, Local 3-10 v. NLRB, 380 F.2d 628, 630, 65
L.R.R.M. 2633 (D.C. Cir. 1967).

[19] NLRB v. American National Insurance Co., 343 U.S. 395, 400, 30 L.R.R.M.
2147 (1952); NLRB v. Denton, 217 F.2d 567, 570, 35 L.R.R.M. 2217 (5th Cir.
1954), *cert. denied,* 348 U.S. 981, 35 L.R.R.M. 2709 (1955).

[20] *See e.g.,* Overnite Transportation Co. v. NLRB, 372 F.2d 765, 770 64
L.R.R.M. 2359 (4th Cir. 1967), *cert. denied,* 389 U.S. 838, 66 L.R.R.M. 2307;
Leeds & Northrup Co. v. NLRB, 391 F.2d 874, 879-880, 67 L.R.R.M. 2793 (3d
Cir. 1968); NLRB v. Frontier Homes Corp., 371 F.2d 974, 981, 64 L.R.R.M.
2320 (8th Cir. 1967).

[21] *See* NLRB v. Marland One-Way Clutch Co., 520 F.2d 586, 89 L.R.R.M.
2721 (7th Cir. 1975); Gas Machinery Co., 221 N.L.R.B. 129, —— L.R.R.M.
—— (1975) (unilateral withholding of Christmas bonuses). *But cf.* Century
Electric Motor Co. v. NLRB, 447 F.2d 10, 78 L.R.R.M. 2042 (8th Cir.
1971) (no violation in elimination of Christmas bonus.).

[22] Amoco Chemicals Corp., 211 N.L.R.B. No. 84, 86 L.R.R.M. 1483 (1974).

free coffee, was ordered to reinstate the previous schedules, reinstate the coffee program, and reimburse employees for lost wages.[23] In like manner, deviation of an employer from his past practice of recalling laid-off employees in order of seniority prompted the NLRB to order the affected employees made whole for monetary losses.[24] Reimbursement will also be ordered to remedy unilateral elimination of overtime work, if there is a "practical way to measure how much overtime would have been available or which employees would have availed themselves of overtime opportunities had they been offered." [25]

In addition to monetary remedies for unilateral changes, the Board will attempt to restore the status quo ante with respect to in-plant conditions.[26] The fact that certain employees may have benefited from the employer's violation does not alter the Board's power to restore previolation conditions, "for it is public and not private rights that are being vindicated." [27] For example, an employer who improperly changed job classifications to exclude some employees from the bargaining unit was ordered to rescind the change and restore the classifications.[28] Where appropriate, however, the Board may require that the employees express a desire for the former conditions before ordering a restoration of the status quo ante. If they accept the new conditions, no make-whole order is warranted. Only if they desire a

---

[23] *See* Missourian Publishing Co., 216 N.L.R.B. No. 34, 88 L.R.R.M. 1647 (1975). *But compare* Ladish Co., 219 N.L.R.B. No. 60, 89 L.R.R.M. 1653 (1975). Although the employer there had violated the Act by refusing to honor the union's request to bargain about vending machine food prices, the employer was not ordered to bargain about every proposed price change, but rather to bargain on price changes only after they were effectuated unilaterally, and upon request by the Union.

[24] Hamilton Electronics, Co., 203 N.L.R.B. No. 40, 83 L.R.R.M. 1097 (1973).

[25] Chemvet Laboratories, Inc., 204 N.L.R.B. No. 40, 83 L.R.R.M. 1405 (1973), *enforced in pertinent part in* Chemvet Laboratories, Inc. v. NLRB, 497 F.2d 445, 86 L.R.R.M. 2262 (8th Cir. 1974).

[26] *See* Fibreboard Paper Products Corp. v. NLRB, 379 U.S. 203, 57 L.R.R.M. 2609 (1964).

[27] *See* Office & Professional Employees v. NLRB, 419 F.2d 314, 70 L.R.R.M. 3047, 3053 (D.C. Cir. 1969); Virginia Electric and Power Co. v. NLRB, 391 U.S. 533, 540, 12 L.R.R.M. 739 (1943).

[28] Office & Professional Employees v. NLRB, 419 F.2d 314, 70 L.R.R.M. 3047 (D.C. Cir. 1969). *See also* Abingdon Nursing Center, 197 N.L.R.B. No. 781, 80 L.R.R.M. 1470 (1972) (employer ordered to reinstate old hours for kitchen employees and reinstitute a hot lunch program); Federal Mogul Corp., 209 N.L.R.B. 343, 85 L.R.R.M. 1353 (1974).

restoration of the earlier conditions will they be reimbursed for losses resulting from the violation.[29]

UNILATERAL DECISIONS TO CLOSE, RELOCATE, OR SUBCONTRACT UNIT OPERATIONS

In the *Darlington* case, the Supreme Court ruled that an employer has the right to terminate his entire business completely for whatever reason he chooses.[30] Such a decision does not free him from his bargaining obligation, however. At the very least, the employer is required to bargain over the *effects* of his decision.[31] Thus, the employer must give notice to the union so that it has an opportunity to bargain over its members' employment status with respect to such items as pensions, seniority, and severance pay.[32] Where an employer is found to have violated this bargaining obligation, the Board will order him to bargain with the union over the effects of the closing.[33]

The employer's bargaining obligation is much broader, however, when his decision involves less than a complete closing but affects his employees' working conditions. Examples of this include transferring work to a new plant, partially closing operations, or subcontracting.[34] Thus, in the *Fibreboard Paper Products Corp. v. NLRB* decision,[35] the Supreme Court found a Section 8(a)(5) violation when an employer failed to bargain with the union about his decision to subcontract unit work, although the decision merely involved replacing employees in the existing bargaining unit with others who would do the same work in the

---

[29] Johnson's Industrial Caterers, Inc., 197 N.L.R.B. 352, 80 L.R.R.M. 1344 (1972), *enforced per curiam in* NLRB v. Johnson's Caterers, 478 F.2d 1208, 83 L.R.R.M. 2847 (6th Cir. 1973).

[30] Textile Workers v. Darlington Mfg. Co., —— U.S. ——, 58 L.R.R.M. 2657 (1965).

[31] NLRB v. Royal Plating & Polishing Co., 350 F.2d 191, 196, 60 L.R.R.M. 2033 (3d Cir. 1965). Under *Darlington*, a partial closing to chill unionism would violate the act.

[32] NLRB v. Rapid Bindery Inc., 293 F.2d 170, 48 L.R.R.M. 2658 (2d Cir. 1961); Morrison Cafeterias Inc. v. NLRB, 431 F.2d 254, 74 L.R.R.M. 3048 (8th Cir. 1970).

[33] NLRB v. Summit Tooling Co., 474 F.2d 1352, 83 L.R.R.M. 2044 (7th Cir. 1973).

[34] *See* Textile Workers v. Darlington Mfg. Co., *supra*, note 30.

[35] 379 U.S. 203, 57 L.R.R.M. 2609 (1964).

same plant.[36] In an order quite unlike that in *Darlington*, the employer in *Fibreboard* was required to resume the discontinued operations, although legitimate business reasons were involved in the decision to close. The Court also ordered that former employees be reinstated with backpay. Rejecting employer arguments that the employees had been discharged "for cause," the Court did not find that Section 10(c)[37] barred reinstatement. This statutory provision, the Court held, was designed to prevent the NLRB from reinstating an individual who had been discharged because of misconduct, and was not intended to curtail the Board's broad power to fashion remedies when the loss of employment "stems directly from an unfair labor practice . . . ."[38]

---

[36] In a sense, *Darlington* and *Fibreboard* present polar illustrations of employer decisions to change operations. The former involved a complete closure; the latter a mere replacement of employees in a continuing unit. Between these extremes fall almost unlimited types of decisions, and there has been continual litigation attempting to determine whether the employer is required to bargain over the operational decision itself, or merely over its effects. *Compare e.g.*, NLRB v. Adams Dairy, Inc., 350 F.2d 108, 113, 60 L.R.R.M. 2084 (8th Cir. 1965), *cert. denied* 382 U.S. 1011, 61 L.R.R.M. 2192 (1966), *with* International Ladies' Garment Workers' Union (McLoughlin Mfg. Corp.) v. NLRB, 463 F.2d 907, 916-917, 919, 80 L.R.R.M. 2716 (D.C. Cir. 1972). Remedies for violations in this area are rather straightforward, and will generally include bargaining, monetary, reinstatement and notice posting orders. Questions regarding substantive violations with respect to these management decisions are quite complex, however, and to discuss them more completely here is beyond the scope of this remedies study. The issues concerning employer decisions to subcontract, automate, relocate, or completely or partially to close operations are fully discussed and analyzed in Report No. 9 of this Labor Relations and Public Policy Series. *See* SWIFT, THE NLRB AND MANAGEMENT DECISION MAKING, Industrial Research Unit (1974).

[37] 29 U.S.C. § 160(c) (1970), provides in part that "no order of the Board shall require the reinstatement of any individual as an employee who has been suspended or discharged or the payment to him of any backpay, if such individual was suspended or discharged *for cause*. . . ." (emphasis added).

[38] 379 U.S. at 217, 57 L.R.R.M. at 2614. *See also* Florida-Texas Freight, Inc., 203 N.L.R.B. 529, 83 L.R.R.M. 1093 (1973); *enforced sub nom.* NLRB v. Florida-Texas Freight, Inc., 489 F.2d 1275, 85 L.R.R.M. 2845 (6th Cir. 1974) (employer ordered to set aside subcontract, reinstate employees, and reimburse them for any loss of pay and bargain with union); and Arnold Graphic Industries v. NLRB, 505 F.2d 257, 87 L.R.R.M. 2753 (6th Cir. 1974) (order to employer to return transferred equipment to its first location, and to reinstate employees. Backpay was denied in view of employer's history of harmonious labor relations with union, the absence of union animus in unilateral change, the economic hardship on the employer, and the employer's willingness to recognize the union).

THE BOARD MAY NOT COMPEL AN AGREEMENT
—THE H.K. PORTER DECISION

In *H.K. Porter Co. v. NLRB*,[39] the Supreme Court held that even though the NLRB has the power "to require employers and employees to negotiate, it is without power to compel a company or a union to agree to any substantive contractual provision of a collective bargaining agreement." [40] The Court observed that even when agreement between the parties is impossible, "it was never intended that the Government would in such cases step in, become a party to the negotiations and impose its own views of a desirable settlement." [41] The Court in *Porter* reaffirmed its previous decisions which held that the Board may not, either directly or indirectly, compel concessions or otherwise sit in judgment upon the substantive terms of collective bargaining agreements,[42] and that Section 8(c) was an attempt by Congress to prevent the Board from controlling the terms of a contract.[43]

In *Porter*, the employer had repeatedly refused to bargain for a clause providing for check-off of union dues. The District of Columbia Circuit ordered the employer to grant the union a contract clause containing such a provision. In reversing this decision, the Supreme Court held that the Board's remedial powers, although broad, are limited to carrying out the policies of the Act itself.[44] Thus, allowing the Board to compel agreement would violate the fundamental premise of the Act—"private bargaining under governmental supervision of the *procedure* alone, without any official compulsion over the actual terms of the contract." [45] The Court concluded its opinion by holding that if the Board's power is insufficiently broad, it is a matter for Congress and not the courts.

> In reaching its decision the Court of Appeals relied extensively on the equally important policy of the Act that workers' rights to collective bargaining are to be secured. In this case the Court ap-

---

[39] 397 U.S. 99, 73 L.R.R.M. 2561 (1970).

[40] *Id.* at 102, 73 L.R.R.M. at 2562.

[41] *Id.* at 103-104, 73 L.R.R.M. at 2562.

[42] NLRB v. American Insurance Co., 343 U.S. 395, 404, 30 L.R.R.M. 2147 (1952).

[43] NLRB v. Insurance Agents, 361 U.S. 477, 45 L.R.R.M. 2704 (1960).

[44] 397 U.S. at 108, 73 L.R.R.M. 2564.

[45] *Id.* (emphasis added).

parently felt that the employer was trying effectively to destroy the union by refusing to agree to what the union may have considered its most important demand. Perhaps the court, fearing that the parties might resort to economic combat, was also trying to maintain the industrial peace which the Act is designed to further. But the Act as presently drawn does not contemplate that unions will always be secure and able to achieve agreement even when their economic position is weak, nor that strikes and lockouts will never result from a bargaining to impasse. It cannot be said that the Act forbids an employer or a union to rely ultimately on its economic strength to try to secure what it cannot obtain through bargaining. It may well be true, as the Court of Appeals felt, that the present remedial powers of the Board are insufficiently broad to cope with important labor problems. But it is the job of Congress, not the Board or the courts, to decide when and if it is necessary to allow governmental review of proposals for collective bargaining agreements and compulsory submission to one side's demands. The present Act does not envision such a process.[46]

THE BOARD MAY COMPEL THE SIGNING OF A NEGOTIATED AGREEMENT

Although *H. K. Porter* holds that the NLRB may not compel the parties to agree to specific contract terms, once a contract has been negotiated and concluded, the Board may require the parties to sign and acknowledge the existence of the agreement and to make whole the employees because of an unfair labor practice. For example, in *NLRB v. Strong Roofing & Insulating Co.*,[47] the employer was found to have withdrawn from a multi-employer bargaining unit too late to escape the agreement negotiated on his behalf. The Supreme Court approved the Board's remedial order which required the employer to sign the agreement,[48] and reimburse the employees for the fringe benefits which would have been paid had the employer initially signed the agreement and abided

---

[46] *Id.* at 108-109, 73 L.R.R.M. at 2564, 2565. *Accord* Moore of Bedford v. NLRB, 451 F.2d 406, 78 L.R.R.M. 2769, 2772 (4th Cir. 1971); NLRB v. Tex Tan Welhausen Co., 434 F.2d 405, 75 L.R.R.M. 2554 (5th Cir. 1970); Ameri-Crete Ready Mix Corp., 207 N.L.R.B. No. 509, 84 L.R.R.M. 1623 (1973). *But see* Hinson v. NLRB, 428 F.2d 133, 74 L.R.R.M. 2194 (8th Cir. 1970) (*H. K. Porter* no bar to Board order requiring employer to pay health, welfare, and retirement benefit contributions, where 8(a)(5) violation was predicated on the employer's unilateral termination of such payments upon expiration of existing contract).

[47] 393 U.S. 357, 70 L.R.R.M. 2100 (1969).

[48] *See also,* H. J. Heinz Co. v. NLRB, 311 U.S. 514, 524-526, 7 L.R.R.M. 291 (1941); NLRB v. Ogle Protection Service, Inc., 375 F.2d 497, 64 L.R.R.M. 2792 (6th Cir. 1967), *cert. denied,* 389 U.S. 843, 66 L.R.R.M. 2308 (1967).

by its terms. The Court rejected the employer's argument that the Board had improperly inserted itself into the enforcement of the contract, contrary to the policy and scheme of the Act. The Court held that, although the Board has no plenary authority to administer and enforce collective bargaining contracts, it "is not trespassing on forbidden territory when it inquires whether negotiations have produced a bargain which the employer has refused to sign and honor. . . . To this extent the collective contract is the Board's affair, and an effective remedy for refusal to sign is its proper business." [49]

Although an employer may have violated Section 8(a)(5) in his bargaining conduct, he will not be ordered to sign a collective bargaining agreement unless it can be shown that there has been a "complete meeting of the minds as to all of the terms to be incorporated in a final contract." [50] Thus, where the employer and union have not resolved their differences, and "were still at loggerheads" [51] over important issues, the *Strong Roofing* rationale will

---

[49] Strong Roofing & Insulation Co., 393 U.S. at 361, 70 L.R.R.M. at 2101-2102 (1969). *And see* NLRB v. K&H Specialties Co., 407 F.2d 820, 70 L.R.R.M. 2880 (6th Cir. 1969) which applied *Strong Roofing, supra,* and held that the Board has jurisdiction to determine the amount of backpay due employees. The court rejected employer arguments that under the terms of the contract, the amount of backpay should have been determined by arbitration. For other cases applying the principles set forth in *Strong Roofing, see* Crimptex, Inc. 221 N.L.R.B. No. 54, 90 L.R.R.M. 1508 (1975) (NLRB order directing employer to sign contract is clarified to require that the contract be effective as of the date on which the agreement would have been executed had it not been for the employer's unlawful conduct); NLRB v. Raven Industries, Inc., 508 F.2d 1289, 88 L.R.R.M. 2103 (8th Cir. 1974) (employer ordered to give retroactive effect to contract, but not to pay sick leave, since evidence failed to show this agreement on this term); NLRB v. Crimptex, Inc., —— F.2d ——, 89 L.R.R.M. 2465, 2468 (1st Cir. 1975); NLRB v. Summit Tooling Co., 474 F.2d 1352, 83 L.R.R.M. 2044 (7th Cir. 1973); NLRB v. Tex Tan Welhausen Co., 434 F.2d 405, 75 L.R.R.M. 2554 (5th Cir. 1970); NLRB v. Stafford Trucking, Inc., —— F.2d ——, 77 L.R.R.M. 2465 (7th Cir. 1971) (employer who refused to sign agreement ordered to pay lost wages and benefits with interest); Southland Dodge, 205 N.L.R.B. No. 54, 84 L.R.R.M. 1231 (1973), *enforced,* 492 F.2d 1238, 85 L.R.R.M. 2768 (3d Cir. 1974) (employer ordered to sign contract, give it retroactive effect and make employees whole for any loss suffered. The Board refused a request for lost union dues, since the employees had not executed check-off authorization); Coletti Color Prints, Inc., 204 N.L.R.B. No. 96, 83 L.R.R.M. 1598 (1973) (order to execute contract and make employees whole). *Accord* NLRB v. Mayes Bros., Inc., 383 F.2d 242, 66 L.R.R.M. 2031 (5th Cir. 1967); NLRB v. M&M Oldsmobile, Inc., 377 F.2d 712, 65 L.R.R.M. 2149 (2d Cir. 1967).

[50] Orion Tool, Die & Machine Co., 195 N.L.R.B. No. 194, 79 L.R.R.M. 1636, 1638 (1972).

[51] *Id.*

not apply. And even where the Board has found that the parties "had reached agreement in principle as to the substantive terms of a collective-bargaining agreement," the employer was not ordered to execute the document, when "there was no agreement as to the language to go into the contract. . . ." [52] In such cases where a contract-signing order is deemed inappropriate, the Board has simply required the employer to bargain in good faith upon the union's request, and if an understanding is reached, to embody it in a signed contract.[53] Furthermore, in order to provide the union sufficient time to bargain for such an agreement, the Board has extended the union's certification for a period of one year from the commencement of the employer's good faith bargaining.[54]

In some instances, the Board has provided an alternative remedy to ordering the employer merely to execute and carry out the terms of the collective bargaining agreement to which he had agreed. In *NLRB v. Huttig Sash & Door, Inc.*,[55] the Board ordered that if the union decided the contract was no longer satisfactory, the contract would not be enforced retroactively against the employer. Rather, the union would be given the option of bargaining for a new agreement. The Fourth Circuit rejected this order as inconsistent with the major basis of the Board's decision that the parties had already entered into an agreement. Subsequent decisions, however, have limited *Huttig Sash and Door* to its peculiar circumstances, noting that the relevant issues were not briefed or argued to the Fourth Circuit, and that the decision was "academic" since the old contract had expired and the parties were required to bargain anyway.[56]

---

[52] Zenith Radio Corp., 187 N.L.R.B. No. 103, 76 L.R.R.M. 1115, 1116 (1971), *enforced per curiam* —— F.2d ——, 80 L.R.R.M. 2768 (7th Cir. 1972); J. W. Praught Co., 212 N.L.R.B. No. 78, 87 L.R.R.M. 1507 (1974) (evidence did not establish that the employer had orally agreed to contract terms). *Cf.* Retail Clerks v. NLRB (Montgomery Ward & Co.), 373 F.2d 655, 64 L.R.R.M. 2108 (D.C. Cir. 1967).

[53] *See* Zenith Radio Corp., *supra*, footnote 52. Orion Tool, Die, and Machine, Co., *supra*, footnote 50.

[54] *Id.*

[55] 362 F.2d 217, 220, 62 L.R.R.M. 2271, 2272 (4th Cir. 1966).

[56] *See* NLRB v. M&M Oldsmobile, Inc., 377 F.2d 742, 65 L.R.R.M. 2149, 2154 (2d Cir. 1967); NLRB v. Beverage-Air Co., 402 F.2d 411, 69 L.R.R.M. 2369, 2373 (4th Cir. 1968). In both cases, the union was given the option of bargaining for a new contract or putting the old contract into effect retroactively with the employees receiving reimbursement for lost benefits. *Accord* General Asbestos & Rubber Div., Raybesto Manhattan, Inc., 183 N.L.R.B. 213,

The "Ex-Cello-O" Make-Whole Remedy

When an employer has not entered into a collective bargaining agreement and has been found to have violated Section 8(a)(5) in his bargaining conduct, unions have often requested that such employer be ordered to make the employees whole for the wages and other fringe benefits which might have been gained had the employer bargained in good faith with the union. This highly controversial remedy is fully discussed in Chapter XIV.[57] To capsulize, the NLRB's constant position has been that it does not have the statutory power to award such a remedy. The District of Columbia Circuit, on the other hand, has held that the Board enjoys this authority. To date, this remedy has not been ordered by the court which has agreed with the Board that in the cases where the remedy has been requested, it has been inappropriate because the employer's defense was debatable rather than not frivolous.

Orders To Provide Bargaining Information

Obviously, one party in collective bargaining gains an unfair advantage if allowed to justify its bargaining positions with data and information not made available to the other side. Accordingly, as the Second Circuit summarized in *Prudential Insurance Co. v. NLRB*:[58]

> It is now beyond question that the duty to bargain in good faith imposed upon the employer by § 8(a)(5) includes an obligation to provide the employees' statutory bargaining representative with information that is necessary and relevant to the proper performance of its duties. E.g., N.L.R.B. v. Acme Industrial Co., 385 U.S. 432, 64 LRRM 2069 (1967); N.L.R.B. v. Truitt Mfg. Co., 351 U.S. 149, 38 LRRM 2042 (1956); Fafnir Bearing Co. v. N.L.R.B., 362 F.2d 716, 62 LRRM 2415 (2d Cir. 1966). And this obligation applies with as much force to information needed by the Union for the effective administration of a collective bargaining agreement already in force as to information relevant in the negotiation of a new contract. N.L.R.B. v. Acme Industrial Co., supra; Fafnir Bearing Co. v. N.L.R.B., supra.

---

[57] —— L.R.R.M. —— (1970); Schill Steel Products Inc., 161 N.L.R.B. No. 83, 63 L.R.R.M. 1388 (1966); NLRB v. Schill Steel Products, 480 F.2d 586, 83 L.R.R.M. 2369, 2386 (5th Cir. 1972).

[57] *Infra*, pp. 230-234.

[58] 412 F.2d 77, 71 L.R.R.M. 2254, 2257 (2d Cir. 1969).

In ascertaining whether certain information must be supplied under the statute, the Board will act "upon the probability that the desired information was relevant, and that it would be of use to the union in carrying out its statutory duties and responsibilities." [59] When the Board finds that such requested information has been illegally withheld, the offending party will be required to provide the information. [60]

---

[59] NLRB v. Rockwell-Standard Corp., 410 F.2d 953, 957, 71 L.R.R.M. 2328, (6th Cir. 1969), *quoting from* NLRB v. Acme Industrial Co., *supra*, 385 U.S. at ———.

[60] *See e.g.*, Prudential Insurance Co. v. NLRB, *supra* (names and addresses of insurance agent who do not belong to union); Stanley Building Specialties Co., 166 N.L.R.B. 984, 65 L.R.R.M. 1684 (1967), *enforced sub nom.* Steelworkers v. NLRB, 401 F.2d 434, 69 L.R.R.M. 2196 (D.C. Cir. 1968), *cert. denied*, 395 U.S. 946, 71 L.R.R.M. 2426 (1969) (financial data); NLRB v. Western Wirebound Box Co., 356 F.2d 88, 61 L.R.R.M. 2218 (9th Cir. 1966) (records relevant to wage increase demands); Tex Tan Welhausen Co. v. NLRB, 419 F.2d 1265, 72 L.R.R.M. 2885 (5th Cir. 1969) (time study information); NLRB v. Rockwell-Standard Corp., 410 F.2d 953, 71 L.R.R.M. 2328 (6th Cir. 1969) (information on job classifications and wage rates of nonunit employees); NLRB v. Twin City Lines, Inc., 425 F.2d 164, 74 L.R.R.M. 2024 (8th Cir. 1970) (information concerning employees' claims filed pursuant to an arbitration award necessary for the union to evaluate the merits of grievances); Detroit Edison Co., 218 N.L.R.B. No. 147, 89 L.R.R.M. 1515 (1975) (copies of employee aptitude tests); NLRB v. Marland One-Way Clutch Co., 520 F.2d 856, 89 L.R.R.M. 2721 (7th Cir. 1975) (information on past methods of computing Christmas bonus); Hawkins Construction Co., 210 N.L.R.B. No. 152, 86 L.R.R.M. 1549 (1974) (information concerning employer's refusal to hire members referred by union). *But compare* the following cases in which employer violations did not result in an order requiring it to furnish the information. C-B Buick, Inc. v. NLRB, 506 F.2d 1086, 87 L.R.R.M. 2878 (3d Cir. 1974) (information denied due to its diluted relevance to negotiations and the administration of the contract caused by passage of time and execution of a new contract); General Electric Co., 188 N.L.R.B. No. 105, 76 L.R.R.M. 1433 (1971) (order requiring employer to correlate wage information data with specific companies involved in survey is limited to disclosure of only such data the employer has in his possession); Fawcett Printing Corp., 201 N.L.R.B. No. 139 (1973) (because of the confidential nature of the information, certain portions need not be furnished, and union access to other portions is limited).

PART SEVEN

*NLRA Sanctions Against The Persistent,
Flagrant, Or Frivolous Violator*

CHAPTER XIV

NLRB Extraordinary Remedies and Proposed Statutory Penalties

Previous chapters have discussed traditional NLRB unfair labor practice remedies. These remedies, although not free from criticism, have become widely accepted as appropriate methods to deal with routine violations of the Act. By and large, NLRB respondents comply with these remedies.[1] Fortunately, there are few respondents who engage in persistent violations of the Act, flagrantly disregard employee Section 7 rights, or delay the implementation of NLRB orders by frivolous litigation. Such conduct requires remedial or other measures that are unnecessary in the vast majority of cases. The remaining chapters deal with NLRB and court sanctions available in these extraordinary situations. Critics of the traditional National Labor Relations Act remedies often argue that these sanctions are inadequate because there are some employers and unions which have continued to violate the Act even after these remedies have been employed against them.[2] As the persistence of some violators, however, has not been deterred by severe contempt of court sanctions,[3] it seems unlikely that harsher NLRB remedies would have much impact on employers or unions

---

[1] In fiscal year 1974, of 8,003 NLRB remedial actions (*i.e.*, informal settlements, formal settlements, ALJ recommendations, Board and court orders), only 266 were by court order, 39 NLRB Ann. Rep. 202 (1974).

[2] The most often cited example is J. P. Stevens & Company. *See* Textile Workers Union of America, AFL-CIO (J. P. Stevens & Co.) v. NLRB, 475 F.2d 973, 82 L.R.R.M. 2471, n. 1 (D.C. Cir. 1973) and cases cited therein. *See also* Food Store Employees, Local 347, (Heck's Inc.) v. NLRB 476 F.2d 546, 82 L.R.R.M. 2955 (D.C. Cir. 1973) (company's campaign against union organization resulted in eleven NLRB proceedings) ; Amalgamated Local Union No. 355 (Russell Motors, Inc.), 198 NLRB No. 58, 80 L.R.R.M. 1757 (1972), *enf'd as modified*, 481 F.2d 996, 83 L.R.R.M. 2849 (2d Cir. 1973) ; Teamsters, Local 705 (Gasoline Retailers Ass'n), 210 N.L.R.B. No. 58, 86 L.R.R.M. 1011 (1974).

[3] Contempt of court proceedings under the NLRA are discussed *infra* in Chapter XV, pp. 245-248.

which, as a matter of policy, repeatedly violate the Act. On the other hand, increasing the severity of remedies used against the majority of respondents who make good faith attempts to abide by the Act and carry out the requirements of NLRB orders appears to be unnecessary to effectuate the purposes of the Act.

Recently, there has been an increasing amount of litigation in which the NLRB has been requested to grant extraordinary remedies for flagrant or persistent violations of the Act. The Seventh Circuit in *NLRB v. Good Foods Corp.*[4] has explained:

> Remedies of the sort claimed by the Union are never granted absent a history of unlawful antiunion conduct (e.g., J.P. Stevens & Co. v. NLRB, 417 F.2d 533, 72 L.R.R.M. 2433 (5th Cir. 1969)), or an obviously frivolous defense of company misconduct (e.g., Tiidee Products, Inc., *supra*), or a clear showing that conventional remedies will be inadequate (e.g., Teamsters Local 992 v. NLRB, 427 F.2d 582, 73 L.R.R.M. 2924 (D.C. Cir. 1970)).

Thus, the Board and courts have continuously expressed concern that the severity of the available penalty may not deter Board respondents from exercising their right to have potentially meritorious claims heard and litigated in the appropriate forum. To do otherwise would entail serious due process problems and bring the fairness of NLRA procedures into question.

We now turn to a discussion of the various types of extraordinary remedies which have been requested of the Board and proposed to Congress.

Extraordinary Notice and Access Remedies

In order to remedy flagrant, repeated, or widespread unfair labor practices, the NLRB has sanctioned, with court approval, a number of "extraordinary" remedies necessitated by the egregious conduct of the company or union. In Chapter III,[5] we discussed the proper utilization of "broad" cease and desist orders which would subject the respondent to potential contempt of court proceedings for future violations. Chapter III also describes situations in which employers and unions had instituted centrally directed and coordinated policies to commit unfair labor practices in several plants or throughout their jurisdiction. In such cases, the Board has expanded the scope of its orders beyond the immediate unit involved in the particular case.[6] Chapter VI deals with in-

---

[4] 492 F.2d 1302, 85 L.R.R.M. 2739, 2742 (7th Cir. 1974).

[5] *Supra*, pp. 18-31.

[6] *Supra*, pp. 34-37.

stances in which flagrant unfair labor practices have prompted the Board to require that copies of the remedial notice be mailed to the employees, bulletin board space be made available to the union, the union be allowed company time to address the employees, the employer or his agent be required to read the notice to the employees, and the notice be included in an appropriate union or company publication.[7]

Attorneys' Fees and Litigation Expenses—
The Tiidee and Heck's Decisions

In *Tiidee Products, Inc.*[8] the Board noted that litigation expenses normally are not recoverable by the charging party in Board proceedings even though the public interest is served when the charging party protects its private interest before the Board. But the *Tiidee* decision further indicated that the Board would order payment of attorneys' fees and litigation expenses when the respondent's defense is "frivolous." The Board stated:

> We agree with the court, however, that frivolous litigation such as this is clearly unwarranted and should be kept from the nation's already crowded court dockets, as well as our own. While we do not seek to foreclose access to the Board and courts for meritorious cases, we likewise do not want to encourage frivolous proceedings. The policy of the Act to insure industrial peace through collective

---

[7] *Supra*, pp. 73-80. *See also* John Singer, Inc., 197 N.L.R.B. 88, 80 L.R.R.M. 1340 (1972) (employer ordered to give union access to bulletin boards, furnish the union with a list of the employees' names and addresses, and keep the list current for one year from the time the company begins to bargain in good faith. The Board also authorized the General Counsel to seek injunction under Section 10(e) if the employer did not comply); The Loray Corp., 184 N.L.R.B. 557, 74 L.R.R.M. 1513 (1970) (remedies included signing and reading notice, mailing notice, access to bulletin boards, access to plant for union speeches, list of employees names and addresses, opportunity for union to request representation election within thirty days of employer's compliance regardless of a showing of interest by 30 percent of employees); Tiidee Products, Inc., 174 N.L.R.B. 705, 70 L.R.R.M. 1346 (1972), *enforced in relevant part* in Electrical Workers (IUE) (Tiidee Products, Inc.), 502 F.2d 349, 86 L.R.R.M. 2093 (D.C. Cir. 1974), *cert. denied*, 417 U.S. 921, 86 L.R.R.M. 2427 (1974) (mailing notice, bulletin board access, furnishing employees with a current list of employees names and addresses); Heck's Inc., 172 N.L.R.B. 2231, 69 L.R.R.M. 1177 (1968), *enforced in relevant part* in Food Store Employees, Local 347 v. NLRB, 476 F.2d 546, 82 L.R.R.M. 2955 (D.C. Cir. 1973) and in NLRB v. Food Store Employees, Local 347, 417 U.S. 1, 86 L.R.R.M. 2209 (1974) (notice to be posted in all stores and mailed to employees, bulletin board access, and current list of employees names and addresses). *But cf.* Longhorn Machine Works, 205 N.L.R.B. 685, 84 L.R.R.M. 1307 (1973), where the Board denied similar requested remedies because the employers' violations did not warrant unusual remedial action.

[8] 194 N.L.R.B. 1234, 79 L.R.R.M. 1175, 1178 (1972).

bargaining can only be effectuated when speedy access to uncrowded Board and court dockets is available. Accordingly, *in order to discourage future frivolous litigation,* to effectuate the policies of the Act, and to serve the public interest we find that it would be *just and proper to order Respondent to reimburse the Board and the Union for their expenses incurred in the investigation, preparation, presentation, and conduct of these cases,* including the following costs and expenses incurred in both the Board and court proceedings: reasonable counsel fees, salaries, witness fees, transcript and record costs, printing costs, travel expenses and per diem, and other reasonable costs and expenses. Accordingly, we shall order Respondent to pay to the Board and the Union the above-mentioned litigation costs and expenses.[9]

As the cases indicate, a "frivolous" defense is one which obviously lacks merit, is not debatable, and not one which fails simply upon the Administrative Law Judge's resolutions of conflicting testimony.[10] The Board's policy set forth in *Tiidee* was approved by the Supreme Court in *NLRB v. Food Store Employees, Local 347 (Heck's Inc.)*.[11] In language suggestive of the Board's rationale in *Tiidee*, the Court explained:

> [I]t cannot be gainsaid that the finding here that Heck's asserted at least "debatable" defenses to the unfair labor practice charges, whereas objections to the representation election in Tiidee were "patently frivolous," might have been viewed by the Board as putting the question of remedy in a different light. We cannot say that the Board in performing its appointed function of balancing conflicting interests, could not reasonably decide that where "debatable" defenses are asserted, the public and private interests in affording the employer a determination of his "debatable" defenses, unfettered by the prospect of bearing his adversary's litigation costs, outweigh the public interest in uncrowded dockets.[12]

The District of Columbia Circuit in *Heck's* found that in view of the Board's *Tiidee* decision, the Board should have ordered the employer to pay legal fees and litigation expenses.[13] The Supreme

---

[9] *Id.* at 1236-1237, 79 L.R.R.M. at 1179 (emphasis added). *See also* Tiidee Products, Inc., 196 N.L.R.B. 158, 79 L.R.R.M. 1692 (1972).

[10] *See* United Steelworkers v. NLRB (Quality Rubber Mfg. Co.), 430 F.2d 519, 521, 74 L.R.R.M. 2747 (D.C. Cir. 1970); Southwest Regional Joint Board, Amalgamated Clothing Workers (Levi Strauss & Co.) v. NLRB, 441 F.2d 1027, 1035-1036, 76 L.R.R.M. 2033 (D.C. Cir. 1970); Ex-Cell-O Corp. v. NLRB, 449 F.2d 1058, 1064, 1065, 77 L.R.R.M. 2547 (D.C. Cir. 1971).

[11] 417 U.S. 1, 86 L.R.R.M. 2209, 2211 (1974).

[12] *Id.*

[13] *See* Food Store Employees, Local 347 (Heck's Inc.) v. NLRB, 476 F.2d 546, 82 L.R.R.M. 2955 (D.C. Cir. 1973).

Court, however, noted that the Board's initial opinion in *Heck's* was decided prior to the Board's *Tiidee* decision, and held that the circuit court should not have decided the legal expense issue itself. Rather the court should have remanded the *Heck's* decision to the Board to allow the agency to reconsider its ruling in light of the subsequent *Tiidee* ruling.[14]

On remand in *Heck's*, the Board found that even if the employer there was found to have engaged in clearly aggravated and pervasive misconduct or flagrant repetition of conduct previously found unlawful, it would not assess attorneys' fees and litigation expenses because the defenses raised were not frivolous, but "debatable." [15] The Board also harmonized its decision with the earlier *Tiidee* decision and further explained its attorneys' fees and litigation expense policy:

> At the outset, we wish to dispel any doubt concerning our policy with respect to extraordinary remedies. We did not, by our subsequent Decision in Tiidee, intend any change or modification of such policy as had therefore been articulated and applied by us. The intendment of our Decision in Tiidee, in which we specifically referred to our earlier Decision in the instant case, was to harmonize the two cases, not to repudiate one of them. Thus, those cases, when read together, indicated our intent to refrain from assessing litigation expenses against a respondent, notwithstanding that the respondent may be found to have engaged in "clearly aggravated and pervasive misconduct" or in the "flagrant repetition of conduct previously found unlawful," where the defenses raised by that respondent are "debatable" rather than "frivolous. . . ."
>
> To be sure, since Congress has invested us, and not the courts, with broad discretion in the exercise of our remedial powers, we feel a concomitant responsibility to be ever mindful of the manner most appropriate for effectuating the policies of the Act in each case to come before us. The Union's pleas for more effective remedies are by no means wholly unmeritorious or without equitable appeal. Yet such equitable considerations do not justify, in our view, retroactive application of a departure from our prior rulings in the case at bar. Whether, for instance, an award to compensate for excess organizational costs ought, in the future, to be considered as necessary to restoring the status quo ante in certain factual contexts rather than as an extraordinary remedy to be applied only in the case involving frivolous defenses, as we have heretofore held, is an issue which we do not intend here to foreclose from thorough consideration in future cases. Nor do we intend to exclude from consideration whether in determining the appropriateness of awards of attorney fees, litigation costs, and excess organizational costs,

---

[14] 417 U.S. at 1, 86 L.R.R.M. 2209, 2212 (1974).

[15] 215 N.L.R.B. No. 142, 88 L.R.R.M. 1049, 1051-1052 (1974).

we ought to apply some more definitive criterion than the distinction between "debatable" and "frivolous" defenses which thus far we have been utilizing.[16]

After the *Heck's* decisions, the Board's *Tiidee* decisions [17] were reviewed by the District of Columbia Circuit which made one interesting modification. Although it found that the Board had properly ordered the employer to reimburse the union for attorneys' fees and litigation expenses,[18] it found that the NLRB had erred by ordering the employer to reimburse the Board for such expenses. The court believed such remedies were inappropriate because the employer was a "stranger" to the processes of the Board and because the scope of the initial court remand limited the Board to considering whether to award legal expenses to the charging party.[19]

Although *Tiidee* and the subsequent cases discussed above establish the principle that legal expenses are recoverable in special circumstances, the Board's application of the rule shows that this remedy is indeed "extraordinary." When such reimbursement has been requested, the Board, for the most part, has found either that the unfair labor practices were not flagrant or the defenses were not frivolous. Accordingly, the requested remedy has not been granted often.[20] The Board has also denied requested legal expenses when the employer had agreed to bring the case directly to the Board on a stipulated record, thereby not only avoiding imposi-

---

[16] *Id.*, 88 L.R.R.M. at 1051-1052.

[17] *See supra*, n. 9.

[18] Electrical Workers (IUE) v. NLRB, 502 F.2d 349, 86 L.R.R.M. 2093, 2096 (D.C. Cir. 1974).

[19] 86 L.R.R.M. at 2098-2099.

[20] *See* Federal Prescription Service, Inc., 496 F.2d 813, 86 L.R.R.M. 2185 (8th Cir. 1974); Amalgamated Local Union 355 (Russell Motors, Inc.) v. NLRB, 481 F.2d 996, 83 L.R.R.M. 2849 (2d Cir. 1973); San Luis Obispo County and Northern Santa Barbara Country Restaurant & Tavern Ass'n. 196 N.L.R.B. 1082, 80 L.R.R.M. 1584 (1972), *enforced* 488 F.2d 664 84 L.R.R.M. 2984 (1973); Int'l Union of Electrical, Radio and Machine Workers, AFL-CIO v. NLRB, 426 F.2d 1243, 1248, 1253 n. 15, 73 L.R.R.M. 2870 (D.C. Cir. 1970); Union Nacional de Trabajadores (Jacobs Construction, Inc.), 219 N.L.R.B. No. 65, 89 L.R.R.M. 1746 (1975); Fuqua Homes Missouri, Inc., 474 F.2d 1341, 82 L.R.R.M. 2976 (4th Cir. 1973); Lang Towing, Inc., 201 N.L.R.B. No. 92, 82 L.R.R.M. 1365 (1973); Marshal Transport, Inc., 199 N.L.R.B. No. 89, 82 L.R.RM 1094 (1972); Teamsters, Local 728 v NLRB, 415 F.2d 986, 71 L.R.R.M. 2646 (D.C. Cir. 1969); Orion Corp., 210 N.L.R.B. No. 71, 86 L.R.RM 1193 (1974); Longhorn Machine Works, 205 NL.R.B. 685, 84 L.R.R.M. 1307 (1973). *Cf.* M.F.A. Milling v. NLRB, 463 F.2d 953, 80 L.R.R.M. 2412 (D.C. Cir. 1972).

tion of excessive litigation costs, but, in fact, eliminating many such costs and expenses.[21]

The Board did order legal expenses paid in *Local 396, etc., Teamsters (United Parcel Service)*,[22] where it found that the union had violated Section 8(b)(1)(A) by refusing to process grievances of a group of employees. The Board ordered the union to take the grievance to arbitration and to furnish the grievants with reasonable fees to allow them to retain counsel for the proceedings. The Ninth Circuit enforced the novel remedy of the Board.[23] The court pointed out that one of the purposes of the Act is to undo the effects of unfair labor practices by bringing about a "restoration of the situation, as nearly as possible, to that which would have obtained but for the illegal discrimination." [24] Unless the employees were relieved of the expenses incurred in securing the independent representation to which they were entitled, the court believed this goal could not be obtained.

Prompted by the Board's *Heck's* [25] and other related decisions, NLRB General Counsel Peter G. Nash sent a memorandum, dated January 22, 1975, to the Board's regional directors.[26] The memorandum advised the directors that in "bad faith bargaining cases" they might appropriately seek "a remedy requiring reimbursement by the respondent of the charging party's bargaining expenses resulting from that unfair labor practice." The General Counsel noted that in two pending contempt cases, the Board was seeking an order compelling employers to reimburse the charging unions for business agents' salaries, lodging, mileage, and other related expenses.

Reimbursement for Lost Union Organizing Expenses, Dues, and Initiation Fees

When union organizing campaigns have been subject to employer unfair labor practices the Board occasionally has been

---

[21] Mailers Union No. 89 (Little Rock Newspapers), 219 N.L.R.B. No. 84, 89 L.R.R.M. 1767 (1975).

[22] 203 N.L.R.B. 799, 83 L.R.R.M. 1472 (1973).

[23] NLRB v. Local 396, Teamsters (United Parcel Service), 509 F.2d 1075, 88 L.R.R.M. 2589, 2591 (9th Cir. 1975).

[24] *Id.*, 88 L.R.R.M. at 2591, *citing*, Phelps Dodge Corp. v. NLRB, 313 U.S. 177, 194, 8 L.R.R.M. 439 (1941).

[25] Heck's Inc., 215 N.L.R.B. No. 142, 88 L.R.R.M. 1049 (1974).

[26] NLRB General Counsel's Memo on Litigation Costs, 99 L.R.R. 136 (1975).

requested to require the employer to reimburse the union for losses in organizing expenses and dues. The litigation history of this remedy parallels that of requests for reimbursement of legal expenses.[27] In *Heck's Inc.*,[28] the Board held that the union had not established that the respondent's conduct had contributed to the loss of any dues or fees. The Board further felt that such a remedy would require finding that if the employer had not refused to bargain, he would have entered into a union-security agreement requiring the payment of dues and fees to the union. The execution of such an agreement did not seem so strong a probability that any loss of dues or fees must be deemed to have resulted from the employer's misconduct.[29] The Board also stated that although "we are not unmindful that the [union] has spent more money on organization costs and attorneys fees than it would have spent had the employer not refused to bargain," it did not necessarily follow that the union was entitled to such costs. Such a remedy was not determined, under these circumstances, to help effectuate the policies of the Act.[30]

Following the *Heck's* decision, the Board issued one of its *Tiidee* holdings [31] in which it denied a similar request for organizing expenses and lost dues and fees. The Board did not state, however, that such a remedy should never be granted, but rather held that there was "no nexus" between the employer's unlawful conduct and the union's pre-election organizing expenses.[32] The Board also noted in *Tiidee* that it was not the union's policy to collect initiation fees and dues until a contract was executed. No reason was seen to make the employer assume the risk for these fees when the union could have elected to assess its members for them.[33]

After the Board issued this *Tiidee* decision, *Heck's* decision reached the District of Columbia Circuit in *Food Store Employees, Local 347 v. NLRB.*[34] The court took note of *Tiidee's* apparent endorsement of reimbursing organizing costs in appropriate cir-

---

[27] *See supra* pp. 223-227.

[28] 191 N.L.R.B. 2231, 77 L.R.R.M. 1513 (1971).

[29] *Id.*, 77 L.R.R.M. at 1517.

[30] *Id.*

[31] Tiidee Products, Inc., 194 N.L.R.B. 1234, 79 L.R.R.M. 1175 (1972).

[32] *Id.*, 79 L.R.R.M. at 1178.

[33] *Id.*

[34] 476 F.2d 546, 82 L.R.R.M. 2955 (D.C. Cir. 1973).

cumstances, and contrasted that holding with the Board's general statement in *Heck's* that such a remedy would not effectuate the policies of the Act. In view of the Board's statement that the conduct of *Heck's* had probably caused the union additional organizational costs, the court, relying on *Tiidee,* ordered such remedies paid the union.[35] The Supreme Court reversed the court of appeals and determined that the case should have been remanded to the Board for a determination of whether or not there existed a nexus between the employer's conduct and the union's pre-election organizing expenses.[36] On remand in *Heck's*,[37] the Board did not deal directly with the merits of the union's claim for organizational expenses. Rather, it determined, as it did with the union's request for legal expenses, that the employer's defenses were debatable rather than frivolous. Therefore, it was inappropriate to reimburse the union for organizing expenses.[38]

As the previous discussion indicates, even when an employer does not have a debatable defense, organizing expenses will not be ordered reimbursed unless it can be shown that there is a nexus between the employer's illegal conduct and an increase in the union's organizing expenses. In practice, this nexus may be difficult to establish. Thus, the union should be required to present a justifiable estimate of the costs of additional campaign propaganda, additional organizers, and other expenses which were necessary to counteract the misconduct of the employer. It may be that the employer's violations actually drove employees to support the union. Moreover, the employer may also have engaged in other intensive *lawful* efforts to counteract the union's campaign which also required the additional union organizing expenses. Even if the union can show a loss of support among the employees, it still has the problem of proving that this loss did not arise for reasons other than the employer's violations. Section 8(a)(1) employer violations, however, are determined by

---

[35] *Id.* at 554, 82 L.R.R.M. at 2959. The court agreed with the Board that the union's claim for lost fees and dues was speculative and was properly denied. *Id.,* 82 L.R.R.M. at 2959, 2960.

[36] NLRB v. Food Store Employees, Local 347 (Heck's Inc.), 417 U.S. 1, 86 L.R.R.M. 2209.

[37] Heck's, Inc., 215 N.L.R.B. No. 142, 88 L.R.R.M. 1049 (1974).

[38] *See* the discussion, *supra,* p. 225-226. *See also* Ameri-Crete Ready Mix Corp., 207 N.L.R.B. No. 79, 84 L.R.R.M. 1623 (1973) (employer's defenses not frivolous, so no organizing expenses ordered reimbursed).

their coercive "tendency" [39] and not by a showing of their actual impact. It appears, therefore, difficult to prove the harm to the campaign by such employer violations and the connection between this harm and alleged increased campaign expenses. Thus, an inquiry into the actual monetary effect of unfair labor practices on the union's organizing campaign might be highly speculative, and result in a Board order that could be considered punitive, rather than remedial.[40] Furthermore, an award of damages based on speculation may invite collateral litigation which could be counter-productive in the administration of the Act.

When the union wins an election campaign in spite of employer unfair labor practices, the Board, with court approval, has denied requests for organizing expenses and union dues and fees. Thus, in *Electrical Workers (IUE) (Tiidee Products) v. NLRB*,[41] the court held that the Board did not err when it refused to order the employer to reimburse the union for organizing expenses since the union was shown to have incurred only normal organizational expenses in its successful representation campaign. Also, the union was deemed adequately protected by its certification as the exclusive bargaining agent for the unit, since the one-year protective period would not commence until the employer began to bargain in good faith.[42]

The "Ex-Cell-O" Make-Whole Remedy.

In cases where employers have been found to have violated Section 8(a)(5) by improperly refusing to bargain with a union, unions often have requested that the Board provide a remedy which would make its members whole for the wages and other fringe benefits which might have accrued from the bargaining process had the employer bargained with the union in good faith.[43]

---

[39] *See* Chapter VII, *supra*, pp. 107-108, footnote 16.

[40] *See e.g.*, Russell Motors, Inc., 198 N.L.R.B. No. 58, 80 L.R.R.M. 1757, *enf'd*, 481 F.2d 996, 83 L.R.R.M. 2849 (2d Cir. 1973) ; Local 60, Carpenters v. NLRB, 365 U.S. 651, 655, 47 L.R.R.M. 2900 (1961).

[41] 502 F.2d 349, 86 L.R.R.M. 2093 (D.C. Cir. 1974).

[42] *Id.*, 86 L.R.R.M. at 2102-2103. The court reaffirmed its previous holding that the Board properly denied the union's request for union dues and fees.

[43] This form of make-whole remedy has received considerable discussion among law review commentators. *See* McGuiness, *Is the Award of Damages for Refusal to Bargain Consistent with National Labor Policy?*, 14 WAYNE L. REV. 1086 (1968) ; St. Antoine, *A Touchstone for Labor Board Remedies*, 14 WAYNE L. REV. 1039 (1968) ; Schlossberg and Silard, *The Need for a*

In *Ex-Cell-O Corp.*,[44] the Board stated the position, that it does not have the statutory power to order such a remedy. There the union had won an NLRB election and was certified as the employees' bargaining representative. The employer advised the union that it would refuse to bargain and would seek appellate court review of the Board's certification of the union. The union filed a Section 8(a)(5) charge and also asked that it receive a make-whole remedy because of the employer's refusal to bargain. The trial examiner recommended that the employer be ordered to pay such monetary damages, but the Board refused to approve the recommended order. The Board relied heavily on the Supreme Court's decision in *H.K. Porter Co. v. NLRB*.[45] There the Court held that although the Board had the power to require employers and employees to negotiate, it was without power to compel a company or union to agree to any substantive contractual provision of a collective-bargaining agreement. The Board in *Ex-Cell-O* found that there was no basis for the requested compensatory remedy because its imposition would require the Board to infer generally, if not entirely speculatively, that employees were deprived of specific benefits as a consequence of their employer's refusal to bargain. The Board would have been required to speculate on how much the employer was prepared to give and how little the union was willing to take, and then assume that a contract favorable to the union's members would result from the negotiations. The Board has consistently held to the opinion expressed in *Ex-Cell-O* that such relief is beyond its statutory power.[46]

Compensatory Remedy in Refusal-to-Bargain Cases, 14 WAYNE L. REV. 1059 (1968); Note, *NLRB Power to Award Damages in Unfair Labor Practice Cases*, 84 HARV. L. REV. 1670 (1971); Fairweather, *The NLRB—Implementer of the National Labor Policy or Vice-Versa?*, 22 LAB. L. J. 294 (1971); Note, *Assessment of the Proposed "Make-Whole Remedy,"* 67 MICH. L. REV. 374 (1968). See also, *The Scope of Good Faith Bargaining and Adequacy of NLRB Remedies: Remarks of Elliott Bredhoff, IUD General Counsel*, DAILY LABOR REPORT, January 9, 1974, p. F-1 (BNA, 1974); Parker, *Employee Reimbursement for an Employer's Refusal to Bargain: The Ex-Cell-O Doctrine*, 46 TEX. L. REV. 758, 764 (1968); Baier, *Rights Under a Collective Bargaining Agreement: The Question of Monetary Compensation for a Refusal to Bargain*, 47 J. URBAN L. 253, 309 (1964); Comment, *The Labor-Management Relationship: Present Damages for Loss of Future Contracts*, 71 YALE L. J. 563, 573 (1972).

[44] 185 N.L.R.B. No. 20, 74 L.R.R.M. 1740 (1970).

[45] 397 U.S. 99, 73 L.R.R.M. 2561 (1970). *See supra*, pp. 212-213.

[46] *See e.g.*, Tiidee Products, Inc., 174 N.L.R.B. No. 103, 79 L.R.R.M. 1175 (1972), 196 N.L.R.B. No. 27, 79 L.R.R.M. 1692 (1972); Heck's Inc., 191

The District of Columbia Circuit has disagreed with the Board's holding in *Ex-Cell-O* and held in a number of cases that the Board possesses the statutory authority to grant this make-whole remedy.[47] The District of Columbia Circuit, however, has never ordered the Board to implement this type of make-whole remedy. Even though the Board and court disagree over the Board's authority to grant the remedy, they have agreed in several cases that, in any event, the remedy was not appropriate because the employer's violation was debatable, and not a "clear and flagrant" refusal to bargain for "patently frivolous" reasons.[48]

N.L.R.B. No. 146, 77 L.R.R.M. 1513 (1971); J. P. Stevens & Co., 205 N.L.R.B. No. 169, 84 L.R.R.M. 1092 (1973); John Singer, Inc., 197 N.L.R.B. No. 7, 80 L.R.R.M. 1340 (1972); Fuqua Homes Missouri, Inc., 201 N.L.R.B. No. 13, 82 L.R.R.M. 1142 (1973). In *Ex-Cell-O*, Members McCulloch and Brown would have granted the compensatory remedy since they viewed such a remedy as within the Board's wide remedial discretion. They argued that the remedy in no way "writes a contract" between the employer and the union, for it would not specify new or continuing terms of employment, and would not prohibit changes in existing terms and conditions. 74 L.R.R.M. at 1743-1752. After the expiration of the terms of Members McCulloch and Brown, the Board, without dissent, reaffirmed the majority position in *Ex-Cell-O*, that the Board does not have the statutory authority to grant this remedy. *See* Tiidee Products, Inc., 194 N.L.R.B. 1234, 79 L.R.R.M. 1175 (1972).

[47] International Union of Electrical Radio and Machine Workers v. NLRB (Tiidee Products, Inc.), 426 F.2d 1243, 73 L.R.R.M. 2870 (D.C. Cir. 1970), *cert. denied*, 400 U.S. 950 75 L.R.R.M. 2752 (1970); Int'l Union, United Automobile Workers v. NLRB (Ex-Cell-O I), 449 F.2d 1046, 76 L.R.R.M. 2753 (D.C. Cir. 1971), *vacated in part* Ex-Cell-O Corp. v. NLRB (Ex-Cell-O II), 449 F.2d 1058, 77 L.R.R.M. 2547 (D.C. Cir. 1971); United Steel Workers of America, AFL-CIO v. NLRB (Quality Rubber Co.), 430 F.2d 519, 521-522, 74 L.R.R.M. 2747 (D.C. Cir. 1970); Southwest Regional Joint Board, Amalgamated Clothing Workers of America, AFL-CIO (Levi Strauss) v. NLRB, 441 F.2d 1027, 76 L.R.R.M. 2033 (D.C. Cir. 1970); Food Store Employees Local 347 v. NLRB, 433 F.2d 541, 542-543, 74 L.R.R.M. 2109 (D.C. Cir. 1970).

[48] Int'l Union, United Automobile, Workers (Ex-Cell-O Corp.), 449 F.2d 1058, 1064, 1065, 77 L.R.R.M. 2547, 2552 (D.C. Cir. 1971); Retail Clerks, Local 1401 (Zinke's Foods, Inc.) v. NLRB, 463 F.2d 316, 79 L.R.R.M. 2984, 2990 (D.C. Cir. 1972). *See* United Steelworkers of America, AFL-CIO v. NLRB (Quality Rubber Co.), 430 F.2d 519, 521-522, 74 L.R.R.M. 2747 (D.C. Cir. 1970); Southwest Regional Joint Board, Amalgamated Clothing Workers of America, AFL-CIO (Levi Strauss) v. NLRB, 441 F.2d 1027, 1035-1036, 76 L.R.R.M. 2033 (D.C. Cir. 1970); Food Store Employees, Local 347 (Heck's Inc.) v. NLRB, 476 F.2d 546, 82 L.R.R.M. 2955, 2960-2961 (D.C. Cir. 1973), *rev'd on other grounds* in NLRB v. Food Store Employees, Local 347, 417 U.S. 1, 86 L.R.R.M. 2209 (1974); Electrical Workers (IUE) (Tiidee Products, Inc.), 502 F.2d 349, 86 L.R.R.M. 2093 (D.C. Cir. 1974). The distinction between "debatable" and "frivolous" defenses is discussed more fully in connection with union requests for attorneys' fees and litigation expenses. *See supra*, p. 224.

The question of the statutory authority of the NLRB to order a make-whole remedy for an employer's illegal refusal to bargain has not been resolved by the Supreme Court.[49] Other circuits have considered such make-whole remedies but have avoided ruling on the NLRB's statutory authority. In *Steelworkers (Metco, Inc.) v. NLRB*[50] Judge Tuttle of the Fifth Circuit indicated that he agreed with the District of Columbia Circuit that the Board had the statutory authority to grant such relief. In that case he found, however, that a remand to the Board was unnecessary because the employer's objections to the union's certification were not frivolous, and the litigation was not undertaken to delay collective bargaining. Judges Coleman and Ainsworth concurred in the result but stated they did not concur with that portion of Judge Tuttle's opinion dealing with the Board's power to enter the make-whole order, and indicated that they intimated no opinion on that subject.[51]

The Second Circuit in *Lipman Motors, Inc. v. NLRB*[52] refused to grant this type of monetary relief and stated that:

> The Company pursued the only procedural course available to secure judicial review of the Board certification. This commonplace attack on the Board's decision certainly does not warrant a direction by us to the Board to undertake the *speculative adventure* of fixing damages by "determining" whether the parties would have reached an agreement if they had bargained in good faith and what the terms of that hypothetical agreement would have been.[53]

---

[49] NLRB v. Food Store Employees, Local 347 (Heck's Inc.), 417 U.S. 1, 86 L.R.R.M. 2209 (1974) was limited to a consideration of litigation expenses and organizing costs.

[50] 496 F.2d 1342, 86 L.R.R.M. 2984, 2988-2992 (5th Cir. 1974).

[51] *Id.*, 86 L.R.R.M. at 2992. *But see* United Steelworkers of America, AFL-CIO v. United Gypsum Co., —— F.2d ——, 85 L.R.R.M. 2962, 2973-2976 (5th Cir. 1974) in which the court held that an arbitrator did not exceed his authority or contravene national labor relations policy when he ordered a successor employer to pay wage increases to which the arbitrator determined the employer would have agreed had negotiations occurred. The successor had refused to negotiate pursuant to a wage reopener clause in his predecessor's contract, and at the time the arbitrator made his decision, the union had been decertified for about five years. The court held that such a remedy was within the arbitrator's authority under an arbitration clause authorizing him to "interpret, apply or determine compliance with the provisions" of the agreement.

[52] 451 F.2d 823, 829, 78 L.R.R.M. 2808 (2d Cir. 1971).

[53] *Id.*, (emphasis added). The court expressly stated, however, that it was not deciding whether or not the Board has the power to grant compensatory

The Ninth Circuit also has reserved judgment on the Board's power to grant such remedies, but has rejected the requested compensatory damages where the employer had not engaged in a flagrant violation of the law and was not engaged in litigation to delay final resolution of the dispute.[54]

Company-Wide Bargaining

Heck's, Inc.[55] marked the eleventh time in which that particular employer had been involved in NLRB proceedings for resisting union organization at various units within its chain of discount stores.[56] The Board rejected the union's argument that the company's history of unfair labor practices warranted ordering it to bargain with the union on a company-wide basis. The Board pointed out that never in its history had it granted such a remedy and it, therefore, intended to examine the request carefully. The Board concluded that the remedy was not warranted because it would have interfered with the free choice of employees by imposing a union on some units where the union had at no time established a majority. Furthermore, the Board noted that the union had received majority support at some of the employer's units and, therefore, the company's actions had not wholly precluded its employees from making their own free choice.[57]

The Board also rejected a similar union proposal to order the company to bargain "at such time in the future when, with

---

damages for refusal to bargain. *Id.*, at n. 11. For a similar result in the Second Circuit, *see* The Herald Company v. NLRB, 444 F.2d 430, 436, 77 L.R.R.M. 2679 (2d Cir. 1971).

[54] *See* Bartenders Local 703 (Restaurant and Tavern Ass'n) v. NLRB, 488 F.2d 664, 84 L.R.R.M. 2984, 2985-2986 (9th Cir. 1973), *cert. denied*, 417 U.S. 946, 86 L.R.R.M. 2643 (1974). The recently enacted California Agricultural Labor Regulations Act of 1975 (Chapter 6, Section 1160.3 of Part 3.5, Division 2 of the California Labor Code), provides in part that the California Agricultural Labor Relations Board has the power to take the remedial action of "making employees whole when the board deems such relief appropriate, for the loss of pay resulting from the employer's refusal to bargain . . . ."

[55] 191 N.L.R.B. 2231, 77 L.R.R.M. 1513 (1971).

[56] *See* the cases cited in Food Store Employees, Local 347 v. NLRB, 476 F.2d 2955, n. 1, 82 L.R.R.M. 2955, 2956 n. 1 (D.C. Cir. 1973).

[57] *Id.*, 77 L.R.R.M. at 1516. The Board, assumed *arguendo*, that it had the power to enter such an order citing by way of caveat its opinion in J. P. Stevens & Co., 157 N.L.R.B. 869, 877, 61 L.R.R.M. 1437 (1966), and comparing NLRB v. Gissel Packing Co., 395 U.S. 575, 612-613, 71 L.R.R.M. 2481 (1969).

respect to any appropriate single-store unit, it either secures a card majority or the respondent becomes lawfully obligated to bargain with respect to such unit." [58] The Board was not convinced that the employees would always be unable to make a free choice with respect to their representatives. The Board also rejected arguments that the remedy would bring speedier relief. Rather, it held that unless the parties were in complete agreement on all representation issues, such issues would still have to be resolved by the Board, or by a special master in contempt proceedings. [59] The Board's rejection of both requested defenses was approved by the District of Columbia Circuit. [60]

Compensatory Damages for Lost Business

The Ninth Circuit has ruled that the Board properly denied an employer's request that a union which had entered into a "hot cargo" agreement proscribed by Section 8(e) should be required to pay compensatory damages for the employer's lost business and costs of redress. The court stated that the language of the statute "at least supports" the union's argument that the Board did not have jurisdiction over the employer involved. Although the court ruled that the unfair labor practice was within the Board's jurisdiction, it felt that the circumstances did not call for the requested award compensating for lost business and costs. The court specifically stated that it expressed no opinion concerning the power of the Board to award such affirmative relief. [61]

Gross Backpay

On occasion, unions have argued that the conventional backpay award is inadequate and that the Board should order the reimbursement of gross backpay, *i.e.*, backpay without the deduction of interim earnings from other employment. The Board and courts have rejected such requests. As stated by the District of Columbia Circuit:

---

[58] Heck's, Inc., *supra*, 77 L.R.R.M. at 1516.

[59] *Id.*, 77 L.R.R.M. at 1516.

[60] *See* Food Store Employees, Local 347 (Heck's, Inc.) v. NLRB, 476 F.2d 546, 82 L.R.R.M. 2955, 2957, 2958 n. 4 (D.C. Cir. 1973).

[61] *See* Marriott Corp. v. NLRB, 491 F.2d 367, 370-371, 85 L.R.R.M. 2257 (9th Cir. 1974), and cases cited therein.

The union readily agrees that the Board's powers are remedial in nature and that it "could not award gross back pay for the purpose of punishing the employer." See Republic Steel Corp. v. NLRB, 311 U.S. 7, 7 LRRM 287 (1940) ; Carpenters Local 60 v. NLRB, 365 U.S. 651, 655, 47 LRRM 2900 (1961). The union further concedes that full back pay is no more directly responsive to the sorts of collateral and intangible harms suffered by discharged employees than is net back pay; its claim is that the former provides "more complete compensation" for the employees' losses. While the union persistently asserts that its proposed remedy falls well on the permissible side of the thin line between compensation and punishment, it makes no effort to place a dollar figure on the inadequacies of net back pay. Nor does it attempt to quantify the difference, as to these discharged employees, between net and gross. In light of the union's contention that the remedy should only obtain in cases of egregious employer conduct, we cannot fault the Board for viewing the *full* back pay alternative, at least based on the union's showing here, as essentially punitive. Contrarily, the net back pay order entered in this case cannot, on this record, be said to be "a patent attempt to achieve ends other than those which can fairly be said to effectuate the policies of the Act." NLRB v. Rutter-Rex Mfg. Co., 396 U.S. 258, 263, 72 LRRM 2881 (1969), quoting NLRB v. Seven-Up Bottling Co., 344 U.S. 344, 346-47, 31 LRRM 2237 (1953).[62]

Debarment of Violators from Federal Contracts—H.R. 8409. Pending before the Labor-Management Relations Subcommittee of the U.S. House of Representatives Labor and Public Welfare Committee is H.R. 8409, which has been presented to Congress as a bill which would "strengthen the remedial provisions of the [National Labor Relations] Act against repeated or flagrant transgressors." [63] In essence, H.R. 8409 provides that if "any

---

[62] *See* Oil Workers (OCAW) (Kansas Refined Helium Co.), 445 F.2d 237, 77 L.R.R.M. 2378, 2742 (D.C. Cir. 1971), *cert. denied*, 404 U.S. 1039, 79 L.R.R.M. 2256 (1972). *Accord* NLRB v. Good Foods Corp., 492 F.2d 1302, 85 L.R.R.M. 2739, 2742 (7th Cir. 1974). *Cf.* Bigelow v. RKO Radio Pictures, Inc., 327 U.S. 251, 263-265 (1946).

[63] H.R. 8409 reads as follows:

A BILL

To amend the National Labor Relations Act, as amended, to strengthen the remedial provisions of the Act against repeated or flagrant transgressors.

Be it enacted by the Senate and House of Representatives of the United States of America in Congress assembled, That section 10 of the National Labor Relations Act is amended by adding at the end thereof the new subsection:

"(n) Whenever it is charged that any person has engaged in or is engaging in a willful and flagrant unfair labor practice, and/or has engaged in or is engaging in a pattern or practice, of unfair labor practices designed to interfere with, restrain, or coerce employees in the exercise of the rights guar-

person has engaged in a willful and flagrant unfair labor practice and/or a pattern or practice of unfair labor practices designed to interfere with, restrain or coerce employees in the exercise" of their Section 7 rights, the Board "shall" certify that finding to the Comptroller General. The Comptroller will then inform all other agencies of the United States government of the finding, and no government contracts will be awarded to the person or business entity for a period of three years from the date of the Board's certification. The only exceptions are those persons or business entities which a governmental agency, after a hearing, certifies to the NLRB as being the sole source for the material or services involved.

There are several serious deficiencies both in the concept of debarment and the wording of this particular proposed legislation. First, it is obvious that the debarment penalty exceeds remedying the particular unfair labor practice found. Instead, debarment would prevent employers who meet the law's criteria from obtaining federal contracts for a three year period. Under this legislation, even after particular unfair labor practices have been remedied, debarment would be mandated without any further inquiry into the sufficiency of the traditional NLRB remedy, or the necessity of the use of debarment against the particular employer. Furthermore, according to the wording of H.R. 8409, once the Comptroller certifies that the employer should be debarred, no appellate or other procedure exists to permit this decision to be revised. Thus, debarment could be based on a

---

anteed in section 7; and, whenever the General Counsel has reasonable cause to believe that such charge is true, he shall include the allegation in the complaint issued pursuant to section 10(b): Provided, That no allegation of a pattern or practice or unfair labor practices shall be based upon any unfair labor practice occurring more than three years prior to the filing of the charge with the Board. If it is determined, upon completion of the procedures available in section 10(b), (c), (d), (e), (f), and (g), that a person has engaged in a willful or flagrant unfair labor practice and/or a pattern or practice of unfair labor practices designed to interfere with, restrain, or coerce employees in the exercise of rights guaranteed in section 7, the Labor Board shall certify the identity of the person to the Comptroller General who shall distribute a list to all agencies of the United States containing the names of persons found by the Labor Board to have engaged in willful and flagrant unfair labor practices and/or a pattern or practice of unfair labor practices. No contracts shall be awarded to such person, or to any firm, corporation, partnership, or association in which such person has a controlling interest, until three years have elapsed from the date of the Labor Board certification; unless, the agency of the United States concerned, after notice and opportunity for hearing to all interested parties, certifies to the Labor Board that there is no other source for the material or services furnished by the person affected by the Labor Board order."

"pattern" based on NLRB findings some of which might be reversed upon court review.[64] This reversal should call for a reassessment of the debarment, but the bill lacks such a provision. Our previous discussions have demonstrated that remedies which exceed neutralizing particular unfair labor practices have traditionally been struck down by the courts as punitive and outside the scope of the Board's remedial power.[65] The debarment penalty is clearly punitive. Since the proposed penalty would give congressional sanction to a remedial method never before adopted by Congress, the courts, or the Board, the "legal and policy considerations bearing on its applicability" should be carefully considered.[66]

Second, the bill lacks standards for defining a *"willful or flagrant* unfair labor practice and/or a *pattern* or *practice* of unfair labor practices." Nothing in the bill helps distinguish an egregious (i.e., flagrant) violation from a "pattern" of violations which might have a minimal impact on the employees in a unit involved. The bill does not define "flagrant" violation in terms of the type or seriousness of the violation. Furthermore, the word "pattern" does not suggest the number of violations necessary, or determine whether the violations must be of the same type, before the sanction would be applied. A "practice" of unfair labor practices conceivably could range from a widespread attempt to undermine a union campaign to a few Section 8(a)(1) violations which would not have appreciable effect on a large unit of employees.

For example, an owner of a small plant who responds to a unionization campaign with contumacious conduct such as illegal discharges, threats to close his plant, and widespread interrogation of his employees is not distinguished from an employer who merely undertakes a "pattern" of questioning a few employees out of several hundred about their knowledge of the union. Quite clearly, there would be no reason to bar the latter employer from federal contracts, but the bill does not provide for graduated penalties. In short, H.R. 8409 does not

---

[64] Only about 70 percent of NLRB orders which were appealed in the last 6 years were enforced in full by courts. *See* 39 NLRB ANN. REP. 240 (1974).

[65] *See* the discussion in Chapter II, *supra*, pp. 12-16.

[66] *See generally* Heck's Inc., 191 N.L.R.B. No. 146, 77 L.R.R.M. 1513, 1516 (1971), *enforced on this ground sub. nom.* Food Store Employees, Local 347 (Heck's Inc.) v. NLRB, 476 F.2d 546, —— n. 1, 82 L.R.R.M. 2955, 2956 n. 1 (D.C. Cir. 1973).

require the Board to consider the size of the unit involved or the impact of the violations on the employees therein. Therefore, the bill offends the well-established principle that the imposition of NLRB remedies intended to have a broad impact must be based on a consideration of the nature and seriousness of the unfair labor practices found, the complete labor relations history of the offender, and the probability of the practices recurring.[67]

Third, the debarment penalty would have a detrimental effect on the fairness of NLRB litigation. Previously in this chapter, we have seen that the Board and courts have held consistently that even in those instances where a flagrant violation has occurred, extraordinary remedies such as payment of attorneys' fees will not be assessed unless the violator also advances a "frivolous" and "nondebatable" defense.[68] Thus, the tribunals which regularly deal in NLRB cases have indicated a strong lack of "desire to take action which could become the basis of chilling the assertion of rights reasonably held in good faith by virtue of imposing a penalty because of failure to prevail in the litigation."[69] This potentially chilling effect is more pronounced in H.R. 8409 than in any of the other remedies previously discussed in this chapter. With enactment of that bill, the employer who litigates a charge alleging that he has engaged in a "pattern" of unfair labor practices does not only face the loss of litigation expenses if his defense should prove frivolous. Rather, the vague standards and definitions of the bill confront the employer with the possible loss of the government contract portion of his business for at least three years, plus the time necessary to regain his lost contracts. This severe penalty would tend to encourage an employer with a *debatable* defense to settle an unfair labor practice charge because of the uncertainty and seriousness of the penalty.

Fourth, H.R. 8409 is not restricted to the particular unit where the unfair labor practices occurred. Rather, debarment would apply to "such person, or to any firm, corporation, partner-

---

[67] *See* Chapter III, *supra*, which deals with the appropriate use of narrow and broad orders.

[68] *See* pages 223-227, *supra*.

[69] *See* NLRB v. F & F Laboratories, Inc., 517 F.2d 551, 89 L.R.R.M. 2549, 2552 (7th Cir. 1975). *Accord* NLRB v. Food Store Employees, Local 347 (Heck's Inc.), 417 U.S. 1, 86 L.R.R.M. 2209, 2211 (1974), cited above, pp. 223-224.

ship, or association in which such person has a controlling interest . . . ." No showing would be required, as in the usual broad order situation, that the employer had instituted a system-wide, centrally directed, and coordinated policy to commit unfair labor practices throughout his entire operation.[70] From this language, it could be easily argued that a flagrant violation at one Chevrolet plant would deprive the entire General Motors Corporation of its federal contracts. The bill clearly would force the debarment of all divisions of one employer, even if each division had a distinct labor relations policy. Obviously, the overly broad language of this bill fails to consider the labor relations structure of the employer involved, or the impact of the unfair labor practices on the employees in units where no violations occurred.

Fifth, the devastating impact of debarment on the employees of the affected employer seems to have been overlooked in favor of a vaguely defined notion of the impact of unfair labor practices. It is easy to conceive that the loss of jobs to employees whose employer has been debarred from federal contracts could be more serious than the effect of the unfair labor practices. Such mitigating factors, however, are not considered in the application of the debarment penalty. Similarly, the impact on the public is not considered. Once debarment is found appropriate, the only instance in which it would not be effectuated is when an agency certifies to the NLRB that there is "no other source for the material or services furnished." Nothing would prevent debarment, however, even if other available sources are more expensive, or provide inferior quality goods or services. Indeed, the concept of federal debarment would necessarily entail increased costs to the public since federal regulations require that the contracts be awarded to the lowest qualified bidder.

In sum, H.R. 8409 is an ill-defined, vague, and overly broad statute. Moreover, the concept of debarment in any form is unacceptable because it provides a penalty which far exceeds the particular unfair labor practice found, improperly discourages respondents from participating in litigation, could easily result in the loss of jobs for employees in the unit and

---

[70] *See* the discussion *supra*, in Chapter III, pp. 34-37.

may increase the cost of supplies and services purchased by the federal government.[71]

Treble Damages for 8(a)(3) and 8(b)(2) Violations—H.R. 8110.

Another bill pending before the House Labor Subcommittee is H.R. 8110 which would amend Section 303 to permit any person who suffers financial injury through a violation of Section 8(a) (3) or Section 8(b)(2)[72] to sue in a U.S. district court to recover treble the damages sustained plus legal costs and attorneys' fees.[73]

As with the proposed debarment penalty discussed above,[74] the proposed treble damage remedy is too broadly drafted and

---

[71] Recently the Administrative Conference of the U.S. recommended that the Office of Federal Contract Compliance drop its debarment sanction. The conference stated that "contract cancellation is in many cases too severe or impracticable as the primary sanction for noncompliance with equal employment opportunity regulations." It pointed out that a broad debarment penalty fails to take into account the special circumstances of major employment categories, and recommended that the Department of Labor develop a system of graduated sanctions for breach of EEO obligations. The conference's recommendations were printed in the July 2, 1975 Federal Register. See also No. 128 DAILY LABOR REPORT, page A-14 (BNA, July 2, 1975).

[72] Section 8(a)(3) [29 U.S.C. § 158(a)(3)] makes it an unfair labor practice for an employer "to discriminate in regard to hire or tenure of employment or any term or condition of employment to encourage or discourage membership in any labor organization. Section 8(b)(2) [29 U.S.C. § 158(b) (2)] makes it an unfair labor practice for a labor organization or its agents

> "to cause or attempt to cause an employer to discriminate against an employee in violation of subsection (a)(3) or to discriminate against an employee with respect to whom membership in such organization has been denied or terminated on some ground other than his failure to tender the periodic dues and the initiation fees uniformly required as a condition of acquiring or retaining membership . . .".

[73] Section 2 of H.R. 8110 reads as follows:

> SEC. 2. Section 303 of the National Labor Relations Act, as amended, is amended by adding the following paragraph at the end thereof:

> "(c) Any person who shall suffer financial injury by reason of any violation of sections 8(a)(3) or 8(b)(2) may sue therefor in any district court of the United States in the district in which the defendant resides or is found or has an agent, without respect to the amount in controversy, and shall recover threefold the damages by him sustained, and the cost of suit, including a reasonable attorney's fee. A final judgment or decree heretofore rendered by the Board to the effect that a defendant has violated said sections 8(a)(3) or 8(b)(2) shall be prima facie evidence against such defendant in any action or proceedings brought by any person under this subsection."

[74] *Supra,* pp. 236-241.

cannot be justified as a proper unfair labor practice remedy. The bill permits "any" person who has suffered financial injury from an 8 (a) (3) or 8 (b) (2) violation to sue for three times the damage suffered. The bill permits such damages when *any* such violation is found, even if the employer or union had a debatable defense, or a defense where the outcome turned upon difficult credibility resolutions.[75] The bill also fails to consider that the violator might have had a mistaken but good faith belief that the affected employee had engaged in misconduct justifying discharge. While such a belief would not be a defense to an unfair labor practice[76] it would also not present a degree of culpability from which an employer or union should be made to bear the reimbursement of damages at least three times as great as those actually suffered.

Furthermore, the bill would place particularly heavy pressure on small employers and unions with limited resources to settle a case in order to avoid the payment of fees to their own and opposing lawyers, and to escape potential triple liability. The result would be a chilling effect on a respondent's right to have potentially meritorious defenses decided by the Board and courts. While some might argue that such a result would have a beneficial effect of decreasing the Board's and courts' caseloads, such an effect would be counterbalanced by the detriment to the respondent's right to litigate, and the increase in cases filed by those seeking to take advantage of the increased money damages and attorneys' fees.[77] In addition, this impact on the

---

[75] The increased damages provided by the bill might make credibility resolutions much more difficult. As the Second Circuit recently noted in a case which overruled the Board's policy of not sequestering witnesses who are alleged to be discriminatees, there is "the danger that [the discriminatee's] financial interest makes the temptation to perjury great." *See* NLRB v. Stark, —— F.2d ——, —— L.R.R.M. —— (2d Cir. 1975).

[76] *See* NLRB v. Burnup and Sims, Inc., 379 U.S. 21, 57 L.R.R.M. 2385 (1964), discussed in more detail in Chapter IX, *supra*, pp. 143-144.

[77] One commentator has pointed out that "[a]bout 70% of all [NLRB] charges against employers are non-meritorious." *See* Samoff, *The Future of the NLRB*, paper delivered at the 26th Annual Meeting of the Industrial Relations Research Association, Friday, December 28, 1973, New York City. This high degree of nonmeritorious charges points out the unfairness of an extremely harsh remedy with the potential to coerce settlements. In addition, as the cumulative figures for fiscal years 1969-1973 show, the courts of appeals often find it necessary to modify (13.6%), remand in full (4.8%), remand in part (1.8%), or set aside (11.5%) orders of the NLRB which come before the courts on review or enforcement. 77.2 percent of appealed NLRB orders were enforced in full in f.y. 1974. *See* 39 NLRB ANN. REP. 240 (1974).

small employer and union would be particularly unfair when it is realized that a treble damage award might seriously harm their financial position, whereas a particularly flagrant violator, however, with strong economic power might easily be able to pay the award and continue his pattern of unfair labor practices.

Also, the bill does not require that the discriminatees first attempt to have the case tried before the NLRB in order to determine whether an unfair labor practice was committed. Neither does it provide that if the NLRB General Counsel or the Board dismiss the complaint that the NLRB's decision will be binding on the district court. H.R. 8110 merely states that a Board determination that a violation occurred "shall be prima facie evidence" against the defendant. Thus, a district court would be able to review issues of substantial evidence and make legal conclusions which might be at odds with the Board's findings on the very same facts. Thus, H.R. 8110 poses the possibility of duplication of litigation and of inconsistent findings by the Board and courts. Not only would H.R. 8100 greatly increase the workload of the U.S. district courts [78] it would also tend to undercut the effectiveness of the NLRB by making the greater district court damages more attractive.

The concept of treble damages assumes that all violators of the Act have a degree of culpability which requires a penalty unrelated to the seriousness of the violation, the relative merits of the allegations and the respondents' defenses, the violator's past history, and the likelihood of future violations. Because of these shortcomings, this penalty entails fundamental inequities and should be rejected as inconsistent with the remedial structure of the Act.

---

[78] In fiscal year 1974, 11,620 cases filed with the NLRB contained allegations of Section 8(a)(3) violations. This figure was about 65 percent of all unfair labor practice charges filed against employers. *See* 39 NLRB ANN. REP. 198 (1974).

CHAPTER XV

Court Contempt and Injunction Proceedings, and Penalties for Frivolous Appeals

The previous chapter discussed extraordinary NLRB remedies used when violators engage in flagrant unfair labor practices or advance frivolous defenses in Board proceedings. The focus of this chapter is on court proceedings and sanctions, provided by the National Labor Relations Act, to supplement the Board's remedial powers. In this chapter, we discuss the increasing use of penalties by the appellate courts to discourage frivolous appeals of NLRB orders. Also, we examine the contempt of court sanction available for use against respondents who defy court-enforced Board orders. Further, we consider court injunctions used against those union violations which Congress has designated as so serious that they require the Board's General Counsel to seek injunctive relief if he determines there is "reasonable cause to believe" that one of these violations is occurring. Next, we deal with court injunctions which the NLRB has the discretion to seek in order either to preserve the status quo, protect the efficacy of the Board's final order, prevent a harmful impact upon the public interest, or prevent the frustration of the purposes of the Act.

THE SMITH & WESSON PENALTY FOR FRIVOLOUS APPEALS

Relying on Rule 38 of the Federal Rules of Appellate Procedure, the U.S. Courts of Appeals have indicated considerable irritation at having to decide NLRB-related cases which, upon examination, are found to be based on frivolous contentions. Thus, in *NLRB v. Smith & Wesson*,[1] the First Circuit found

---

[1] 424 F.2d 1072, 1073, 74 L.R.R.M. 2173, 2174 (1st Cir. 1970).

that the Board's findings were clearly supported, and the employer's resistance thereto was frivolous. It stated that "some penalty should attach to taking up our time with such a meritless contention." [2] The court not only awarded the Board its regular costs, but added the sum of $250 for expenses.[3] In *NLRB v. Sauk Valley Mfg. Co.*,[4] the Ninth Circuit declined to assess the penalty, but reserved the right to do so in appropriate future circumstances. The Seventh Circuit also recognized the availability of the penalty, but refused to award it in the case at bar because the outcome turned on credibility resolutions, and the court did not want to chill the assertion of rights which were held in good faith.[5] The Fifth Circuit in *Monroe Auto Equipment Co. v. NLRB*,[6] held that where the law was clearly contrary to the employer's position, it was appropriate under FRAP 38 to direct the assessment of double costs and a reasonable award of attorneys' fees. In that case the employer had attempted to convince a U.S. District Court to reopen the record in an NLRB representation case. The court indicated that if the parties could not agree on attorneys' fees, it would appoint a special master to do so.[7] Further, the court stated that this penalty was "without prejudice to the institution of contempt proceedings for failure of the [e]mployer to obey the order of [the court]." [8]

CONTEMPT OF COURT PROCEEDINGS

Orders of the NLRB are not self-enforcing. Rather, Section 10(e)[9] of the National Labor Relations Act gives the Board the

---

[2] *Id.*

[3] *Accord*, NLRB v. United Shoe Machinery Corp., 445 F.2d 633, 635, 77 L.R.R.M. 2719 (1st Cir. 1971); General Tire & Rubber Co. v. NLRB, 451 F.2d 257, 259, 78 L.R.R.M. 2836 (1st Cir. 1971); NLRB v. Ramada Inns, Inc., 190 N.L.R.B. 450, 77 L.R.R.M. 1681, 1971, *enforced*, —— F.2d ——, 79 L.R.R.M. 2929, 2928 (1st Cir. 1972); NLRB v. Hijos de Ricardo Vela, Inc., 475 F.2d 58, 82 L.R.R.M. 2967, 2970 (1st Cir. 1973); NLRB v. Bedford Discounters, Inc., 484 F.2d 923, 84 L.R.R.M. 2332 (1st Cir. 1973).

[4] 486 F.2d 1127, 1133-1134, 84 L.R.R.M. 2674 (9th Cir. 1973).

[5] NLRB v. F&F Laboratories, Inc., 517 F.2d 551, 89 L.R.R.M. 2549, 2552 (7th Cir. 1975).

[6] 511 F.2d 611, 89 L.R.R.M. 2104, 2106 (5th Cir. 1975).

[7] *Id.* at n. 2.

[8] *Id.* at 614, 89 L.R.R.M. at 2106.

[9] 29 U.S.C. § 160(e).

power to apply to the appropriate United States Circuit Court of appeals for enforcement of its orders. Once the court enforces an order of the Board, that order becomes a lawful decree of a court which has the inherent power to enforce compliance through the civil contempt sanction, upon request of the Board.[10] Thus, if a respondent either refuses to comply with the affirmative requirements of a particular order which the court has enforced, or commits a violation of the same nature as one included in the court-enforced NLRB cease and desist order, he may be subject to contempt of court proceedings. This makes available powerful sanctions beyond the purely remedial power of the Board.

It is well established that the courts "should impose whatever sanctions are necessary under the circumstances to grant full remedial relief, to coerce the contemnor into compliance with [the] court's order, and to fully compensate the complainant for losses sustained." [11] Thus, in NLRB-related civil contempt proceedings, the courts will routinely order respondents to pay the Board all fees, costs, and expenditures incurred during the contempt proceedings. These include counsel fees incurred in investigation, preparation, presentation, and final disposition of the contempt case.[12] Further, in order to assure that the respondent complies with the terms of the decree, the courts consistently order a fine for each further violation plus a fine for each day each violation continues. For example, in *NLRB v. Amalgamated Local Union 355 (Robin Ford)*,[13] the court anticipated future violations and ordered compliance fines

---

[10] *See e.g.*, NLRB v. Sheet Metal Workers, Local No. 80, 491 F.2d 1017, 85 L.R.R.M. 2490 (6th Cir. 1974) (violation of a consent judgment ordering union to cease running a hiring hall in a discriminatory manner) ; Teamsters, Local 745 (Farmers Co-op. Gin Ass'n) v. NLRB, 500 F.2d 768, 86 L.R.R.M. 2110 (D.C. Cir. 1974) (employer violation of a bargaining order) ; NLRB v. J. P. Stevens & Co., 464 F.2d 1326, 80 L.R.R.M. 3126 (2d Cir. 1972) ; NLRB v. J. P. Stevens & Co., ——— F.2d ———, 81 L.R.R.M. 2285 (2d Cir. 1972) ; NLRB v. Mooney Aircraft, Inc., 366 F.2d 809, 61 L.R.R.M. 2163 (5th Cir. 1966).

[11] NLRB v. Vander Wal, 316 F.2d 631, 52 L.R.R.M. 2761, 2763 (9th Cir. 1963), *Accord*, United States v. United Mine Workers, 330 U.S. 258, 19 L.R.R.M. 2346 (1947).

[12] *See e.g.*, NLRB v. Nickey Chevrolet Sales, Inc., ——— F.2d ———, 76 L.R.R.M. 2849, 2853 (7th Cir. 1971) ; NLRB v. J. P. Stevens & Co., 464 F.2d 1326, 80 L.R.R.M. 3126 (2d Cir. 1972). *Cf.* NLRB v. Mooney Aircraft, Inc., 366 F.2d 809, 61 L.R.R.M. 2164, 2165 (5th Cir. 1966) (counsel fees excluded).

[13] ——— F.2d ———, 77 L.R.R.M. 2989 (E.D.N.Y. 1971).

of $10,000 from the union, and $2000 from each of two union officers. Also, in that case, if such future violations were of a continuing nature, the union and officers would have been required to pay fines of $1000 and $200 per day respectively.[14] Another illustration is found in *NLRB* v. *Johnson Mfg. Co.,*[15] wherein the employer who had refused to bargain in good faith with the union was fined $50,000, which was to be returned if the employer presented within 60 days satisfactory evidence of compliance with the new court order. Similarly, in *NLRB v. F. M. Reeves & Sons,*[16] the court enforced a fine of $1,000 for the employer's past acts of contempt.

In contempt proceedings involving employer refusals to bargain, the Fifth Circuit has devised remedies which surpass those employed by the Board in similar violations. In *NLRB v. Schill Steel Products, Inc.*[17] the employer was ordered to bargain until full agreement or bona fide impasse was reached. The existence of such impasse was to be decided by the court, and the failure to find such an impasse was to be considered a failure to bargain in good faith. Such a failure would subject the employer to compliance fines of $5,000 for the violation, plus a fine of $1,000 for each day the violation continued. In addition, the employer was not permitted to refuse to meet with the union at reasonable times, or to withdraw recognition from the union until further order of the court. Also, unless the union gave written permission otherwise, bargaining sessions were to be held at least fifteen hours per week. Sworn reports signed both by the employer and union were to be filed with the court clerk and the Board every thirty days detailing the nature and course of the bargaining. If the Board determined that the employer was not bargaining in good faith, it was required to submit a report and supporting brief to the court and propose appropriate sanctions. If the company was found to have en-

---

[14] *See also* NLRB v. Schill Steel Products, Inc., 480 F.2d 586, 83 L.R.R.M. 2669, 2672 (5th Cir. 1973); NLRB v. Sheet Metal Workers Local No. 80, 491 F.2d 1017, 85 L.R.R.M. 2490 (6th Cir. 1974); NLRB v. Ambrose Distributing Co., 382 F.2d 92, 65 L.R.R.M. 3057 (9th Cir. 1967).

[15] 511 F.2d 153, 88 L.R.R.M. 3553 (5th Cir. 1975).

[16] 273 F.2d 710, 47 L.R.R.M. 2480 (10th Cir. 1961).

[17] 480 F.2d 586, 83 L.R.R.M. 2669, 2670-2671 (5th Cir. 1973). *See also* NLRB v. Johnson Mfg. Co., 511 F.2d 153, 88 L.R.R.M. 3553 (5th Cir. 1975).

gaged in bad faith bargaining, the compliance fines mentioned above would then be imposed.

A further alternative available to the court in dealing with the persistently recalcitrant violator is to issue a writ of body attachment under which the appropriate officer or agent of the offending respondent will be confined to jail until compliance with the court's decree is forthcoming.[18]

Finally, if it can be shown that the respondent "knowingly, willfully and intentionally" violated the court's decree, the Board may petition the court to find the respondent criminally liable for his conduct.[19] Sentences for criminal contempt include monetary fines and imprisonment.

As shown, contempt of court proceedings provide powerful sanctions to use when employers and unions violate Board orders which have been enforced by the courts of appeals.[20]

SECTION 10(l) INJUNCTIONS

The National Labor Relations Act provides certain exemptions to the Norris-LaGuardia Act's [21] general prohibition of injunctions in labor disputes.[22] The Board itself does not have the power to issue injunctions. Sections 10(l) and 10(j), however, describe various conditions under which the NLRB and its General Counsel may apply to the appropriate U.S. District

---

[18] *See* NLRB v. Savoy Laundry, Inc., 354 F.2d 78, 61 L.R.R.M. 2021, 2023 (2d Cir. 1965); and NLRB v. Schill Steel Products, Inc., 480 F.2d 586, 83 L.R.R.M. 2669, 2672 (5th Cir. 1973).

[19] *See e.g.,* Winn-Dixie Stores, Inc., 386 F.2d 309, 66 L.R.R.M. 2427 (5th Cir. 1967); NLRB v. Star Metal Mfg. Co., 187 F.2d 856, 27 L.R.R.M. 2437 (3d Cir. 1951).

[20] A description of the NLRA contempt process and an analysis of its effectiveness can be found in Bartosic and Lanoff, *Escalating the Struggle Against Taft-Hartley Contemnors*, 39 U. Chi. L. Rev. 255 (1972).

[21] 47 Stat. 70 (1932), 29 U.S.C. §§ 101-105 (1970).

[22] *See generally* Section 10(h) of the NLRA [29 U.S.C. § 160(h)] which provides that:

> When granting appropriate temporary relief or a restraining order, or making and entering a decree enforcing, modifying, and enforcing as so modified, or setting aside in whole or in part an order of the Board, as provided in this section, the jurisdiction of courts sitting in equity shall not be limited by the Act entitled "An Act to amend the Judicial Code and to define and limit the jurisdiction of courts sitting in equity, and for other purposes," approved March 23, 1932 (U.S.C., Supp. VII, title 29, secs. 101-115).

Court for injunctive relief. Injunctions issued under these sections are by no means designed to provide a final unfair labor practice remedy, rather they are designed to give provisional relief which expires upon the issuance of a final Board order.[23] The provisional nature of these injunctions consummates the intent of Congress to give the NLRB the primary authority to remedy unfair labor practices. Even though these injunctions do not constitute remedies of the Board itself, it seems appropriate to mention them here because their use may preserve the status quo and thus complement the Board's remedial authority. Section 10(1) provides in part that:

> Whenever it is charged that any person has engaged in an unfair labor practice within the meaning of paragraph (4) (A), (B), or (C) of section 8(b), or section 8(e) or section 8(b)(7), the preliminary investigation of such charge shall be made forthwith and given priority over all other cases except cases of like character in the office where it is filed or to which it is referred. If, after such investigation, the officer or regional attorney to whom the matter may be referred has reasonable cause to believe such charge is true and that a complaint should issue, *he shall*, on behalf of the Board, petition any district court of the United States (including the District Court of the United States for the District of Columbia) within any district where the unfair labor practice in question has occurred, is alleged to have occured, or wherein such person resides or transacts business, for appropriate injunctive relief pending the final adjudication of the Board with respect to such matter. Upon the filing of any such petition the district court shall have jurisdiction to grant such injunctive relief or temporary restraining order as it deems just and proper, notwithstanding any other provision of law: *Provided further,* That no temporary restraining order shall be issued without notice unless a petition alleges that substantial and irreparable injury to the charging party will be unavoidable and such temporary restraining order shall be effective for no longer than five days and will become void at the expiration of such period: .... (emphasis added)

Thus, Section 10(1), sets forth situations in which the NLRB General Counsel is required to seek injunctive relief.[24] Pursuant to 10(1), the Board must allege the following: (1) an

---

[23] Section 10(1) permits the court to enter appropriate injunctive relief "pending final adjudication of the Board with respect to such matter." *See also* Sears, Roebuck & Co. v. Painters, Local 419, 397 U.S. 655, 658-659, 74 L.R.R.M. 2001, 2002-2003 (1970). *Cf.* Building & Construction Trades Council of Philadelphia v. Samoff, 414 U.S. 808, 84 L.R.R.M. 2421 (1973); Vincent v. Teamsters, Local 294, 424 F.2d 124, 73 L.R.R.M. 2983 (2d Cir. 1970).

[24] In fiscal year 1974, the NLRB's General Counsel sought 233 10(1) injunctions. *See* 39 NLRB Ann. Rep. 241 (1974).

unfair labor practice charge has been filed; [25] (2) a preliminary investigation of the charge has been undertaken; [26] (3) there is reasonable cause to believe one of the specified violations has occurred; (4) the evidence warrants granting relief; (5) the court has jurisdiction; and (6) the parties are subject to the Act.

Although the Board must establish a prima facie case, this may be done merely by producing evidence sufficient to lead a reasonable person to believe that an unfair labor practice has occurred.[27] Nevertheless, it must be remembered that 10(1) injunctive remedies have been statutorily defined to apply to certain specified unfair labor practices. Consequently, any request for relief must clearly reflect evidence of those illegal acts to avoid the possibility of enjoining lawful conduct.[28]

---

[25] *See* LeBaron v. Los Angeles Building & Construction Trades Council, 84 F. Supp. 629, 24 L.R.R.M. 2131 (S.D. Cal. 1949), *aff'd mem.*, 185 F.2d 405, 27 L.R.R.M. 2184 (9th Cir. 1950), *vacated on other grounds*, 342 U.S. 802, 28 L.R.R.M. 2625 (1951).

[26] Since a preliminary investigation is a prerequisite to injunctive relief under § 10(1), LeBaron v. Kern County Farm Labor Union, Local 218, 80 F. Supp. 156, 23 L.R.R.M. 2077 (S.D. Cal. 1948) ; the Board must comply with its own procedures and requirements or face dismissal of its suit. *See* Madden v. Masters, Mates & Pilots, Local 3, 259 F.2d 297, 42 L.R.R.M. 2792 (7th Cir. 1958). However, neither the failure of the Board to allege that a preliminary investigation had been conducted, McLeod v. Local 239, Teamsters, 180 F. Supp. 679, 45 L.R.R.M. 2302 (E.D.N.Y. 1959) (technical defect in Board's petition which could be readily cured) ; nor proof as to the sufficiency of the investigation, *see* Buildings & Construction Trades Council of Metro District v. Alpert, 302 F.2d 594, 50 L.R.R.M. 2154 (1st Cir. 1962) (allegations as to the scope, nature, and extent of the investigation not required) ; Madden v. Hod Carriers, Local 41, 277 F.2d 688, 46 L.R.R.M. 2181 (7th Cir. 1960), *cert. denied*, 364 U.S. 863, 46 L.R.R.M. 3091 (1960) (union request for production of files and records pertaining to an investigation denied), may be raised by a respondent union as a defense.

[27] *See, e.g.*, Hull v. Teamsters, Local 24, 148 F. Supp. 145, 39 L.R.R.M. 2370 (N.D. Ohio 1957) ; LeBaron v. Los Angeles Building & Trades Council, 84 F. Supp. 629, 24 L.R.R.M. 2131 (S.D. Cal. 1949) ; Styles v. Local 760, Electrical Workers, 80 F. Supp. 119, 22 L.R.R.M. 2446 (E.D. Tenn. 1948).

[28] *See* Potter v. Houston Gulf Coast Building Trades Council, 482 F.2d 837, 841, 83 L.R.R.M. 3042, 3044 (5th Cir. 1973), wherein the Fifth Circuit stated that "whenever possible, a grant of equitable relief should be carefully tailored so as to permit the continuation of primary activities while stamping out the illegal secondary conduct and its deleterious impact." This view is exemplified by the district court decision in Kaynard v. Local 707, Teamsters, 73 L.R.R.M. 2575 (E.D.N.Y. 1969). In that case, the court enjoined union-sponsored picketing where one of its primary purposes was recognitional, despite the claim that it was in support of discharged employees to gain reinstatement. The court, however, refused to grant a blanket injunction

The "reasonable cause to believe" standard of 10(1) is applicable only to the unfair labor practices charged; [29] factual proof of all other matters, such as jurisdiction over the parties sought to be restrained, is required.[30] For example, although an international union may be made a proper party to the suit,[31] it cannot be made responsible for a local's misconduct without

against picketing, noting that the discharged employees retained the right to picket on their own behalf in order to gain reemployment.

On the other hand, when union activity has both an unlawful, as well as a lawful objective, it will be enjoined. *See* Greene v. Bangor Building Trades Union, 165 F. Supp. 902, 42 L.R.R.M. 2713 (D. Me. 1958); Getreu v. Teamsters, Local 327, 37 L.R.R.M. 2133 (N.D. Tenn. 1955).

[29] In mandatory suits pursuant to § 10(1), the "reasonable cause to believe" standard is limited to questions concerning the alleged unfair labor practice and whether a party should be enjoined; it is an insufficient standard to establish whether such a party is subject to the Act. LeBaron v. Kern County Farm Labor Union, 80 F. Supp. 156, 23 L.R.R.M. 2077 (S.D. Cal. 1948). On the other hand, the standard has been applied to questions as to whether a group of employees who engaged in secondary activities was a labor organization within the meaning of the Act. *Compare* Madden v. Masters, Mates, & Pilots, Local 28, 166 F. Supp. 862, 42 L.R.R.M. 2793, (N.D. Ill. 1958) (no reasonable cause to believe that organization composed exclusively of supervisory personnel was subject to the Act), *with* Madden v. Masters, Mates, & Pilots, Local 47, 259 F.2d 297, 42 L.R.R.M. 2742 (7th Cir. 1958) (reasonable cause to believe employee organization subject to the Act where its members were employed to give technical advice and assistance).

[30] A court's jurisdiction in 10(1) proceedings, is not dependent upon the dollar volume of commerce affected, IBEW, Local 501 v. NLRB, 341 U.S. 694, 28 L.R.R.M. 2115 (1951); but rather is based upon the question of whether interstate commerce is affected by the allegedly unlawful activities in question. Kaynard v. Nassau & Suffolk Building & Construction Trades Council, 61 L.R.R.M. 2674 (E.D.N.Y. 1966); *cf.* Local 74, Carpenters v. NLRB, 341 U.S. 947, 28 L.R.R.M. 2121 (1951). *But see* Madden v. Teamsters, Local 364, 40 L.R.R.M. 2595 (N.D. Ind. 1957) (injunction denied where court doubted Board would assert jurisdiction under current monetary standards). *Compare* McLeod v. Local 1199, Drug and Hospital Union (666 Cosmetics, Inc.), 80 L.R.R.M. 2503 (S.D.N.Y. 1972), *with* McLeod v. Building Service Employees Union, Local 32E, 227 F. Supp. 242, 55 L.R.R.M. 2380 (S.D.N.Y. 1964).

[31] Brown v. Oil & Chemical Workers, 80 F. Supp. 708, 23 L.R.R.M. 2016 (N.D. Cal. 1948). *Compare* Matson Navigation Co. v. Seafarers Union, 100 F. Supp. 730, 29 L.R.R.M. 2364 (D. Md. 1951) (supervisors, union, ordinarily outside the jurisdiction of the Act, will be enjoined where it is acting as a "front" for a national labor federation which is subject to the Act), *with* Humphrey v. Local 639, Teamsters, 369 F. Supp. 730, 86 L.R.R.M. 2968 (D. Md. 1974) (fact that mixed unit composed of guards and other employees is noncertifiable does not render it immune to injunction). *See also* Alpert v. Int'l Typographical Union, 161 F. Supp. 427, 41 L.R.R.M. 2704 (D. Mass. 1958), at note 41, *infra*, for an explanation of the rationale for making internationals responsible for the acts of their locals.

evidence that the international participated, authorized, ratified, or engaged in the unlawful conduct.[32]

Finally, relief will be granted where the court deems it "just and proper" [33] and where its denial may result in irreparable injury [34] either to the charging party [35] or to the public interest.[36]

SECTION 10(j) INJUNCTIONS

Unlike Section 10(l), the provisions of Section 10(j) are not mandatory, but rather grant the NLRB the discretionary power to apply to a U.S. district court "for appropriate temporary relief," and authorize the court to grant such relief "as it deems just and proper." [37]

---

[32] Sperry v. Operating Engineers, Local 6-6A-6B, 43 L.R.R.M. 2167 (W.D. Mo. 1958).

[33] Douds v. Local 24368, Wire & Metal Lathers, 86 F. Supp. 542, 24 L.R.R.M. 2487 (S.D.N.Y. 1949).

[34] *E.g.,* Goldfarb v. Rochester St. Bd. of the Amalgamated Clothing Workers, 85 L.R.R.M. 2622 (W.D.N.Y. 1974). In *Goldfarb,* unlawful picketing by the clothing workers, who were engaged in bitter organizational struggle at Farah Mfg. Co., directed at a retailer, subjected the neutral to "irreparable damage" by interference with its business "and by damage to its good name [*i.e.,* good will], a critical element to a major retailer."
See also Douds v. ILGWU, Local 66, 124 F. Supp. 919, 34 L.R.R.M. 2540 (S.D.N.Y. 1954); Getreu v. District 50, Mine Workers, 30 L.R.R.M. 2048 (E.D. Tenn. 1952). In both of these cases, the court determined that a union seeking to force an employer to recognize it, by engaging in work stoppages or picketing, despite the valid certification of a rival union, causes the employer irreparable harm.

[35] *See* Douds v. Milk Drivers & Dairy Employees, Local 584, 154 F. Supp. 222, 40 L.R.R.M. 2669 (2d Cir. 1957), *stay denied,* 154 F. Supp. 222, 40 L.R.R.M. 2673 (2d Cir. 1957), wherein the Second Circuit denied the union's request for a stay of a direct court injunction where such a request, if granted, would have compelled the charging employers either to yield to the union's demands or to go out of business.

[36] Cosentino v. Longshoremen (ILA), 107 F. Supp. 235, 30 L.R.R.M. 2683 (D.P.R. 1952) (economic life of Puerto Rico threatened by Longshoremen attempt to obtain control of all organized labor on island); Brown v. Roofers, Local 40, 86 F. Supp. 50, 24 L.R.R.M. 2472 (N.D. Cal. 1949) (jurisdictional strike involving rights of six craftsmen properly enjoined to permit four to five hundred other employees to remain on job to complete public housing project).

[37] The provisions of Section 10(j) [29 U.S.C. § 160(j)] are as follows:

The Board shall have power, upon issuance of a complaint as provided in subsection (b) charging that any person has engaged in or is engaging in an unfair labor practice, to petition any district court of the United States (including the District Court of the United States in the District of

Under 10(j), the Board's petition must allege that the following conditions exist: (1) an unfair labor practice charge has been filed; [38] (2) a complaint has been issued; [39] (3) the facts presented support the charge; (4) there is a likelihood that the unfair labor practice will continue unless restrained; (5) the district court has jurisdiction; [40] and (6) the persons sought to be restrained are subject to the Act. [41] Of course, the primary prerequisites are whether the unlawful conduct, as a matter of law, constitutes an unfair labor practice and whether

---

Columbia), within any district wherein the unfair labor practice in question is alleged to have occurred or wherein such person resides or transacts business, for appropriate temporary relief or restraining order. Upon the filing of any such petition the court shall cause notice thereof to be served upon such person, and thereupon shall have jurisdiction to grant to the Board such temporary relief or restraining order as it deems just and proper.

The Board sought Section 10(j) injunctions on eighteen occasions in fiscal year 1974. *See* 39 NLRB Ann. Rep. 341 (1974). A thorough review of the use of the Section 10(j) injunction during the recent term of former General Counsel Peter G. Nash can be found in the *Report of the NLRB General Counsel on Section 10(j) injunction proceedings under Taft-Hartley Act in Period from August 1971 to July 1 1975.* 90 L.R.R. 12-37 (1975); DAILY LABOR REPORT No. 161 (BNA, 1975).

[38] *Cf.* Douds v. Longshoremen, ILA, 147 F. Supp. 103, 39 L.R.R.M. 2110 (S.D.N.Y. 1956), *aff'd,* 241 F.2d 278, 39 L.R.R.M. 2388 (2d Cir. 1957). A union contention that a complaint based on a defective charge precluded the granting of jurisdiction was rejected on the grounds that the initial defect, admittedly a technicality, was cured by subsequent events.

[39] *See, e.g.,* Kaynard v. Bagel Bakers Council of Greater N.Y., 68 L.R.R.M. 2140 (E.D.N.Y. 1968); Reynolds v. Marlene Industries Corp., 250 F. Supp. 722, 61 L.R.R.M. 2342 (S.D.N.Y. 1966); Evans v. Typographical Union, 76 F. Supp. 881, 21 L.R.R.M. 2375 (S.D. Ind. 1948).

[40] The courts have been rather lenient in terms of the requisite notice which is afforded to charged parties under the terms of the Act. *Compare* Reynolds v. Marlene Industries Corp., 250 F. Supp. 724, 63 L.R.R.M. 2097 (S.D.N.Y. 1966) (service of process upon president of subsidiaries sufficient to bind loosely integrated company), *with* Douds v. Anheuser-Busch, 28 L.R.R.M. 2277 (D.N.J. 1951) (sufficient notice given where Board agent rather than federal marshall served process on respondent employer).

[41] *See* Kaynard v. Bagel Bakers Council of Greater N.Y., 68 L.R.R.M. 2140 (E.D.N.Y. 1968) (injunction issued against employer association properly extended to include successor member); Alpert v. Int'l Typographical Union, 161 F. Supp. 427, 41 L.R.R.M. 2704 (D. Mass. 1958) (international union, which approved unlawful strike by member local union, was proper party defendant in injunction suit). The *Alpert* case is particularly important because it prevents an international union, which has supported illegal practices by one of its locals, from escaping all liability for its misconduct. In effect, the international is made a surety for the observance of the injunction by the local which may be virtually judgment-proof in any subsequent contempt proceedings.

the record shows a reasonable probability that the acts alleged were in fact committed. As the Eighth Circuit in *Minnesota Mining & Mfg. Co. v. Meter* [42] has indicated, when both of these questions have been answered in the affirmative, a district court may properly assume jurisdiction to entertain a request for injunctive relief.[43]

As a matter of proof, the General Counsel must first establish reasonable cause to believe that the statute has been violated.[44] The Board then must show that the injunction would be "just and proper" under the circumstances. Pursuant to this criterion, injunctions have been issued on various grounds, for example: prevention of frustration of the purposes of the Act,[45] preservation or restoration of the status quo pending final adjudication by the Board,[46] a reasonable expectation that the efficacy of the Board's final order may be nullified if the injunction does not issue,[47] or a harmful impact on the public interest.[48]

In a recent case, the Third Circuit highlighted the importance of swift administrative action by the Board once a Section 10(j)

---

[42] 385 F.2d 265, 269, 66 L.R.R.M. 2444, 2447 (8th Cir. 1967).

[43] *See also* McLeod v. Construction Workers, Local 147, 292 F.2d 358, 48 L.R.R.M. 2655 (2d Cir. 1961); Elliott v. Dubois Chemicals, Inc., 201 F. Supp. 1, 50 L.R.R.M. 2279 (N.D. Tex. 1962); Jaffee v. Newspaper and Mail Deliverers Union of N.Y., 97 F. Supp. 443, 27 L.R.R.M. 2583 (S.D.N.Y. 1951).

[44] *E.g.*, Brown v. Pacific Telephone & Telegraph Co., 218 F.2d 542, 35 L.R.R.M. 2346 (9th Cir. 1954). In this case, the Board made a prima facie showing when it established that the employer had granted recognition to a noncertified union as the exclusive bargaining representative of employees formerly included in a unit certified by the NLRB.

[45] Angle v. Sachs, 382 F.2d 655, 659, 66 L.R.R.M. 2111, 2114 (10th Cir. 1967); Minnesota Mining and Mfg. Co. v. Meter, 385 F.2d 265, 272, 66 L.R.R.M. 2444 (8th Cir. 1967); Jaffee v. Henry Heide, Inc., 115 F. Supp. 52, 58, 31 L.R.R.M. 2634 (S.D.N.Y. 1953).

[46] *See* the cases cited *supra*, footnote 45, and Johnston v. J.A. Hackney & Sons, Inc., 300 F. Supp. 375 (E.D.N.C. 1969); McLeod v. General Electric Co., 366 F.2d 847, 849, 63 L.R.R.M. 2065 (2d Cir. 1966); Johnston v. J.P. Stevens & Co., 341 F.2d 891, 892, 58 L.R.R.M. 2457 (4th Cir. 1965).

[47] Angle v. Sachs, *supra*, footnote 45; Minnesota Mining and Mfg., *supra*, footnote 45; Lebus v. Manning, Maxwell and Moore, Inc., 218 F. Supp. 702, 705-706, 54 L.R.R.M. 2122 (D. La. 1963); Reynolds v. Curley Printing Co., 247 F. Supp. 317, 323-324, 60 L.R.R.M. 2413 (D. Tenn. 1965).

[48] *See* Penello v. United Mine Workers, 88 F. Supp. 935, 942, 25 L.R.R.M. 2368 (D.D.C. 1950); McLeod v. General Electric Co., 257 F. Supp. 690, 708, 62 L.R.R.M. 2809 (S.D.N.Y. 1966), *rev'd*, 366 F.2d 847, 63 L.R.R.M. 2065 (2d Cir. 1966).

injunction issues. In *Eisenberg v. Hartz Mountain Corp.*,[49] the court held:

> In our view, a six-month period from the date of issuance of a Section 10(j) injunction should suffice, save in the most extraordinary circumstances, for the completion of expedited action by an administrative law judge on the underlying complaint. Accordingly, we hold that in this circuit such an injunction should include an explicit time limitation, not longer than six months, on the restraint it imposes. If it is believed that injunctive relief or its continuation is warranted after the findings and recommendations of the administrative law judge have been entered, upon proper petition in an appropriate case a district judge may grant or continue a Section 10(j) injunction for an additional period of not more than six months to permit Board action upon those recommendations. Moreover, these six-month limitations shall not preclude a district judge from extending the life of any Section 10(j) injunction for an additional thirty-day period upon a showing that administrative action on the underlying controversy seems to be imminent.[50]

SECTION 10(e) INJUNCTIONS

Section 10(e) and (f) of the Act [51] authorizes the U.S. Court of Appeals to "grant such temporary relief or restraining order as it deems just and proper" pending the outcome of proceedings pursuant to the Board's application for enforcement of an unfair labor practice order.[52] The legal standard applicable to NLRB requests for Section 10(e) relief were set forth by the Fourth Circuit in *NLRB v. Aerovox*,[53] as follows:

> As the first prerequisite for relief pending appeal, the Board must establish reasonable cause to believe the Act had been violated. This alone, however, is insufficient to show why the normal processes

---

[49] —— F.2d ——, 89 L.R.R.M. 2705 (3d Cir. 1975).

[50] *Id.* For a discussion of the split in court opinions on the Board's requests for 10(j) injunctions to compel an employer to bargain with a union pending the outcome of the NLRB unfair labor practice proceeding, *see supra*, Chapter XI, footnote 125, p. 183.

[51] 29 U.S.C. § 160(e) and (f).

[52] NLRB orders are not self-enforcing. Hence they become legally binding upon respondents only upon enforcement by the appropriate court of appeals. A further discussion of the legal effect of court-enforced NLRB orders is found on pages 245-248, *supra*, which describes contempt proceedings against respondents who fail to comply with such orders.

[53] NLRB v. Aerovox, 389 F.2d 475, 67 L.R.R.M. 2158 (4th Cir. 1967). *See also* International Union, UAW v. NLRB (Ex-Cell-O Corp.), 449 F.2d 1046, 76 L.R.R.M. 2753, 2756, n. 29 (D.C. Cir. 1971).

of court enforcement should not be followed. A second test should be applied. It must appear from the circumstances of the case that the remedial purposes of the Act will be frustrated unless relief pendente lite is granted. These standards, we believe, will generally satisfy the Act's requirement that temporary relief be just and proper.[54]

It should be emphasized that 10(e) relief is requested sparingly by the Board and is not generally available in NLRA enforcement proceedings. Only two such requests were filed in each of the 1973 and 1974 fiscal years.[55]

---

[54] Further explication of the requirements for Section 10(e) relief can be found in Minnesota Mining & Mfg. v. Meter, 385 F.2d 265, 270-271, 273, 66 L.R.R.M. 2444 (8th Cir. 1967); McLeod v. Compressed Air Workers, 292 F.2d 358, 48 L.R.R.M. 2655 (2d Cir. 1961); Firestone Synthetic Rubber & Latex Co. v. Potter, 400 F.2d 897, 69 L.R.R.M. 2415 (5th Cir. 1968); Angle v. Sachs, 382 F.2d 655, 66 L.R.R.M. 2111, 2114 (10th Cir. 1967); Sears, Roebuck and Co. v. Carpet Layers Local No. 419, AFL-CIO, 397 U.S. 655, 659 (1970); NLRB v. Beverage Air Co., 391 F.2d 255, 257, 67 L.R.R.M. 2763 (4th Cir. 1968); NLRB v. ILGWU, 274 F.2d 376, 44 L.R.R.M. 2003 (3d Cir. 1959).

[55] 38 NLRB Ann. Rep. 252 (1973); 39 NLRB Ann. Rep. 241 (1974).

PART EIGHT

Conclusion

CHAPTER XVI

Altering the Scope and Severity of NLRB Remedies

Throughout this study, this legal principle has constantly recurred: the NLRB has been granted broad authority by Congress to fashion unfair labor practice remedies in order to effectuate the policies of the National Labor Relations Act. This power is subject to the stipulation that its use be restricted to undoing the effects of unfair labor practices found to have been committed. Stated in another and perhaps more conclusory fashion, Board orders must be remedial and not punitive or confiscatory.

For the most part, the remedies utilized by the Board are accepted by the users of the Board's processes as appropriate manifestations of the Board's remedial powers. For example, bargaining orders, backpay, reinstatement, notice posting, and cease and desist orders are all considered to be "traditional" remedies which the Board may apply with flexibility and discretion. Of course, the Board's application of these sanctions is neither perfect nor free from criticism. At various places throughout the study, we have suggested what we believe would be improvements in the NLRB remedial process. Our criticism emphasizes areas wherein analytical lapses by the Board have resulted in uncertain or inconsistent application of some remedies. We have tried to highlight areas where the courts of appeals have severely criticized the Board's analytical approach. Such criticism has been especially harsh regarding the proper use of the *Gissel* bargaining order [1] and concerning decisions to reinstate employees who have engaged in proven acts of misconduct or violence.[2] Furthermore, we expressed in Chapter

---

[1] *See* Chapters XI and XII, *supra.*

[2] *See* Chapter IX, *supra.*

IV particular concern for the enervation of increasingly strained resources of the agency and of the courts that pursuit of insignificant or de minimis violations may cause.

NLRB and judicial decisions have also recognized that respondents who engage in repeated or flagrant violations, or who advance frivolous defenses to unfair labor practice charges, deserve to receive harsher and more imaginative remedies. Thus, the Board has fashioned remedies designed to confront the particular circumstances of the violations found. For example, where a respondent has demonstrated a proclivity to violate the Act, and where it can be anticipated that future violations will occur, the Board will issue a "broad" order which requires that the Act not be violated "in any other manner." Also, special notice provisions may be ordered to inform the employees that an unfair labor practice has been found and is being remedied. The respondent may be required to mail the notice to the employees, give the union access to company bulletin boards, or read the notice aloud to the employees. Where a flagrant unfair labor practice is unaccompanied by a debatable defense, the respondent may be ordered to pay attorneys' fees and litigation expenses.

The Act also provides the NLRB with authority to seek injunctions to prevent the continuance of unfair labor practices where it can be shown that such relief is "just and proper." If such an injunction issues, the unfair labor practice will be restrained until the Board issues a final order which will then contain the appropriate NLRB remedy. Under Section 10(1) of the Act, the General Counsel is required to seek an injunction from a U.S. district court against certain specified union unfair labor practices. Injunctions against other unfair labor practices are covered by Section 10(j). While the injunction is in effect, a breach of the injunction will subject the defendant to powerful contempt of court sanctions.

Other contempt sanctions are available for use against a respondent who violates a Board order which has been enforced by the appellate courts. The NLRB order has then become the order of the court and a refusal to comply with that order, or the commission of a similar future violation, will subject the contemnor to "whatever sanctions are necessary under the circumstances to grant full remedial relief, to coerce the contemnor into compliance with [the] court's order, and to fully compensate the complaint for losses sustained." [3] These sanctions in almost all NLRA civil contempt cases will include payment to the Board of fees, costs, and litigation expenses incurred. Additionally, the court can coerce compliance by fining the contemnor and even placing his responsible officer or agent in jail through a writ of body attachment. Willful violations may be prosecuted by way of criminal contempt, with its attendant penalties of fines and imprisonment. [4]

As shown, harsher remedies presently are available for use against the flagrant or recalcitrant violator. But availability is not the only touchstone for their utilization. In dealing with requests for these extraordinary remedies, the Board and courts have recognized that when the severe remedy is ordered, they must address questions involving the fundamental fairness of the proceeding. One basic problem is the possibility that harsh remedies and penalties tend to coerce respondents with potentially meritorious claims into settling the case in order to avoid the remedy. [5] In order to minimize this chilling effect on the assertion of possibly valid defenses, the Board and courts have rejected requests for attorneys' fees, litigation costs, union organizing expenses, and "make whole" remedies for refusals to bargain, where the respondent has been able to present a "debatable," or nonfrivolous defense. [6]

The potential unfairness becomes more pronounced when considering that high financial penalties will most affect litigants with small financial resources. A flagrant violator with a sound economic position, however, may be able to pay the price and continue violating the Act. If such a violator is undeterred by potential contempt of court compliance fines and jail terms, the possibility of paying treble damages may not deter him either. While valid reasons exist for concern about those respondents who repeatedly commit serious unfair labor practices,

---

[3] *See* NLRB v. Vander Wal, 316 F.2d 631, 52 L.R.R.M. 2761, 2763 (9th Cir. 1963). *Accord*, United States v. United Mine Workers, 330 U.S. 258, 19 L.R.R.M. 2346 (1947).

[4] The contempt sanction is discussed more fully in Chapter XV, *supra*, pp. 245-248.

[5] This objection is especially applicable to proposed penalties which would prevent certain NLRA violators from receiving federal government contracts for a three-year period, and would permit victims of Section 8(a)(3) and 8(b)(2) violations to sue in federal court for treble damages. *See* Chapter XIV, *supra*, pp. 236-243.

[6] *See* Chapter XIV, *supra*, pp. 223-234.

those concerns should be balanced by recognizing, as the Board and courts have done, that certain proposed remedies in this area are unacceptable because they may unfairly coerce settlements and hinder a full determination of whether the alleged violation actually occurred.

Cogent arguments have maintained that certainty in the application of remedies and promptness and efficiency in their administration would provide better deterrence than would increasing the severity of the remedies. Former Board Chairman Edward B. Miller has addressed this problem several times and his views deserve full examination. Miller has argued that:

> The other criticism—that our remedies provide too little, too late—is doubtless sometimes valid. But I think the emphasis is more properly placed on the "too late" rather than the "too little." It is important to remember that the primary purpose of our remedial orders is to bring persons and entities into compliance with our law, in the hope that the compliance will extend to the spirit as well as to the letter of our law.
>
> It will, for example, accomplish precious little if an employer, at our command, enters upon a bargaining relationship with the union, convinced in his own mind that he is there only under protest and determined only to go through the motions of bargaining because he has been forced to do so. On the other hand, if he goes there, perhaps not liking it, but determined to follow our directives in good faith and to learn to live with his new situation, then there is hope that we have achieved genuine, rather than superficial, compliance.
>
> Similarly, a union which abandons picketing which we have found to be of a prohibited secondary nature but remains determined to find some means, legal or illegal, to bring improper pressure to bear upon the protected neutral employer, may honor the letter of our law but by subsequent conduct may very well frustrate the law's objective.
>
> Thus we must always be conscious of the fact that our remedial orders are not designed as penalties, and should not be evaluated in a penal context. They are, rather part and parcel of an administrative effort to shape viable and continuing relationships among the parties who appear before us and who must often live together long after our file on their case has been sent to the archives.
>
> The empirical data which is available is not as comprehensive as I would like, but such as there is seems to bear out the wisdom of this caveat. It tends to show that a Respondent, whether union or employer, who is so hostile to the requirements of our law and our processes of implementing it that he will deliberately and repeatedly engage in improper conduct both before and after he has appeared before us is not likely to achieve the kind of industrial stability that our Act envisions, even after having been the target of the full thrust of our remedial powers. While it is possible to conclude

from this data—and some have—that we therefore need bigger and better monetary remedies, I am more inclined to conclude that we must face up to the fact that big monetary remedies—or penalties —are not really effective in deterring the true recalcitrant in this field.

Our experience has been, however, that when we are able to move with both firmness and dispatch, the results are much more encouraging. . . .

The emphasis, therefore, in my view, should be more heavily placed on prompt and efficient case handling than on belated expanded remedies, no matter how imaginative or inventive those remedies might be.[7]

In response to the widely held belief that NLRB remedies would be more effective if less time elapsed between the filing of an unfair labor practice charge and ultimate Board or court resolution of the dispute, Board Chairman Betty Southard Murphy recently announced the formation of a chairman's Task Force on the NLRB to review and evaluate the Board's existing structure, practices and procedures, and rules and regulations for the investigation, prosecution, hearing, decision, and enforcement of NLRB cases. The task force is also charged with advising the Board and General Counsel of its recommendations on the means and methods of improving the Board's processes and making recommendations on the recruitment and productivity of its Administrative Law Judges.[8] The House of Representatives Education and Labor Committee also has expressed concern over this delay issue. Its Labor-Management Relations Subcommittee is now considering several proposed solutions in the course of general oversight hearings concerning the National Labor Relations Act, its remedies and administration.

---

[7] *See* Miller, *The NLRB—Hero or Villain?* 1970 LABOR RELATIONS YEARBOOK 214, 217-218. *See also* the remarks of former NLRB Member Gerald A. Brown, 14th Annual Institute on Labor Law of the Southwestern Legal Foundation, Dallas, Texas, 1967 LABOR RELATIONS YEARBOOK 251, 258 ("I became completely convinced that the certainty of punishment was more significant as a deterrent to law violations than the severity of the punishment."); *and compare* Morris, *Labor Court: A New Perspective* 24 N.Y.U. CONF. ON LAB. 27, 40 (1972), wherein the author observes that "[c]ertainty of enforcement would encourage more voluntary compliance, which would in turn reduce the case load and also shorten the time required for handling of contested cases." *with* Ordman, *The National Labor Relations Act: Current Developments,* 24 N.Y.U. CONF. ON LAB. 115, 128 (1972) (". . . if the litigational process would be substantially shortened without forfeiting minimal due process, the need for drastic remedies would in large part be obviated.")

[8] *See* No. 223 DAILY LABOR REPORT A-10 to A-11 (BNA, November 18, 1975). Notice of the Task Force's establishment appeared in the November 18, 1975 Federal Register.

Such proposals include giving greater finality to Administrative Law Judge decisions, making NLRB orders self-enforcing, expanding the number of Board members, increasing the use of Section 10(j) injunctions, and amending Section 10(a)[9] to increase the discretion of the Board to cede its jurisdiction in appropriate circumstances.

Generally agreed to is the conclusion that NLRB remedies would be more effective if there were no premium which Board respondents could enjoy by delaying their compliance with Board orders. It is also generally accepted that a diminution of the time period required to resolve an unfair labor practice case would increase the effectiveness of the Board's remedies. Analysis, however, of these proposals should consider that a large portion of charges filed with the Board are nonmeritorious, and, further, that about 70 percent of appealed Board orders are enforced in full by the courts.[10] NLRB respondents cannot, therefore, be presumed to have committed the unfair labor practice charged. Thus, not all proposals which would decrease the time lag in Board proceedings would necessarily result in increased fairness to Board litigants. An analysis of proposed solutions to resolve the delay issue must give full consideration to assuring that respondents are provided with due process sufficient to enable them to present proper defenses to the charges against them.

It also cannot be assumed, *ipse dixit,* that the Board's caseload will automatically be lightened if present remedies are made more severe, or new harsher penalties introduced. Skepticism about such an assumption was expressed by Bernard Samoff, a former Board regional director, who made the following analysis:

> Would stricter, harsher, costlier remedies diminish case intake? We just don't know. Although several unions, a minority of the NLRB and at least one circuit court endorse a financial reparations remedy in certain refusal-to-bargain cases, their aim is not to

---

[9] Section 10(a) (29 U.S.C. 160(a)) (1972) now provides that:

. . . the Board is empowered by agreement with any agency of any State or Territory to cede to such agency jurisdiction over any cases in any industry (other than mining, manufacturing, communications, and transportation except where predominantly local in character) even though such cases may involve labor disputes affecting commerce, unless the provision of the State or Territorial statute applicable to the determination of such cases by such agency is in inconsistent with the corresponding provision of this Act or has received a construction inconsistent therewith.

[10] *See* 39 NLRB ANN. REP. 240 (1974). *See supra,* p. 242, n. 77.

diminish intake but to achieve other goals. Even if potential wrong-doers were deterred by the certainty of a costly remedy, this might reduce only a few cases. More likely, if experience is a helpful indicator, even more union, employer and individual charges would be filed to exploit the new remedies. Each time the Board establishes a new pattern of violations or orders new remedies, this causes disorder rather than order and the intake climbs.

Although modern penology does not believe that capital punishment diminishes murders, we might grant that costlier remedies against employer (and unions too) would deter prospective law-breakers and reduce repeat violators. But would this curb intake? Although this is not the place to discuss harsher remedies, I doubt whether they are likely to yield fewer cases. Whatever diminution would occur would be equaled by new cases stimulated by the expectation of the desirable remedies. Interacting influences, particularly market forces and the attitudes of workers, public and employers toward unionism, are more likely on balance to add to the swelling intake than the new remedies are likely to reduce it.[11]

As Miller and Samoff have pointed out, it should not be facilely assumed that harsher remedies would deter unfair labor practices or reduce the Board's caseload.

While there is good cause to be concerned about serious violations of the Act, and the mounting caseloads of the Board and the courts, we should refrain from embracing solutions "which could become the basis of chilling the assertion of rights reasonably held in good faith."[12]

---

[11] *See* Samoff, *The Case of the Burgeoning Load of the NLRB,* 22 LABOR LAW JOURNAL 611, 623 (October 1971). Bernard Samoff is a well-known commentator on NLRB practices and procedure, and formerly was regional director of Region 4 of the Board in Philadelphia, Pennsylvania.

[12] NLRB v. F & F Laboratories, Inc., —— F.2d ——, 89 L.R.R.M. 2549, 2552 (7th Cir. 1975).

Index of Cases